A BOOK IN THE SERIES

Radical Perspectives

A RADICAL HISTORY REVIEW BOOK SERIES

SERIES EDITORS: *Daniel J. Walkowitz, New York University*

Barbara Weinstein, New York University

Grand Designs, Lara Kriegel's brilliant study of the politics of cultural production in early and mid-Victorian Britain, is precisely the kind of book we hoped to publish when we conceived of a series on radical perspectives in history. Kriegel's interpretation revises what has been the dominant account in design culture of "a spectacular modernity characterized by commodity display and consumerism," an interpretation that reifies the place of machinery and machine production in exhibits. Kriegel demonstrates both the centrality of artisanal labor in exhibition culture and the deeply contested nature of design reform. Close readings of an extraordinary cache of visual and literary representations plumbed from contemporary journals and newspapers wonderfully illuminate the discourse of design reform as it emerged in the Great Exhibition of 1851 and at the South Kensington Museum.

Kriegel's accomplishment also represents a radical intervention into the debate on historical method. Besides offering a wide-ranging account of political economy and state and imperial imaginings, *Grand Designs* effectively responds to recent calls to embed cultural history in social and economic history. Kriegel unites the economic and the cultural domains of Victorianism by investigating copyright and aesthetic principles in museological practice, by tying consumption to discourses of production, and by demonstrating both the constructed and contested nature of market ideology and the imperatives to order, categorize and "reform." Kriegel's innovative perspectives reshape, in her own words, "not just the story of design reform, the chronology of nineteenth-century Britain, or the linguistic turn, but the very contours of historical practice."

GRAND DESIGNS

Lara Kriegel

GRAND DESIGNS

Labor, Empire, and the Museum in Victorian Culture

DUKE UNIVERSITY PRESS   *Durham & London*   2007

© 2007 DUKE UNIVERSITY PRESS

All rights reserved

Printed in the United States of America

on acid-free paper ∞

Designed by C. H. Westmoreland

Typeset by Tseng Information Systems, Inc.

Library of Congress Cataloging-in-Publication Data

appear on the last printed page of this book.

FOR MY PARENTS

CONTENTS

ILLUSTRATIONS

Figures

Illustrations

Plates (*Following page 142*)

ACKNOWLEDGMENTS

Education of many varieties, generosity of every sort, friendships in several places, and support on all levels have allowed this book to take its shape. It is tempting to trace its roots to the House on the Hill, where colored beads and Benthamite strictures may have sparked a preschooler's interest in British design reform. Its beginnings are more clearly evident, however, in the education I received at St. Mary's Episcopal School in Memphis, which proved to be the perfect place for a nice Jewish girl to become enchanted with the Victorians and their values. Subsequent training at Emory, York, and Johns Hopkins Universities went a long way toward shattering some of my girlish notions about the Victorians, but in the process they became all the more compelling.

It is fitting that this book embodies the genealogy of an education, for it is, in many ways, a history of just that. *Grand Designs* is also a study of institutions, the ideas that grow inside them, the currents that flow against them, and the afterlives that develop beyond them. As such, it has facilitated an appreciation for my own affiliations, both past and present. I am very much a beneficiary of the intellectual vibrancy and true friendship that characterized the overlapping cohorts in British history, nineteenth-century studies, and women's studies at Johns Hopkins University. I remain especially thankful for the continuing friendship and collegiality of Rachel Ablow, Nadja Durbach, Karen Fang, Alison Fletcher, Elke Heckner, and Natalie Zacek.

Postdoctoral fellowships at the Pembroke Center for Teaching and Research on Women at Brown University and the Huntington Library, Gardens, and Art Museum in San Marino provided important opportunities for this project to mature. For their direction of fellowship programs, I am grateful to Ellen Rooney, Elizabeth Weed, Roy Ritchie, and their staffs. I wish to thank those fellows, friends, and scholars who enlivened my experiences on both coasts, especially Susan Amussen, Elizabeth Barboza, Gail Bederman, Christy Burns, Juilee Decker, Dian Kriz, Mary Ann O' Donnell, and Andrea Volpe. This project and I have also benefited from the financial and intellectual support of the North American Conference on British Studies; the Winterthur Library, Museum, and Gardens; the Yale Center for British Art; and the Paul Mellon Centre for Studies in British Art.

It has been a treat—intellectual, aesthetic, and tactile—to work with incomparable collections at the aforementioned institutions. For these opportunities, I wish to thank the staffs of the Huntington Library, the Winterthur Library, and the Yale Center for British Art. Across the Atlantic, I am particularly grateful to the librarians and archivists at the National Art Library and the Archive of Art and Design. Thanks are due, too, to the staffs of several other collections, including, but not limited to, the British Library, the Kensington Local Studies Library, the National Archives, the National Gallery Archives, and the New York Public Library.

The discussions that transpire at the coffee table and the conference session often find their ways into print only years later. I am glad, at long last, to be able to offer my thanks to several colleagues and mentors who have helped give shape to this book, some deliberately and others unwittingly. On this score, I am indebted to Timothy Alborn, Sally Alexander, Jeffrey Auerbach, Bryan Callahan, Nina Caputo, Rafael Cardoso Denis, Anna Clark, Dan Cohen, Deborah Cohen, Charles Delheim, Toby Ditz, Brigid Doherty, James Epstein, Pamela Fletcher, Margot Finn, Oz Frankel, Ellen Handy, David Harvey, Anne Helmreich, Ian Hunter, Dian Kriz, Fred Leventhal, Vernon Lidke, Dianne Sachko Macleod, Peter Mandler, Mary Catherine Moran, John Plotz, Jordana Pomeroy, Mary Poovey, Tori Smith, Peter Stansky, Gareth Stedman Jones, Whitney Walton and Martin Wiener. Thanks are due as well to the many conferences and universities that have provided productive venues for discussing works in progress.

At Florida International University, I have been lucky—very lucky—to have the sort of colleagues, past and present, who would literally go to battle for me. They and their families have provided invaluable collegiality, impeccable hospitality, and even shelter from storms. In truth, they and the departmental staff all deserve mention by name for good deeds, goodwill, and good humor. For help with this book, however, I must especially thank Darden Pyron for his authorial exhortations, Alan Kahan for his keen reading, Victor Uribe for his effective advocacy, David Cook for his assiduous follow-up, and Mark Szuchman for his generous funding. I would also like to recognize Rebecca Friedman, Kirsten Wood, and Aurora Morcillo for their encouragement in the endgame. Ken Lipartito has been a peerless advocate, mentor, colleague, and friend. Without him and Elisabeth, I can honestly say, I wouldn't be where I am today. Had it not been for Mickey Wolfson's inimitable collection of design and propaganda arts, I might not have made it to Miami. And, for their assistance and partnership, I am sincerely grateful to the entire staff of the Wolfsonian-FIU. Finally, I wish to thank the Department of History, the College of Arts and Sciences, the Office of the Provost, and the Florida International University Foundation for funding this project.

I have been the beneficiary of tremendous generosity from four scholars and friends who came enough before me to clear a path but not too soon for it to grow over. Their support has opened up crucial opportunities for funding, publication, and more. My wish to locate the origins of this project in my toddler years notwithstanding, it was, in truth, Louise Purbrick's wonderful dissertation on the display of design that provided a decisive and enduring inspiration. An inimitable impresario, Tim Barringer has made British art an ever broader tent that has welcomed me and other historians, too. I consider it a privilege to have shared extended time in Baltimore with Antoinette Burton during the headiest days of the new imperial history, which she did so much to pioneer. It has been an honor and a pleasure to be Erika's doppelgänger, especially since this role has allowed me to declare—in the best of humor and on more than one occasion—that "I'm not Rappaport."

Accolades are due to Jordanna Bailkin, who has been the ideal companion from day one for excursions into libraries, restaurants, and, of course, museums. And my most heartfelt appreciation goes to Judith Walkowitz, whose unwavering belief in me and this project has been as essential as it has been long-standing. Myriad innovations in telecommunications have allowed us to log countless hours of conversations over the past decade. Without these discussions, this book would not have taken its present shape. Nor would it have turned out in the end to be such fun.

There are many people who deserve recognition for their help in the publication process. For their assistance in the image rush, I am grateful to Nicholas Blaga, Jean-Robert Durbin, Melissa Gold Fournier, Emily Guthrie, Paul Johnson, Alan Jutzi, John Knaub, Francis Luca, Elaine Morris, and Mil Willis. Sincerest thanks are due to the two anonymous readers for Duke University Press for their keen and constructive suggestions. The enthusiasm of the series editors, Danny Walkowitz and Barbara Weinstein, was absolutely invaluable. Finally, I wish to thank my editors, Valerie Millholland and Miriam Angress, as well as assistant managing editor Katharine Baker and designer Cherie Westmoreland, for the genial and professional attentiveness that they have given to me and this book.

Many friends outside the academy have offered welcome diversion and good humor at times when I needed it. Finally, my family has provided critical support as it has grown and changed, to my great delight, over the course of writing this book. My sister Mirm and my new brother-in-law Bryfy provided infectious energy and enthusiastic encouragement at crucial junctures. I cannot imagine this book—or many other things—without my husband Alex Lichtenstein. This project came to fruition as we came to know one another. It was reborn in California, where he read aloud from nineteenth-century newspapers so that I could transcribe them; it grew in Texas, where he offered his inimitable critiques of drafts; and it achieved completion in Florida, where he made every milestone his own, so much so that he wanted to be here with me to put it in the mail. Hannah and Max have leavened scholarship with irreverence, wit, and curiosity. Finally, my most overdue thanks are for my parents, who know the academic life well and encouraged an uncanny career choice through thick and thin. With the Victorians chronicled in these pages, my father shares an affection for good writing and rational thinking, and, along with them, my mother believes in the edifying qualities of hard work and good taste. But their particular brand of compassion, humanity, generosity, and humor may be more characteristic of other places and other times. For all of this and more, I dedicate this book to them.

Introduction

On a May evening in 1865, Benjamin Lucraft, a cabinetmaker, made a rousing speech at the South Kensington Museum. Opened to acclaim in 1857, this predecessor to the Victoria and Albert Museum boasted a formidable collection. Its riches included Indian silks, English paintings, and French porcelain. With these holdings, this state-sponsored museum located in a West London suburb aspired to transform its visitors into elevated subjects, skilled producers, and discerning consumers. Those local worthies who joined Lucraft at the 1865 meeting deemed the museum's mission so important that they hoped to enhance access for the working classes. After the dignitaries had spoken, Lucraft, a self-described "artisan," assumed the stage. He endorsed the museum, for it had made him a "better workman." Its rare cabinetry allowed him to study the finest masterpieces of European civilization. Its gothic treasures helped him to provide his customers with the best goods they desired. Finally, its pastoral environs provided a welcome respite from London's gritty East End, where he and his brethren lived and toiled. For the good of his class and the good of the nation, Lucraft exhorted his listeners to make collections such as South Kensington's ever more available to the "working man."[1]

Had it not been for a weighty parliamentary report compiled thirty years before, Lucraft might never have ascended the stage at the South Kensington Museum. In 1835 and 1836, the Select Committee on Arts and Manufactures had elevated artisanal producers such as Lucraft and the goods they made into objects of national concern. Those who testified had complained of shoddy calicoes, inelegant cutlery, and garish wallpaper. One exemplary witness was James Morrison, a member of Parliament (MP) and proprietor of a London firm that dealt in such fancy goods as shawls, silks, ribbons, and gloves. While England's manufactures were sturdy, Morrison reported, they were notably inferior in design. To Morrison, the causes of these shortcomings were all too clear. Britain lacked the drawing schools, museum culture, and copyright protection enjoyed on the Continent, especially in France. It was, he argued, an "absolute necessity" to address these travesties in the face of the influx of overseas goods, the invasion of foreign designers, and the industrialization of the Continent.[2] Countless others endorsed Morrison's conclusions about the deplorable "taste in design" that plagued Great Britain in the 1830s.[3] The time had come, they agreed, to improve "the hand and the eye" of the people, especially the artisanal and industrial classes.[4] Although they did not speak before the committee themselves, these forerunners of Benjamin Lucraft gave every possible indication that they were eager and ready to receive such an education.

The agenda set by Morrison and the select committee provided the inspiration for the mid-nineteenth-century movement for design reform examined in this book, which is, essentially, a prehistory of the Victoria and Albert Museum. Its beginning in the mid-1830s preceded the better-known arts and crafts movement by half a century. Like the arts and crafts movement, which sought to cure the ills of industrialization, it placed labor and aesthetics at its center. Unlike the arts and crafts movement, which eschewed a broad marketplace, it was concerned with large-scale economic reform. This was the case from the outset, when the Government School of Design opened in London in 1837 to teach Lucraft's forbears how to make patterns for manufactures. Between 1839 and 1842, a second supply-side intervention aimed to correct degenerate practices of trade by extending industrial copyright laws and so to protect manufacturers and merchants such as Morrison.

At midcentury, this reforming movement would attain a larger stage and aspire to grander designs. The turning point was the Great Exhibition of 1851, which employed spectacular display to put the ornamental manufactures of Britain and the world on view. The results were twofold. On the one hand, the exhibition celebrated Britain's industrial progress; on the other, it cast renewed doubt on the nation's aesthetic prowess. Given these concerns, reformers' priorities shifted to demand-side improvement following the exhibition. This was evident at the Museum of Ornamental Art, which opened just one year after the exhibition with the hope of bettering consumer taste. Design reform's midcentury efforts would culminate with the 1857 opening of the South Kensington Museum, which was pioneered by the utilitarian reformer Henry Cole. There design reform attained a roomier estate and a larger mission. It was no longer concerned simply with improving production or reforming consumption. Instead, the South Kensington Museum engaged in the spiritual elevation of the nation's populace and with the grand enterprise of imperial collecting. The institution would grow and flourish in a new suburban location, where it was rechristened the Victoria and Albert Museum in 1899.

The South Kensington Museum's status as a hub of imperial display is made luminously clear in an 1882 tribute penned by Moncure Daniel Conway, an American abolitionist and unitarian who was a longtime London resident. By the time Conway published *Travels in South Kensington*, the museum had become a venerable institution. This fixture on the museological landscape of the metropolis boasted the world's largest array of the industrial arts or, as the institution variously referred to its holdings, of "ornamental art," "practical art," "decorative art," and "applied art."[5] Its cabinets overflowed with Italian lace, Indian jewelry, and Chinese porcelain, which provided exotic complements to England's arts. Filled with goods redolent of oriental luxury, the hallways of South Kensington evoked faraway lands for the American writer. In a familiar Victorian conceit, Conway argued that it was possible to travel the earth without leaving the museum. As he touted the collection's virtues, Conway invited readers to join him on a leisurely ramble through the institution and, ultimately, across the globe.[6] Conway's fanciful text is a tribute to collecting, pleasure, and display. Only rarely and incidentally do the concerns about trade voiced by Morrison or the preoccupations with labor articulated by Lucraft intrude.[7]

Conway's view of the South Kensington Museum as a fantastical treasure trove devoted to displaying the globe has become a prevalent one. It ratifies understandings of the late nineteenth century as an era of visual pleasure and imperial spectacle.[8] Moreover, it endorses a narrative of the midcentury design reform campaign as a movement from market-place to museum or, at least, from supply to demand. Bookends on an epoch of aesthetic improvement that spanned nearly half a century, the methodical select committee report and Conway's whimsical travelogue epitomize these differences. The select committee report is a product of the 1830s, when questions of economy, production, and utility came to the fore in an industrializing and reforming Britain. Published in 1882, Conway's travelogue is the fruit of an era whose immediate preoccupations seemed to lie elsewhere, namely, with connoisseurship, travel, and empire. These transitions were reflective of broader nineteenth-century transformations in aesthetics, economics, and public culture.[9] In fact, they have come to dominate histories of the period, especially those written under the rubric of cultural history, which has highlighted exhibitions, museums, and department stores—along with the increasingly mobile populations that frequented them—as hallmarks of the late nineteenth century's modernity.[10]

Grand Designs provides an alternate view of the South Kensington Museum and the broader cultural landscape of which it was a part. By examining midcentury design reform, this study exposes the links between markets and museums and between aesthetics and economics. It demonstrates that nineteenth-century cultural institutions such as the South Kensington Museum arose out of a complex and long-standing engagement with labor and trade.[11] As it propounds this view, *Grand Designs* expands on the cast of characters that has taken center stage in a well-rehearsed story of design reform, not to mention in the mid-nineteenth-century public arena. Design reform, of course, concerned artists, consumers, museumgoers, and civil servants such as the middle-class reformer Henry Cole. But these figures, often the protagonists of cultural history, toiled and campaigned alongside a broader range of characters. *Grand Designs* restores merchants such as Morrison and artisans such as Lucraft—long the protagonists of social history—as leading actors in a saga of aesthetic reform and cultural formation. Alongside these metropolitan figures, it incorporates Manchester manufacturers and provincial critics who clung fiercely to the nineteenth-century liberal faith in unfettered markets. Finally, it brings into view those imperial laborers from the Indian subcontinent who dazzled visitors to the Great Exhibition and the South Kensington Museum with visions of oriental splendor.

By resuscitating these historical actors, *Grand Designs* argues that marketplace concerns about trade, labor, and manufacturing resided at the "heart of Victorian public discourse," not to mention the reform campaigns and civic institutions of the era.[12] In the process, it seeks to challenge orthodoxies in museum studies, imperial history, and Victorian culture. Ultimately, *Grand Designs* suggests a reconsideration of the very contours of historical practice at a moment when critics are calling for a new synthesis of social and cultural history.

THE MUSEUM AND THE MARKETPLACE

Because it has occupied a place of prominence in old and new cultural histories, the South Kensington Museum provides an ideal venue for embarking on the intellectual project described above. South Kensington has long been considered a landmark institution of Britain's mid-nineteenth-century cultural revolution. This revolution accompanied the better-known political, economic, and social transformations of the day. In fact, liberal political reform provided its very conditions of possibility, for the committee that spurred it on was forged by members of a reformed Parliament, most notably the radical William Ewart, and sustained by middle-class civil servants, especially the utilitarian Henry Cole.[13] The nascent relationship between art and government in the nineteenth century has been a concern of institutional, cultural, and architectural historians since the 1970s. As they examined state patronage and imperial city building, they placed South Kensington at the center of a nineteenth-century reform movement that shaped aesthetic education and grand collections alike.[14]

More recently, new directives from the fields of cultural studies, museum studies, and political history have encouraged scholars to reconsider the relationship between art and government.[15] One of the most influential theorists for this revitalization of inquiry has been Michel Foucault, who urged scholars to understand nineteenth-century liberal reforms as efforts to manage populations that were increasingly reaping the spoils of democracy.[16] Building on Foucault and adding in a measure of Gramsci, the cultural critic Tony Bennett showed that museums and exhibitions were ideal vessels for this project. With their spectacular displays, they brought populations at the threshold of political representation under the succoring arm of the state. In the process, they promoted order, obedience, and social solidarity. To capture this understanding, Bennett introduced the notion of the "exhibitionary complex" in a seminal 1988 essay. With its collections designed to educate and amaze, Bennett argued, the South Kensington Museum represented the exhibitionary complex par excellence.[17] Over the past decade and a half, Bennett's schema has served as a springboard for studies of art institutions that have examined the cultural manifestations of state formation and nation building.[18] But these works have not, for the most part, espoused the dynamic view of labor that is advanced in the pages of this book.

The nation to which the South Kensington Museum ministered was avowedly imperial, especially as the nineteenth century wore on. This is evident in Moncure Daniel Conway's tribute, which located South Kensington squarely within a trajectory of Victorian high imperialism. The American writer employed the familiar narrative conceits of orientalism as he portrayed London, and the South Kensington Museum especially, as the heart of an empire.[19] South Kensington attained its greatest stature as the storehouse of empire when an Indian section, filled with jewels, thrones, and firearms, debuted there in 1880. Like the world's fairs that contributed to its collections, the South Kensington Museum has attracted considerable attention from practitioners of the new imperial history. Once an embattled enterprise, this now established scholarly movement has examined the cultural manifestations of imperialism in the metropole to great effect.[20] Working in this vein, several scholars have analyzed the objects of empire aggregated at South Kensington, not to mention the museum's collection policies.[21] In the process, they have portrayed South Kensington as the epitome of the "imperial archive," to use the words of Thomas Richards, devoted at once to classifying the goods and kindling the imagination of empire.[22] *Grand Designs* builds on these insights, but it also shifts attention from the consumption and display of overseas goods to their manufacture and trade.

The exhibitionary complex suggests that the late-nineteenth-century preoccupation with collecting had everything to do with managing an expanding political sphere. The imperial archive indicates that collections were integral to stimulating an appetite for an exotic yet governable empire. Together these concepts have become a shorthand for South Kensington and the spectacular urban landscape of which it was a part. Whether implicitly or explicitly, they guide the many assessments of the museum that have filled anthologies, catalogues, and even exhibitions over the past decade or so.[23] *Grand Designs* moves beyond these two shibboleths, as it foregrounds the concerns with labor and trade that were so pervasive in the 1835 select committee report, not to mention in Benjamin Lucraft's 1865 speech.[24] To begin, this book offers a more animated view than that implied by Tony Bennett's exhibitionary complex. Rather than a top-down formation, it shows that the exhibitionary complex was a contested locale, at least in its rendition at South Kensington. There Lucraft and his ilk used their positions as laborers to gain access to museum collections. Similarly, this book offers a new understanding of the imperial archive and imperial culture more generally, as it explores the role played by oriental labor within midcentury design reform. The South Kensington Museum brought oriental production, especially as it was embodied in the figure of the Indian laborer, to the attention of its visitors. At the museum and its predecessors, those Indian wares that contributed to the spectacle of empire informed notions of honest labor and good design.

As it brings labor and trade to the fore, *Grand Designs* locates South Kensington and the preceding innovations squarely within the "culture of industrial capitalism."[25] Whether as discursive categories or material concerns, I argue, trade and labor played decisive roles in shaping South Kensington and the cultural terrain of Victorian Britain more generally, driving the form of its collections, providing a logic for its geography, and even informing the character of its critiques. As it carries out this line of argument, *Grand Designs* participates in an ongoing reconsideration and revision of historical categories. Specifically, it brings aesthetics and the marketplace—two concerns that are often severed by the disciplinary conventions of contemporary historiography—into a common analytical frame. In the mid–nineteenth century, design reform was no mere defensive bulwark against changes in production, trade, and industry. This book shows instead that preoccupations with trade and labor lay at the heart of Victorian public debates and cultural institutions. Moreover, it demonstrates that marketplace actors—whether artisans, tradesmen, or manufacturers—were protagonists in the design reform movement that culminated at South Kensington.[26]

By advancing this argument, *Grand Designs* joins scholarship on the culture of the market that has developed over the past two decades. Notable works in history and literary criticism have sought to understand the far-reaching cultural effects of market development in Europe and the

Americas, especially during the long transition to industrial capitalism from the sixteenth century to the nineteenth.[27] Influential scholarship has linked the birth of market societies to such wide-ranging matters as theatricality, humanitarian sensibilities, abstract space, and aesthetic theory.[28] In the process, it has illuminated the "reciprocal influence and interpenetration" of cultural practice and economic activity.[29]

Because nineteenth-century design reform in Britain operated at the crossroads of aesthetics and economics, and at the interstices of production and pleasure, it offers an intriguing and fruitful opportunity to engage with market culture. The story of midcentury design reform builds on the insights of scholars who have uncovered the complicated relationships between economic change, aesthetic innovation, and cultural formation. But it also deepens the understandings offered by earlier works that privileged discourse, theory, and abstraction over everyday commerce, daily life, and material possessions.[30] Notably, this book demonstrates that market developments gave rise to the very aesthetic conundrums and economic anxieties that design reform sought to redress. Waged between 1839 and 1842, the campaign for design copyright extension, discussed in chapter two, provides a case in point. During the early nineteenth century, calico printers and merchants complained that the rise of mechanization and the growth of the export trade facilitated "design piracy." This practice, whereby some printers stole the designs of their more venerated counterparts, threatened a struggling British tradition of original design, not to mention the very health of the calico trade. To rectify this matter, advocates of extension looked to the strong arm of the law for protection. Marketplace changes produced demand-side conundrums as well, as chapter four demonstrates. During the early 1850s, Henry Cole would argue, the democratization of consumption led to the aesthetic decay of manufactures. In order to rehabilitate such household goods as wallpapers, carpets, and chintzes, Cole and his circle enumerated a series of taste principles, many of which were derived from Indian design. At the Museum of Ornamental Art, founded in 1852, they put decorative objects, both good and bad, on display. By so doing, they hoped to teach consumers from the middle classes, broadly construed, the rules of good taste. In the process, they aimed to cure the ills of the marketplace through aesthetic reform.

Provincial printers, metropolitan merchandisers, and London artisans joined in these contentious campaigns. To insert themselves into the discussions, they looked for authority to their trades. In the process, these market actors, traditionally the protagonists of social history, attained influence by drawing on earlier radical discourses of the property of skill identified by John Rule.[31] That is, by portraying themselves as venerable manufacturers, honorable merchants, and skilled laborers, they gained entry into philosophical and aesthetic debates of national import. Their positions as producers afforded them a measure of cultural capital, to use the words of Pierre Bourdieu.[32] This was especially the case for artisans such as Lucraft who sought access to the South Kensington Museum. He derived the power and authority to speak at the May 1865 meeting expressly by framing himself as a craftsman. Not incidentally, Lucraft's predecessors had themselves looked to design reform's pedagogical innovations to gain cultural capital. This was especially evident at the School of Design, discussed in chapter one. There artisans clamored to learn to draw not just from geometrical illustrations but also from the figure. By so doing, they sought to gain a training reserved traditionally for artists and so to secure their places in an industrial marketplace that threatened to degrade their skills. Often, the school itself forestalled their aspirations. As it chronicles these episodes, *Grand Designs* demonstrates the importance of artisanal skill, artistic prowess, and aesthetic knowledge as forms of cultural capital.

Artisanal skill, artistic prowess, and aesthetic knowledge all assumed center stage at the Great Exhibition of 1851, which represents a turning point in the midcentury campaign chronicled in this book. The Great Exhibition brought the industrial arts, including English cutlery, French porcelain, and Indian jewelry, to a public unprecedented in its scope. Among these, we can count not only the six million exhibitiongoers but also the immeasurable numbers who read the catalogues produced for the event. There is a long-standing notion that the mid-nineteenth-century design reform campaign began in earnest at the Great Exhibition of 1851, but this study places the first world's fair in a longer, broader trajectory of aesthetic improvement.[33] In the process, it challenges two prevailing orthodoxies about the exhibition, namely, that it was the epitome of mechanized production and the apotheosis of spectacular society.

To begin, *Grand Designs* demonstrates the centrality of artisanal labor at the Great Exhibition. Although the machinery courts occupied a place of prominence at the Crystal Palace, the great show valorized artisanal skill and hand labor, too. Some have argued that these tendencies foreshadowed Britain's industrial decline later in the century.[34] Regardless, they are particularly evident in the discussions of the goods from France, famed for its artistic workmen, and the riches from India, esteemed for its craft tradition. This brings us to a second challenge. Current orthodoxy has it that the Great Exhibition inaugurated the society of the spectacle, that modern form of representation in which, the theorist Guy Debord once argued, the fetishized commodity reigned supreme. At the exhibition, and in spectacular society more generally, the understanding goes, the commodity spoke for itself and obscured its own conditions of production.[35] *Grand Designs* joins recent work that refines this formulation. To do so, it looks to the catalogues, journals, and periodicals that discussed the Crystal Palace's displays. These texts ultimately produced a popular discourse of design that relied on idealized laborers—whether English, French, or colonial—for its expression.

These reassessments of the exhibition and spectacular society have broader consequences for the master narratives of the nineteenth century. A tendency to privilege 1851, the year of the exhibition, is evident not just in scholarship on Victorian museums and design but in British cultural history at large.[36] As Louise Purbrick and Tim Barringer have both observed, this foregrounding of 1851 marks a change from earlier traditions in social and economic history, which took 1848, the year of rebellion and revolution, as a watershed. With this shift has often come a privileging of cultural innovation over the class politics that were once so prevalent within nineteenth-century historiography.[37] The dominating story of the nineteenth century has thus become the move to a spectacular modernity characterized by commodity display and consumerism. This has replaced a narrative of the continuing, if frustrated, attempts of labor to adjust itself to industrial capitalist regimes of production. Because of its very chronology and the concerns it entertained, the movement that engendered South Kensington provides an ideal opportunity to create a revised account of the nineteenth century, which understands trade and labor not simply as economic enterprises but as central concerns of Victorian culture.[38]

As it reconsiders the nineteenth century, this book joins in a broader critical assessment of Victorianism's organizing notions.[39] Together design reform, the Great Exhibition, and the South Kensington Museum provide fertile ground on which to do so. In the popular imagination, mid-nineteenth-century design, with its florid ornament suggestive of wealth, propriety, and stability, has long stoked an appetite for Victorian things, even as its aesthetic stock has ebbed and flowed with the changing assessments of critics and the museum establishment. It was, notably, at the Great Exhibition of 1851 that the term *Victorian* was first used as the self-conscious marker of an age.[40] Moreover, museum scholarship and public exhibitions have recently enshrined the South Kensington Museum as the "most Victorian" of nineteenth-century institutions and perhaps the most imitated and influential as well.[41] Observed in 2001, the sesquicentennial of the Great Exhibition and the centennial of the death of Queen Victoria together prompted a reexamination of Victorianism, not to mention numerous retrospectives on the field of Victorian studies. One important line of assessment reviewed the prevailing modes of academic inquiry for Victorian studies in the English-speaking academy. The Victorians provided ready candidates for exploration by social historians in the 1960s and 1970s, as many scholars have noted. More recently, however, the field has become the province of literary studies, the new cultural history, and the linguistic turn.[42]

When it comes to nineteenth-century British historiography, these twists and turns themselves constitute a saga of heady debates that fill journals, monographs, and even personal correspondences.[43] Beginning in the early 1980s, important advances came from notable historians of labor and radicalism, including Gareth Stedman Jones and Patrick Joyce.[44] Along with scholars of modern France, they critiqued an earlier variety of cultural history that had itself challenged crude base-superstructure models of social formation.[45] Namely, Raymond Williams had sought to address culture as a "whole way of life" and E. P. Thompson to understand social class as a "relationship and a process."[46] Critics of these frameworks, especially Thompson's, questioned the assumption that texts are transparent communicators of historical experience. They argued for a new history of political culture based in language. In the process, class, once an "objective historical category," became for many scholars a "cultural, historical, or discursive construct."[47] Ultimately, these developments led some historians to reject the very category of class, whether as a cultural or economic affiliation.[48] They also fed a broader neglect of the leading materialist concerns of social history, including labor, mechanization, capitalism, and skill.[49]

In a related yet distinct project, feminist historians, including Joan Scott, Judith Walkowitz, and Carolyn Steedman, challenged the underlying assumptions of social history as they pioneered the cultural turn. Not only did they bring gender to the fore as a social and cultural category. They also demonstrated how representational practices themselves acted as the agents of historical change. Finally, they called attention to consciousness and subjectivity as historical concerns.[50] One collective effect of these innovations—feminist, linguistic, and cultural—has been a move away from the topics that flourished under the hand of social history, including work and industry, in favor of such issues as identity and performativity.[51] With its rich archives of texts and images, the Victorian era has proven especially facilitative of this move. As testimony to the force of these developments, Martin Hewitt notes that cultural history has, of late, become the "spine of Victorian studies."[52]

Recently, several historians have advocated a new synthesis of cultural method and social concerns. For instance, James Epstein has advocated "taking the turn without forgetting what we still have to learn" from earlier historical traditions.[53] *Grand Designs* takes up this directive as it integrates the long-standing preoccupations of social history with the current methods of cultural studies, most notably an analysis of a range of texts and images. Moreover, it allows us to see how some of the leading characters of social history—namely, artisans, manufacturers, and tradesmen—found their ways into cultural institutions, where they became consumers and critics themselves. By framing themselves as market actors, they pressed for an extended copyright, questioned aesthetic directives, and critiqued the museological geography of Victorian London. In keeping with the dictates of an age of equipoise, these interlocutors sought not so much to oppose the innovations that grew out of the *Report of the Select Committee on Arts and Manufactures* as to stake out their own interests within this project.[54] This said, their pleas for inclusion on the cultural landscape complicate notions of the monolithic rise of a liberal project of design reform, not to mention of a liberal state more generally.[55] On the one hand, design reform transitioned from a radical project that sought to give artisans cultural capital into a liberal one that stressed market responsibility and social obedience. But, on the other, this was never an unchallenged movement, as the contests over such diverse matters as collecting, aesthetic hierarchy, curriculum, and geography that are chronicled in this book will show.

At issue here, finally, is not just the story of design reform, the chronology of nineteenth-century Britain, or the linguistic turn, but the very

Introduction

contours of historical practice. *Grand Designs* is part of a movement "beyond the cultural turn." Victoria Bonnell and Lynn Hunt have noted that cultural history has tended toward the "obliteration of the social" in its attempt to escape a crudely materialist determinism. In the face of this development, some have exhorted scholars to return to the "hard surfaces of life" and to reaffirm the concerns of social history.[56] What is needed, I contend, is a reappraisal of the priorities and interpretive possibilities of cultural history. Design reform provides an ideal subject for taking up this task. Because they traverse the domains of production, consumption, and display, design reform's literal objects of concern require that we restore a "sense of social embeddedness" to cultural history.[57]

FROM THE SCHOOL OF DESIGN TO THE
SOUTH KENSINGTON MUSEUM

In the chapters that follow, I take up the challenge issued long ago by Moncure Daniel Conway, who called for an examination of the "great revolution" in aesthetic culture that began at the School of Design and culminated at the South Kensington Museum. To narrate the institution's rise, Conway recommended that South Kensington's future chroniclers sift through the *Report of the Select Committee on Arts and Manufactures*, personal correspondence, and committee minutes.[58] *Grand Designs* engages with this archive, which by now is as voluminous as it is well trod. In the process, it seeks to unite a number of previously studied episodes in aesthetic reform into a seamless institutional narrative.[59] It also accompanies an account of design reform from above with an analysis of design reform from the outside and below. To do so, it considers a larger body of print and visual culture.[60] This includes drawing manuals and workmen's periodicals that whetted an appetite for aesthetic improvement among Lucraft's predecessors; affordable catalogues, many of them illustrated, that aided the growth of a public culture of display; and neighborhood newspapers that allowed artisans and tradesmen to enter national debates as producers and purveyors of goods, not to mention as consumers of culture. Together these texts allow us to see design reform as a series of contests, whether metropolitan, local, or national, that addressed the issues of artisanal skill, cultural capital, and aesthetic acumen in the face of the rise of commodity capitalism. In the process, they en-able a reconfiguration of our accounts of Victorian cultural formation that pays heed to social history's categories, concerns, and champions.

Our tale begins at the Government School of Design, whose early career I chronicle in chapter one, "Configuring Design: Artisans, Aesthetics, and Aspiration in Early Victorian Britain." Opened in London in 1837, the School of Design marked the first attempt to address the complaints lodged before the Select Committee on Arts and Manufactures. The school began modestly, counting a handful of students in its entering class, but it grew by midcentury into a network of institutions instructing fifteen thousand pupils. Its economic aims were as grand as its institutional aspirations. By educating putative designers, the school aspired to salvage a marketplace that was marred by shoddy industrial wares. For all of the hope bestowed on artisanal training at the school, however, there was little consensus about what constituted a proper curriculum for training in design. Instructors, bureaucrats, students, and artists thus engaged in a series of vitriolic disputes. The most explosive issue had to do with whether students should study the human figure, then the apogee of fine art. Those who argued in its favor, including the renegade artist Benjamin Robert Haydon, saw art education as the road to manly ennoblement. Skeptics such as Director William Dyce, himself a painter, regarded design as a modest vocation. The figure dispute precipitated resignations, impassioned letters, and even a suicide. It also sparked revolts among those students who brought their own aspirations for improvement to the school and its provincial outpost at Manchester. As it chronicles these fracases, chapter one shows that the figure question was more than a rarefied aesthetic matter. At stake instead were broader matters of cultural capital and aesthetic hierarchy for artisans in a changing marketplace and a nascent reforming regime.

Manufacturers and merchants argued that the infant School of Design would prove useless without a companionate effort devoted to curing design piracy. This evil pervaded Britain's industrial towns, where unscrupulous manufacturers, traders, and laborers stole patterns from their more illustrious rivals. It was especially rampant in the Lancashire trade in printed cottons, or calicoes, purchased by consumers in Britain and overseas. To the chagrin of honorable printers, accelerating mechanization and expanding commerce made this practice ever more prevalent, as the shabby and garish patterns flooding the market evinced. In the face of this blight, an unlikely coalition of manufacturers, economists, and members of Parliament galvanized a campaign between 1839 and 1842 to extend the three-month copyright to a year. Extending the copyright, proponents argued, would not only prevent piracy. It would also enhance a tradition of original design that they equated with a moral marketplace. As they made their case, those calico printers who favored extension engaged in a process of self-fashioning in which they framed themselves as bearers of an artisanal tradition and defenders of the national patrimony. Chapter two, "Originality and Sin: Calico, Capitalism, and Copyright of Designs, 1839–1851," examines their efforts, which met a boisterous opposition from a coterie of Manchester economists and manufacturers. These opponents placed their faith not in original design but rather in the free marketplace. The debate between these antagonistic interests provides a window onto the aesthetic conundrums that arose from changes in productive practice within a commercial and industrial society.

Before midcentury, design reform concerned a select few artists, civil servants, manufacturers, and artisans who were preoccupied largely with supply-side matters. The Great Exhibition of 1851 would bring the industrial arts to a constituency of unprecedented proportions by transforming the strategies of design reform. At this first world's fair, progenitors Henry Cole and Prince Albert placed a matchless display of raw materials, machinery, and industrial arts on display for the millions to see. By so doing, they hoped to uphold the virtues of skilled labor and to celebrate the glories of a moral marketplace, just like the early Victorian design reformers had. These continuities notwithstanding, their methods of improvement differed starkly from the preceding efforts. Rather than educating a select group of artisans or curing the ailments of a particular trade, the exhibition's leadership sought to elevate the public taste through spectacular display. Chapter three, "Commodification and Its Discontents: Labor, Print Culture, and Industrial Art at the Great Exhibition of 1851," addresses this shift. At the same time, it challenges dominant understandings that suggest that the commodity displaced labor as the preeminent mode of representation at the exhibition. To be sure, the finished goods from Britain, its empire, and the globe attracted considerable attention at the Crystal Palace. But these installations—and especially the ornamental art manufactures—also featured prominently in the sizable print corpus that accompanied the exhibition. In exhibition catalogues, artisans and craftsmen assumed center stage. To bring the industrial art wares to life, exhibition literature invoked ideal laboring figures, including the English operative, the French artisan, and the Indian craftsman. Rather than eliminating labor from view, the exhibition's texts ultimately located it at the center of Victorian discourse. The great spectacle thus invigorated labor as a discursive category that would be available to many different interests in the ensuing decades. Most notably, in the exhibition's perorations on labor, working men such as Lucraft would soon find a measure of cultural capital that allowed them to stake their claim to the national collections.

For all of its success among the general public, the Great Exhibition left contemporary aesthetes with the unsettling awareness that Britain failed to rival its continental counterparts, and even its imperial possessions, in the industrial arts. It thus signaled to reformer Henry Cole and his London-based circle the necessity of a revised approach. Ever the pragmatist, Cole looked to a new audience and new strategies. Rather than focusing on supply, Cole argued for demand-side reform, thereby anticipating the priorities of neoclassical economic theory, which would privilege consumption above production just a few decades later.[61] Cole's new collection in London's West End, the Museum of Ornamental Art, placed the consumer front and center. Chapter four, "Principled Disagreements: The Museum of Ornamental Art and Its Critics, 1852–1856," examines this museum, which sought to educate consumers by promulgating the "correct principles" of design. Based on the aesthetic thought of the preceding decades, these principles were available in the museum's *Catalogue*, which offered digestible consumer directives through a series of aphorisms. If they learned these principles, Cole envisioned, buyers from the middle classes would become educated market actors. His most expressly didactic display was a Gallery of False Principles, which gibbeted travesties in home furnishings, including rugs, wallpapers, and chintzes. Together, Cole's principles, his market assumptions, and his strategies for showing became the focus of a vehement debate that took place in tracts, short stories, and newspapers. There, detractors who championed laissez-faire dismissed the aesthetic principles as fatuous. By so doing, these challengers hearkened back to the sentiments of copyright's opponents, who had argued that the free market was the true arbiter of good taste and good design. Like these predecessors, the museum's critics employed an equally vitriolic rhetoric, which was evident in their attacks on the Gallery of False Principles, also known as the

Chamber of Horrors. In the face of these attacks, the chamber would be short-lived, lasting only a year. Although it proved ephemeral, the larger museum did not. It was, in fact, the immediate predecessor to the South Kensington Museum and later the Victoria and Albert.

In 1857, Cole moved the Museum of Ornamental Art just a few miles west to his newly constituted South Kensington estate, where it would become the centerpiece of a new district. With the move came yet more transitions in the grand logic of collecting and the broader project of design reform. At South Kensington, Cole flanked extravagant displays of ornamental art with other collections, most notably a gallery of British paintings. With considerable aplomb, he sought to lure the national collections of art and natural history to South Kensington over the coming years. At South Kensington, Cole frequently carried out his centralizing ambitions in the name of the working man, and especially the skilled artisan, who was quickly becoming an object of political and cultural reform. Men such as Lucraft did not hesitate to point out, however, that the museum stood far from the dwellings of metropolitan laborers. In the face of this geographical iniquity, they maintained that their status as producers entitled them to the cultural wealth of the nation. When they made such claims, they drew on the concerns articulated in the *Report of the Select Committee on Arts and Manufactures*; they also looked to the virtues popularized at the Great Exhibition. Their challenges spurred Cole to establish a satellite collection in the working-class neighborhood of Bethnal Green, which was home to thousands of laborers. I chronicle these developments in the final chapter of *Grand Designs*, "Cultural Locations: South Kensington, Bethnal Green, and the Working Man, 1857–1872."

When they made claims on the collections at South Kensington, working men like Benjamin Lucraft recalled the priorities of the School of Design, which had opened in 1837. This first inroad to state-sponsored reform placed artisans front and center as it sought to improve their productive practices. By so doing, it aimed to exert a salutary influence on the industrial arts. This would prove to be a more complicated and contentious enterprise than the School's progenitors had envisioned. The project of improving production impinged, it turned out, on matters of individual aspiration and cultural capital. These were especially potent concerns in an era of industrial transition, liberal reform, and popular radicalism. Disputes about hierarchies of aesthetics and class manifested themselves in the myriad curricular struggles that plagued the School in its early years, as the institution looked to design education for the purpose of market improvement. Let us see what sorts of questions and conflicts arose when early Victorian artists, manufacturers, civil servants, and artisans tried to configure design.

Configuring Design

ARTISANS, AESTHETICS, AND ASPIRATION IN

EARLY VICTORIAN BRITAIN

As the summer of 1837 drew near, a handful of young men gathered at London's Somerset House to embark on a new pedagogical venture. They went seeking training in drawing and design. The fledgling institution in which they enrolled would soon minister to thousands, but in June 1837 the Government School of Design opened to little acclaim.[1] In its early months, it counted a scanty seventeen students, many of them mere boys.[2] These modest beginnings notwithstanding, the infant school carried a heavy burden and an awesome responsibility. It was the first response to the Select Committee on Arts and Manufactures. In 1835 and 1836, this committee, led by the radical member of Parliament William Ewart, had called countless witnesses to investigate art academies, public museums, and aesthetic education in Britain.[3] Its 1836 report outlined a litany of criticisms. Most notably, Ewart's committee had expressed grave concern about the quality of Britain's industrial art wares, including such staples as silks, china, and wallpaper. In the face of its apprehensions, the committee had urged the formation of an academy devoted to instructing would-be designers in the "application of the arts to manufactures."[4] It looked to the putative school, which debuted just a year later, as the salvation of Britain's industrial arts. The infant school, like the protean notion of design itself, would carry a heavy burden.[5]

Given these lofty goals, it is no surprise that the school's early years were rocky ones, marred by derision and plagued by disagreements. When they looked back on its infancy, later Victorian critics referred to the institution as the "despised School of Design."[6] In his 1882 *Travels in South Kensington*, the chronicler Moncure Daniel Conway noted that the "poor little school" at Somerset House had become a "thing to make fun of."[7] From the vantage point of 1882, when Conway wrote, the meager enrollment at Somerset House appeared pitiable and its grand designs seemed laughable. Yet it had considerable staying power. By the time Conway penned his *Travels*, the once embattled Government School of Design had moved to South Kensington, where it had grown into the National Art Training School. This institution was the lynchpin of a network of 7 schools in the metropolis and 150 across the nation. Young artisans, would-be designers, aspiring artists, and even lady students flocked to the National School and its branches. Still grander things were in store for the school, which was renamed the Royal College of Art in 1896.[8] As such, it holds a prominent place on the landscape of London's South Kensington district to this very day.

Eventual success notwithstanding, estimations such as Conway's have cast a pall over the early years of the School of Design, inflecting the historiography of the school, of Victorian art institutions, and of drawing more generally. As a result, the School of Design receives scant attention in histories of nineteenth-century arts training and Victorian aesthetic culture. More often than not, it appears as a discouraging prelude to eventual triumphs in industrial education or as a disheartening denouement to the polite practice of drawing so prevalent among elites in the early modern period.[9] And those who do give heed to the school's early years find themselves caught, by and large, in teleological narratives that seek to explain the institution's inevitable failures or anticipate its ultimate triumph.[10]

Singular in the depth of analysis and the drama it ascribes to the institution, Quentin Bell's *The Schools of Design* remains the exception to this historiographical rule. In 1963, Bell penned what endures as the authoritative narrative of the institution's early years. This meticulous text cast the school as a stage for tense contests among "incalculable and enigmatic" men. Many of these squabbles were petty intrigues that involved "political chicanery" and "office seeking."[11] Often, however, more substantial matters lay at the heart of these struggles. These had to do, specifically, with the curriculum for educating designers, which turned out to be as contentious as it was open-ended. The school's proponents agreed that students should learn to draw. But what they were to draw, and to what larger purpose, remained subject to debate. The question of whether students should study from the human figure, particularly the nude, proved especially divisive.[12] This was a charged matter in the waning days of an era in which drawing served "to identify and locate individuals in the social order."[13] Whether in Renaissance Italy or Victorian Britain, life drawing represented the apogee of training in art.[14] Its pursuit conferred claims to taste, authority, power, and even masculinity. These matters would turn out to be noticeably fraught at an institution that sought to extend the cultural capital of artisans in an age of political upheaval, uprooting, and unrest.

At the School of Design, two competing models of study came to the fore. The first, the academy, placed a premium on figure study so that pupils could attain their highest aesthetic potential. The second, the workshop, eschewed the figure in favor of a trades-based education that would prepare students for practical employment.[15] Each of these had its own champion. Advocating the academy was the artist Benjamin Robert Haydon, a historical painter, a devotee of the Elgin marbles, and a gadfly to the art world. He argued for training that focused on the figure and culminated with the nude. According to Haydon, such a course of study would tap into the "genius of Britain" and elevate the people.[16] William Dyce, a Scottish fresco painter and longtime superintendent of the School of Design, promoted the workshop. In contrast to Haydon, he understood design training as a means to vocational ends. During the first decade of the school's existence, these two men staked their positions in impassioned speeches, bureaucratic reports, and instructional manuals. But there was more in question in their competing models than drawing itself. When they sparred over the figure, those on both sides of the matter argued about the place of the artisan in aesthetic and cultural hierarchies at a time of sociopolitical transition. While Haydon viewed design education as a vehicle for nurturing aspiration, Dyce upheld industrial art training as a regime of containment. Given the stakes of this disagreement, the ripple effects were especially dramatic. In London and the provinces, drawing masters, students, and council members struggled between the positions offered by Dyce and Haydon as they sought to define a curriculum for design training. During the first decade of the school's existence, their contentious dispute inspired splinter academies, incited student revolts, and ruined careers. In sum, the figure was a nakedly political issue at the School of Design.[17]

The School of Design was just one component of a broader extension of cultural capital and visual literacy among the working and middle classes during the early Victorian era. At that time, parliamentary radicals sought to make the nation's monuments, museums, and churches accessible to the populace; mechanics' institutes endeavored simultaneously to expand the intellectual and aesthetic worlds of artisans.[18] Most notable for our purposes, an explosion of print culture brought aesthetic appreciation and artistic pursuits to an expanding public sphere in unprecedented ways. The School of Design's early years coincided with a watershed moment in the proliferation of affordable drawing books, which made the onetime polite practice of ladies and artists accessible to mechanics, businessmen, and youths.[19] The era also witnessed an increase in illustrated periodicals for laborers, most notably the utilitarian *Penny Magazine of the Society for the Diffusion of Useful Knowledge*. Like the School of Design, these publications participated in the broader contemporary project of providing their consumers with visual literacy, aesthetic acumen, and work ethics. Riddled with contradictions themselves, their pages amplify the conflicts that played out at the School of Design. On the one hand, they advertised the seductions of the artistic ambition that Haydon so revered; on the other, they urged the wisdom of the modest pursuits that Dyce firmly proposed.[20]

This chapter addresses the fractious early years at the School of Design in an attempt to understand the volatile relationships between institutional development, aesthetic theory, and cultural capital in early Victorian England. It locates this struggle within the broader cultural matrix of which it was a part, especially the print culture of the day. Placing the School of Design in this larger context allows us to move beyond the narratives of success and failure that have long characterized the history of the institution. The Government School was a staging ground for important discussions about aesthetic principles and artisanal practices that would inform the project of design reform in the decades to come. When they advanced their arguments regarding the figure, Haydon offered notions about the beauty of curvilinear design and Dyce proposed ideas about the instrumentality of minimal ornament that would find their way into aesthetic canons later in the century.

Moreover, when they offered their programs for artisanal training, Haydon provided visions of artistic uplift and Dyce suggested lessons about working diligence that would eventually inform cultural politics at the South Kensington Museum.

Design reform found one of its most prescient, passionate, and tragic advocates in Benjamin Robert Haydon. Haydon was an artist, iconoclast, and debtor who devoted a lifetime to challenging the art establishment.[21] He waged his battle on the page and the canvas alike. In young adulthood, Haydon imagined that he was involved in a grand struggle against privilege and corruption in art. Haydon's passion is evident in his voluminous diaries, where he confided in 1804, "I must believe myself destined for a great purpose, a great purpose. I feel it, I ever felt it, I know it."[22] Haydon's crusade met an early setback in 1809, when he exhibited at the Royal Academy for the first time. The academy dealt Haydon a major blow when it removed his beloved *Dentatus* from a place of prominence. It replaced Haydon's painting of the dramatic assassination of a classical hero with an academician's portrait of a little girl donning a pink sash. The slight only added fuel to Haydon's campaign against the Royal Academy, which he likened to a "ruthless, calculating coiled snake" and denounced as the "constituted imbecility of art."[23] As he battled the academy, Haydon sought to resurrect history painting as the proper vehicle for the visual expression of the British national character. According to Haydon, this manly form represented the British spirit far better than effete portraiture could.[24] Convinced of history painting's importance, Haydon brought the urgency of a military maneuver to its resuscitation.[25] Ardently and passionately, he painted such figures as the Duke of Wellington and Marcus Curtius. These subjects embodied the patriotism, masculinity, civic duty, and sacrifice that Haydon so revered.[26] Given the artist's proclivities, it is hardly surprising that he viewed himself as the "Napoleon" of art—the ultimate warrior, hero, and martyr.[27] Indeed, like Napoleon, Haydon was undone by his ambition, frustrated when his reach exceeded his grasp. A romantic hero and a tragic martyr, Haydon would take his own life in 1846.[28]

A wretched man with grandiose aspirations, Haydon might seem, at first, an unlikely progenitor for the School of Design. Yet it was Haydon "more than any other man" who spurred Britons to "take a practical interest in art."[29] His role had as much to do with accident as calculation. It was equally indebted to the painter's rancor and his convictions. In the wake of the Reform Bill of 1832, Haydon gained a strategic audience for his grievances against the Royal Academy. At that time, he received a commission to paint a commemorative portrait of the Reform Banquet of 1832, which was held at London's Guildhall. While he sketched leading Whigs and Liberals whose ascendance marked a new era in politics, Haydon offered a vision of a new day in art.[30] He found an especially sympathetic ear in William Ewart, a radical and a new member of Parliament for Liverpool.[31] An opponent of monopoly and privilege, Ewart shared Haydon's dislike for the Royal Academy. Haydon was pleased to come across this "keen little man" who had a sharp understanding of the "presumption" of the academicians.[32] The two men wrought an alliance out of their shared antipathies. Together political radical and radical artist joined ranks to fuel the Select Committee on Arts and Manufactures, the very body that would inspire the School of Design.

With Ewart in the chair and Haydon as a witness, the Select Committee on Arts and Manufactures mounted a radical critique of the aesthetic establishment in Great Britain. In the process, it sought to do nothing less than reconfigure the relationship between art and state. This involved attacking old institutions and championing new ones. First and foremost, the committee sought to expose the Royal Academy's privilege and mismanagement.[33] It called countless witnesses who charged that the academy deadened talent, promoted mediocrity, and encouraged mannerism. One of the most dramatic was Haydon himself, who used his testimony as an official platform to attack the Royal Academy. Haydon decried the academy as a "despotism," "a House of Lords without appeal," and an "anomaly in the history" of a "constitutional people."[34] In sum, it was a blight on the English nation. If the committee was concerned to expose old corruption in art, it also envisioned a new aesthetic order. This effort became ever more pressing in light of the mounting evidence that the trades in shawls, ribbons, and wallpapers were in decline. Haydon was, predictably, among those who promoted public access to art in the face of this apparent crisis.[35] In particular, he championed drawing as a universal pursuit and a surefire way to improve industrial design.

Haydon brought this radical platform to an audience far broader than the committee's meeting room. While Ewart's committee interviewed its witnesses, Haydon toured the nation, preaching his radical vision for art. At the London Mechanics' Institute, and later across the provinces, Haydon extolled the twinned virtues of access to art and education in drawing. He offered his message to respectable laborers and middle-class listeners. In these meetings, the outcast Haydon found the audiences that he had "so eagerly desired," as well as the hearing that he had been "so long and pertinaciously denied."[36] Time and again, Haydon recounted in his diaries with delight how the crowds "smothered" him and the minions "crowded round" to show their drawings after the lectures.[37] To be sure, Haydon was an appealing figure for these audiences. He parlayed his position as outcast, rebel, and radical into great advantage within the brotherhood of the lecture hall in both London and the industrial north. "We are all mechanics in varying degrees," he claimed.[38] He relayed to these audiences the dream of a day when art would cease to be a "mystery" for the humble mechanic, the artisan, or the journeyman.[39]

More than mere public performances, the speeches provide a window onto Haydon's aesthetic thought and his pedagogical principles. When he lectured, Haydon claimed that "the same principle regulated the milk jug as the heroic limb."[40] This pithy pronouncement reflected his deeply held conviction about the connections between high art and industrial design. If the two were connected, they demanded the same pedagogical practices. To allow artisans to reach their highest potential, Haydon argued, it was imperative for them to follow a course of study that was identical to that pursued by artists. Namely, they should learn from the figure, long considered the "cornerstone" of high art.[41] Just like aspiring artists, Haydon advised that artisans study from anatomical models, his beloved Elgin Marbles, and finally, the nude.[42] On this score, Haydon actually endorsed the hierarchies enshrined by the Royal Academy, which had elevated the figure, and especially the nude, as the pinnacle of high art. But Haydon differed in his desire to extend the reach of figure study. It was, at bottom, the "first great step in the reform of design." He recognized, of course, that it was the rare cloth printer, bricklayer, or carpenter who would use the figure in his labors. Nonetheless, he found indisputable utility in such a pursuit. When students learned to draw the figure, Haydon explained, everything else became easy, even effortless.[43] It was a position that lent itself well to sloganeering in the "manly, forcible language" for which Haydon was so well known. In a letter to the *Manchester Courier*, Haydon asked, "What is the first requisite in design? The figure.—What the next? The figure.—What the third?—the figure."[44]

Haydon's passion for the figure may have been singular, but he was not alone in advocating its merits. His campaign coincided with an explosion of drawing books for women, children, tradesmen, and artisans. Several of these books advised figure study for this widening constituency. They espoused a range of courses, which included learning from proportional formulas, geometric shapes, the antique, and the nude.[45] More than an end in itself, they argued, figure study held out a number of virtues. Among the most important were lessons in curvilinear design and its fundamentals: the ellipsis and the circle. Haydon, himself, had endorsed curves as the basis of figure drawing, as his own preliminary sketches show (fig. 1). In his penchant for curvilinear design, Haydon joined contemporaries who found the curved line far more pleasing than the straight line. Their preference was an inheritance from William Hogarth, who had endorsed the S-curve as the so-called line of beauty in the eighteenth century. Drawing books, aesthetic treatises, and even the Select Committee on Arts and Manufactures would ratify this hierarchy in the early years of the nineteenth century. In fact, one witness, Edward Cowper brought to the committee drawings and diagrams that endorsed the superiority of curvilinear design over its geometrical counterpart.[46] According to Cowper, works so mundane as terra cotta flowerpots were more pleasing to the eye when their contours were curved (fig. 2).[47] This proclivity proved to be more than a fleeting fashion; such preferences would be all too evident at the Great Exhibition of 1851, where curvilinear design reigned supreme.

For Haydon, there were far greater matters at stake in art education than curves, however. Haydon believed that figure study had the potential to unlock latent genius.[48] This, in itself, presented a challenge to aesthetic hierarchy. When the School of Design was in its infancy, genius was an especially charged, if tenuous, category. It was considered to be the province of art rather than design. Correspondingly, it suggested originality, inspiration, and the aesthetic. Design, on the other hand, involved copies, toil, and the marketplace.[49] Mindful of these distinctions, many of Haydon's contemporaries disavowed genius. When they did so, they endorsed the understandings of the eighteenth-century painter and aesthetic theorist Joshua Reynolds, who had warned against the seduc-

1   Benjamin Robert Haydon's curvilinear figure studies. Pen and brown ink on wove paper. Yale Center for British Art, Paul Mellon Collection.

2   Progress in curvilinear design. Lithograph of vases by J. Basire in *Report from the Select Committee on Arts and Their Connection with Manufactures* (1836). Yale Center for British Art, Paul Mellon Fund.

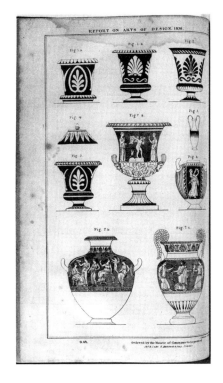

tions of genius. Nineteenth-century drawing books similarly cautioned readers about the dangers of genius. In its place, they proclaimed the virtues of perseverance, care, and discipline.[50] Ever the iconoclast, Haydon repeatedly flew in the face of Reynolds and his popularizers. Their excessive love of method and industry was sure to lead capable youths "to misery and a mad-house."[51] Unlike many of his day, Haydon clung to the promise of genius, preaching its virtues in his lectures and proclaiming its wonders in his diaries.[52] For Haydon, genius was a quest, a dream, and an obsession. "I awoke saying what is genius?" he recounted in his diary with florid language. "It is a spark from the Deity's Essence which shoots up into the Heavens fiery and blazing over an astonished World, & when it has reached its elevation, drops back into his Being like lava from a Volcanic Mountain."[53]

Haydon's desire to unleash "British genius" was part and parcel of a broader aesthetic and political project that involved elevating the English artisan.[54] It was a timely intervention that reverberated in contemporary radical political, pedagogical, and artistic circles. Haydon's heady rhetoric resonated with political radicals of the 1830s and 1840s, who had their own penchant for melodrama.[55] It also struck a chord with those contemporaries who romanticized popular instruction as a tool for rescuing the "genius" that was "buried in cellars and attics" from "thraldom."[56] Finally, it found correlatives in fictional works that romanticized artisans at the very moment when they faced increasing routinization and eroding autonomy in the workplace.[57] A historical idyll entitled *The Artisan of Lyons* provides a case in point. This tale recounted the saga of the formidable Pierre Renais, a Huguenot blacksmith whose life testified to the virtues of freedom and self-determination. Renais combined pride in his "humble birth" with chivalry and heroism. As a testament to his strength and virtue, he managed to rescue a maiden—and the city of Lyons, too—from a philandering noble. When he defeated the noble, Renais boasted, "That I am a mechanic is my pride, since it doth teach me my superiority over such a thing as thee!'"[58] This was, unquestionably, a rhetorical flourish worthy of Haydon.

While Haydon encountered sympathy in radical circles, his grand designs made him easy fodder for ridicule in the more elevated reaches of the press. For example, the Tory periodical *Blackwood's Edinburgh Magazine* mocked Haydon's grandiloquence. There an author who wrote under the pseudonym "The Sketcher" dismissed the notion that artisans should train as artists. This contributor deemed it ludicrous for artisans to draw from the Elgin Marbles, study from skeletons, and attend lectures on high art. As the critic mocked this path of training, he laid bare the futility of Haydon's educational model. Namely, he exposed the fundamental discontinuities between classical Greece and industrial Britain. "If you want to know how to plane a board, study the Torso; build a wall according to the contortions of the Laocoon," the Sketcher jested, all the while scoffing at Haydon's curriculum.[59] The satirical magazine *Punch* took aim at Haydon similarly, as it emphasized the incongruities between figure training and artisanal toil. In an article entitled "Drawing from Models," it imagined a laborer who studied from children's toys and extracted teeth. This was just one prong of *Punch*'s long-standing attack on high art in inappropriate places, a transgression for which Haydon was only the best-known perpetrator.[60]

These charges would follow Haydon throughout his career, but satirical critique was the least of his concerns in 1837, when the Government School of Design opened at long last at Somerset House on the Strand (fig. 3). When the school became a reality in August of that year, Haydon's hopes for a radical vision of design education appeared to be in shambles. In an ironic reversal, the school had become the fiefdom of the Royal Academy.[61] To use the words of Thomas Gretton, it was a spectacular "conservative hijack of a radical project."[62] The academicians on the Governing Council made it their goal to distinguish the fledgling institution from the Royal Academy. Invested as it was in maintaining a distinction between art and design, the council determined early on that "the figure was of no use to the mechanic." To ratify this understanding, it passed a measure forbidding figure study, whether from casts or from the nude.[63] Moreover, the school required that students promise in writing not to pursue painting, whether of portraits, landscapes, or historical scenes. A visit to the school only confirmed Haydon's disappointment. In a letter to a council member, he bemoaned, "Nine poor boys drawing paltry patterns—no figures—no beautiful forms!"[64] Although he was the most impassioned critic, Haydon was not alone in his grievances about the foreclosure of the radical vision of design education. Dismay registered from other quarters devoted to artisanal uplift, too. For instance, the *Mechanics Magazine*, whose editor had only just testified before Ewart's committee, charged that the school made a "mockery" of the report. Its disregard for the realities of laboring life was shameful.

SOMERSET HOUSE & ST MARY LE STRAND.

Strand
Nº 20

London, Tead & Cᵒ 16 Johnsons Cᵗ Fleet Sᵗ
Paris, M.Mandeville, 42 Rue Vivienne

3   Etching of Somerset House by Chavanne. *Views of Mighty London* (ca. 1854). Yale Center for British Art, Paul Mellon Collection.

This was especially evident in the institution's hours, which were inconvenient for working youths and men, and its fees, which were out of their reach.[65] In the end, the School of Design was deemed to be "open to the laboring classes in name alone."[66]

These concerns in hand, Haydon, Ewart, and Joseph Hume, a fellow radical, joined forces against the Government School of Design.[67] Together they founded a splinter organization, the Society for Promoting Practical Design, and along with it a rival school at Saville House. Saville House offered a radical alternative to the Government School of Design in many ways. To begin, its location held out tantalizing promises for students. Leicester Square was the heart of London's popular entertainment district, a hotbed for political radicalism, and the center of the artisanal engraving trade, which included a pornographic element.[68] As such, it was far more seductive than Somerset House, a onetime royal residence,

Chapter One

the home of the Royal Academy, and the epicenter of governmental and civic London.[69] It was not just the environment, of course, but the curriculum that offered new opportunities. At the splinter school, Haydon encouraged students to draw the figure from the antique and from life. To facilitate this endeavor, he hired both male and female models. Haydon's introduction of female models was daring in aesthetic and sexual terms alike. The use of the female model reflected Haydon's aspiration to explode aesthetic hierarchies, for even more than her male counterpart she connoted high art. Moreover, the female nude carried particular sexual insinuations during the Victorian era. At that time, female models shared their skills and visual repertoire with the *tableaux vivants*, *poses plastiques*, and anatomy shows that were popular entertainments in and around Leicester Square. With its promises of high art and sexual adventure, it is no surprise that the splinter institution drew students away from Somerset House. This was a trend that the Government School of Design was desperate to halt. To stop the hemorrhaging enrolments, the Government School soon broke with the strict regime that forbade figure study. In 1838, Somerset House introduced an evening course in the figure featuring male and female models as a "counterattraction" to the follies at Leicester Square.[70] It also lowered admission costs. Foiled by these adjustments, the Society for Promoting Practical Design would close the Saville House academy in 1839.[71]

WILLIAM DYCE, THE INDUSTRIAL ARTIST, AND THE WORKSHOP

William Dyce, the most ardent proponent of the workshop, would play a decisive role in undoing the splinter institution and its radical vision.[72] An Aberdeen-born painter of frescoes and portraits, Dyce would assume the directorship of the school in 1838. In that year, the Scot introduced a course in the figure at Somerset House. This was a starkly pragmatic move for Dyce, who did not endorse figure study as an end in itself among designers. Instead, he advised the pursuit only when it was necessary for trades such as house decorating, wood carving, or silver chasing.[73] For his antagonism to the figure and his attack on the splinter school, Haydon derided his rival as a "most vicious artist." Later, he would charge Dyce with turning the Government School of Design into a "precious case of fiddle faddle."[74]

Configuring Design   **31**

These colorful invectives reflected important philosophical and pedagogical differences between Dyce and Haydon. The figure was only the most particular expression of their divergences. More broadly, the two men split on the fundamental question of industrial design's place within the realm of the arts. Haydon, who linked the "milk jug" and the "limb," understood art and design as parts of a great, unbroken chain. Dyce, on the other hand, sought to carve out an independent space for the "art of the ornamentist."[75] In fact, it was he who coined the neologism "industrial artist" in the year 1839. For Dyce, the so-called industrial artist occupied a discrete, if hitherto unidentified, place in the pantheon of art. Dyce's designer held a "middle rank" between the "mere workman" and the "professor of fine art."[76] In the 1830s and early 1840s, Dyce devoted himself to identifying this intermediate space. His very efforts to define a curriculum for design differed from Haydon's. While the passionate Haydon had promulgated his notions in colorful lectures and emotive writings, the measured Dyce employed a series of disciplined and systematic works, including tracts, surveys, and drawing books, to develop his particularly industrial vision.[77]

Dyce made his first significant foray into design in 1837 when he co-authored the *Letter to Lord Meadowbank* with the watercolorist Charles Heath Wilson. Here, Dyce and Wilson sought to define a curriculum for the industrial arts in Scotland.[78] Their curricular ideal differed in two important ways from Haydon's. Rather than an end in itself, Dyce and Wilson claimed that genius was valuable solely as an inspiration for those "incapable of treading a path of their own." When it came to design, luminaries such as Raphael were noteworthy precisely for the guidance they might offer to those of an "inferior order."[79] Upholding Raphael as an exemplary teacher, Dyce and Wilson longed for a system of education that operated like a Renaissance workshop, where masters steered students along their proper courses. This view leads us to the second difference between the Scots and Haydon. In distinction to Haydon, Dyce and Wilson did not wish to cultivate artistic ambition or the radical sympathies that could be associated with it. The pursuit of high art, they warned, routinely led to ill, for it encouraged a man to discard a certain livelihood in the humbler arts in favor of a "precarious," often "hopeless" existence as a painter. As they urged against the excesses of artistic aspiration, they expressly steered students away from this "rambling, desultory, and unprofitable course of study."[80] In sum, if Haydon viewed design education as a vehicle for creative uplift, Dyce and Wilson conceived of it as a regime of careful discipline.

These timely admonitions struck a chord among the mainstream of aesthetic theorists. One such theorist, David Ramsay Hay, echoed his fellow Scots when he derided the "widespread mania of becoming artists."[81] Other contemporaries joined in sounding this warning. "Many a man whose life is now spent, miserably enough, caricaturing the human countenance and spoiling good canvas," another cautioned, "might under better auspices have lived in comfort and aided in advancing the manufactures of his country." By the 1840s, such notes of caution had found their way into trade journals.[82] One such publication was the *Decorator's Assistant*. In an 1847 article entitled "Artistic Ambition," this workman's periodical counseled against excessive "zeal" and "laziness." Forlorn, penniless figures on the street attired in "thread-bare coats" warned against these vices. Far better to be cautious, the *Assistant* argued, than to suffer the lamentable fate of an "ambitious man."[83]

Timely and methodical, the *Letter to Lord Meadowbank* garnered attention in London from the council of the faltering School of Design. Eager for direction, the council asked Dyce to embark on a grand tour of France, Prussia, and Bavaria to study the Continent's much vaunted design training. There the Germanic schools won his admiration. Concerned with producing designers rather than artists, they were well suited to the "exigencies of industry."[84] These impressions found their way into Dyce's *Report Made to the Rt. Hon. Poulett Thompson on Foreign Schools of Design for Manufacture*, which was eventually anointed as policy in a Government School of Design resolution.[85] Although the school's actual adherence to the Germanic curriculum is debatable, the resolution marked an important step in making design education a form of vocational training rather than a vehicle for aesthetic edification in Britain.[86] It was, in the end, a great disappointment for Haydon, who found in Dyce's report and its reception yet another obstacle to his radical notion of design. He decried the report for its embrace of "German crudity," but he reserved his choicest declamations for Dyce himself, defaming the artist as "German to the bone and marrow."[87]

Undaunted by Haydon's repeated aspersions, Dyce assumed the directorship of the Government School of Design in June 1838 after he returned from the Continent. His five years in office were fruitful ones marked by dramatic growth and transformation for the school.[88] However, Dyce complained frequently and bitterly throughout his tenure. Haydon was the least of his woes. Repeatedly, he denounced the "obstructive, useless," and "pernicious" Governing Council. But for Dyce the largest problem lay with the students, who came to the school unable to draw. Time and again, Dyce complained of their "disappointingly slow" progress.[89] The odds were stacked against success, for the School of Design stood "isolated" as the lone state engine for improving art and industry.[90] Students arrived armed with little, if any, prior education in design. Consequently, Somerset House was a mere drawing school. "We have established a *university* before we had any grammar schools," lamented Dyce. For the school to flourish, he recognized, "it must begin by teaching the ABC" of drawing and design.[91]

Ever the pragmatist, Dyce sought to redress this problem by encouraging elementary education in drawing throughout the nation. To do so, he published the *Drawing Book of the Government School of Design*, which was distributed originally as a series of drawing sheets in 1842 and 1843 by Charles Knight, one of the foremost early Victorian promulgators of cheap literature and useful knowledge.[92] Dyce's text took its place alongside other affordable drawing books released from the 1820s onward and directed to artisans, laborers, youths, and children. Together these works preached that drawing was "indispensable." It was, after all, an "assistant to words" and even a "universal language."[93] Such sentiments echoed the sorts of pronouncements made by Haydon, but here the similarities ended. Dyce's *Drawing Book*, like so many of its contemporaries, upheld the "utility" of drawing.[94] These texts sought to ready young men for a vocation, not to unleash genius. They aspired to inculcate discipline, not to fuel enthusiasm. To these ends, the authors of utilitarian drawing books looked to pedagogical practices that differed starkly from Haydon's. They emphasized gradual study, beginning with simple lines and moving to curves. These tools provided the building blocks for such prosaic objects as dogs, pipes, birds, and shoes but never the figure (figs. 4 and 5). There was more on offer in these texts than delineative skill, however. By prescribing such a course of study, utilitarian drawing books sought to impart the Victorian virtues of patience, perseverance, and obedience.[95] Dyce followed a similar formula as he stressed the necessity of incremental learning for producing an educated eye and an obedient hand. His sheets proceeded methodically, beginning with such elements of geometry as right lines, geometrical shapes, and curves, and

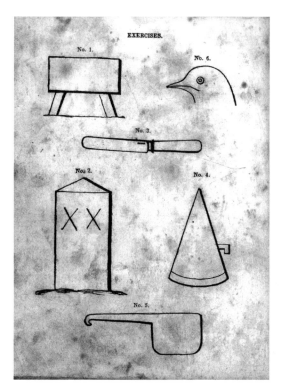

4   Exercises 1–5 in Grant's *Drawing for Young Children, Containing One Hundred and Fifty Drawing Copies and Numerous Exercises* (1848). Reproduced courtesy of the Huntington Library, San Marino, California.

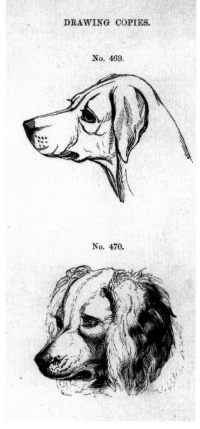

5   Drawing copies of dogs in Grant's *Drawing for Young Children* (1862). Reproduced courtesy of the Huntington Library, San Marino, California.

then advancing to freehand design. Like the scales studied by musicians, these rudimentary exercises provided the ornamentist with a foundation for later endeavors.[96]

On one important score, however, Dyce's text stood apart from these contemporary productions. According to Rafael Cardoso Denis, Dyce's *Drawing Book* was the first to impart an industrial sense of vision and to define a training expressly for design.[97] Here Dyce described design as a pursuit lying "midway" between artistic rendition and mechanical drawing. Neither art nor geometry, it was an endeavor wholly distinct in its purpose, principles, and effect.[98] Dyce had long concerned himself with defining industrial art, but in the *Drawing Book* he delineated this particular province in more technically precise terms than ever before. The author crystallized his understanding in his discussion of the lily, a simple flower that performed markedly discrete functions in art and design. Sculptors or painters who depicted the lily sought to make the flower "more beautiful and perfect" than any single specimen in nature. But the designer employed the lily differently, transforming it into a wholly new form. In the field of design, the lily was no longer a flower but "a cup, a vase, the bowl of a candlestick, or . . . a hundred other articles of common use."[99] This notion would have lasting effect, shaping the collections of the Museum of Ornamental Art, discussed in chapter four. Not only did the *Drawing Book* influence the collections. It would also guide the direction of art education in Britain for years to come. The text became a staple in elementary classes well after Dyce's resignation from the directorship in 1843.[100] When he penned the *Drawing Book*, little did Dyce know that he was "sentencing generations of school-children to mechanical copying."[101] His text proved to be a vehicle for containment par excellence.

INDUSTRIAL APPLICATION, PROVINCIAL EDUCATION, AND THE NUDE

During his years as director of the School of Design, Dyce was equally concerned with a second issue, the application of design to industry, or *mise en carte*.[102] To address this pressing matter, Dyce looked to the branch institutions, which were becoming important cogs in the Government School of Design's bureaucratic machinery. Beginning in 1841, branch schools for young men and women had developed in London, provincial England, Ireland, and Scotland. Whereas Somerset House sought to train students at the highest levels, the branch institutions ministered to the particular needs of manufacturing districts. Given this important difference, Somerset House and the branch schools drew varying constituencies. The former attracted the metropolitan professional classes, especially the sons and daughters of manufacturers, tradesmen, and architects; the latter ministered to humbler students, including those destined to apply their knowledge in such trades as carpentry, calico printing, and housepainting. In the face of this vocational audience, curricular matters assumed an ever greater significance. Nowhere was this more evident than at the Manchester School of Design, founded as an independent academy in 1838 and subsumed under Somerset House in 1843. Advocates pinned great hopes on this institution, which was located in the hub of a textile industry that marketed its goods across the world. Its success was especially critical given the lamentable state of Manchester's calico trade, as discussed in chapter two. Despite these great hopes, the Manchester school did not meet expectations during its first decade, which was characterized by fractious disputes and even sexual scandal. As in London, the question of the figure took center stage. In distinction to London, however, the matter at hand involved more than choosing between Haydon and Dyce. Instead, an especially heated curricular contest pitted local elites against the metropolitan bureaucracy. Broadly speaking, Manchester demonstrates the pedagogical challenges of *mise en carte*, which had to do as much with local politics as with aesthetic principles.

Even before Somerset House initiated its plan to establish branch institutions, Haydon played an influential role in inaugurating design training in Manchester. The artist had found fertile ground for extending his vision in the industrial north, where he lectured during the 1830s and 1840s. He found the tours thrilling, if arduous. "Lecturing till I am sick. I am not happy in Manchester," confessed Haydon, who recounted the depredations of the industrial milieu with its "hideous mill prisons for Children" in his diary. Given Haydon's propensity to link the aesthetic and the social, it is fitting that he declared the town itself in a "dreadful condition of Art."[103] With its intertwined social and aesthetic ailments, Manchester appeared ripe for the sort of aesthetic uplift that Haydon had earlier preached in London. To realize such a plan, Haydon oiled the civic machinery of the provincial metropolis. He spoke to artisans at the Mechanics' Institute and to middle-class elites at the Royal Manchester Institution, which sought to promote literature, science, and art.[104] He appealed to a sense of civic pride as a contributor to the *Manchester Guardian*. There he cajoled a town famed for its "vast capital" and "vast credit" to support the aesthetic training of its artisans and operatives, lest it wished for ruin in the face of an industrializing France.[105] Never deterred from his course, Haydon cultivated local elites at private dinners, winning the support of eminent calico manufacturers such as Edmund Potter and James Thomson and a member of Parliament, Mark Philips, all of whom we will meet in chapter two. Finally, in the house decorator and writer George Jackson, Haydon found an especially energetic local purveyor of his rhetoric who lobbied for training in design.[106]

With the support of these leading men, a school for artisans opened in the dank and dark basement of the Royal Manchester Institution in 1838. The cellar school, which began with thirty-six students, would have a long history, metamorphosing into the Manchester School of Design and eventually into the Manchester College of Art. Like the London school, this institution was riddled from the outset with curricular conflict, especially as it pertained to study from the nude. The school's first master, an artist named John Zephaniah Bell, insisted on teaching students to draw the figure. Under Bell, tutelage culminated with lessons from his own female model. In truth, Bell's practice pleased eminent Lancashire manufacturers such as Potter and Thomson, who had been skeptical about design education. These entrepreneurs wished to employ skilled artisans, but they remained concerned that the school would become a "manufactory of patterns" and hence a commercial competitor.[107] By teaching the figure, Bell offered a seemingly safe alternative. He imparted drafting skills to the students without threatening the integrity of the cotton trade, where designs from the figure were apostasy.

Local support notwithstanding, Bell ultimately met censure from Somerset House and especially from William Dyce. The showdown came in January 1843 when Manchester's application for a government grant provided the occasion for a visit from the director, who was then approaching the end of his tenure. In Manchester, Dyce found a school that ranged far from his workshop ideal and an institution that had signally failed to carve out a curriculum expressly suited to local industry. As a response, he issued a formal remonstrance that dismissed the renegade institution as a mere drawing school. Above all, Dyce criticized Manchester's focus on the figure, deeming it a decidedly superfluous attainment for the calico trade. "It is termed a school of *design*, not a school of *drawing*," he chided. If the Manchester School wished continued funding from London, it would have to curtail its forays into figure drawing and opt, instead, for William Dyce's brand of useful knowledge.[108]

It was not Dyce, however, but a local imbroglio that rendered the decisive blow to figure study in Manchester. The incident in question concerned one of Bell's female models. It unleashed early Victorian anxieties about the dangers of the life class. Hearsay has it that a student encountered the model in a corridor where she was "seized with a fit." The distressed lady caused such a stir that the council put an end to the life class—whether to ensure the model's safety or to protect the students' propriety we cannot be sure. Then, in a gesture of defiance that mimicked the radical politics of the day, the students in the life class defected to form a splinter academy. Their master followed, leaving the school for London.[109] These successive defections delighted Haydon, who likened the uproarious students to martyrs. "This is going on like the early Christians," he intimated in a letter to his wife. Inspired by the affair, he predicted that the school would embrace the figure again someday.[110] Haydon would not see this in his lifetime, however, for the life class at the Manchester School of Design did not reconvene until the 1850s. Yet again the imperatives of bureaucracy, utility, and respectability had foreclosed the pursuit of high art.

CHARLES HEATH WILSON, THE ANTIQUE,
AND THE "REVOLT OF THE STUDENTS"

This episode did not mark the end of the troubles at the Manchester School of Design, which would see a revolving door of drawing masters over the coming years. Nor was it the last controversy over the figure. An even more dramatic fracas broke out in London in 1845, just as the Manchester controversy was reaching its denouement. This so-called Revolt of the Students—or the Rebellion of Forty-Five—was a decisive firestorm in the school's history.[111] Like the provincial dispute, the rebellion involved a dueling director, a beloved figure master, and a student secession. And, like the Manchester struggle, the Rebellion of Forty-Five demonstrated that curricular disputes involved far more than mat-

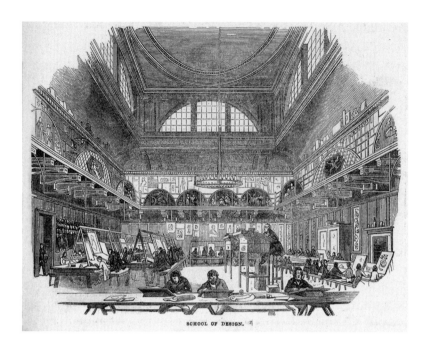

SCHOOL OF DESIGN.

6 Discipline and toil at the School of Design. *Illustrated London News*, 15 March 1843. Department of Special and Area Studies Collection, George A. Smathers Library, University of Florida.

ters of aesthetic principle. In Manchester, curricular struggles had pitted provincial interests against metropolitan bureaucracy. In London, they would hinge on the peculiarities of personality.

The chief antagonist in the Rebellion of Forty-Five was the water-colorist Charles Heath Wilson, Dyce's onetime coauthor and later his successor as director of the School of Design. Lasting from 1843 to 1847, Wilson's reign was known as the "Pompeiian Dictatorship" for the new director's love of discipline and devotion to the antique. Wilson preached the virtues of "steady industry" and "hard study." He brought "order, silence, and regularity" to the school, pictured here in the *Illustrated London News* with a vigilant master and decorous students at the time of the directorship's transition (fig. 6).[112] In his adherence to such ideals, Wilson resembled Dyce, who sought to train disciplined students. Unlike Dyce, however, Wilson was poorly attuned to the exigencies of trade. This was all too evident in his tedious curriculum, which took stu-

Chapter One

dents away from practical study, sending them instead down dead ends of mindless copying from Etruscan vases, Pompeiian pots, and Chinese baubles. Ill suited for industry, Wilson's curriculum drew the ire of drawing masters such as Charles Robinson, who bemoaned the director's tendency to treat such everyday items as carpets, mugs, and tea trays like "cartoons for historical pictures, or designs for regal palaces."[113]

In the face of this internal disagreement, the school descended to its nadir in public estimation during Wilson's regime. The director's notoriety extended into periodicals as wide-ranging as the moderate and measured *Edinburgh Review* and the bohemian and outlandish *Punch*, both of which mocked Wilson's slavish adherence to the antique.[114] In its inimitable style, *Punch* rendered studentship under Wilson into graphic satire through two figures who would have held great currency among its readership. The first was a comic Dickensian schoolboy sentenced to toilsome elementary studies and the second a diligent young man left to laconic copying from chinoiserie (figs. 7 and 8).[115] *Punch* accompanied these drawings with ludicrously tragic tales of students with thwarted talents and dashed aspirations who withered under the Wilsonian regime. While such tales exemplified the hyperbole of *Punch*, they also reflected the realities of the school under Wilson, which many students left in frustration before completing their training.[116]

Already in disfavor among advocates of practical training, Wilson also alienated himself from devotees of the figure. Suspicious of artistic ambition, Wilson stipulated that "no persons studying to become artists" be admitted to the school.[117] In the face of this declaration, a confrontation with the figure master, John Rogers Herbert, a Royal Academy associate, seemed inevitable. A popular, charismatic, and talented teacher, Herbert was beloved among those mechanics and gentlemen who comprised the most senior students at the school. Envious of Herbert's skill and celebrity, Wilson retaliated against his figure class during the spring of 1845. The director removed casts from the figure room; he ordered the gas and heat to be extinguished; and, finally, he commanded Herbert's students to draw from a model who was partially draped rather than nude. When Herbert's minions refused to obey this last order, Wilson suspended them. A showdown followed, with Herbert calling Wilson a "snob" and Wilson denigrating Herbert as a "liar and a scoundrel."[118] When Herbert was removed, a crisis of secession reminiscent of Manchester ensued. Herbert's devotees left the school to begin

7 "The School of Bad Designs."
Punch 9 (1845): 70.

8 Study at the School of Design
under the Wilsonian regime. *Punch*
9 (1845): 115.

Both reproduced courtesy of the
Huntington Library, San Marino,
California.

THE SCHOOL OF BAD DESIGNS.

The Study of "High Art" at Somerset House.

their own independent life class at a studio on Maddox Street just west of the bohemian and foreign quarter of Soho, long the haunt of artists. The outcome of the revolt resembled that of the Manchester scandal. Instead of a radical triumph, it became another victory for bureaucracy, order, and regularity. When the trouble had ended at Somerset House, Wilson held a banquet to celebrate the revolt's successful containment.[119]

Ample treatment of the incident in the press suggests the significance of design pedagogy in the public imagination. What might have been an internal squabble became an expression of larger concerns about artisanal aspiration and institutional containment; such concerns riddled the project of extending cultural capital in the early Victorian era. The press, inevitably, came out divided on the revolt, with the establishment *Art Union* sympathizing with the school and the practical *Builder* taking up the cause of the students.[120] Even *Punch* joined in to defend the renegade students, as it pilloried Wilson and the cowardly council. Predictably, however, Haydon was the revolt's most vigorous defender. Under the pseudonym Alpha, he published his last public statements on the school in a series of letters to the *Times*. If, for *Punch*, the rebellion was fodder for satire, for Haydon it was pure melodrama, redolent of the radical political struggles of the early nineteenth century. The School of Design was "Old Corruption" all over again. It was nothing more than a "tool to cramp the English citizen in his thirst for knowledge." A far cry from the engine of edification and uplift that Haydon had once imagined, the school seemed to be a tool of jealous class privilege just like his despised Royal Academy. But even in his waning days Haydon longed for a time when "every Briton" might have as easy access to figure study as to the "ABC." Writing in the *Times*, he invoked the "spirits" of Raphael, Michelangelo, and Cellini as guarantors for his dream.[121] Simultaneously, in his diary, Haydon imagined that the "genius of Britain," so evident in bygone days, would rise again someday, "fresh and vigorous," to vanquish "the Aristocratic Demon of Pride & Pomposity."[122]

ASPIRATION, CONTAINMENT, AND
THE *PENNY MAGAZINE*

Such perorations are typical of Haydon, not only for their emotiveness but also for their tendency to cast the students as ideal vessels for carrying out his own grand designs. To be sure, the same tendency is evident in the writings of Haydon's adversaries, though in drier, more prescriptive form. However, the Manchester melee and the London rebellion together remind us that the curricular contests at the School of Design were not simply theoretical discussions. Instead, they involved students' hopes and demands. On both occasions, students voted with their feet when the schools failed to meet their expectations. Their decisions likely had less to do with hard and fast principle than with other factors. Among these we might count pedagogical loyalty, group camaraderie, or individual ambition, whether of an artistic or vocational variety. Ultimately, the students brought their own expectations and aspirations to the schools. More often than not, these are difficult to discern within the official archives, which include minutes, speeches, and reports. To be sure, these sources inform us about the constituencies that attended the schools, their numbers, and their vocations.[123] They also reveal practices of attendance, which were often spotty, or habits of comportment, which could be "unruly."[124] On a more laudatory note, the minutes recount student successes, whether in prize competitions or the marketplace. It turns out that some students managed to sell designs to manufacturers or even to rival their masters among patrons.[125] But within the official archive of the School of Design firsthand accounts of students' expectations are all too rare.[126]

Given this limitation, contemporary diaries and memoirs help us flesh out students' hopes and ambitions. These turn out to be as wide-ranging as the school's constituency itself. In his diary, for instance, William Andrews, a midcentury provincial student, welcomed the modest mobility that the Coventry School of Design provided. For ribbon designs made at the school, Andrews won several medals and prizes, most notably a trip to the Great Exhibition of 1851.[127] A different evaluation appears in the autobiography of Fred Miller, who would later associate himself with the arts and crafts movement. Miller recalled his education at the West London School of Art in a manner that vindicated the hyperbole of Haydon. It "was of a very rule-of-thumb character," he recollected as he bemoaned nights spent "drawing from uninteresting casts in a heated, fetid underground cellar." In the end, he found the study to be "so deadening" that he "dropped going to the school altogether."[128]

Why did some students regard the schools as valuable launching pads and others as detainments or derailments from greater ambitions? Some contrasts, of course, can be written off to individual aspiration, social background, and historical moment. But there are broader, more intangible matters that have to do with the cultural ideals about art and vocation that the students brought to the schools. The unyielding nature of the school's archives coupled with the spare qualities of artisanal autobiography require that we look elsewhere. One source, the *Penny Magazine*, provides an especially rich window onto the respectable artisanal culture of the day. The magazine was part of the expanding range of print culture for the laboring classes that developed contemporaneously with the School of Design. Like the school, the *Penny Magazine* sought to expand the visual literacy of mechanics and to extend the cultural capital of workers.[129] In this way, it participated in Haydon's project of artisanal uplift. At the same time, the *Penny Magazine* sought to convey work discipline for laborers. As such, it echoed Dyce's efforts at vocational training. In its own pages, the *Penny Magazine* thus contained many of the very contradictions that riddled the School of Design and shaped the expectations of students.[130]

In 1836, the Select Committee on Art Manufactures had looked with great hope to the *Penny Magazine* for its potential to improve the artistic acumen of the masses. Like other affordable illustrated weeklies, it used the innovation of steam printing to bring instruction to the laboring classes in unprecedented ways. The select committee had praised the *Penny Magazine* and its contemporaries as engines of the "paper circulation of knowledge" and welcomed their engravings as the "paper currency of art." Witnesses lauded these new publications for their potential to raise the cultural capital of the mechanic and artisan. One witness, the printing machine patentee William Cowper, welcomed the magazine's rich array of engravings from old masters such as Raphael, Michelangelo, and Rubens. He also praised its powers of dissemination. For instance, Cowper lauded a recent series on the Raphael cartoons. Thanks to the magazine's efforts, "hundreds of thousands of people" with no chance of seeing the originals gained the opportunity to admire the treasures. In a manner reminiscent of Haydon, Cowper explained that the *Penny Magazine*'s images could awaken slumbering genius. Views like this one from the British Museum, for instance, might encourage budding artists along a path of devoted study (fig. 9). If this proved too grandiose a hope, such images could at least teach the people to "respect and venerate the name of 'Artist.'"[131]

Cognizant of these possibilities, the printing maverick Charles Knight placed views from museums and paintings by old masters front and center in the *Penny Magazine*. No mere embellishments, these images were integral to the publication itself. To show as much, its editors located the magazine at the pinnacle of a history of popular illustration. For instance, an 1833 supplement entitled "The Commercial History of a *Penny Magazine*" extolled Knight's application of mechanical reproduction to wood engraving. Such an innovation made the magazine an agent for the democratization of visual culture. The magazine, it boasted, had the ability to reproduce images at the staggering rate of eight hundred per hour or ten thousand per day. Thanks to this capacity, art treasures were no longer "confined to the cabinets of a very few." They could reach thousands through engravings, which had merits all their own. In this proto-Benjaminian moment, it seems that the copy, not the original, carried an aura. The commentary that accompanied the image of Raphael's *Madonna* certainly suggests as much. The text did not laud the old master himself. Instead it showered praise on the engraving for its true conveyance of the great master's style (fig. 10).[132]

The *Penny Magazine* reproduced these images with the hope of imparting visual literacy and cultural capital to the "intelligent artisan" and the "plain man" who perused its pages.[133] But there were other lessons, too, that readers were to glean from its accounts of art. Those artisans who read about high art in the *Penny Magazine* found an inventory of virtues that they could apply to their lives and labors.[134] Much like the tales of the prophets of biblical days, the annals of artists offered parables and morals. Artists became figures for emulation, towering men whose lives provided maps for aspiration. First and foremost was Leonardo da Vinci, "handsome, well-formed, and possessed of great bodily strength" to accompany his genius. From Leonardo, readers could learn about patience; he was known for excellence rather than haste, "his object" being "less to do much than to do well."[135] The magazine lauded English masters, too. In Gainsborough, it found an exemplar of painterly execution and charitable magnanimity. There was also much to be garnered from decorative luminaries such as Bernard Palissy, the French porcelain painter whose works would eventually gain a place of prominence at the South Kensington Museum. In Palissy's life, those who labored without recognition or reward could find a germ of hope. According to the *Penny Magazine*, Palissy had passed a life of "toil, privation, and misery." He lived as a debtor and died as a prisoner. Fortuitously, posterity had rec-

[Gallery of Athenian Antiquities in the British Museum.]

9   Antiquities in print. *Penny Magazine of the Society for the Diffusion of Useful Knowledge* 1 (1832): 305. Reproduced courtesy of the Huntington Library, San Marino, California.

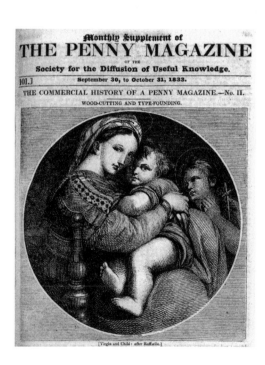

Monthly Supplement of
THE PENNY MAGAZINE
OF THE
Society for the Diffusion of Useful Knowledge.

[101.]   September 30, to October 31, 1833.

THE COMMERCIAL HISTORY OF A PENNY MAGAZINE.—No. II.
WOOD-CUTTING AND TYPE-FOUNDING.

[Virgin and Child: after Raffaelle.]

10   The work of art in the age of mechanical reproduction. *Penny Magazine of the Society for the Diffusion of Useful Knowledge* 2 (1833): 420. Reproduced courtesy of the Huntington Library, San Marino, California.

ognized him as a "zealous and persevering man of genius." Perhaps even Haydon might have found a grain of consolation here.[136]

These sketches offer just a few examples of the ways in which the *Penny Magazine* provided working men with figures for Haydonian emulation in the artists it profiled. Simultaneously, though, it urged the readership to modest pursuits that recalled the philosophy of Dyce. The writer of an article entitled "Little Things" exhorted laborers to content themselves with finding their rightful places on the great chain of the division of labor, regardless of where these might fall within its vast hierarchy. "Things small in themselves are often great in their consequences," it announced, as it upheld the virtues of the silkworm, whose eggs were "the source of employment and wealth to multitudes."[137] Like the silkworm, the *Penny Magazine* argued, working men should be modest, or at least realistic, in their pursuits. To press this point, it looked again to the lives of the artists. It found a cautionary tale in the person of Benjamin West, whose life verged on tragedy. West was a "very worthy man" and a "very respectable artist," too. His single flaw was artistic ambition. According to the *Penny Magazine*, Benjamin West had "overreached himself" by pursuing history painting, a branch deemed by many—Haydon among them—to be the "highest walk in the profession."[138] Of its readers, the magazine counseled more restrained ambition, especially when it came to art. It found a case in point in an anonymous deaf-mute who gained a livelihood as a sign painter after he purchased a fourpenny box of watercolors.[139]

The *Penny Magazine* thus revealed a number of contradictions that seemed to encapsulate the views of both Haydon and Dyce. It recommended aesthetic pursuits while also preaching utilitarian vocation. It provided models for aspiration while imparting tales of caution. Such contradictions are reminiscent of the curricular contests that gripped the School of Design. They are also indicative of a broader ambivalence about education as uplift. Such mixed feelings likely extended well beyond the purview of the pedagogues. Artisans in mid-nineteenth-century Britain might have carried similar ambivalences as they sought to better themselves without betraying craft or class.[140] It should be no surprise, therefore, that the students at the School of Design brought a set of fraught imperatives to an already contentious enterprise. This was par for the course in an era whose leading figures valued heightened access to culture even as they policed the lines between aspiration and containment, not to mention the boundaries between art and design.

Such concerns would bedevil philosophers and reformers throughout the century. Perhaps they were only resolvable in fiction, as a text by the French aesthetic philosopher and restorer Emanuel Viollet-le-Duc, which was published in 1881, suggests so well. *Learning to Draw; or, the Story of a Young Designer* is a novel and a drawing treatise rolled into one.[141] It tells the story of Jean, a French youth rescued from rural poverty by a capitalist benefactor who recognized his drafting skills. Viollet-le-Duc peppered his discussion of Jean's education with his own meditations on drawing; to all of this, he added diagrams for study. As his education reached its culmination, Jean faced the ultimate decision: whether to parlay his training into a career as a painter or a livelihood in trade. In the end, the hero chose to pursue industrial art despite the scorn of his less talented peers. Viollet-le-Duc's text concludes with the image of a vindicated Jean, whose choice allowed him to prosper, to buy his poor parents a home, to find situations for his brothers, and to provide dowries for his sisters.

CONCLUSION

In the heady early days of the School of Design, the choice between fine art and industrial design was not so easily resolved. It certainly had not been decided by 1849, when a Select Committee on the School of Design convened to assess the young institution's progress. According to the 1849 report, the schools had fallen well short of their purported mission of improving designs for manufactures. Time and again, witnesses branded them an "utter and complete failure."[142] The leading aesthetic periodical of the day, the *Art Journal*, summed up the feeling on the occasion of the report's release when it declared, "In place of the glorious sun-burst of expectancy and promise which beamed upon their pristine efforts, the shadow of a twelve years' disheartening failure casts its gloom."[143]

It is, perhaps, no surprise that the figure remained as murky, if not as contentious, a question in 1849 as it had in the foregoing years. In fact, by 1849 neither the academy nor the workshop had emerged victorious.[144] What is striking, however, is the rise to prevalence in the report of another matter. Rather than curricular principle, marketplace efficiency became the driving concern for design education with the publication of the 1849 select committee report. This marked a real departure from a skepticism about the marketplace that had characterized the early years of the School of Design, when critics feared that the institution would turn into a state-sponsored pattern manufactory that could threaten free trade. Time and again, advocates had assured detractors that the school's mission was to "produce designers and not designs."[145] Yet, in the face of its attempts to squelch this criticism, the school had become "nearly useless" as a training ground for the marketplace.[146] The witnesses who testified certainly supported this notion. A textile manufacturer told the committee that there was scarcely a pattern produced at the school that would be useful in his trade. Eminent decorators such as J. G. Crace echoed these assessments. Moreover, a ribbon and shawl designer charged that the school was out of step with the public taste. In the more than ten years of the school's existence, he could think of only one student who had produced what he called a "good marketable design." These assessments help us to decipher an enigmatic charge made by the founder of the South Kensington Museum, Henry Cole, who took the reins of the school in 1849. While the school had not "totally failed," Cole argued, it had "totally failed as a School of Design."[147] What was needed, clearly, was training informed less by aesthetic principles and invested more in commercial utility. In the future, success would mean ministering to the market itself, not following a particular pedagogical model. The dream of aesthetic uplift would take a backseat to the production of patterns.

The growing preoccupation with marketable patterns marks an important shift from the earlier curricular disputes, which concerned themselves, uniquely, with the skilled working man. Their particular stances on the figure aside, Haydon, Dyce, and their contemporaries had placed the artisan front and center as they debated a curriculum for the School of Design. To be sure, they differed when it came to the specific contours of this education. When they sparred, however, they engaged in a conversation about the aesthetic, cultural, and productive capacities of skilled labor. When a concern for pattern prevailed in 1849, the imperative of improving the artisan, whatever the method, diminished. In the embrace of the market, we find yet another example of the foreclosure of design education's radical potential. As we shall see, however, the calls for vocational competency made by Dyce, as well as the pleas for artistic uplift advanced by Haydon, would prove useful for working men later in the century. They would draw on both, it turns out, when they sought access to the metropolitan museums discussed in chapter five.

These long-term implications notwithstanding, we should note that the select committee report of 1849 was just part and parcel of a broader discussion of pattern among manufacturers, artists, and others that developed in the 1840s. In fact, pattern had itself been the subject of a great parliamentary contest, not to mention another select committee report, earlier in the decade. At that time, aesthetes, manufacturers, MPs, and economists had immersed themselves in an ancillary design debate. Between 1839 and 1842, they argued at fever pitch over the question of design copyright. They contested the length of protection for designs on consumer wares, especially the cheaply printed cottons called calicoes. In the process, the protagonists weighed the worth of patterns and the integrity of the marketplace. Much like the School of Design disputes, the copyright contest provides a portal onto a larger set of aesthetic issues and marketplace anxieties. At the school these matters coalesced around the figure, but in the copyright debate they would center on the ever vexing matter of originality.

CHAPTER TWO

Originality and Sin

CALICO, CAPITALISM, AND THE COPYRIGHT

OF DESIGNS, 1839–1851

In February of 1840, Edmund Potter, a calico printer, traveled down to London from Manchester. A combination of personal interest and national concern spurred him to make the journey. While in London, Potter had a date to testify before the Select Committee on Copyright of Designs. When he spoke before this committee, Potter revealed an evil that was weakening his trade and threatening Britain's industrial arts. "Notorious pirates" were preying on this honorable printer's stock and copying his goods, which were distinguished for their original patterns, fine colors, and impeccable execution. When they did so, they compromised his trade, causing "very serious loss." Countless other printers and merchants joined Potter in testifying before this new select committee, which was chaired by James Emerson Tennent, MP. There they reported a widespread plague that was debilitating wallpaper, porcelain, chintz, and calicoes. The dismal reports revealed a piracy so widespread that it threatened to debase the industrial arts wholesale. Ultimately, it promised to render the nation's nascent network of design schools—which Potter himself had a hand in creating—useless. In the face of pervasive piracy, Potter and his compatriots beseeched Parliament to strengthen its ineffective design copyright laws. Only this sort of intervention could save their trades, the nascent enterprise of design reform, and the possibility of original design.[1]

Between 1839 and 1842, an unlikely coalition of men mounted an impassioned campaign to extend the copyright of designs. Led by Conservative member of Parliament for Belfast, James Emerson Tennent, this group included legislators, manufacturers, merchants, and economists whose interests surpassed party and region. They centered their case for extension on the trade in calicoes, cheaply printed cottons that had a long and storied history in Britain from the seventeenth century onward. Calicoes were integral to the consumer revolution, the industrial revolution, and the export trade. By the 1830s, leading printers such as Edmund Potter argued that piracy was running rampant in the industry. Given its prevalence, they asked for a longer and stronger copyright. Parliamentary intervention would protect individual livelihoods and improve the nation's trade. Just as important, it promised to safeguard a tradition of original design, which copyright's proponents associated with good taste, high morals, and a strong marketplace.[2] The efforts of this coalition would meet with modest success in 1842, when the copyright on calicoes was extended from three to nine months, though not the twelve its members had advocated. But this was no foreordained victory. Instead, the proponents of extension fought for it with alacrity and vigor in the face of a boisterous opposition mounted by rival Lancashire MPs, merchants, and calico printers. Advocates of the free market, these men questioned the necessity of extension, not to mention the possibility of original design.

To press their cases, those on both sides of the matter generated a massive archive, enumerated afterward as "a pile of pamphlets, a heavy Parliamentary report, several heavier debates, a clever 'Digest of Evidence,'" and "files of Lancashire papers."[3] These pages chronicle a neglected epoch in nineteenth-century design reform. Like those better-known minute books and speeches that recount the early years of the School of Design, these texts provide a view onto a contentious culture of aesthetic reform. While the protagonists at the School of Design argued over curriculum, the leading figures in the copyright campaign sparred over the period—not to mention the very logic and viability—of protection.

In both instances, bureaucratic disputes engendered heated arguments

Originality and Sin

because they hit on larger issues confronting an industrializing marketplace. The curricular matters debated by Haydon, Dyce, and their ilk had proved contentious because they addressed the changing place of the artisan in an industrial regime of production. In the case of the copyright, protagonists locked horns over the importance of patterns—and those who produced them—within a particular industry in transition. The arguments mounted by each side bring the textile manufacture into sharp focus.[4] Notably, the campaign sheds light on a mechanizing industry and a growing marketplace. But the participants in the debate illuminated far more than the market dynamics of one particular trade. The literature produced in the course of the copyright contest offers us an entry into the cultural world of calico printers and merchants. Like the artisanal protagonists discussed in chapter one, these men were not only producers of patterns and dealers in goods. They were also cultural actors who engaged in a complex process of self-fashioning when they sought to style themselves as venerable producers. In tracts and testimony, they showed themselves to be the defenders of original design and the attendant virtues of artisanal production and private property. When they presented themselves as the protectors of a venerable aesthetic tradition, they branded their opponents as plagiarists and pirates—men of questionable character who preyed on the nation's stock of good designs and compromised its industrial future. In the face of this piracy, men such as Edmund Potter called on Parliament to protect original design.

The valorization of originality on the part of extension's proponents is one of the many ironies in a campaign that focused its concerns on the calico manufacture. The calico trade, we shall see, was predicated on copying of manifold varieties. The mechanical reproduction made possible by innovation, the mimesis of the fashion system, the imitation that was part and parcel of imperialism, and, of course, the illicit duplication of piracy all played a part in calico's commodity history.[5] Given these realities, perhaps it was the opponents of the copyright, rather than the advocates, who were closer to the mark in their estimations of the trade. They questioned the very possibility of original design in a regime of mechanical reproduction. Rather than original design, their *summum bonum* was the free marketplace. Ultimately, when they sparred over the period of protection, these antagonists engaged in a dispute over the aesthetic and ethical stakes of mechanical reproduction. And when they questioned the hierarchies of original and copy, they contested the nature of industrial modernity in early Victorian Britain.

From its very introduction into Britain, the calico trade relied on copying of all sorts.[6] The link between calico and copies dates to the seventeenth century, when the English and Dutch East India Companies began importing the cloth from the Indian subcontinent.[7] Along with such goods as Chinese porcelain, calico transformed the visual and material culture of urban Britain, providing growing ranks of consumers with an unprecedented "cornucopia" of "colors, patterns, and qualities."[8] Calicoes were especially beloved by women, whose passion for the colored cloth galvanized a fashion frenzy during the late seventeenth century and the early eighteenth.[9] At that time, ladies from the upper and middling ranks avidly sought out the imported cottons for clothing and furnishings.[10] Servants who aimed to emulate their superiors joined in this pursuit. Their desires were sated, at least in part, by hand-me-downs from the ladies who employed them. Such adulation of Indian cottons led critics to lament the impossibility of distinguishing the mistress from the maid and so to suggest the disruptive potential of the calico trade.[11]

Eighteenth-century writers branded the craze, and the essentially mimetic pursuit of fashion, as deceptive, reprehensible, and dangerous.[12] Female consumption and feminine desire occupied a central place in their criticisms, but cultural commentators also looked with disdain on oriental production. One eighteenth-century writer derided the Indian products as "tawdry, bespotted, flabby, [and] ragged." If their aesthetic was reprehensible, their producers were despicable. They were, in the mind of the same critic, "a parcel of Heathens and Pagans that worship the Devil and work for a half-penny a day."[13] Although he was a strong advocate of a vigorous domestic marketplace, Daniel Defoe expressed a similar distaste when he portrayed calico as a foreign invasion. Like the plague, calicoes had "crept" into "houses," "closets," and "bedchambers," he noted, until "curtains, cushions, chairs, and at last beds themselves were nothing but calicoes or Indian stuffs."[14]

Representatives of the domestic silk and woollen industries effectively harnessed these critiques, deploying a patriotism based on protectionism as they sought to salvage their livelihoods in the face of the calico invasion.[15] Beginning in 1700, Parliament responded to their woes by passing a series of acts that prohibited the importation of fabrics that had been dyed, stained, or painted.[16] Despite the threat of a fine of two hundred pounds, eighteenth-century merchants persisted in smuggling calicoes into Britain, and customers continued to buy them.[17] Parliament sought to discourage this practice wholesale in 1720 when it passed a stringent sumptuary law that prohibited the "use or wear of any printed or dyed calicoes." It softened the law in 1736 but did not strike it from the books until 1774.[18]

In one of the many ironic turns in calico's commodity history, the acts passed to protect the domestic woollen and silk trades gave rise to an indigenous cotton manufacture.[19] An artisanal printing trade began near London with the express goal of copying the outlawed Indian productions.[20] Thanks to the metropole's role as an import center, printers found ready examples of Indian wares. Working with wooden blocks and later with copper plates, printers imitated these goods and sold their high-end productions to consumers from the middling and upper ranks. It was a distinctly artisanal enterprise, as this early-nineteenth-century engraving suggests (fig. 11).[21] The enterprise of copying Indian cottons would grow to industrial proportions in Lancashire, where the calico manufacture found a new home in the 1760s and 1770s. There, and in Scotland, too, a mechanized trade devoted to large-scale production developed. It flourished thanks to innovations in spinning, dyeing, bleaching, and, most important, printing.[22] The most crucial of these developments was the cylinder, or roller, which allowed printers to copy long, continuous pieces of cloth as never before.[23] By the mid–nineteenth century, the block could print six pieces per day while the roller could produce between two and five hundred.[24]

The enormity of this development was not lost on nineteenth-century commentators, who marveled at the cylinder's productive capacities. Equally interested in industry and art, the *Penny Magazine* conveyed the wonder of the trade. It applauded the "cylinder machine," which printed three-quarters of a mile of cloth per hour, effectively substituting "*miles for yards*" as the measure of production (fig. 12).[25] This acceleration of production changed the character of consumption. By the time the *Penny Magazine* spotlighted the trade in 1843, members of the laboring classes, and women especially, had become the chief consumers of cali-

The Calico Printer.

11   Calico printing by block. Woodcut.
*The Book of English Trades, and Library
of the Useful Arts* (1821). Yale Center for
British Art, Paul Mellon Collection.

12   Calico printing by roller. *Penny
Magazine of the Society for the Diffusion
of Useful Knowledge* 12 (1843): 296.
Reproduced courtesy of the Huntington
Library, San Marino, California.

[Cylinder-printing.]

coes within Britain. This ascendancy was a long time coming. From the mid–eighteenth century onward, laboring women had delighted in the dress prints, shawls, bandannas, and handkerchiefs produced by the provincial trade.[26] Provincial manufacturers also sold similar, if bolder and more garishly colored, wares abroad. By the middle of the nineteenth century, the provincial trade would supply the markets of Africa, Asia, the United States, South America, and, in what D. A. Farnie once called a "gesture of supreme presumption," even the Indian subcontinent.[27]

Taken together, these developments enabled the provincial calico manufacture to prosper and eventually to outstrip the metropolitan trade. By the end of the eighteenth century, provincial printers presented a real threat to London.[28] They produced more cottons, with greater rapidity and cheapness, than their metropolitan counterparts.[29] But, although the provincial trade easily surpassed that of London in sheer quantity, it did not enjoy the same renown for tasteful designs.[30] Ever the entrepreneurs, provincial printers sought to rectify this shortcoming by garnering inspiration from London. Printers from Lancashire, and even Scotland, took the practice of copying that had governed the trade's development to yet another level. In a widespread practice, they imitated the designs of their metropolitan counterparts, often copying these patterns wholesale.[31]

Metropolitan printers lashed out against the imitative practices of their provincial competitors, which they branded as piracy. The printer Charles O'Brien was one of the first to lambast the activities of provincial manufacturers. He decried their "piratical practices" as "unwarrantable in intention, disgraceful in execution, and destructive in their tendency." Inveighing against his provincial competitors, O'Brien conceived an imaginative geography of the trade that pitted the moral and tasteful London printer against the debased Lancashire manufacturer. His formulation elevated the so-called original designs of the metropole above the pirated wares of the provinces. As O'Brien saw it, London's productions surpassed Lancashire's on aesthetic, economic, and moral grounds. Along with other metropolitan printers, he maintained that piracy threatened this hierarchy because it deprived original design of its value. O'Brien and his allies found sympathetic ears in Westminster. There Parliament would respond to their concerns with an early effort at design reform. It passed a two-month copyright on printed designs in 1787 and extended this protection to three months in 1794.[32] This would prove an effective stopgap measure at best. By the time Tennent, Potter, and their allies mounted their campaign, calico printing had become, by and large, a provincial concern. The Lancashire manufacture, especially, had "swallowed up" the venerable London trade.[33]

MECHANIZATION, MODERNITY, AND THE MARKETPLACE

The acts of 1787 and 1794 were emblematic of the "fitful attempts" to improve the industrial arts in eighteenth-century Britain.[34] Such efforts would attain new vigor, legitimacy, and coherence in the 1830s thanks to the Select Committee on Arts and Manufactures, which spurred Parliament to revisit the issue of design copyright.[35] In 1839, just two years after the School of Design opened its doors at Somerset House, Parliament passed a new copyright law.[36] This statute established a central designs registry in London and extended the copyright to Ireland and Scotland. Ultimately, however, this act would prove to be a feeble response to complaints delivered to the select committee. It was especially disappointing to representatives of the calico manufacture, whether printers, merchants, or traders. While the new law extended a twelve-month copyright to woven fabrics, it granted only three months' protection to calicoes. Advocates of the calico manufacture complained about this statutory distinction. In what may seem an ironic deployment of popular radicalism, Tennent held that the 1839 statute attested to the "impolicy" and "injustice" of Parliament.[37] Printers, politicians, and political economists united behind him as they argued that calicoes should carry a twelve-month term of protection. The three-month period of protection had become a "dead letter," they explained, as they illuminated the changes in a marketplace where originals and copies were becoming increasingly indistinct. To drive their case home, they would raise the specter of an aesthetic and artisanal France, which was just recovering from the Napoleonic wars.[38]

Tennent and his allies enumerated the myriad changes within the calico manufacture. Most notable was the acceleration of production due to mechanization. It was not that mechanization itself deteriorated design, they explained.[39] Instead, the increased productive capacity of Britain's manufacture presented designers with a paradox that inventor Charles Babbage had identified in his *Economy of Machinery and Manu-*

factures, published in 1832. There, Babbage had noted that mechanical reproduction enhanced the value of original design.[40] For historians and cultural critics, Babbage's words are instructive because they challenge Walter Benjamin's influential notion that the original loses its aura in a regime of mechanical reproduction.[41] For contemporaries, Babbage's understanding was useful because it provided theoretical heft for their arguments. In fact, the advocates of copyright extension took Babbage's theories a step further. If mechanization made designs more valuable, it also rendered originals increasingly vulnerable. In a mechanized marketplace, honest printers found themselves daily at the mercy of pirates who could produce wares with staggering and unprecedented speed. To show as much, Tennent and his allies peppered their pleas for extension with striking vignettes. Tennent, for instance, told the tale of a pirate who "surreptitiously obtained" the new dress patterns of an eminent house. Just eight days later, he sold shoddy copies at a shockingly lower price.[42]

The growing export trade also made patterns increasingly vulnerable. It was impossible, extension's advocates held, to protect stock in both the domestic and overseas markets under the three-month copyright. This was due to the fact that sales at home and abroad occurred at different times of the year, as the printer Salis Schwabe explained so well.[43] Schwabe, who catered to clients in the Americas, the Mediterranean, the Levant, and Europe, outlined the yearlong trade cycle of one dress pattern. Schwabe designed the pattern in June, engraved it in September, sent it overseas in October, marketed it at home in January, and delivered it in February and March for sales that extended to the following July.[44] Such predicaments promised to become only more prevalent in the nineteenth century's globalizing marketplace. Once "so distinct," the "tastes" of consumers across the globe seemed to be converging, albeit within limits. To be sure, "gaudy" large prints remained in vogue in the Americas, where calico clothed slaves.[45] Such exceptions notwithstanding, the tastes of all nations seemed yearly to be "growing more assimilated."[46]

If the three-month copyright presented a problem for the garment trade, it proved an even more insurmountable obstacle in home furnishings and paper staining. Here goods did not merely "pass off with the season."[47] Furniture patterns remained "valuable" for at least four or five years, the printer Edward Brooke explained to the select committee.[48] Others followed Brooke by stressing the particular rhythms of the

13   Regent Street by Thomas Hosmer Shepherd. Graphite and watercolor. *One from A Series of 41 Drawings to Illustrate the Work "London in the Nineteenth Century."* Yale Center for British Art, Paul Mellon Collection.

furniture trade. Thomas Clarkson, a high-end upholsterer, deemed the three-month copyright ludicrous in a market in which it took him a full year merely to ascertain if a pattern might be successful. In response, Clarkson and others went so far as to advocate a two- or even a three-year copyright.[49]

When they commented on the rhythms of the furniture trade, men like Clarkson and Brooke illuminated a dynamic consumer marketplace. The very cadences of its retail culture necessitated a longer copyright. The same could be said for its practices of display. When they pressed for a stronger copyright, the advocates of extension pointed to the "general opening up of visual culture" that was so central to consumption practices in the eighteenth and nineteenth centuries. Shop windows, like those in the arcades in Regent Street pictured here, displayed patterns for all to see (fig. 13). The display of design was not, however, restricted to London's West End. Throughout the nation, the rise of traveling merchants, illustrated periodicals, trade catalogues, and display techniques gave design a new and unparalleled visibility.[50] Of late, the very modernity of this retail culture has become a subject of contention among historians.[51] Certainly, the development of a culture of

Originality and Sin

display was incremental in character. Given this fact, it is all the more intriguing that the proponents of extension brought a rhetoric of shock to their discussions of retail culture, which they described as an abrupt development. In the 1830s and 1840s, they noted, the products of calico printers filled London's shopwindows. Although intended to promote the wares of manufacturers and retailers, these displays left producers vulnerable to attack. One opponent of the bill, John Brooks, confessed before the select committee that he employed a pattern drawer to "look through the windows" in the City of London and the West End, where he would find designs worthy of reproduction. Men such as Brooks's assistant devised an ingenious approach to pattern production. Instead of copying patterns wholesale, they pieced them together through accumulation, using "a little bit from one and from another" and making what one witness called a veritable "jumblement."[52] For eminent printers, this practice exemplified patterns' insecurity as property. It was the very "*immateriality*" of a pattern on display that allowed it to be "stolen through a window, without cutting out a pane of glass," or "carried off by the eye, without being traced, or found upon the person."[53]

It was not just visual spectacle but alienation too that marked the calico marketplace as distinctly modern. Witnesses who testified before the select committee made it clear that alienation, like the culture of display, endangered the trade. Printers such as Thomas Clarkson reported that they had fallen victim to the depersonalization wrought by commerce's expansion. In fact, Clarkson avowed before the select committee that his very customers had betrayed him, albeit unknowingly. The unwitting pawns of pirates, they had inadvertently passed Clarkson's designs to men of questionable character, whom he deemed "mean enough to do anything."[54]

The proponents of extension thus argued that the very developments that had enriched the calico trade posed a threat to original design. As they pressed for extension, Tennent and his allies cast the copyright as a shield against the depredations of a modern marketplace. Yet they also maintained that a stronger copyright was essential to the trade's growth, especially in the face of an industrializing France.

Like the advocates of the School of Design, extension's supporters added geopolitical weight to their claims by looking across the English Channel to France, whose recovery from the Revolution and the Napoleonic wars made a new British law all the more imperative. To date,

Chapter Two

Britain had benefited from France's struggles, as its prowess as an export power suggested. However, the proponents of extension warned that France would soon challenge Britain's market dominance.[55] For decades, printers had taken comfort in a pervasive understanding that Britain excelled on the "useful" side of the trade while France had achieved supremacy in the "ornamental" aspects of textile production.[56] This understanding would persist at the Great Exhibition of 1851. There French artisans garnered praise for their skill and taste. At times, exhibition critics would even consign French production to an artisanal past. Still, France's newfound industrial vigor appeared ominous to extension's advocates in the 1830s and 1840s. To them, it seemed inevitable that a France that married industrial strength to aesthetic prowess would certainly deal a commercial blow to Great Britain.[57]

For all of the attention given to the subject, French superiority in design confounded several contemporary commentators. When asked about French aesthetic prowess, for instance, John Brooks testified, "I cannot give any reason for it, only they have got the taste some how or other, and we seem to follow it." This understanding proved ludicrous to Tennent. Taste was not, he argued, the fruit of some mysterious "configuration of nature." Rather, it was the result of cultivation. Whereas the English regarded "taste in design" as "common-place and valueless," Tennent held, the French had "nurtured" it with "all the tenderness bestowed upon a rare exotic."[58] As he drew this analogy, Tennent denied that there might be anything innate about good taste. His ally, the barrister George Brace, put it well when he maintained, "We possess no strictly *natural taste* whatever."[59] Like Tennent, Brace held that social and cultural institutions shaped aesthetic practices.

James Thomson, a leading figure in the debate, an "indefatigable pamphleteer," and a man touted as the "Duke of Wellington of calico-printers," provided the most comprehensive analysis of those institutions.[60] The first was, of course, the Catholic Church. In France, he argued, "beautifully decorated" churches gave the people a sense of "form and color." Second, France's long-standing drawing schools, recently investigated by William Dyce, elevated design to a "liberal art" and venerated designers as "gentlemen." These institutions, Thomson argued, provided a welcome contrast to those in Britain, where design was considered a mechanical employment. Finally, and most critically, Thomson listed among those institutions devoted to ennobling design a strong copyright dating to the 1730s. When it came to design copyright, France boasted the "most comprehensive and effectual" law in Europe. In France, extension's advocates noted, periods of protection ranged from one year to the life of the designer. Given these advantages, Thomson forecast that Britain would stand "on a footing of equality" with France only when it granted a twelve-month period of protection to its calico printers.[61]

Katie Scott's scholarship on the French case suggests that Thomson, Tennent, and their allies may have exaggerated the legal might of the copyright across the channel.[62] This idealization is just part and parcel of the striking brand of Francophilia deployed in the copyright campaign. In the interest of safeguarding British design, extension's supporters mobilized a mélange of French symbols. These ranged from the Catholic Church, a frequent emblem of despotism among Britons, to the call for equality, a potent rallying cry for English radicals. The copyright campaign thus places the Franco-British opposition that so many scholars have discussed in a new light.[63] It suggests a certain pragmatism, not to mention a hybridity, to this discourse. Proponents of extension, we find, strategically deployed Francophilia to advance their cause. Regardless of their political alignments, they found in ancien régime institutions such as "Papism" and protectionism mechanisms for redressing the ills of a modern marketplace, especially design piracy.

SELF-FASHIONING, ARTISANAL PRODUCTION, AND PROPERTY

When they outlined developments within the calico trade, Tennent and his allies demonstrated that a stronger law had become requisite for their livelihoods and the national health alike. Yet their arguments eclipsed mere matters of supply and demand. As they pressed for a new law, the proponents of extension engaged in a process of self-fashioning wherein they styled themselves as the defenders of original production.[64] This intricate enterprise relied on the rhetoric of imperiled masculinity, it looked to statistics, it drew on political discourse, and it exploited literary heritage. When they fashioned themselves the protectors of originality, moreover, copyright's proponents showed themselves to be the guardians of artisanship and property. In the process, they marshaled a set of associations that allowed them to distinguish themselves—morally, politically, and aesthetically—from the pirates they so reviled.

To press their cause, extension's advocates portrayed themselves as "creative and conscientious printers," "enterprising men," risk takers, and "speculators or adventurers in goods."[65] When they sold original designs, Tennent and his allies contended, they braved an uncertain marketplace. Those who pioneered new styles never knew which designs would "take the public taste," "strike the public," or "hit" the market. The odds of success, the printer Edmund Potter lamented, were slim to none in a trade in which only one in five hundred designs flourished.[66] Its likelihood appeared all the more bleak in a market fraught with piracy. To press this point, the printer and merchant Augustus Applegath likened the current marketplace to a rigged lottery. It was useless, he mourned, to design new patterns in a market in which a pirate was likely to run away with his "prize."[67] The irrational market wrought by piracy compromised revered traditions of vigorous trade and gentlemanly commerce. The printer confessed that he had "suffered" at the hands of copyists, who had "entirely destroyed" his designs. Others, too, bemoaned the "untoward events" of the piratical marketplace. Like the virtue of a compromised maiden, their trades had deteriorated "beyond telling."[68] The rhetoric of imperiled masculinity deployed by Applegath and his allies is striking. It bears a close resemblance to that employed among risk-taking merchants in colonial America. This continuity indicates that those on both sides of the Atlantic were bound in a common culture of trade. Even more appositely, it suggests that crises of masculinity were part and parcel of the upheavals of industrial production and commodity capitalism during the eighteenth and nineteenth centuries.[69] These changes would not only shape the identities of producers. They would inform the self-conceptions of consumers, too, as we will see in chapter four's examination of the Museum of Ornamental Art and its critics.

Yet, design piracy's injuries went far beyond ruining livelihoods and assaulting masculinity. The practice also denigrated a broader tradition of honorable production that copyright's advocates sought to define as they made their case for extension. This extended beyond the artisanal production of the small workshop to the venerable manufacture of the modest firm. Thomson and Potter, two Lancashire worthies who were among the foremost supporters of extension, conceived of themselves as proprietors of such firms, and they went to great lengths to distinguish their businesses from those of the pirates. They presided over "houses of the first magnitude" that represented the vestiges of an honorable but vanishing trade. Men of "small capital," they ran modest enterprises that allegedly retained the structure of artisanal workshops.[70] They catered to high-end constituencies; they preferred the block to the roller.[71] Friendly to aesthetic improvement—as their involvement with the Manchester School of Design indicates—these two Lancashire gentlemen employed their own designers.[72] They did not rely on products from the outside, whether bought or stolen. In stark contrast stood the businesses of the "notorious pirates," which served Britain's lower classes and the export market. The men of "large capital" who operated them lived nearby. They poached the designs of Thomson, Potter, and their ilk. Favoring the rolling machine over the block, they also threatened a venerated tradition of hand labor.[73] With their challenges to originality and hand labor came other travesties, including shoddy patterns, runny dyes, and discordant colors.

Potter and Thomson tried to shore up their discussion of artisanal manufacture with numeric data and even their own "statistical accounts." This was a timely enterprise, especially in the industrial north of England. At the moment of the copyright debates, the social investigators James Philips Kay and Edwin Chadwick were weaving "figures of arithmetic" together with "figures of speech" as they pioneered the science of statistics to understand social conditions in Manchester.[74] By employing numbers from the trade, Potter and Thomson hoped, similarly, to illuminate the productive condition of Lancashire. Simultaneously, they aimed to hone an image of themselves as protectors of artisanal manufacture, not to mention originality. In 1839, Potter's firm printed 83,000 pieces, and Thomson's produced 168,181. Potter employed 380 hands, and Thomson 930.[75] According to Thomson and Potter, these figures suggested the great credence they gave to design, aesthetics, and labor. These numbers were especially striking in comparison to those provided by James Kershaw, a man branded as the consummate pirate. One of the bill's foremost opponents, Kershaw boasted that his firm was the "largest" in Britain and that he produced "in very large quantities, indeed." Between 1834 and 1836, for instance, he printed over 880,000 pieces per year. In the face of these numbers, Thomson and Potter were quick to point out that Kershaw was no friend to artisanal practice. Although he produced calico in staggering amounts, Kershaw employed only 200 men.[76] These numbers were effective for their stark divergences. Less compelling would be the "statistical account" that Potter presented to the select committee. It did not provide a convincing delineation of the trade writ large. As Potter explained, he had surveyed eighty-eight firms in Lancashire, which employed 410 machines for roller printing and 8,601 tables for block printing. Twenty-six firms, together accounting for 133 machines and 3,940 tables, supported the bill. In opposition stood thirty-two firms with 155 machines and 2,661 tables. This said, Potter's statistics suggest the great efforts to which the defenders of the copyright would go to define themselves as the friends of artisanal production and original design.[77]

Not only did the advocates of extension portray themselves as defenders of small-scale production. They also framed themselves as the protectors of property in its manifold varieties. In tracts and testimony, extension's advocates sought to make the claim for property in design "as clear as the sun at noonday."[78] They would draw on many types of property, but one had especial resonance with their claims to be the true guardians of craft production. This was the notion of "property of skill," analyzed by John Rule. Artisans had put forth this idea in the late eighteenth century and early nineteenth, especially following the parliamentary repeal of statutory apprenticeship in 1814. When they invoked this notion, artisans had grasped for a measure of security in the face of a deregulated marketplace.[79] The annals of design reform suggest an even broader appeal. The idea resonated with students at the School of Design who sought to draw the figure. The design copyright debate attests even further to its flexibility. When they made their case for extension, the middle-class proponents also deployed property of skill strategically, if implicitly. Like the artisans who had preceded them, they sought to stake their ground in aesthetic debates and parliamentary struggles specifically by portraying themselves as venerable producers.

If they relied on implicit understandings of property of skill, extension's supporters looked far more explicitly to other forms of property. Notably, they relied on literary copyright law. Here they found an effective vehicle for making a claim to nascent notions of intellectual property.[80] Literary copyright had been the subject of great debate in the eighteenth century in the face of technological strides in printing, the growth of a literary marketplace, and the development of Romantic notions of the author. When they looked back to the eighteenth-century literary copyright contests, Tennent and his allies saw market circumstances that resembled their own. They also found cultural capital and moral authority in the notion of the heroic author.[81] Renowned printers such as Thomson and Potter harnessed this ideal for their own purposes by translating it into the figure of the original printer. The literary copyright debates thus offered the proponents of extension an apposite rhetorical strategy. They also provided a claim to relevance. Thanks to the continued growth of book consumption, both at home and abroad, literary copyright had surfaced once again as an issue of domestic and international concern at the very moment of the design copyright debate.[82] Its foremost champion, Charles Dickens—who would, incidentally, later dedicate *Our Mutual Friend* to Tennent—had raised the issue of international copyright law in his *American Notes* (1839).[83] It was Tennent, a published author himself, who used the comparison between literature and design most effectively in his *Treatise on the Copyright of Designs*.[84] There he ridiculed a regime in which a worthless literary trifle, whether a farce, a ballad, or a waltz, enjoyed a twenty-year copyright, while designs for calicoes held only three months' protection.[85]

Finally, Tennent's allies also likened patterns to long-standing forms of property such as "merchant's capital" and land. To fashion themselves as property's guardians, several printers looked especially to agrarian metaphors. Augustus Applegath was just one witness who portrayed himself as a yeoman farmer to argue that the copyright would render the market more predictable. If granted a longer period of protection, Applegath envisioned, "the more I sowed, the more I should reap."[86] The *Art Union* echoed Applegath when it used agricultural metaphors to uphold the claim for intellectual property. It was preposterous, it maintained, to allow protection to the "productions of the hand" while leaving the "work of the head" vulnerable to "every invasion of fraud and plunder."[87]

The savvy resort to the language of agriculture allowed the proponents of extension to carve out an advantageous political space, albeit one that stood at odds with their claim to property of skill. By emphasizing the sanctity of land as property, extension's advocates curried favor with landed members of Parliament. This maneuver was particularly attractive to men such as Edmund Potter, a fixture in Manchester's efforts to achieve design reform. A committed Lancashire liberal, Potter had lobbied for the repeal of the calico duty; he was also a supporter of the Anti–Corn Law League.[88] Potter's endorsement of laissez-faire, which he and others abandoned to advocate for the copyright, separated him from more conservative members of Parliament such as Tennent. By upholding property in land, Potter and his allies found a way to bridge the ideological gap that distanced them from the Tories. This process of framing themselves as property's guardians had other political uses as well. As they aligned themselves with Tory England, the advocates of extension distanced themselves from the radical causes of the industrial north. James Thomson went so far as to liken his opponents to Chartists, who disputed the sacredness of "property in land," and socialists, who attacked the private ownership of "goods and chattels." When he framed the pirates as property's enemies, Thomson placed them at not one but at two political extremes. By drawing on a popular variety of orientalism, Thomson compared the bill's challengers to unyielding tyrants. In their oppressive universe, the "insecurity of property" produced a "withering effect." It was detrimental to market progress regardless of whether the "spoiler" was a "Turkish Pacha in the despotic East" or an "English Pirate" in a "land of liberty and law."[89]

SERVILE COPYISTS AND NOTORIOUS PIRATES

As the foregoing discussion suggests, the process of self-fashioning undertaken by Thomson and other printers was a complex, even contradictory one. The proponents of extension marshaled a set of associations that traversed economics, politics, and literature as they sought to portray themselves as the stewards of artisanal practice, the friends of private property, and the guardians of original production. In the process, they did not hesitate to draw on opposing political traditions. There was another prong to their enterprise, too. It involved discrediting the bill's opponents, and it proved just as essential to the printers' endeavor of "self-fashioning," or so the literary critic Stephen Greenblatt suggested in his seminal discussion of the topic. Self-fashioning occurs, Greenblatt noted, "in relation to something perceived as alien, strange, or hostile."[90] The tracts and testimony produced by extension's supporters bear out this insight. When they depicted their challengers, Thomson and other printers invented foils who preyed on them, and also the national economy, in a moral drama of the marketplace. In the process, they sought to place their opponents at the boundaries of respectable trade, aesthetic improvement, and even the English nation. To do this, the proponents of extension mobilized a theatrical rhetoric, circulated didactic narratives, and deployed the notion of the predatory pirate. In the process, extension's advocates would strengthen their claims to be the guardians of aesthetic improvement and the protectors of design reform.

Extension's supporters employed a melodramatic rhetoric as they sought to brand their opponents in the copyright contest. According to James Thomson, the struggle pitted a group that exhibited "high principle, correct taste, and refined execution" against a set of opponents who acted with "avarice," "impunity," and "unscrupulous morality." The bill's opponents were "servile copyists" who showed no respect for originality. Parasites, they sat "lying in wait" to assail their more virtuous competitors.[91] They tended to congregate in Manchester, which had become infamous as the very "nest and nursery of piracy."[92] When he testified before the select committee, Charles Warwick embroidered Thomson's portrayal of the bill's opponents, characterizing them as "persons of very little character, who did not like to be seen in daylight."[93] Warwick, Thomson, and their colleagues sustained a common eighteenth-century association of the quality of goods with the morality of their producers. According to extension's advocates, the very copies wrought by piracy were themselves "deceptive and delusive," "evil," "immoral," "mean," and "servile."[94]

The liberal journalist William Cooke Taylor, a contributor to *Art Union*, cast the pirates in a particularly disadvantageous light by exploiting infamous literary and historical referents. Cooke Taylor compared the unethical pirates to Fagan's gang, which had captivated readers of Dickens's contemporary novel *Oliver Twist*. With their cunning thievery and artful dodgery, the band of pickpockets preyed on the "earners and possessors of money." The piratical printers, Cooke Taylor argued, committed equally egregious infractions. Worse, the pirates resembled the slave traders of recent times, who had dealt in human flesh until an act of Parliament outlawed their depraved practices in 1807. Slave traders and piratical printers shared more than a tendency toward debased morality. Both displayed a "splendid contempt" for "logics and ethics." Like their ignominious forbears, the pirates relied on specious arguments in their defense. Like the slave traders, the printers who opposed the copyright

Chapter Two

abused the notion of free trade. In their defense, piratical printers maintained that copying had the virtue of keeping the prices of printed cottons in check. Such an argument, Cooke Taylor claimed, was tantamount to the notion that slavery was a necessity because it provided "cheap sugar."[95] All told, design piracy was a reprehensible market practice.

As he continued his assault, Cooke Taylor likened design piracy to the high-seas piracy so prevalent in bygone days. It tended, as calico printers did not hesitate to note, to "produce sameness" and "retard the march of improvement in art." Several proponents of extension held that investment in patterns was not worth the "risk" it required in the face of piracy. It was foolish to invest in the production of expensive and tasteful patterns when they could be so easily copied.[96] According to Cooke Taylor, patterns remained "careless and hasty productions" for the very reasons that the coasts of England and France had remained uncultivated in the "times of Northmen." "People will not expend labor, time, and money for the benefit of pirates," he explained.[97] High-seas piracy of the sort that Cooke Taylor described was once the officially sanctioned practice of states and later the province of bands of renegade marauders. By the time of the copyright debate, however, it had long been an antiquated practice. The stuff of legend and didactic tales, piracy carried indeterminate meanings. On the one hand, it recalled the masculine vigor of an earlier era. Often practiced by the dispossessed, piracy was a form of ingenious, and even heroic, adaptation to inhospitable environments.[98] On the other hand, piracy connoted parasitism, degeneration, and marginality.[99] This association continued into the nineteenth century, when it extended well beyond the seas. If latter-day pirates did not transgress the boundaries of polite trade, they challenged the limits of respectability. A serially published tale called "Social Piracy," which appeared in the *New Monthly Magazine* in 1844, suggests as much. "Social Piracy" told the story of a parasitical family, the Hawkes, who lived off of the hospitality of their friends and relatives to the ruin of those around them.[100] In all of its nineteenth-century variants, then, piracy was a degenerative practice that led to decay.

As they sought to tarnish the reputations of their opponents, the proponents of extension built on these understandings. In particular, Edmund Potter deployed vignettes from the trade to illustrate the workings of "piratical economy." "It is always the low that copies the first-class printer," he claimed. Potter proposed a scenario in which printer

A lost his trade to pirates B, C, and D, each of whom executed in shoddier colors than his predecessor. By the time D got a hold of the pattern, A's "first-class" design had degenerated into something "servile" and "low."[101] Others similarly brought the analogy of class to bear on design's deterioration. According to Thomas Clarkson, piracy compromised the "patrician character" of originals, rendering them "common" and "plebeian."[102] The merchant Augustus Applegath also emphasized the market deterioration wrought by piracy. "I do not buy my patterns with any confidence," he bemoaned, as he staged himself as a subject at risk. "The draper who employs me does not order with any confidence; the retail draper does not buy with any confidence; the lady who buys the dress buys it almost with the impression that it is hardly worth while to buy it." As if to confirm that impression, the lady's servant managed to acquire a pirated copy almost immediately after her employer's purchase. "How we manage to get a trade, I hardly know," he mused.[103]

Applegath's narrative is remarkable for its incorporation of women and consumption into the nineteenth-century debate. Consumption had been a dominant concern among eighteenth-century critics of the calico craze. It was less so in the first half of the nineteenth century, when advocates of extension—and design reformers more generally—concentrated on supply-side matters. Still, there were anecdotal exceptions that featured ladies, servants, and shoddy English prints.[104] Such anecdotes remind us that consumption remained a preoccupation in the nineteenth century, especially for merchants, as the domestic and global consumer base continued to grow and change. At the time of the debate—and, in fact, from the mid–eighteenth century onward—working-class women were the chief consumers of calicoes within Britain.[105] They purchased machine-wrought designs like the "cheap cylinder print" pictured here (fig. 14). Together the combination of cheap prints and uneducated consumers made reputable merchants such as Applegath and ally Leo Schuster ever more sanguine about the copyright. Perhaps it would protect humble consumers from the vicissitudes of the marketplace—or at least safeguard the market from these very consumers.[106] In the eighteenth century, foreign producers and fashionable women compromised the marketplace, but in the nineteenth English pirates and working-class women threatened to do the same. In sum, when they pled for extension, its supporters maintained that the copyright promised to guard "true taste" from those plagues of the modern consumer marketplace—"fash-

Chapter Two

10　CHEAP CYLINDER PRINT,

Manufactured by Messrs. Devas, Minchener, and Routledge,
24 Lawrence Lane.

Exhibited by them in Class 18 (Woven, Felted, and Laid Fabrics, dyed and printed),
at the Great Exhibition of 1851.

This specimen is also a cheap print for the working classes: it too is effective as
a design, owing to the flat treatment of the background and the somewhat conven-
tional arrangement of the principal forms.

14　Calico print for
the working classes.
*Journal of Design and
Manufactures* 6 (1851):
10. Reproduced courtesy
of the Huntington
Library, San Marino,
California.

ion," "the tinsel of fancy," and "the passion of novelty."[107] In the face of
these depredations, only a strong law could protect the nation from the
rank degradation of piracy.

THE POLICY OF PIRACY

In tracts and testimony, the proponents of extension tried to dis-
credit their opponents through melodramatic rhetoric and marketplace
vignettes. Partial to Thomson and his allies from the outset, the Select
Committee on the Copyright of Designs also sought to vilify the so-
called pirates. As David Greysmith explains, extension's opponents
found themselves "reduced to petulance" when they testified before a
body that had come to a foregone conclusion.[108] If we sustain the meta-
phor of piracy, we might consider the select committee a latter-day bureaucratic counterpart to those punitive spectacles designed to condemn
high-seas pirates in earlier centuries. This parallel was not lost on James
Emerson Tennent, who relied on the committee's evidence to produce

Originality and Sin

two anonymously published tracts, *Argument Made Easy* and *The Policy of Piracy*.[109] Here Tennent strategically excerpted the select committee testimony of two of his most vociferous opponents, the Manchester printers Daniel Lee and James Kershaw. By circulating the words of his adversaries, Tennent sought to portray them to the reading public as rogues and even cuckolds.

A close analysis of Tennent's tracts reveals that he was not successful in this effort. Rather than coming off as idiots or schemers, the opponents of the bill showed themselves to be adherents of a different industrial logic. When they spoke before the select committee, the boisterous constituency of Lancashire printers and MPs who challenged the bill marshaled their own arguments about originals and copies. In strategic terms, they may have been defeated and disorganized, bulldozed as they were by the partisan committee. Yet their responses did not want for logic.[110] Instead they reveal that the "policy of piracy" was itself a market strategy. Rather than looking to protection, the opponents venerated the free market. In place of craft, they celebrated mechanization. And instead of distinctiveness they valorized imitation. Ultimately, they would call into question the very possibility of original design.

Like the bill's supporters, copyright's challengers addressed the issues of market expediency and foreign competition. They advocated what they touted as a theoretically pure, unadulterated version of laissez-faire. Echoing contemporary campaigns against the Corn Laws and the East India Company, the so-called pirates accused the advocates of extension of fostering "monopoly."[111] As they saw it, it was not copying but the copyright itself that harmed market health. Its extension would raise prices, increase litigation, and stymie the printing trade, not to mention the spinning and dyeing industries connected to it.[112] Louis Lucas, a merchant who opposed the bill, argued as much before the select committee. There he warned that extension would prove more debilitating to the nation's commerce than any amount of copying. Specifically, he predicted that the trade would grind to a halt in the face of the multitude of legal "scrapes" resulting from the new law.[113]

Just as the bill's supporters had, the so-called pirates looked overseas to make their case. They warned that the proposed law would place the English manufacturer on an unequal footing with foreign competitors. William Ross shrewdly cautioned that the copyright would present foreigners with a "bounty" that was off-limits to English printers.[114] While the proposed legislation punished British printers for copying, it contained no provisions for disciplining overseas firms. This was no small concern given the industrialization of continental Europe, which was aided in large part by the importation of British machinery. With this in mind, the bill's opponents looked with alarm to Germany, Switzerland, and even Belgium. Mark Philips, a liberal MP for Manchester, member of the select committee, and staunch opponent of the copyright, claimed that he could not shake the "bug bear" of overseas competition from his mind.[115] Others noted that foreign manufacturers even attacked Britain's trade from the inside. The engraver John Royle reported that it was customary for American firms to employ agents in Britain, especially in Manchester. Charged with obtaining swatches of British patterns, these agents provided an aesthetic lifeline to the United States. "Native Germans" did the same for their motherland. This sort of practice was certain to grow under the proposed law.[116]

It is telling that the pirates looked with seemingly prophetic concern to the United States and Germany rather than France. When they did so, the opponents of the bill espoused a distinct industrial strategy. While Tennent and his allies prized a quality trade as the key to Britain's market health, the bill's challengers favored bulk production or, as they put it, the trade in "medium goods" rather than "fine ones."[117] Moreover, when they pointed to the likelihood of foreign theft, the opponents of extension portrayed the English calico manufacture differently than the bill's supporters had. The pirates imagined Manchester as a fertile design field, while Tennent and his allies envisioned the city as an aesthetic wasteland, much as Benjamin Robert Haydon had on his visit there. This is all too evident in the dismissive responses to the concerns about foreign competition offered by Tennent and his allies. Why would continental printers copy English designs, one supporter of extension had asked, when they regarded these prints with the "greatest contempt" from the outset?[118]

These differences informed the contrasting degrees of significance that those on opposing sides of the issue accorded to design itself. The proponents of extension had pressed the importance of originals by likening them to different sorts of property, whether skill, literature, or land. The pirates attacked this understanding when they argued that patterns carried "very little value," especially in comparison with books or paintings. In the minds of the pirates, patterns did not fall within the domain of art. Instead, they were "common" things—commodities of "insignificant character" with "no talent in them," the residue of casual labor to be hawked about on the street. Hasty creations, a designer could produce between six and eight patterns during a day's work.[119] This strategy is evident in the designs registered by opponents after the bill's passage, which show little variety and variation.[120] Even James Thomson, whose patterns were remarkably distinct from one another, compared patterns to "soap-bubbles blown in the sunshine." "Glittering and iridescent," they tended to "burst" just as they came into being.[121]

Ultimately, when they testified that patterns were things of a "trifling" nature the pirates challenged the hierarchy of original and copy as laid out by extension's supporters—and they did so in several ways.[122] As he brought the labor theory of value to bear on the process of copying, printer Daniel Lee interrogated one of the orthodoxies held by extension's advocates. Tennent and his allies had repeatedly noted that designing an original required more time, labor, and creativity than making a copy. They based their claim on the fact that the process of translating an original design from pattern to roller—called "making out" within the trade—was a time-consuming one.[123] Lee argued, instead, that tracing a copy was "more tedious and unpleasant" than designing an original.[124] It was, perhaps, a skill in its own right.[125] Elsewhere, the printer John Brooks posed an alternate hierarchy of original and copy by drawing on the logic of fashion: the mimetic enterprise to which calico had been linked since its entry into Britain. He invited printers such as Thomson to copy his patterns outright. "It exalts my name," Brooks proclaimed. "We thrive better under people copying us than otherwise."[126] Brooks suggested that it was the copy, not the original, that conferred value within the marketplace. By so doing, he displayed a far better understanding of the fashion system and its reliance on imitation than had his opponents.[127]

The pirates even went so far as to confound the distinction between original and copy.[128] Once the bill passed, they warned, it would be impossible to distinguish originals from copies. When he spoke against the bill in the Commons, the Manchester MP Mark Philips pointed to the problems magistrates might face. They would meet a tremendous obstacle, he warned, for it was "difficult, if not utterly impossible, to decide when originality in design ended, and copying commenced."[129] John Heathcoat, another liberal MP, expressed a similar concern. As he marshaled the familiar association between women and fashion, Heathcoat suggested that ladies—who certainly loved novelty if not originality—might be the judges in copyright disputes.[130]

Given these associations, perhaps originality was nothing but a rarefied, metropolitan pursuit—or so the challengers of the bill argued as they cannily redeployed the politics of region that had characterized the copyright struggles of the eighteenth century. "I have heard very little of copying, never so much as I have heard since I came to London on this business," claimed the printer Daniel Lee. "We want enlightening on the subject, to make things work in Manchester, and in the trade generally, as they ought to do," he jestingly asserted. Lee confessed that he did not know exactly what a copy was. Even after consulting with an eminent Manchester merchant, and Samuel Johnson's *Dictionary* too, he remained at a loss. He presented two patterns to the committee and informed its members that he could not tell which was the copy and which the original. Surely, he suggested, such matters could not be decided in court.[131] To use the words of a modern-day critic, Hillel Schwartz, perhaps the distinction between "fair copy" and "forged copy" was tenuous at best.[132]

Finally, the pirates constructed a layman's aesthetic philosophy as they sought to stake their ground. When he testified before the select committee, James Kershaw, a Manchester printer, challenged the very categories of original and copy. Asked if he "copied patterns," Kershaw replied:

> No further than as every man is a copier, by taking the ideas which various patterns present to his mind, and endeavouring to adapt them anew, to constitute what is termed a new pattern, but which I contend, nevertheless, is not an original pattern. *Violations of the law of copyright I endeavour studiously to avoid*; and my invariable instructions to our pattern designers are TO COPY NO MAN'S PATTERNS, but to improve upon other men's ideas.[133]

In Kershaw's testimony, we find a popular iteration of the words of eighteenth-century aesthetic theorists for whom imitation was an organizing principle. To name one, Sir Joshua Reynolds had asserted that "originality" was produced "by imitation only."[134] Maxine Berg has noted that such notions get to the heart of the "tension between imitation and innovation" that was so central to product development and design in the eighteenth century.[135] This was not lost on those calico printers who had testified before the Select Committee on Arts and Manufactures. When he spoke before this body just a few years before, one witness had boldly stated, "We borrow from each other."[136] Yet it was Kershaw's crony Daniel Lee who went the farthest in disavowing the possibility of originality. Lee claimed that originality was not a matter of rearranging "old objects." As he explained it, a pattern was not original unless it contained elements that were themselves original.[137] He joined the printer John Brooks, who avowed that he had only seen two original designs over the past thirty years—Hoyle's Wave and the Diorama. In the case of the Diorama, a mistakenly creased cloth yielded a "new and unexpected effect" in which parallel stripes were repeated at an angle. Legendarily, the pattern sold twenty-five thousand copies in one day. In the end, perhaps originality was so elusive that it could only occur as the result of "pure accident."[138]

ORIGINAL DESIGN, NATIONAL STYLE, AND THE INDUSTRIAL REVOLUTION

When they discussed originality and its possibilities, the protagonists in the copyright debate engaged everyday commerce in philosophical terms. Ultimately, even those printers and manufacturers in the opposition fashioned themselves as market critics and aesthetic philosophers. This was certainly the case with the proponents of extension, who responded to the challenges of their adversaries with aesthetic notions of their own. James Thomson went to great lengths to salvage the category of original design in the face of the attack by the bill's opponents. To do so, he advanced what he called the "doctrine of Permutation." This rule dictated that, by using as few as six lines, a printer could produce an "infinite" number of designs, all of them entitled to copyright protection.[139] To press this point, Thomson employed the example of Lane's Net, a geometric pattern designed for the London market in the early nineteenth century and pictured here (fig. 15). Nowhere on this stark pattern was Hogarth's curved "line of beauty" to be found. Still, the pattern attained great "celebrity" in its day, enjoying "universal success" in England and abroad. This was not due to aesthetic merit, Thomson suggested. Rather, it was because Lane's Net bore "no resemblance" to anything produced before in Britain's print trade. Lane's Net was, unques-

Chapter Two

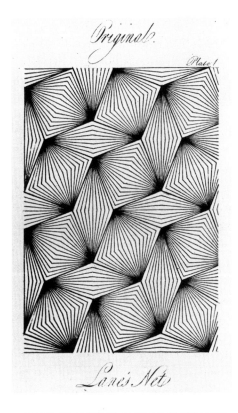

Original.

Plate 1

Lane's Net

15 Lane's Net. Plate 1 and
16 Plate 12 in Thomson,
*A Letter to the Rt. Hon. Sir
Richard Lalor Sheil* (1841).

Both reproduced courtesy
of the British Library, CT
180 (4).

Plate 12.

tionably, an original. But this pattern itself opened up a new style, giving "birth to more imitations and varieties than any other individual pattern in existence." Because copyright defended patterns, and not styles, all of these varieties were entitled to protection, including the variant shown here (fig. 16). A pattern in its own right, it was not an infringement on original design.[140]

Other advocates of extension rallied behind Thomson, claiming that a pattern could be considered "new" even if it contained "all the objects of another."[141] As they saw it, such building blocks of design as flowers, leaves, lines, and curves were common property out of which printers could fashion original patterns. They looked once more to pastoral metaphors as they stressed the cumulative and collective nature of design. Like the agriculturalist who learned his "best modes of tillage" from prior custom, the designer produced good patterns only by drawing on the work of others.[142]

These defenses of original design as a collective enterprise get us back to the origins of the calico trade and to the industrial revolution itself. It was the very desire to imitate, or to copy, Indian cottons that had given rise to the English calico manufacture, not to mention to much of the machinery that enabled Britain's industrialization. The fact of this indebtedness rarely surfaced within the debate, but historians of the cotton industry such as Edward Baines, who wrote contemporaneously, were well aware of it all the same. Baines grappled with this legacy in his 1832 *History of the Cotton Trade in Great Britain*. Through a series of rhetorical maneuvers, he sought to naturalize the industry as an unmistakably English one and ultimately to quash the romantic opposition between culture and industry.[143] The historian described India as the "birthplace" of the cotton manufacture and England as the "second birthplace" of the art. According to Baines, this did not mean that the English trade was opprobrious in the way that a forged copy might be. England had revived the trade, giving it new life with those mechanical innovations that would allow the industrial nation to "surpass" its oriental forbears.[144] By the mid–nineteenth century, in fact, English and Scottish printers had filled Britain with paisley handkerchiefs, which enjoy a prominent place in the designs registry established in 1839 (fig. 17). They also flooded India with printed cloths, which were brightly colored so that they might attract the fancies of buyers from the subcontinent.

Despite the fact that England had eclipsed India's productive capaci-

Chapter Two

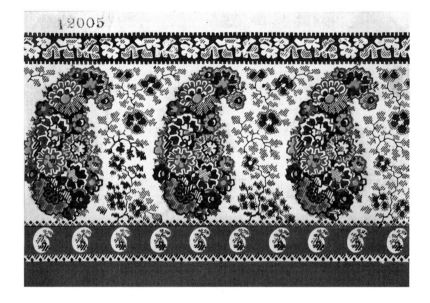

17   Paisley handkerchief design. BT 43/195/12005, National Archives, Kew, United Kingdom.

ties by the moment of the debate—as the phenomenon of reverse export indicated so well—the advocates could not erase their indebtedness to the subcontinent. When they reckoned with this material history, they looked to the copyright as a measure for redressing their debt, albeit in a somewhat convoluted fashion. As part of their philosophical defense of copyright's viability, the proponents of extension had distinguished between patterns and styles. Patterns, they had claimed, should be entitled to copyright protection, while styles, as more general aesthetic expressions, should not. This had been evident in Thomson's discussion of Lane's Net.[145] This qualification notwithstanding, the proponents of extension saw the copyright as a way to improve style, and they imbued the category of style with national significance. It was a Scottish MP, William Morison, who made the connection most explicit when he expressed the hope that a stronger copyright would engender an "English style." Under the present regime, he bemoaned, there was "no English art of design." In fact, Morison noted, all English prints were "wholly or in part foreign."[146] When he made such a claim, Morison picked up on a broader anxiety about national style expressed in the pages of the *Report of the Select Committee on Arts and Manufactures* and in the writings of aesthetic critics.[147] Like these contemporaries, Morison acknowledged Britain's aesthetic debt to France. But he took this line of discussion a step further, noting the influence of India, and even Africa, in England's stockpile of designs.

Others, including the pattern designer Thomas Barker Holdway, expressed similar concerns. When he testified before the Select Committee on Copyright of Designs, Holdway discussed the pine pattern so popular in ladies' wares such as shawls and scarves. The pine, Holdway had claimed, was not "original." Instead, it was "Indian." In the copyright, Holdway saw a mechanism that would foster a national tradition of design. Like Holdway, Edmund Potter looked nostalgically to India, and even more expressly to Africa, as locations whose artisanal crafts epitomized so-called national styles. Potter mobilized long-standing historical fictions surrounding material culture as he evoked an Africa that was an original culture and a blank slate.[148] When he meditated on the so-called Negro print, Potter noted what he took to be a paradox. It was the "lowest specimen" of manufacture on the globe, yet it was also original in every regard: untouched by "machinery, steam, or artificial heat" and unadulterated by other styles.[149] It is ironic that the celebration of the African print as the epitome of originality came from one of the foremost supporters of the copyright. Potter's veneration points to the impossibility of originality in an industrial and trading nation such as Britain with its cosmopolitan commercialism. Still, it is not surprising. In his longing for a preindustrial past, Potter underscored the anxieties about industrial modernity that motivated the call for originality, the defense of artisanship, the campaign for extension, and the struggle for design reform itself.

CONCLUSION

In August of 1842, Parliament extended the copyright for industrial designs from three to nine months rather than the twelve that Tennent and his allies had sought. Still, at a banquet celebrating the bill's passage held at Manchester's Albion Hotel in January 1843, Tennent would call the triumph the "most gratifying" of his "public life," in large part because a constituency whose interests often opposed his own had embraced his

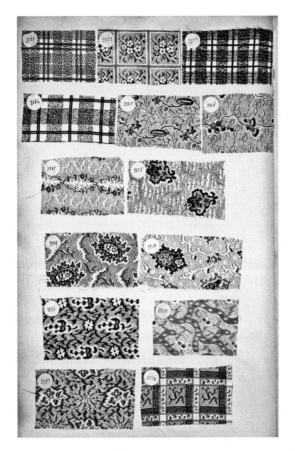

18 Calico prints by Kershaw, Leese, and Company. BT 43/188/2221–2234, National Archives, Kew, United Kingdom.

efforts. He predicted improvements in the marketplace and the aesthetic domain. For him, the sixfold increase in the registration of printed fabrics at the designs office on the Strand augured as much.[150] Tennent did not note, however, that some of the most frequent registrants turned out to be the so-called pirates themselves. In the pattern books, a multitude of entries from such firms as Kershaw, Leese, and Company take their place alongside the more modest number of submissions by Thomson Brothers and Company (fig. 18, plate 1). When placed side by side, the respective samples provide material testimony to the different values accorded to pattern by the proponents of extension and their adversaries. The designs of James Thomson show great variation, strong color, and careful workmanship. Those of Kershaw, on the other hand, display definite monotony, runny hues, and shoddy execution. Perhaps Tennent had been overly sanguine when he equated design registration with aesthetic improvement.

This said, the rate of registration would continue to increase throughout the decade, as the stacks of pattern books now held at the National Archives demonstrate.[151] Furthermore, several manufacturers found recourse under the new law, which allowed them to bring pirates to justice.[152] These registrations and prosecutions notwithstanding, Tennent's self-pronounced victory proved to be an unfinished triumph. In the following years, countless manufacturers bemoaned the inadequacy of the law. Calico printers cursed the fees required for litigation.[153] Representatives of other trades, too, joined their ranks to criticize the law. Ornamental metalworkers protested the cost of registration.[154] Silk manufacturers complained of the short duration of the copyright.[155] Finally, damask makers penned petitions beseeching Parliament to extend the copyright on their costly productions.[156]

In 1850, Parliament would revisit the matter of design copyright. This was thanks in part to the cajoling of the new *Journal of Design and Manufactures*, which had played the watchdog role well, reporting with avidity the ineffectiveness of the law. But the more immediate impetus was the upcoming Great Exhibition of 1851, the first world's fair, which was soon to open in London's Hyde Park. The looming exhibition, many argued, necessitated a more forceful and efficient law, one that would prevent the "pillage" that remained so common.[157] As it stood, one manufacturer warned that none of his peers would show the "best and newest designs" at the exhibition, for they were sure to be copied. Such fears turned out to be unfounded, but in the face of these portents Parliament passed a revised Designs Act in August of 1850. This law sought to encourage exhibitors, both English and foreign, by providing a year's provisional registration. It met a critical reception in the *Art Journal* and the *Journal of Design and Manufactures*, which both castigated the new law with a strident language reminiscent of Tennent's campaign.[158]

Such vigorous critiques were exceptional in 1850, however. It would be difficult to match the fervor of the debate that had transpired between 1839 and 1842. But there are other reasons, too, for this change. By 1850, the copyright did not seem to hold the utopian possibilities that so many supporters had ascribed to it in Tennent's day. By the time of the Great Exhibition, in fact, reformers and manufacturers were looking to a grander stage for improving design and venerating production. Rather than placing their faith in the transforming potential of the design copyright, they turned to the captivating power of exhibitionary practice and spectacular display. The exhibition's organizers sought to include a broader public within the endeavor of design reform by showcasing the world's treasures. This is not to say, however, that they abandoned an interest in productive practice by embracing a fetishizing spectacle. Chapter three will show us that the literature produced for the exhibition cultivated an appreciation of artisanal practice and industrial process. Not incidentally, it also reconfigured the national histories and economic rivalries that had informed the copyright contest. When they described the goods on display at the Crystal Palace, the exhibition's texts popularized the figures of the British workman, the French artisan, and the Indian laborer. And for the length of the exhibition season, at least, these figures would coexist in spectacular harmony rather than economic competition.

Commodification and Its Discontents

LABOR, PRINT CULTURE, AND INDUSTRIAL ART

AT THE GREAT EXHIBITION OF 1851

Between May and October of 1851, the French political economist Jerome Adolphe Blanqui published a series of letters to commemorate the Great Exhibition, held in the famed Crystal Palace in London's Hyde Park (fig. 19). Never before had there been such a "magnificent spectacle" of "human industry," the Frenchman proclaimed of the first world's fair. Although they were penned expressly to convince a French audience of the merits of free trade, Blanqui's letters became remarkably popular in Britain, where they were reproduced widely in 1851.[1] The Frenchman's missives proved satisfying for English readers on many scores. There they could find endorsements of the liberal values of free trade and hard work that the exhibition sought to underwrite. They could also enjoy descriptions of the exhibition as a truly enchanted event. As Blanqui explained, visitors to the Crystal Palace found themselves "carried away by magic from country to country, from East to West, from iron to cotton, from silk to wool, from machines to manufactures."[2] This journey gave exhibitiongoers an unprecedented entry into a world of goods. In Blanqui's understanding, it also provided them with an unparalleled view onto the "laboring populations" of the earth.[3] Sturdy cotton indicated the seriousness of the able English laborer, beautiful porcelain exhibited the taste of the artistic French craftsman, and glorious silk revealed the skill of the dextrous Indian spinner. At bottom, the spectacle of industry rendered by Blanqui was truly remarkable in its suggestiveness.[4]

The exhibition that Blanqui so vividly described was the brainchild of a civil servant, Henry Cole, and the prince consort, Albert, two leading design reformers who had risen to prominence in the 1840s. In 1849, Cole had become the anonymous editor of the *Journal of Design and Manufactures*; he had also taken the helm of the Government School of Design. Earlier in the decade, Cole had made his name as a designer with his line of Felix Summerly's Art Manufactures, which won prizes at exhibitions sponsored by the Royal Society of Arts, where Prince Albert was a noted patron. With the backing of the Society of Arts, Cole and Albert built on the tradition of national exhibitions of manufactures, a longtime practice in France and a more recent development in England. Together they brought a matchless collection of art and industry from across the globe to an audience of historic proportions. Their plan became an unprecedented success, with a staggering six million pilgrims visiting the Crystal Palace during the exhibition season. They swarmed the building, especially on the affordable Shilling Days, as the rendition in the *Illustrated London News* suggests (fig. 20). There they beheld a stockpile of over one hundred thousand objects, which included raw materials, machinery, and manufactures, to use the taxonomy of the exhibition's classificatory system.[5] This last section comprised the greatest number, including magnificent porcelain, ornate silks, and elegant silver, which delighted visitors to Hyde Park.

Recently, scholars have looked to the exhibition as a landmark moment for refashioning class relations, promoting national identity, and forming spectacular society.[6] The exhibition was also a punctuating event in the history of nineteenth-century design reform. It inaugurated important changes in reforming strategy and design discourse. The exhibition's progenitors advertised the show as a celebration of labor and a validation of free trade. Yet the turn to collecting and display marked a shift from earlier supply-side interventions. With this move came important modifications in the intended audience, geographical purview, and governing concerns of design discourse. Before 1851, the ornamental arts had preoccupied a cadre of reformers, whose ranks included manufacturers, MPs, merchants, and artists. Together, they had framed design reform as an economic concern for a competitive European marketplace. By contrast, the exhibition introduced a broader lay audience to the industrial

342. VIEW OF THE GRAND ENTRANCE TO THE EXHIBITION.

19   The Crystal Palace. Plate 342 in *The Official Descriptive and Illustrated Catalogue of the Great Exhibition* (1851). V & A Images, Victoria and Albert Museum, London.

20   Crystal Palace crowds on a Shilling Day. *Illustrated London News* (1851). Department of Special and Area Studies Collections, George A. Smathers Library, University of Florida.

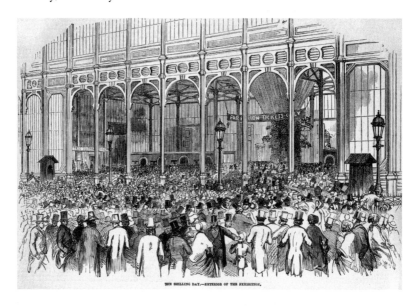

THE SHILLING DAY.—EXTERIOR OF THE EXHIBITION.

arts of the globe. No longer a specialized interest, design became the stuff of enchantment, edification, and entertainment in 1851.

These understandings were evident in Blanqui's missives, which married economic concerns to fantastic reveries and melded aesthetic critique with patriotic commentary. English readers could find the Frenchman's assessments excerpted in the divers publications that described the grand collection and commemorated the hallowed event.[7] Artisans would encounter Blanqui's letters in John Cassell's *Illustrated Exhibitor*, a twopenny weekly featuring woodcut illustrations. Elevated connoisseurs could enjoy the same texts in John Tallis's *History and Description of the Crystal Palace*, a lavish three-volume masterpiece showcasing steel engravings.[8] These are but two of the catalogues that conjoined text and image to memorialize the great show.[9] Others included the three-volume *Official Illustrated Catalogue of the Great Exhibition*, which touted itself as a work "without precedent" for philosophers, merchants, and manufacturers.[10] Art aficionados might have found more lively accounts of the exhibition's ornamental riches in Matthew Digby Wyatt's two-volume *Industrial Arts of the Nineteenth Century*, which featured colored lithographs, or the *Art Journal Illustrated Catalogue*, with its plentiful engravings.[11] Finally, middle-class readers with broader interests could peruse the weekly supplements to the *Illustrated London News*. Other "permanent tokens" of the exhibition included lavish serials, domestic periodicals, personal travelogues, and entertaining ephemera.[12] For all of their claims to distinctiveness, these texts had a good deal in common. To begin, they literally shared copy, shamelessly excerpting from one another and explicitly featuring the same commentators.[13] But, more notably, they shared a larger worldview.[14] Despite their professed differences, the Great Exhibition's catalogues collectively embraced the broad liberal values of hard work, free trade, imperial expansion, and democratic consumption that have come to characterize the mid-nineteenth century in the historiography of modern Britiain.[15]

Although they endorsed the exhibitionary order, these texts sought to take their readers beyond the glass walls of the Crystal Palace. They endeavored to relocate the goods on display within "their modes of manufacture."[16] Blanqui joined several writers who used the exhibition's displays, and especially its ornamental art, as inspirations for examinations of labor practices and productive regimes. The pervasiveness of this tendency challenges a longtime understanding of the exhibition as the triumph of spectacular society. The critic Thomas Richards once influentially asserted that the commodity seemed to speak "for itself" and "by itself" at the exhibition. There, the argument goes, the fetishized commodity became the dominant mode of representation, while the labor involved in its production disappeared from view.[17]

This chapter joins with recent scholarship that rejects the conception of the exhibition as an "awesome, subjugating spectacle."[18] To do so, it examines the print culture produced for the exhibition, including Cassell's *Illustrated Exhibitor*. This serial employed descriptive texts and plentiful illustrations to glorify the "working human presence" in the face of the fetishized commodity.[19] More than any other publication, it sought to redress the "tragic irony about labor" that characterized nineteenth-century exhibitions.[20] Published for artisans, the *Exhibitor* was singular in its prominent graphic renditions of productive processes and matchless in its explicit glorification of skilled labor. Catalogues for more privileged readers followed suit in telling tales about production. Granted, they often highlighted the ingenuity of entrepreneurs rather than the dexterity of workers. Even so, they showed entrepreneurial innovation and artisanal skill to be integrally conjoined virtues in 1851.

As they meditated on the displays at the exhibition, English contributors relied on narrative strategies similar to those employed by Blanqui, whose putative laborers represented the nations that exhibited their wares.[21] They drew on design reform's familiar oppositions as they invoked the mechanical English workman and the tasteful French artisan. In an important enlargement of design discourse, English writers joined Blanqui by taking object lessons from civilizations that spanned the globe. Like Blanqui, English commentators marshaled idealized laborers from Europe, India, and the Orient. But at an event where patriotism was the lingua franca and design was an index of national character, they did not simply ratify Blanqui's worldview. Instead, they would refine Blanqui's understandings to fit English productive concerns, aesthetic predilections, and imperial impulses in 1851.

ENGLISH WORKMEN, MECHANICAL GENIUS,
AND ARTISANAL IDEALS

For Blanqui, the impressive displays of the United Kingdom, with its copious raw materials, its imposing machinery, and its sturdy manufactures, suggested the distinctive characteristics of the English workman. In contrast to his counterparts on the Continent, the English laborer, whether the Manchester printer, the Sheffield cutler, or the Leeds weaver, was a singularly private figure with a natural affinity for family and home life. It was, however, his "mode of working" that provided the true measure of distinction and explained the wondrous productivity of the premier industrial nation. Industrious, serious, and modest, Englishmen valued work for "its own sake." They went about their labors "conscientiously and perseveringly." Blanqui's English workman tended toward efficiency, exactitude, and regularity, bringing "mathematical precision" to his tasks.[22] Given these tendencies, it was no wonder that Great Britain's displays of ingenious machinery and bulk manufactures were preeminent at the Crystal Palace. If Blanqui found English laborers admirably diligent, however, he also regarded them as excessively absorbed in their tasks. Of late, the English laborer had fallen prey to the regime of the factory system, becoming as much an automaton as the machine that he worked.[23]

Exhibition catalogues published for England's reading public echoed Blanqui's understanding of English mechanical distinctiveness. Time and again, these publications upheld Britain as a nation whose "genius" was "peculiarly mechanical."[24] But rather than leading to drudgery, as Blanqui charged, several English commentators argued that machinery facilitated mastery and even liberation. Thanks to English mechanical prowess, one writer maintained, the nation had harnessed those "monsters of nature" — "fire, air, water, steam, electricity" — "to the triumphal car of the human will." Visitors to the Crystal Palace would find confirmation of this fact in the Machinery Courts, whose cotton and steam engines dazzled visitors. In the Machinery Courts, such displays announced the majesty of English ingenuity to the cross-class audience that came to admire these motors of productivity and prosperity. There they could find England displayed "in all her splendor."[25]

These assessments were widespread, penetrating even into the artisanal *Illustrated Exhibitor*, which was especially prolix about the mechanical triumphs on display in the Machinery Courts.[26] In a notable accommodation to bourgeois interests, the *Exhibitor* aligned itself with machinery and even capital. "The day has passed," it noted, "when the operative looked with gloomy jealousy on the introduction of every new mechanical invention, as being likely to deprive him of a portion of his hard-earned bread." No friend to the Luddites of a bygone era, Cassell took pains to distance himself from earlier radical movements. It was time, his *Exhibitor* held, for a new, patriotic appraisal of mechanization that underscored its liberating potential. Rather than oppressing or impoverishing workers, machines promised to relieve "labor from its drudgery" and to delegate "to iron, and steam, and water, the real weight and burden of toil."[27] This was one among several significant revisions of artisanal thought about mechanization at midcentury. In the heady years before the exhibition, laboring radicals had criticized machines not only for their dehumanizing potential but also for the threat they posed to artisanal skill.[28] Cassell reversed this equation in 1851 as he sought to align machinery with artisanal values. He reframed machine labor as a matter of skill, requiring its own variety of dexterity, precision, and art. Indeed, with its two operatives placed on either side of the image, the *Exhibitor*'s rendition of Queen Victoria's and Prince Albert's visit to the Machinery Courts suggests the skill and adroitness involved in running the *Illustrated London News*'s printing machine. Even when he located machines at the center of his images, Brian Maidment notes, John Cassell depicted the laborers who worked them with a "certain heroic presence," or at least a truly essential function (fig. 21).[29]

Cassell's strategies support a time-honored notion of the Great Exhibition as the decisive embrace of both industrial modernity and Victorian stability.[30] Several historians have pointed out, however, that this endorsement was limited and even waning in 1851.[31] Understandings of the heroism of labor and the triumph of machinery would meet numerous challenges in the literature that surrounded the Great Exhibition. Blanqui, for one, had questioned whether mechanization could liberate workmen. He found sympathetic ears among British commentators who shared his skepticism. W. H. Smith, a contributor to the Whig periodical *Blackwood's Edinburgh Magazine*, called mechanization into question by addressing the ironies of the locomotive. His ingenious "Voltaire in the Crystal Palace" recounted a fictive visit to the exhibition on the part of the philosophe, who had returned from the dead for the great event. "Your iron slave wants many other slaves, unfortunately not of iron, to attend on it," the spectral Voltaire, once an admirer of all things English, proclaimed. "On this condition only will it serve you."[32] In the character of the resurrected Voltaire, Smith found a shrewd vehicle for casting doubt on the unqualified virtues of the very mechanization that the ex-

21 Mechanical ingenuity in the Machinery Courts. *Illustrated Exhibitor* 7
(26 July 1851): insert. Reproduced courtesy of the Huntington Library, San
Marino, California.

hibition aimed to glorify. Such critiques extended beyond the written
word and into graphic satire, too. The bohemian magazine *Punch* cast
doubt on the event's promise of dignifying labor with its "Specimens
from Mr. Punch's Industrial Exhibition," pictured here (fig. 22).[33] Not
only did this critique call into question the representational strategies
of the exhibition's commodity spectacle. It also disputed the attendant
narrative of progress with its array of figures who epitomized the exploi-
tation of industrial capitalism and the unevenness of mechanization.[34]

   This uneasiness about the machine age and its effects was not restricted to the printed page. In his now classic *English Culture and the
Decline of the Industrial Sprit*, the historian Martin Wiener noted that
the exhibition, which seemed to represent the apogee of English mechanical confidence, contained within its own halls a critique of the
mechanization it purportedly celebrated. Wiener locates an alternative
vision of society in the famed Medieval Court, designed by the architect
and Gothic revivalist Augustus Welby Pugin.[35] In the Medieval Court,

Commodification and Its Discontents   **93**

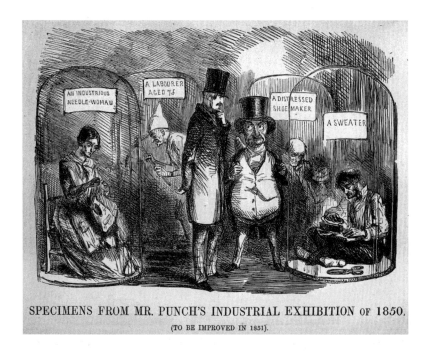

SPECIMENS FROM MR. PUNCH'S INDUSTRIAL EXHIBITION OF 1850.
(TO BE IMPROVED IN 1851).

22   A Crystal Palace critique. *Punch* 17 (1850): 145. Reproduced courtesy of
the Huntington Library, San Marino, California.

Pugin, who would help to found the Museum of Ornamental Art discussed in chapter four, offered exhibitiongoers a rich handicraft showcase whose warm colors and lavish fabrics contrasted starkly with the
functional Machinery Courts (plate 2). With this ocular feast, Pugin
hoped to suggest the virtues of an organic society untarnished by the
alienated labor and unforgiving work regimes that allegedly pervaded
industrial society.[36] Its prescience notwithstanding, Wiener's argument
stops short, for ambivalence about mechanized production extended far
beyond the Medieval Court. The displays of England's manufactures—
and, of course, the writings that discussed them—suggested the prevailing importance of hand labor, workshop production, and even artisanal
virtuosity in 1851.[37]

For all of the refrains about the mechanical genius of Great Britain,
it is important to note that an artisanal ideal persisted in 1851. Alongside their paeans to machinery, exhibition catalogues paid homage to
the skilled workman who produced tasteful products by hand. Given its

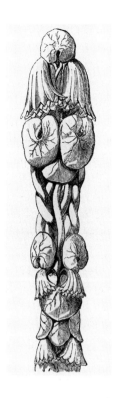

23 Fish knife handle. Engraving. *The Art Journal Illustrated Catalogue* (1851): 222. Yale Center for British Art, Paul Mellon Collection.

audience and values, it is not at all surprising that the *Illustrated Exhibitor* sought to celebrate the artisan. But similar accolades also filled elite publications. Time and again, Matthew Digby Wyatt pointed readers to the "labor and troubles" involved in producing the masterpieces in the Crystal Palace, not to mention the everyday goods contained therein.[38] Similarly, the *Art Journal Illustrated Catalogue* called attention to those "clever designers" and "industrial artisans" whose works filled the Crystal Palace. Although their names would remain unknown to posterity, the *Art Journal* urged readers not to take their "skill and labor" for granted. Its treatment of an ornamented silver fish knife is exemplary in this regard (fig. 23). "The number of hands employed upon the production of a single article, even of common use," the *Art Journal* explained in its assessment of the utensil, "is greater than would be supposed by one unacquainted with the art and mystery of manufacture."[39] Contributors to other costly publications followed suit as they heaped further praise on silver goods, which provided object lessons in skill, refinement, and execution.[40]

Commodification and Its Discontents

This embrace of the labor theory of value on the part of connoisseurs was not mere altruism. Pointing out the crafted virtues of the fish knife and similar goods served the interests of elite publications and their readerships. Writing a century after the exhibition, John Steegman noted that the event's planners had aspired to show Britain to be the "richest nation in the world."[41] Similarly, Nikolaus Pevsner held that the displays in the Crystal Palace reflected well the ascent of the "prospering, well-fed, self-confident class" concerned with wealth and emulation that predominated at midcentury.[42] In such ornate wares, the bourgeoisie found a means of asserting its own dominance.[43] Suggestive of both productive skill and consuming might, luxury goods embodied the aesthetics of the age of equipoise, which sought to balance the interests between classes.[44] As we shall see in chapter four, however, this aesthetic of equipoise, with its florid designs, would meet censure at the Museum of Ornamental Art, where Henry Cole and his circle sought to inaugurate a more modest, streamlined taste that eschewed ornamental excess. But in 1851 such criticisms were restricted to the pages of the *Journal of Design and Manufactures* and to the musings of budding aesthetic radicals such as William Morris, who legendarily refused to enter the Crystal Palace.[45]

If ornament provided an ideal vehicle for class reconciliation, it also enabled the "domestication" of the industrial revolution in 1851.[46] While the steam engine and the power loom gave way to a stark narrative of mechanical progress, ornamental art suggested another trajectory that held its own appeal and provided its own reassurance. Notably, the productions that received the most fulsome praise at the exhibition were those that fused artisanal skill and manufacturing innovation. Among these we can count the contributions from the hardware and metal trades. As the historian Maxine Berg has noted, these trades did not follow the path of the textile manufacture, that "historical archetype" of industrialization that was characterized by wholesale mechanization, deskilling, and large-scale production. Instead, they melded skilled labor, workshop production, and process innovation in the service of art and industry.[47]

The ornamental iron trade provides a case in point. Visitors to the exhibition could find a shrine to this manufacture in the Coalbrookdale Dome, which occupied pride of place in the transept of the Crystal Palace. The *Exhibitor* touted this monument as "the triumph" of Britain's "peculiar institutions visible in a single object." The Coalbrookdale Dome showed what was possible when technical ingenuity was married to artistic taste. "Here we have iron fashioned into the semblance—and not the semblance merely, but the reality—of beauty," Cassell effused (fig. 24).[48] Other productions by the Coalbrookdale Company that graced the main throughways of the Crystal Palace received similar accolades. An iron fountain tickled the fancy of Matthew Digby Wyatt. It offered proof of the "skill" of the maker and the "high degree of perfection" in the trade. Moreover, by joining the talents of the "highest class of artists" with the energies of the boys who hauled coal to the furnace, it evoked the great unity of labor. Labor's exertions, Digby Wyatt noted, might yield "ambitious" showpieces like the fountain. But even more important, they could provision a broad range of consumers with attractive articles for daily use, whether stoves, chairs, vases, or inkstands.[49]

Even more than the Coalbrookdale Company's showpieces, the workshop trades of nearby Birmingham epitomized the "other face" of the industrial revolution in 1851.[50] Famed as the "toy shop" of Europe, Birmingham made a strong showing at the Crystal Palace.[51] The town's papier-mâché was "unrivaled."[52] Its ornamental glass reassured critics that "the British workman need fear no competitor."[53] Above all, the practice of electroplating—a "hallmark of 1851," to borrow from Pevsner—typified the artistry and innovation of Birmingham.[54] The result of accident, this process of recent vintage enabled the gilding and plating of metals using electricity. As the patent holder of the process since 1840, the celebrated Birmingham firm of Elkington and Mason carried the palm here.[55] Its ingenious contributions—which included fruit dishes, communion services, commemorative vases, claret jugs, and even an ornamental stand made by an alumnus of the Birmingham School of Design—filled the Crystal Palace. According to the *Exhibitor*, these works were the "perfect *chefs d'oeuvre* of skillful manipulation, scientific application, and elegant design." Perhaps even better than the cotton manufacture, this great "show of electroplate" represented the fusion of all that the exhibition held dear: "skillful design, untiring energy, unflagging industry," and, of course, "persevering labor."[56]

The case of Birmingham reminds us that manufacturing was a distinctly localized enterprise in 1851. For all that its founders did to frame the exhibition as festival of nations, the Crystal Palace was ultimately a show ground for civic pride, with its selections assiduously collected and organized by local committees.[57] Local distinctiveness had not been lost on Blanqui, who maintained that the representatives of different

COALBROOK DALE DOME AND EAGLE SLAYER.

24 Coalbrookdale Dome. *Illustrated Exhibitor* 1 (7 June 1851): 11. Reproduced courtesy of the Huntington Library, San Marino, California.

trades were like tribes unto themselves, recognizable by distinct physiognomies. English commentators were similarly aware of local distinctions, however differently configured than in the acrimonious copyright debate, in which an artisanal London and a mechanized Manchester had appeared to be locked in bitter combat. In keeping with the exhibition's patina of brotherhood, 1851's rivalries took the form of friendly competition. This was captured well by a representative of Birmingham who looked admiringly on nearby Sheffield, that "metropolis of steel" whose productions were esteemed the world over. "If we were not Birmingham," he declared, "we would be Sheffield," as he heaped praise on the neighboring court (fig. 25).[58]

Sheffield's wares provide one final example of the marriage of "ingenious mechanism" and "skillful workmanship" that was so valued by the exhibition's commentators.[59] Not only did the Sheffield contributions win the high praise of Englishmen; they also enjoyed the accolades of foreign visitors such as Blanqui, who exclaimed, "Sheffield cutlery! What admirable variety! What richness! What amazing cheapness!"[60] To be sure, these effusions did much to obscure the lived experience of the smoky, gritty city and the working conditions of its dangerous, unhealthy trades, which would attract public concern in the 1860s.[61] In 1851, however, it was the very variety of Sheffield goods, ranging from costly centerpieces worthy of noble homes to "humble" table knives found in the most modest "cottages," that preoccupied Blanqui and other commentators. Fascinating in its variation, the trade was also mind-boggling in its intricacy. Each commodity required its own workers and methods. The *Illustrated Exhibitor*, which offered its readers plentiful wood engravings of the phases of the manufacture, tried to impart a sense of the various processes involved in the making of Sheffield's scissors, knives, and files. The entire enterprise demanded muscle, discipline, and perseverance, as this rendition of the file cutting process suggests (fig. 26).

Perhaps the most involved of all was the scissors trade, which called for "very skillful and ingenious workmen" who could master fourteen productive stages.[62] Sheffield scissors garnered praise for their elegant workmanship, if not their ergonomics, as these images from the *Art Journal Illustrated Catalogue* indicate (fig. 27).[63] If any doubt lingered about the "skill" of its artisans, visitors could admire the Sheffield Town Razor, which was crafted expressly to promote the productive capacities

SHEFFIELD COURT: FROM A DAGUERREOTYPE BY FEHRENBACH.

25   Sheffield Court. *Illustrated Exhibitor* 12 (23 August 1851): 210. Reproduced courtesy of the Huntington Library, San Marino, California.

FILE CUTTING AND HARDENING.

26 Sheffield workers. *Illustrated Exhibitor* 11 (23 August 1851): 207. Reproduced courtesy of the Huntington Library, San Marino, California.

of the town. An exemplar of artisanal virtuosity, the celebrated razor was also a souvenir of the great event, sporting a view of the Crystal Palace itself.[64]

THE EMERALD ISLE, RUSTIC MANUFACTURE, AND LADIES' WORK

The United Kingdom's displays hailed not only from England's manufacturing towns but also from Ireland. Because it did not have its own court, Erin's showings were "lost in the general splendor" of the United Kingdom's collection.[65] In fact, the showing of Ireland escaped mention by Blanqui. This was not the case among British commentators, for whom the "Emerald Isle," its contributions, and its laborers carried a range of particularly charged meanings. In the wake of the famine of the 1840s, Ireland was frequently portrayed as a rural hinterland with undeveloped natural resources and a primitive manufacturing system. Time and again commentators characterized the Irish contributions as

SHEFFIELD has been long famous for its manufacture of cutlery, and the improvement exhibited in all its various branches of the trade we have already had occasion to note. Mr. G. WILKINSON, one of its best SCISSORS-MAKERS, has contributed some specimens of his own peculiar art which fully bear out the deserved reputation of that enterprising town. The first on our page has been manufactured by him for the "Indian Steel Company," and is of much delicacy and elegance of design. The group which follows presents great novelty of form; the flowing curves of the handle,

formed of the lily of the valley and its leaves, are very tasteful. There is quaintness, as well as elegance, in the other designs. In fact, restricted as design may appear to be when applied to so simple a thing as the handle of a pair of scissors, it is surprising how varied it may be made through the aid of a clever designer. We present an ingenious adaptation of so unpromising a subject

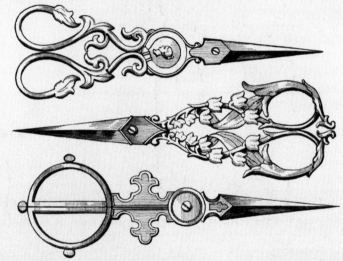

as a coat-of-arms to this purpose. The arms, supporters, crest, and motto of the Cavendish family are made to do duty in this way without any disagreeable result. We conclude our series with a large pair of scissors, which also have "the charm of novelty." Sheffield, in this branch of Industrial Art, has maintained its supremacy, and defied the world, for more than

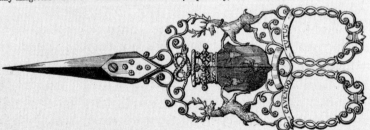

a century. We have no fear of its losing the rank it has obtained. During a recent visit, we were offered, by one manufacturer of scissors, the means to examine no fewer than 7000 executed designs. Mr. Wilkinson has not only studied to improve the forms of objects of a comparatively costly character; he has very essentially improved the commonest articles of

27   Sheffield scissors. Engraving. *Art Journal Illustrated Catalogue* (1851): 93. Yale Center for British Art, Paul Mellon Collection.

expressions of rudeness and sloth.[66] An American visitor to the Crystal Palace dismissed the Irish as poor, "unskilled, and helpless," much like the Choctaw and Sioux of his home continent.[67] To use the words of Tallis, the Irish peasant was "destitute" of the energy, industry, and enterprise that were hallmarks of English labor. The graphic satire *Mr. Goggleye's Visit to the Great Exhibition* put a comic gloss on this understanding. Its image of a tattered scarecrow labeled "Irish Contributions to the Great Exhibition" catered to the metropolitan imagination of Ireland as the abode of rudeness and rusticity (fig. 28).[68] Even children's literature penned for the exhibition upheld such notions as it cast the island's potato-eating poor as a merry, if backward, people who loved to "laugh, sing, and joke."[69]

It was a different matter for Cassell's *Illustrated Exhibitor*, in which Ireland was featured as a cause célèbre. In its pages native industry figured as a vehicle for uplift. "There is hope for Ireland," the *Exhibitor* declared at the outset of the first of two issues that spotlighted the contributions to the world's fair on the part of that "long-oppressed sister of Erin."[70] Cassell's assessment challenged the pervasive notion of an idle Ireland by recasting rusticity as a virtue. The *Exhibitor* effused over furniture carved out of bog wood, which was unparalleled in its quaint design, curvilinear lines, and excellent workmanship (fig. 29).[71] In the decorated linens, it found evidence of Ireland's "inventive genius and industrial skill." Buoyed by his own assessment of Ireland's craft traditions, Cassell adopted the providential rhetoric that pervaded the exhibition as he augured the island's future. Ireland's proud showing at the Crystal Palace gave every reason to hope for a "brighter day" in the "Sister-land" when "famine and despair" would no longer hold sway.[72]

According to the *Exhibitor* and other contemporary publications, the contributions of Ireland's women best embodied this hope. Embroidery, crochet work, and lace made by poor Irish girls joined contributions by women of the English middle classes in the exhibition's displays of ladies' crafts. These displays translated the dexterity, precision, and patience that were hallmarks of skilled labor in 1851 into the domain of the feminine.[73] If the contributions by English ladies embodied the exemplary use of leisure hours, the works of Erin's fairer sex suggested the promise of uplift through industry.[74] In the wake of the famine, a coalition of English women and Irish nuns had revivified the Irish needle trades in a philanthropic campaign that established schools and workshops. The

28   Ireland's comic contribution to the Great Exhibition of 1851. Litho-
graph by Thomas Onwhyn in *Mr. Goggleye's Visit to the Exhibition of National
Industry to Be Held in London on the 1st of April 1851* (1851). Yale Center for
British Art, Paul Mellon Collection.

29   Bog wood chair. *Illustrated
Exhibitor* 9 (2 August 1851):
143. Reproduced courtesy of
the Huntington Library, San
Marino, California.

doilies, carpets, and tablecloths on display at the Crystal Palace attested to the ameliorative potential of such efforts and augured well for the future of Irish industry.[75]

More than philanthropic verve drove these enterprises, however. In 1851, lace making provided an avenue for artistic and entrepreneurial innovation on the part of middle-class ladies. This is particularly important given women's vexed relationship to the Great Exhibition. As a vocation, designing remained primarily the preserve of men at mid-century. It was, therefore, difficult for women to gain entry to the Crystal Palace as exhibitors. As Colin Cunningham has noted, the feminine presence at the exhibition manifested itself in the form of ornamental motifs on Sèvres porcelain, decorative screens, and carved bedsteads.[76] Lessons in lace thus enabled women to become more than decorative emblems in 1851. In philanthropic efforts, they found an avenue into the restrictive world of design and even an entry into Digby Wyatt's exclusive *Industrial Arts of the Nineteenth Century*. Digby Wyatt conferred praise, for instance, on the philanthropy and artistry of Miss Jane Clarke, whose point lace is pictured here (fig. 30). A designer and entrepreneur in her own right, Miss Clarke ran a Belfast school where "distressed needlewomen" executed her designs. Equally laudable were the efforts of Mrs. Treadwin, whose school at Honiton simultaneously provided a means for uplifting the poor women of Devonshire and preserving the local craft.[77]

Whether philanthropic designers or distressed needlewomen, these lace-making ladies ranged far from the somber mechanical workman identified by Blanqui as the archetypical English producer. Together the diligent operative, the skilled artisan, and the female lace maker remind us that a range of productive regimes coexisted in nineteenth-century Britain. To use the words of Prince Albert, the mid–nineteenth century was indeed a time of "most wonderful transition."[78] With its displays of machinery and manufactures, the exhibition sought to capture production in its glorious diversity. The exhibition's catalogues aided in this process as they marshaled a range of British laborers. When they did so, they challenged Blanqui's workman ideal, not to mention the master narrative of English industrial modernity. This said, the exhibition's texts bore out the Frenchman's assertion that there existed an indisputable association between national character and productive practice in 1851.

Commodification and Its Discontents

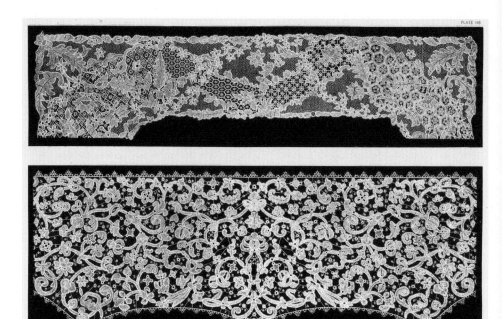

30 Miss Jane Clarke's lace designs. Plate CLVI in Digby Wyatt, *The Industrial Arts of the Nineteenth Century* (1851–53). Reproduced courtesy of the Winterthur Library, Printed Book and Periodical Collection.

FRENCH CRAFTSMEN, REVOLUTIONARY SKILL, AND ROYAL SPLENDOR

Those exhibitiongoers who turned to the French Courts could find porcelain, tapestries, fans, and furniture that bore an unmistakable "stamp of elegance." These goods reflected the "immortal fire of French genius," to use the words of Blanqui.[79] They presented a stark contrast to the English Courts with their ingenious machinery and sturdy manufactures. "They shine with the compass—we with the pencil," explained Blanqui, as he distinguished between the mechanical operatives of England and the artistic workmen of his native France.[80] In Blanqui's schema, matters of character undergirded the productive distinctions that were on display in the Crystal Palace. While Blanqui's English operative was

Chapter Three

a "profoundly serious, silent, and voracious" figure, his ideal Frenchman appeared as a "more gay, more lively, [and] more talkative" character espousing public sensibilities. If the English workman tended toward stoicism, his Gallic counterpart was a "petulant" man with a predisposition for radicalism and even revolution.[81]

English design reformers had become well acquainted with Blanqui's venerable French artist-workman long before the exhibition through a series of official reports and inquiries. In 1835, witnesses who testified before the Select Committee on Arts and Manufactures had recognized French workmen for their matchless knowledge of the art of design. William Dyce had expanded on their understanding in his *Report on Foreign Schools of Design*, discussed in chapter one. When he visited the Continent, Dyce was struck by the designers of the famed Lyons silk trade, who had trained as artists. They enjoyed a level of cultural capital and economic livelihood unimaginable in England. In fact, they exhibited regularly at the Louvre's annual exhibitions.[82] Finally, a tradition of national exhibitions dating from 1798 also gave design its due while infusing taste into the "very essence of the spirit of the people."[83] In English aesthetic circles, these exhibitions had become so central to understandings of Frenchness that Matthew Digby Wyatt compared them to the Olympics of old.[84] If the Olympic Games exemplified the spirit of the classical empires, France's exhibitions conveyed something of the national character through their displays of manufactured treasures. At these events, France's art workmen gave material form to this spirit with works that evinced a "practiced hand," an "ever-thoughtful head," and a "tender manipulation." Digby Wyatt praised these efforts in his report on the eleventh of these expositions, which was held in 1849. In a rhetorical flourish, he concluded that the French artisans who displayed their productions there performed their work "*con amore.*"[85]

If we are to judge by Leora Auslander's landmark *Taste and Power*, such portrayals were exaggerated on several counts given concerns about declining skill in France, the meager livelihood of its workers, and the breakdown of an artisanal culture in the years following the Revolution of 1789. They are, indeed, ironic in light of Auslander's assertion that industrial exhibitions were fundamentally at odds with a traditional artisanal culture.[86] This said, the Great Exhibition brought the understandings of artisanal virtue expressed by Dyce and Digby Wyatt to an ever wider audience. At the Crystal Palace, the six million visitors from all nations could view Sèvres porcelain, Beauvais tapestry, and Parisian jewelry that had long been the envy of English manufacturers. British workmen could admire the famed productions of their French counterparts. Even those who did not behold the "wondrous works" might read about them in the copious publications that accompanied the great show.[87] These texts reinforced the notion so pervasive among design reformers and the broader public alike that the French were the "incontestable masters" of taste and design. At the Crystal Palace, its art workmen stood "preeminent."[88]

Still, the exhibition's texts reveal a modulation in design discourse and the attendant portrayal of the French artisan. In the years preceding the exhibition, the French laborer had appeared as an economic actor concerned primarily with supply and demand. This characterization would change at the Great Exhibition, where design became the stuff of didactic lessons and respectable entertainment. Exhibition writers replaced the theoretical economic men who had filled the earlier discussions with more compelling, if threatening, ideal types. This was especially notable in the writings of Blanqui, who had contrasted the serious, stoic, and exact English workman to the spirited, emotive, and artistic French artisan. English writers endorsed Blanqui's portrayal as they expanded upon his thumbnail sketch. Given its sympathies with artisanal independence, the *Illustrated Exhibitor* found much to admire in France's laborers. Energetic and free, the French artisan provided a foil to the orderly operative of England in its pages. "With them, labor is not always condemned to the treadmill of mechanism, but is allowed frequently to stretch its limbs and try its unaided strength," the *Exhibitor* declared with admiration.[89] Others, too, found in France's workmen a true "vivacity," not to mention an "activity of imagination indicative of a highly developed social and political vitality."[90] Enlarging on this understanding, a contributor to *Fraser's Magazine of Town and Country* explained, "The habits of most Europeans are more free and open than ours." While Englishmen were staid, continentals tended to be "mercurial and excitable." This pervasive understanding proved unsettling to the English middle classes and especially to those aristocrats who opposed building the Crystal Palace in Hyde Park. They had feared the havoc that mustachioed Frenchmen, and with them lascivious Italians and smoking Germans, might wreak on the city. This could mean seducing young English maidens, bringing contagions such as cholera, or, worst of all, inciting political instability and even revolution.[91]

At the exhibition, the orderly crowds allayed all fears of insurrection and reassured skeptics that the era of revolution had passed. Still, revolution cast a specter over the great show, especially when it came to assessments of French laborers and their arts. This was certainly the case in the writings of Blanqui. "Oh, matchless workmen!" he implored the famed furniture makers of Paris's Faubourg St. Antoine. "Why do you not make more furniture and fewer revolutions?"[92] More than a mere rhetorical flourish, this very question bears out an assessment made by Whitney Walton, who argued that Blanqui and other midcentury French political economists were unable to reconcile the intimate relationship between "skill and subversiveness" that was so evident in the furniture trades and other consumer goods industries. Similarly, Leora Auslander has noted, the furniture makers of the Faubourg had participated disproportionately in the revolutions of 1789, 1830, and 1848. This may have had something to do with the moral economy of luxury production, in which the meager livelihoods of artisans contrasted starkly with the lavish goods they produced. This penchant for revolution, Walton claims, also spoke to the deleterious effect of industrialization on handicraft labor and skilled work.[93] These nuances of artisanal livelihood were similarly lost on English commentators. Even so, some did note a relationship between political and aesthetic upheaval. Digby Wyatt proclaimed, for instance, that 1848 had brought "disastrous consequences to the industrial arts."[94] Happily for him and Blanqui, such tensions seemed to be on the wane in 1851. They joined others, including the artisanal *Exhibitor*, when they reported reassuringly that France's showing at the Great Exhibition boded well for its recovery from "that dreadful crisis."[95] Exhibitiongoers could find comforting evidence of this newfound stability in the goods from that former epicenter of revolution, Paris. Although it had gained infamy as a breeding ground for socialism and communism, this capital of the nineteenth century also enjoyed a reputation as the very pinnacle of "fashion and taste" with its matchless bronzes, wallpaper, silver, and fans.[96]

For all of the attention that Parisian workmanship garnered, however, it was the displays from France's Royal Manufactories, showcased in the "Gobelins and Sèvres Room," that announced themselves as the

31   Sèvres Room. *Illustrated Exhibitor* 24 (15 November 1851): 442. Reproduced courtesy of the Huntington Library, San Marino, California.

GOBELIN TAPESTRY—THE WORKMAN.

32 Gobelins craftsman. *Illustrated Exhibitor* 22 (1 November 1851): 396. Reproduced courtesy of the Huntington Library, San Marino, California.

very "triumph of France" (fig. 31).[97] M. J. Lemmoine, a compatriot of Blanqui and an exhibition chronicler in his own right, effused, "Here we are incontestably masters."[98] The beauty of Sèvres china was not lost on Matthew Digby Wyatt, who celebrated its exquisite coloring, excellent execution, and elegant detail.[99] If the treasures of Sèvres and Gobelins inspired, the legendary workshops proved equally fascinating. Cassell brought readers of the *Illustrated Exhibitor* on tours of the Royal Manufactories with his copious engravings, which described the famed production processes and showcased their venerated laborers. One in a series, this engraving featured a spectral artist who worked behind his Gobelins loom, making a tapestry just as his predecessors had done some generations before (fig. 32).[100]

In the end, admiration of the timeless manufactures cut two ways. On the one hand, it lay the groundwork for venerating France's artisans. On the other, it portrayed France's wondrous works as fruits of an anachronistic culture of production more characteristic of the ancien régime than of the nineteenth century. As Auslander has shown, by the mid-nineteenth century, France's absolutist stylistic order was in decline. For all of their pride, this fact did not elude the French, whose taste professionals would mount their own campaign for preservation and improvement in the decades following the exhibition.[101] Nor did this reality escape English commentators, who noted in 1851 that Britain seemed to be catching up to a static France in decorative elegance.[102] When critics examined the ribbons, shawls, and even calicoes on display at the Crystal Palace, they found indications of real improvement. These displays led Matthew Digby Wyatt to credit the School of Design with "diffusing sounder and better principles" of taste throughout the nation.[103] Such optimism would fade after the exhibition, when aesthetic critics turned their attention once again to the bulk goods produced in these trades. But the euphoria of the exhibition season led aesthetic critics to recast France, a former foe, as a partner in the forward march of economic prosperity, if only for a summer.[104]

INDIAN ARTISANS, ORIENTAL ALLURE, AND WASTED LABOR

According to Blanqui, there was one civilization that provided a "contrast, in every respect, to the energetic and laborious habits of the European workman."[105] This was the Indian subcontinent, the jewel in England's imperial crown.[106] For the exhibition, the East India Company had assiduously collected and painstakingly arranged the raw materials, machinery, and manufactures of the subcontinent. The company's project was one part imperial propaganda, another part domestic persuasion. At the exhibition, Britain sought to proclaim to foreign visitors such as Blanqui its status as the foremost colonial power.[107] Simultaneously, the East India Company endeavored to convince the British populace of the worthiness of engagement on the subcontinent at a moment when the very future of empire was in question.[108] To this end, it had amassed a staggering collection of such raw materials as cotton, tea, flax, and peas. For all of their economic significance, however, the raw goods did not steal the show. Instead, the "gorgeous manufactures" of India pro-

Chapter Three

duced the greatest "sensation" at the Crystal Palace. There a veritable "fairyland" of jewels, shawls, and regalia, including the elephant canopy, or howdah, pictured here, captivated English and foreign visitors alike (fig. 33, plate 3).[109] Among those struck by these treasures was Blanqui, who brought his fair share of awe and reverence to bear on the magical skill of its laborers.

The Indian manufactures that intrigued Blanqui also enchanted British commentators, who sought assiduously to impart the magic of the East. To do so, they relied heavily on techniques of visual reproduction. In chromolithography Matthew Digby Wyatt found an effective medium for conveying the "richness and beauty" of the subcontinent's silks, the "exquisite workmanship" of its crystal vases, and the "gorgeous color and elaborate execution" of the famed shawls.[110] A "Lady Contributor" to the *Illustrated London News* proposed that images were, perhaps, more effective than words for capturing the staggering magnificence. A blue cashmere shawl, for instance, proved "too beautiful for any description to do it justice."[111] Such remarks suggest a particularly orientalist version of hyperbole, for the lady journalist and her compatriots did not want for responses to the Indian Courts. Instead, they filled catalogues, newspapers, and periodicals with lavish prose that immortalized the display. "India, the glorious glowing land, the gorgeous and the beautiful," waxed Cassell, as he introduced his artisanal readers to the velvets, jewels, thrones, and arms of the subcontinent. For Cassell and others, this oriental splendor recalled the tales of the *Arabian Nights*, not to mention those stories of conquest that joined myth, history, and thick description.[112] In the end, commentators could not say enough about the magnificent wares that evoked such encomia. Of the displays, Cassell concluded, "How suggestive they are, and what stories they tell."[113]

These "stories" placed the artisans of India front and center. Like the transfixing goods they produced, India's laborers assumed a place of prominence in the exhibition's texts, becoming a source of wonder themselves.[114] Even before the exhibition opened, the *Illustrated London News* featured engravings of the ivory carvers of Bengal in the act of preparing goods for the Crystal Palace. Seated with legs crossed, draped in simple loincloths, and situated in primitive environs, these figures whet an appetite for an artisanal India in advance of the great show (fig. 34).[115] During the exhibition season, commentators repeatedly lauded the "patience, ingenuity, and dexterity" of the native craftsmen pictured

ELEPHANT-HOWDAH, PRESENTED TO HER MAJESTY BY HIS HIGHNESS THE NEWAB NAZIM.

33 Howdah from the Indian subcontinent. *Illustrated Exhibitor* 11 (16 August 1851): 196. Reproduced courtesy of the Huntington Library, San Marino, California.

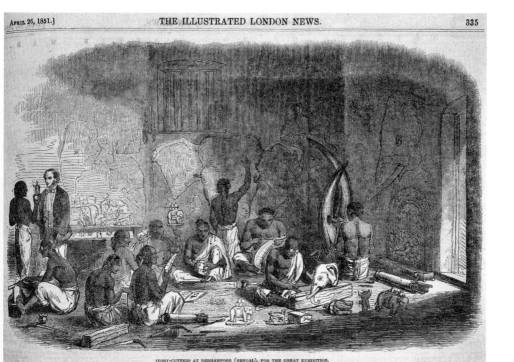

IVORY-CUTTERS AT BERHAMPOOR (BENGAL), FOR THE GREAT EXHIBITION.

34   Bengal's ivory carvers preparing for the Great Exhibition. *Illustrated London News*, 25 April 1851, 335. Department of Special and Area Studies Collections, George A. Smathers Library, University of Florida.

in the *Illustrated London News*'s rendition.[116] Such praise is reminiscent of that offered to the workmen of France and even, at times, the artisans of England. This similarity notwithstanding, the discussion of Indian labor differed in distinct ways from characterizations of European workers. Exhibition commentators adorned their assessments of Indian artisans with an explicit romanticism and a discernable orientalism. This practice, evident in both images and texts, allowed the exhibition press to elevate the laborers of the subcontinent to a mythic status while simultaneously confining them outside of industrial modernity.[117] The *Illustrated Exhibitor* provides a case in point. When it rhapsodized about India's artisans, it deemed them "ignorant in the world's estimate, yet wise in all that is necessary to life."[118]

Commodification and Its Discontents   115

Many endorsed Cassell's assessment.[119] When they extolled India's artisans, critics evoked timeless productive traditions that defied historical change. In their texts, the subcontinent became a living museum that preserved habits of industry in ancient form. There laborers transmitted traditions of making umbrellas, gold cloth, and bejeweled robes "from generation to generation." Artists began to study the secrets of these trades in their "earliest infancy."[120] Perhaps this practice of transmission explained the seeming instinctual quality of Indian labor and the magical goods that resulted. India's muslin, for instance, resembled the "woven wind." It took its place among several wares that even the most renowned European craftsmen failed to rival. "Designed for eternity in the unchanging East," India's celebrated cashmere shawls were unmatched in coloring and execution.[121] For all of his national pride, even Blanqui deemed these productions "more beautiful than those of Paris."[122] Digby Wyatt similarly pointed out the "marvelous sensibility of touch" so evident in the embroidery of Dacca. Even the "delicate fingers" of the Belgian needleworkers, the best in Europe, could not render such magic.[123]

For exhibition commentators, the quotidian habits of labor that gave rise to these matchless goods were themselves a source of fascination. Decidedly preindustrial and markedly romantic, India's productive processes depended on the rhythms of nature and the efforts of families. One exemplary figure was the Indian weaver, who worked under a tree, where he was aided by his wife and children. More than the weaver, the female Hindu spinner embodied the artisanal, natural, and preindustrial. The sun, rather than the clock, regulated her workday. This laborer rose before the sun had "dissipate[d] the dew on the grass" so that she could spin her best thread before dawn. As she toiled in the open air under a pine or mango tree, she relied on rude tools, including fish jaws, iron rollers, and rough bows.[124]

The fact that this "wonderfully simple machinery" yielded such ornate results fascinated English writers.[125] Repeatedly, they noted a marked disparity between the "rough and primitive" tools—many on display in the Crystal Palace themselves—and the intricate results.[126] Digby Wyatt was constantly intrigued by the seeming incongruity between the simple implements and the ornate works. He deemed it a "wonder" that such "rude instruments" as steel chisels and iron rollers had wrought "admirable and elaborate" productions such as the lavish, colorful crystal vases that he featured in his publication (plate 4).[127] The exhibition's practice of collapsing the distance between civilizations crystallized this understanding. For instance, one commentator noted that Nasmyth's steam hammer provided a striking contrast to the anvils wielded by the blacksmiths of Bengal.[128] Even literature for children remarked on the simplicity of Indian tools in comparison to English machinery.[129] Illustrated periodicals only intensified the apparent distance between the two civilizations. To understand the differences, readers of the *Illustrated Exhibitor* needed only to compare the subcontinent's manual loom, pictured with its dextrous and erect worker, to the English power loom, shown in its mechanical glory (figs. 35 and 36).

If such meditations were insufficient to bring India's artisans to life, exhibitiongoers could find at the Crystal Palace a collection of "ethnographic models." Together, these clay and wood carvings offered a "lively representation of Indian life and character," which presaged the human showcases at later exhibitions.[130] According to Tallis, the sixty clay figures from Kishnagur illustrating India's trades and occupations were the most provocative.[131] Among those immortalized in clay were the cotton spinner, the blacksmith, the cook, the snake charmer, and the potter, whose cross-legged and effeminate form exemplified the orientalist iconography of Indian labor (fig. 37). Of these figures, Blanqui effused, "We see them in their attitudes of work, their implements in their hands, their miniature looms before them—they really live before us!" Yet, even as he admired India's magical craftsmen, Blanqui could not help but call attention to their apparent indigence.[132] He thereby joined several commentators who pointed out the "pitiful and precarious" existence of the subcontinent's laborers.[133] John Cassell, for instance, described Indian artisans as "a lean, starved-out regiment of squalid beggars, half naked, or with scanty folds of coarsest cotton flung around their wasted limbs."[134] Another writer professed "repulsion" toward the "distorted," thin, and effeminate models. While the renditions in Cassell's *Illustrated Exhibitor* certainly substantiate these descriptions, the squat and sturdy figures in *Tallis's History and Description* do not.[135] Even so, the disparity between text and image provides us with a sense of the wide-ranging effects of orientalism on both narrative strategy and graphic practice at midcentury (fig. 38).

At bottom, these responses to the ethnographic models ranged far from an idealization of Indian labor. For all of those who celebrated Indian workmanship, there were others who characterized it as barbarism.[136]

INDIAN LOOM.

35 Oriental industry as archaic practice in 1851. *Illustrated Exhibitor* 18 (4 October 1851): 323.

36 English industry as mechanized promise in 1851. *Illustrated Exhibitor* 16 (20 September 1851): 285.

Both reproduced courtesy of the Huntington Library, San Marino, California.

POWER LOOM.

THE POTTER.

37   India embodied in 1851. *Illustrated Exhibitor* 18
(4 October 1851): 323. Reproduced courtesy of the
Huntington Library, San Marino, California.

38   Ethnographic models. *John Tallis's History and
Description of the Crystal Palace*, vol. 3 (1851), after
p. 66. Reproduced courtesy of the Winterthur
Library, Printed Book and Periodical Collection.

Engraved by G.Greatbach, from a Drawing by H.Mason.

INDIAN FIGURES.
FROM THE EAST INDIAN DEPARTMENT.

Such discussions recall an earlier practice of denigrating Indian production. It had been all too evident in the caviling of those eighteenth-century critics of calico, who had called the fabric's producers "a parcel of Heathens and Pagans that worship the Devil and work for a halfpenny a day."[137] Over a century later, such a view persisted among those who discussed the ethnographic models. But the denigration of Indian production did not stop there.[138] Time and again critics pointed out the primitivism of India's productive regime. Nowhere was this more marked than in discussions of Indian weaponry, which suggested to many a certain "barbaric pomp." For a contributor to the liberal *Westminster Review*, the ornate daggers, arrows, and guns in the Indian collection appeared to be the work of an "idle people" who "indulged in cruel and morbid fancies."[139] In the formulation of the Cambridge scientist William Whewell, such goods represented the immoderation of a mode of production in which "tens of thousands" labored for a handful of tyrants.[140] Along with inordinately lavish fabrics and ornate jewels, they provided material evidence of the "wasteful and ridiculous excess" that marred oriental production.[141]

It is important to note that such tendencies extended well beyond the Indian Courts. At the exhibition, it was not India but rather China that represented the apotheosis of wasteful labor. Like India, China was renowned as an ancient and enduring civilization. However, critics did not accord to Chinese snuffboxes, ivory carvings, and porcelain cups any level of aesthetic value. Digby Wyatt determined that China's wares lacked a "fertility of imagination."[142] Others concurred, noting that Chinese design tended toward the grotesque, the whimsical, the fantastic, and the capricious. A "national" predilection for "imitation and patient perseverance" did not translate into works of great merit.[143] Instead, it yielded useless baubles. The most notable of these were the nested ivory balls carved by Chinese craftsmen. Practitioners of this labor-intensive, time-consuming, and intricate craft spent countless hours, days, and even months carving sets of up to twenty concentric balls. More than any other object at the exhibition, these balls seemed to exemplify the painstakingly detailed, if useless, character of Chinese labor.[144]

Critics endorsed the assertion that China represented the quintessence of wasteful toil in 1851, but the Celestial Empire did not have a monopoly here. Indeed, signs of what Tallis called "misplaced labor" abounded throughout the exhibition. Even Englishmen, he noted, displayed a tendency toward folly, whimsicality, and absurdity. Such lean-ings were especially evident in the fruits of recreation submitted by in-dependent exhibitors, especially those members of the petty bourgeoisie who tinkered in their leisure hours. "Quang Sing, of Canton" may have carved and engraved peach stones, but "Mr. Jacob, of Coventry-Street" did the same on eggshells. Together with mutton fat vases and cardboard cathedrals, these goods suggested to Tallis a misunderstanding, or even a perversion, of the exhibition ideal.[145] Other critics similarly lamented the "waste of human labor" so evident at the Crystal Palace. John Cassell found offenses among those knitted, crocheted, and embroidered cre-ations submitted by ladies. Erroneously, the exhibitors of these goods had believed that "the size or number of years wasted in their labor en-titled them to display."[146] Perhaps they had mistaken the intent behind progenitor Henry Cole's call for everyone to become an exhibitor in 1851, the humblest cottager and his daughter included.[147]

Crafted by Chinese artisans, English ladies, and modest gentlemen, such exemplars of misplaced labor occupied a marginal place in the Crystal Palace. But the critique of excessive flourish extended to such leading contributions as this bedstead in zebrawood produced by a Vien-nese furniture maker for the state bedroom of a German prince. It was a star attraction not only at the exhibition but also in its catalogues, which used their reproductive capacities to their best effects to showcase the bedstead (fig. 39). Whether wood engravings or color lithographs, they accompanied the images of the showpiece with lively and suggestive prose. In the estimation of Cassell, it was a veritable "cathedral dedicated to sleep—so grand in conception, so massive in proportion, so deeply rich in carved glories, so evident an invocation of the artist." Digby Wyatt had nothing but praise for the "great facility and command" so evident in its craft, though he found fault with the "florid" design. For him, it suggested the "intensely aristocratic" culture of Austria if not the excesses of high Victorian style. Blanqui put it more bluntly when he suggested that the intricate carving showed a "sheer waste of talent and ability."[148] Unfortunately, this very tendency was evident, too, in England's "cumbrous" furniture, which pandered to "flashy taste."[149] In the end it was no better than the ornate oriental and aristocratic prod-ucts that so troubled English critics such as William Whewell, who saw in the arts of different nations the very differences between liberty and despotism.

39 Austrian state bed. *Official Descriptive and Illustrated Catalogue of the Great Exhibition*, vol. 4 (1851), after p. 1040. Reproduced courtesy of the Winterthur Library, Printed Book and Periodical Collection.

CONCLUSION

Such criticisms of the English furniture trade anticipated the critiques of English design mounted at the Museum of Ornamental Art, which opened in 1852. With the hope of promulgating lessons about good taste, this predecessor to the South Kensington Museum showcased some of the exhibition's most notable works at Marlborough House in London's West End. Like Cassell, Blanqui, and Digby Wyatt, the museum's leadership would find fault with the excessive ornamentation that has come to be associated with high Victorian design. It did not, however, promulgate its criticisms as express concerns about misplaced labor. Instead, the museum identified a series of taste principles that warned against extravagance and insincerity.

The resort to principles of taste marks the foreclosure of a remarkably

Chapter Three

open discourse on design that flourished at the Great Exhibition and in the accompanying literature. As this chapter has shown, the industrial arts attained unprecedented prominence in 1851 thanks to the exhibition and its texts. When they discussed the displays in Hyde Park, a broad range of interlocutors marshaled laboring figures from across the globe to bring the installations to life. This rhetorical practice would have mixed effects. On the one hand, it would challenge the fetishizing power of the great commodity spectacle. On the other, it would sentimentalize labor, ultimately rendering it a part of the great display. But even if the effort to uncover what Blanqui had called a "mystical relationship" between the laborer and his wares did not challenge commodity capitalism, it gave industrial art an extraordinary resonance in a growing public sphere. Moreover, by making labor ever more available in public discourse, the exhibition's texts offered important rhetorical tools that working men would employ in the years to come. They would look to their positions as producers to gain a measure of cultural capital in the ensuing decades, especially at the South Kensington Museum.

If the exhibition's texts marked a wellspring of great creativity and openness in design discourse, they also showed 1851 to be a moment of uncharacteristic optimism.[150] The confidence about Britain's industrial arts—and the sense that the Government School of Design, with its endlessly proliferating branches, was doing its job—would quickly fade, even in the exhibition's waning months. In lectures, in prize-winning essays, and in newspaper articles, authors reasserted the well-known lament that Britain could not rival France in the industrial arts. Additionally, an industrializing Germany and even an artisanal India posed formidable challenges.[151]

How are we to explain this optimism and its subsequent demise? It may be that the euphoria and wonder that pervaded accounts of the exhibition and the magical Crystal Palace colored discussions of the industrial arts. More to the point, however, are the exhibition's strategies of showing. Those manufacturers and local committees who offered contributions to the Crystal Palace tended, whenever possible, to showcase the finest examples of their trades—the "crowning representation[s]" rather than the articles of everyday use.[152] This tendency did not escape Robert Ellis, the editor of the *Official Catalogue*, who remarked that the installations in the Crystal Palace were better suited for palaces than ordinary dwellings.[153] Take, for example, the Coventry ribbon, an exqui-

40 Coventry town ribbon by
Dalziel. Engraving. *Art Journal
Illustrated Catalogue* (1851): 13.
Yale Center for British Art, Paul
Mellon Collection.

site specimen of design that surpassed its peers in beauty and price (fig.
40). Local worthies had organized its manufacture to showcase the highest capabilities of their trade. It was an exemplary showpiece, not a representative production. Digby Wyatt noted that it differed greatly from
the "cheap ribbons" for middle- and lower-class consumption that were
characteristic of the trade. With a censure reminiscent of the copyright
campaign, the architect charged that the majority of Coventry's manufacturers paid little attention to "originality in design." Moreover, they
exhibited a base "tendency to copy or recombine French patterns."[154] In
this regard, they resembled those pirates who had been the scourge of
the calico trade just a decade before.

The exhibition's catalogues only corroborated the tendency to feature
works of virtuosity. Presumably, images of Austrian bedsteads and tales
of Indian weavers offered better copy than laments about bad British
design. This said, the Crystal Palace held its share of "very ordinary"
calicoes.[155] Its halls also included "real slop shawls" so despicable that

Chapter Three

"respectable chamber-maids" in Paris would have refused to wear them, or so Blanqui alleged. When the glimmer of the great show had faded, it was these goods—worn by those "millions" who comprised Britain's consuming masses—that occupied the attention of artists, critics, and reformers.[156] Even if the School of Design had enabled aesthetic improvement, critics charged, it had not done enough. The dross that remained at the exhibition's end thus led a new coalition of reformers to try a different tack. For salvation, they turned to another collection, albeit one of much smaller scale with more discrete ambitions. Opened in 1852, the Museum of Ornamental Art sought to offer lessons in good design. But far from the object of adoration that its magical predecessor had been, this institution would find itself, from the very outset, a center of controversy.

CHAPTER FOUR

Principled Disagreements

THE MUSEUM OF ORNAMENTAL ART AND ITS

CRITICS, 1852–1856

In December 1852, the domestic periodical *Household Words* relayed the cautionary tale of Mr. Crumpet, a fictive City of London countinghouse clerk. By his own admission, Crumpet had recently become a "very miserable man." Just a few months earlier, he had delighted in his lower-middle-class life, in which polite sociability and modest domesticity defined the routine rhythms.[1] After his days in the city, this prototypical "man on the Clapham omnibus" eagerly returned to his rented accommodations in suburban South London. There he spent evenings in his small parlor, flanked by an adoring wife and loving children. Recently, however, Crumpet had found himself "haunted." He lived a nightmarish existence in which "frightful objects" and "ghastly shapes" assaulted him. Nowhere was this more the case than in the English clerk's home. Formerly a comfort, it now appeared "full of horrors."[2]

Aesthetic enlightenment had precipitated Crumpet's demise. Recently he had had the unfortunate privilege of acquiring some "Correct Principles of Taste." A visit to a new London collection, the Museum of Ornamental Art, had provided him with these precepts. Established in the wake of the Great Exhibition, this West End museum showcased treasures that had previously filled the Crystal Palace. By displaying the silver of England, the porcelain of France, and the silks of the Orient, the museum sought to promulgate lessons in good design. To convey these lessons, it employed an affordable *Catalogue*. Here visitors such as Crumpet could find enumerated simple rules of ornamentation. Together they recommended a design ideal that ranged far from the ornate showpieces that had filled the Crystal Palace, on the one hand, and the ill-conceived travesties that marred the consumer marketplace on the other. The *Catalogue* enshrined three rules—the geometry principle, the "direct imitation of nature" principle, and the "stuck-on" principle of ornamentation—which were to guide good design. In sum, these laws upheld an aesthetic that was symmetrical, abstract, and organic.

If Crumpet's saga is any indication, the *Catalogue* was a forceful pedagogical instrument. In *Household Words'* bitingly satirical narrative, the effects of the *Catalogue* arguably exceeded its authors' intentions. After visiting the museum, the clerk came to despise his once beloved dwelling with its "hideous" paper hangings and garish carpets. In the formerly welcoming streets of London, unsightly waistcoats and ghastly ties assaulted him. And when he stood in front of the mirror the clerk could only look with shame on his "own trowsers." England itself had become anathema. In the pages of the *Catalogue*, Crumpet had learned about the superiority of "Oriental ornamentation," which was preferable to that of the West due to its adherence to the principles of design. Tortured by his surroundings, Crumpet longed to escape his native Brixton, a cozy London suburb, for the fictional imperial locations of Palampore and Amberabad.[3]

This chapter examines the Museum of Ornamental Art, which altered the lens through which the fictional Crumpet viewed his domestic environs. The museum opened in London's West End in May 1852, just half a year after the Great Exhibition of 1851 had closed in nearby Hyde Park. The Benthamite civil servant Henry Cole, a mid-Victorian paragon of reform and discipline, spearheaded the museum's foundation. By using his collection as a tool of reform, Cole aspired to improve the "public taste in Design."[4] As an attempt to rehabilitate the industrial arts, Cole's efforts were of a piece with such earlier innovations as the School of Design and the campaign for copyright legislation. The museum differed from these predecessors, however, in significant ways. If the earlier endeavors sought, primarily, to rework supply-side habits of production and trade, the museum elevated the metropolitan consumer to a place of primary importance. Presaging such developments in economic thought as the marginal revolution, which shifted attention from production to consumption, those at the forefront of the Museum of Ornamental Art conceived of design as an issue of marketplace demand.[5] It was useless, they would argue, to train producers without educating consumers. They deemed this enterprise all the more necessary in the mid–nineteenth century, when rising prosperity had empowered new cadres of buyers for whom taste was not a birthright.[6]

This pivotal difference aside, the reforming effort at Marlborough House resembled its predecessors in several regards. Like its forbears, the Museum of Ornamental Art was the stage for a heated cultural contest. Like earlier participants in the design debates who argued over the figure and the copyright, midcentury critics waged their own battle at fever pitch. Their contest focused on questions of principle. As part of an effort to make the museum a useful engine of reform, Cole and his allies codified the series of design principles that Crumpet would absorb on his visit. The museum's *Catalogue* propounded these principles as self-evident truths. It was through these guidelines that Cole endeavored to educate consumers, improve the economy, and produce a British industrial aesthetic. If the principles of design promised salvation to Cole, they were heresy for critics, who took issue with the museum's excessive didacticism, its privileging of oriental ornamentation, and its disregard for their own highest good: the free marketplace.

One critic of the museum's principles was the journalist Henry Morley, who penned Crumpet's saga.[7] According to Morley, the principles of design alienated Crumpet from his environs. In turn, Crumpet estranged himself from the polite world of lower-middle-class sociability that he inhabited. The crowning blow occurred at a dinner hosted by Mr. Martin Frippy, Crumpet's friend and client. There Crumpet broke the rules of civility in favor of the principles of ornamentation. He informed Frippy that his trousers were "beasts" and his shirt a "hideous rag." But it was a tea tray showing a Landseer picture and a teacup enameled with a butterfly on the inside that provided the coup de grâce. These violations of the "direct imitation of nature" principle reduced Crumpet to a state of "mental apoplexy." Rationality, propriety, and perspective deserted him. The representative economic man, the London counting-house clerk, transmogrified into an emasculated figure obsessed with the domestic and particular. When Frippy delivered Crumpet home, he remonstrated gently that his friend might have "swallowed" the museum's principles far too eagerly.[8]

Henry Morley employed the story of the chastened Crumpet to suggest the shortcomings of the museum's principled approach. Writing in a journal directed to a domestic reading public, Morley claimed that the state-sponsored museum intruded unnecessarily into household affairs. In the process, he denounced the museum's reforming zeal, its didactic nature, and its reliance on foreign designs to produce a British industrial aesthetic. Other critics also used the print culture of the day—newspapers, tracts, and even novels—to express their misgivings about the museum and its taste principles. One notable antagonist was F. J. Prouting, a staunch advocate of free trade from industrial Manchester who wrote under the pseudonym Argus. He exploited the medium of the political tract to launch a sustained attack on the museum and its principles. In a series of pamphlets, Argus decried the museum as a "taste dictatorship." As he saw it, the metropolitan museum displayed an excessively cosmopolitan preoccupation with taste. By so doing, it threatened the ideals of English liberty and market freedom that were so dear to members of the provincial middle classes.

Together Morley, Argus, and others charged that the museum and its principles compromised boundaries that were fundamental to the mid-Victorian order. Among these, we can count public and private, domestic and foreign, provincial and metropolitan, and finally aesthetics and economics. Mid-Victorian Britons understood these divisions to be essential to daily life and national culture. They also held these dichotomies to be crucial to the maintenance of gender roles. Given this understanding, it is hardly surprising that the language of masculinity provided the rhetorical currency for the debates that rocked Marlborough House. As they challenged the museum, critics such as Argus and Morley galvanized a rhetoric of imperiled masculinity.[9] When they criticized Marlborough House's principles of taste, midcentury writers expressed anxiety about the vexed place of men—whether lower-middle-class Londoners, middle-class provincials, or wellborn metropolitans—in a changing marketplace. They did not frame these men simply as producers but as consumers, too. Such an understanding allows us to see, yet again, that debates over design allowed mid-Victorian Britons to articulate diverse anxieties about a marketplace in transition. And, like the marketplace whose ailments it aimed to solve, design reform proved to be a cultural battleground par excellence.

AESTHETIC TRAVESTIES, WAYWARD CONSUMERS,
AND THE MUSEUM'S MISSION

The Great Exhibition of 1851 provided the shock that catapulted the Museum of Ornamental Art into existence. This hallowed show left two seemingly divergent understandings about design and material culture in its wake. The previous chapter demonstrated that the showpieces on display at the Crystal Palace, whether English, French, or oriental, prompted commentators to wax lyrical about the inspiring goods and the labor that went into them. As the exhibition came to a close, however, a different assessment of design emerged in the art press and in popular newspapers. At that time, aesthetes and journalists turned their attention to chintzes, calicoes, and wallpapers produced for mass consumption. These goods had crowded the British Courts at the Crystal Palace, but the exhibition press had overlooked them by and large. After the exhibition closed, these commodities continued to flood the domestic marketplace, where they were available to consumers such as Crumpet and Frippy. Aesthetes and journalists were appalled when they compared these shoddy wares to the masterful installations at the Crystal Palace. These calicoes, wallpapers, and rugs were travesties or capricious fashions at best.[10] In the end, such assessments went a long way toward extinguishing the euphoria that surrounded the Great Exhibition.

In the wake of these discoveries, contributors to the popular press reported that British manufactures faced challenges from all sides. The Great Exhibition gave "palpable" evidence of the unsettling truth that other European nations excelled Britain in many industrial arts.[11] The specter of France, so evident during the 1830s and 1840s, continued to loom.[12] Even more notable was the growing strength of other nations whose goods threatened Britain's industrial dominance.[13] The *Morning Chronicle* observed that the manufactured wares of Germany, Belgium, and Russia put England's industries to shame.[14] More "startling" was the increasingly prevalent lament that the ornaments from "'savage' India and 'barbarian' China" surpassed Britain's in aesthetic merit.[15] Some even pronounced with shock that the seeming "barbarity and imbecility" of African wares—"head-dresses of dead men's scalps, earrings of

No. 146.   MEN OF THE DAY, No. 29.
                          "King Cole."

41 Henry Cole caricatured. Lithograph. *Vanity Fair*, 19 August 1871. Yale Center for British Art, Gift of Mr. Michael H. LeWitt, Mr. Peter A. LeWitt, and Mr. Erwin Strasmick.

live snakes, and skin decorations of purple tattoo"—paled in comparison to England's monstrosities.[16]

A discomforting discovery to many, these assessments were no surprise to Henry Cole, the utilitarian reformer who had established himself as a leading figure in aesthetic circles over the previous decade. Driven by relentless efficiency, improving zeal, and personal ambition, Cole was the target of biting critique and satirical comment throughout his long career, as this *Vanity Fair* caricature suggests (fig. 41). These very characteristics were evident in Cole's rise to prominence. As the first prong of his campaign to reconcile art and utility, Cole had released a line of art manufactures under the name of Felix Summerly.[17] His most notable production was a teacup, which won a prize from the Society for the Encouragement of Arts and Manufactures. Summerly was not simply notable but notorious, too, as this notice from the irreverent pages of

Principled Disagreements   131

Punch indicates (fig. 42). After Summerly's triumph, Cole conceived of the Great Exhibition of 1851 with Prince Albert. Not content to stop there, he masterminded the attack on the School of Design by the 1849 select committee and maneuvered himself into the secretaryship of the institution.[18] Finally, Cole found an effective engine for this assault in the six volumes of the *Journal of Design and Manufactures*, which he edited anonymously from 1849 to 1852. There he brought his improving mission to an audience of workmen and manufacturers.

When the Great Exhibition closed, Cole would embark on the next phase of his reforming career. Amid calls to save the Crystal Palace, which would be torn down in 1852 and rebuilt at Sydenham, South London, in 1854, Cole purchased articles from the Great Exhibition for study at the ailing School of Design.[19] A committee comprised of the artist Richard Redgrave, the architect Owen Jones, and the Gothic revivalist Augustus Welby Pugin assisted Cole. Together they trawled the Crystal Palace as if it were a flea market, acquiring Indian shawls, Italian cabinetry, Turkish carpets, French porcelain, and Birmingham metalwork with funds from the Great Exhibition's surplus.[20] Sympathetic to this endeavor, Prince Albert proposed in early 1852 that a permanent state-sponsored museum be made out of these displays. Amenable to her husband's idea, Queen Victoria granted Cole the use of the royal residence of Marlborough House in London's West End, and in May the Museum of Ornamental Art debuted there (fig. 43).[21]

The infant museum would become the centerpiece of a renewed effort to improve the industrial arts in the wake of the aesthetic disenchantment that followed the exhibition. A new Government Department of Practical Art formed in 1852 and renamed the Department of Science and Art in 1853 took up this charge.[22] There Cole served as general superintendent and Redgrave as associate art superintendent. Together they sought to improve on the beleaguered schools of design, which they critiqued in a manner reminiscent of Haydon as schoolrooms filled with "weary artisans" who sat "fagging at elementary drawing on winter evenings." But they also sought to change the very focus and strategy of design education. The schools had erred in manifold ways. Their curriculum was ineffective; their audience was narrow. But even more significant was the fact that they had begun at the wrong end: they trained producers without educating consumers.[23]

Cole drove this critique home in his introductory lecture at the Mu-

DESIGNS FOR ART MANUFACTURES.

WE have looked in vain for the carrying out of the idea we threw out some time back, of supplying articles of real utility amongst the Art Manufactures of MR. FELIX SUMMERLY. "UNA and the Lion" are all very well for those who like to turn their mantel-piece into a Zoological Garden; and a card-tray by a first-rate artist may be welcome enough to those who have a pack of visiting cards left with them every day to fill the ornamental receptacle; but a clothes-horse would be preferable to UNA's Lion, and a tea-tray far more acceptable than a card-tray in the eyes of those whom the Art Manufactures ought to be adapted for. We shall therefore agitate for the application of the principle to matters of humbler pretension than merely ornamental works; and we begin by proposing a series of implements for the fire-side, including hearth-

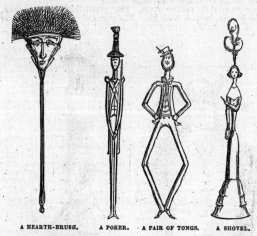

A HEARTH-BRUSH.   A POKER.   A PAIR OF TONGS.   A SHOVEL.

broom, coal-scuttle, and shovel, so that if the projectors will go at it poker and tongs, a successful result will be accomplished. The stiffness of the poker will afford an ample opportunity for the introduction of that starched military erectness that is so effective in our iron-work; while the tongs, by their graceful pliability, are at once suggestive of the easy hornpipe with which the other service is identified. The shovel, by its undulating curve, and the broom, by its elegant sweep, may be easily made subservient to the purposes of Art; and as to the scuttle, it offers a scope, not to say scoop, to the most refined handling.

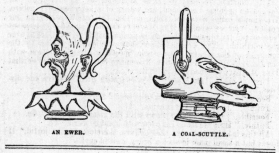

AN EWER.   A COAL-SCUTTLE.

42 Felix Summerly's art manufactures. *Punch* 13 (1847): 227. Reproduced courtesy of the Huntington Library, San Marino, California.

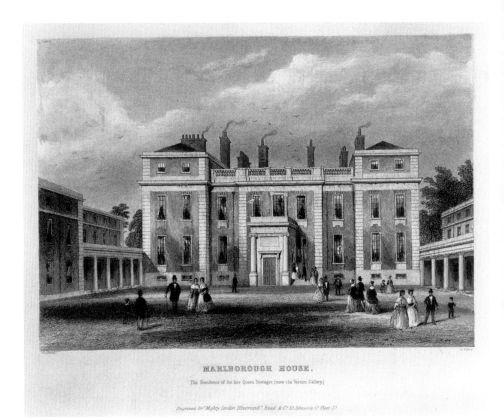

MARLBOROUGH HOUSE.

The Residence of the late Queen Dowager (now the Vernon Gallery.)

Engraved for "Mighty London Illustrated." Read & Co. 10, Johnson's Ct. Fleet St.

43 Etching of Marlborough House by Le Petit. *Views of Mighty London* (ca. 1854). Yale Center for British Art, Paul Mellon Collection.

seum of Ornamental Art, delivered in November 1852. There he exhorted his audience to reconsider the workings of the marketplace. "Why are manufactures produced? Why are more Cotton fabrics woven than Silk ones?" Cole asked rhetorically. "Why does the manufacturer decorate fabrics for the South American market in one way, and the metropolis in another?" He found the answer in "the will of the consumer." The improvement of manufactures depended on "the public ability" to distinguish "between what is good and bad in art." As Cole understood it, it was consumers, and not producers, who drove the market. Therefore, it was sheer "folly"—indeed, "worse than useless"—to continue educating the designer without elevating the consumer.[24]

Chapter Four

A cunning rhetorician, Cole implied that he had discovered "the consumer" as an economic force and a social entity. However, his characterizations relied on pervasive contemporary notions. Together the art press and the popular press bemoaned the dangers of the unreformed consumer in a time of increasing prosperity. They held that the growing ranks of new buyers from the middle and working classes represented the true impediment to artistic progress. These buyers forced manufacturers, artisans, and shopkeepers to pander to the lowest common denominator. Their demands produced a downward aesthetic spiral in the market. Reversing common conceptions of the relationship between supply and demand, several critics accused the "ignorant public" of filling stores with "bad designs." The *Art Journal* bore out this charge with its woeful tale of market-savvy manufacturers who "vulgarized" carpets and tablecloths to meet consumer demand.[25] For instance, they desecrated tasteful Gothic patterns by adding superfluous bunches of tulips. According to Cole's *Journal of Design and Manufactures*, this practice was a real travesty. The *Journal* castigated this sort of "mixture of styles," evident in the plate pictured here, with its crude amalgam of Louis Quatorze, Alhambra, and Italian qualities (fig. 44).[26] Others joined in this lament about the nation's low-end porcelain, which was purchased by the "millions" and sold overseas. With its deplorable designs, it displayed "the very bathos of European art."[27]

Given this preponderance of bad design, the infant Museum of Ornamental Art had a weighty task ahead. To embark on its mission of educating consumers of all classes, the museum conjoined decorative practices reminiscent of the elite collector's romantic interior to the expressly didactic functions of the modern museum.[28] The department filled the lower apartments with the museum's holdings. Richly arrayed in elegant display cases, they brought the domestic milieu of the private connoisseur, with its historicist and romantic overtones, to a broad public (fig. 45).[29] Even as it evoked a world of privilege, the department transformed Marlborough House into a utilitarian schoolroom of sorts.[30] It converted the upper quarters into classrooms. Cole and company transformed the kitchen into a lecture hall and stocked the cellars with ornamental casts.[31] For all of this, it levied liberal admissions fees and even offered free days.[32] Notably, the department allowed paid entrants to handle and examine the collections, provided that they washed their hands. In the next few years, the museum would extend its commit-

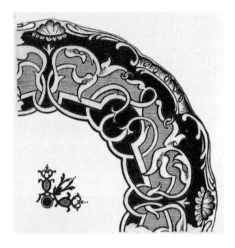

44 Dessert Plate produced at the School of Design showing a mixture of styles. *Journal of Design and Manufactures* 1 (1849): 21. Reproduced courtesy of the Huntington Library, San Marino, California.

45 Marlborough House interior by W. L. Casey (1856). V & A Images, Victoria and Albert Museum, London.

ment to accessibility in several ways. It sold redundant articles to provincial schools of design.[33] In an especially well regarded effort, it formed a traveling collection that would visit Britain's industrial centers.[34] Finally, as an early pioneer in photography, it circulated images for the purpose of study.[35] It was no wonder that the *Morning Post* lauded the Museum of Ornamental Art as a "step in the right direction" on its opening.[36]

THE CATALOGUE, SOUND CANONS, AND THE MUSEUM'S COLLECTION

When it praised the museum, the *Post* called particular attention to the *Catalogue* written by Cole, Redgrave, and Jones. The text was sure to disseminate a "practical national taste" among those consumers, manufacturers, and laborers who visited. If Mr. Crumpet's burlesque tale is any indication, the *Catalogue* was a powerful, even perilous, instrument of instruction, although it did not boast illustrations. As the *Post* suggested, its force rested on two virtues. First, the *Catalogue* was an affordable text, costing sixpence in its first edition and threepence in later printings. Second, the *Catalogue* was an effective treatise, distilling "sure and correct principles" of design in order to "render the beauties and defects" of the objects on display easily comprehensible to uninitiated viewers such as Crumpet. In sum, the *Catalogue* married cheap literature and aesthetic theory in the service of propounding what contemporaries called "sound canons of design."[37]

As a work of affordable and didactic literature, the *Catalogue* followed on earlier utilitarian publishing ventures, including Henry Cole's own enterprise, undertaken during the 1840s under the illustrious pseudonym Felix Summerly. Sold for a penny or a shilling, Summerly's works included drawing books, metropolitan guides, and museum compendia. Like the art manufactures, they were part of Cole's larger enterprise of reconciling beauty and utility.[38] This endeavor was especially evident in Summerly's guides to museums and picture galleries, among them the National Gallery, the Soane Museum, and the British Museum.[39] With their sparse, utilitarian inventories, these pocket manuals sustained the efforts of publications such as the *Penny Magazine* as they sought to communicate the "art of seeing" to readers.[40]

If the *Catalogue* partook of an earlier tradition of affordable literature, it also drew on existing theories of art and design. In fact, it distilled writings on art and design from the previous decades into a succinct "grammar of ornament" that would govern the decorative arts in the years to come.[41] It boasted a formidable lineage which included aesthetic theorists, design periodicals, and exhibition writings. One writer whose thinking had a formative influence on the *Catalogue* was a Scotsman and decorative painter to the queen, David Ramsay Hay. During the 1830s and 1840s, Hay had published several treatises and manuals on design where he asserted that there were "irrefragable laws" of form and color.[42] These were evident in nature, which left "nothing unadorned" but instead exhibited purpose and truth in all of its embellishments. To Hay's chagrin, the lavish carpets and garish paper hangings that dominated the marketplace violated nature's dictates. Hay aspired, therefore, to propound the "rules" of taste and so to check the "fanaticism and false practice" so evident in the consumer goods of the day.[43]

In the late 1840s and early 1850s, several authors propounded the necessity of principled design to an audience that extended well beyond Hay's specialized readership. Cole's *Journal of Design* took up the mission of disseminating laws of ornament to a manufacturing audience. Its editors proceeded in the most tangible of ways, pasting swatches of wallpaper, calico, and cambric into its very pages. As it adjudicated these consumer goods, the *Journal* itself consolidated and disseminated principles of design. Based loosely on the writings of Hay and other contemporaries, these principles had to do with harmonious coloring, proportional form, and flat ornamentation. French arts such as porcelain and wallpaper tended to follow these rules flawlessly, as one sample from across the Channel suggested (plate 5).[44] To the editors' chagrin, however, the majority of goods produced in Britain were not so law abiding. Essays published and lectures delivered in the Great Exhibition's wake thus urged the importance of principled design with heightened urgency. According to a prize-winning essay by Ralph Nicholson Wornum, the rules of decoration were as sacrosanct as the "mechanical laws" of the universe.[45] Building upon this understanding, the Department of Science and Art would hold that design principles carried a moral imperative. In a recent study, Deborah Cohen has demonstrated that this notion persisted well into the twentieth century. Certainly, at the Museum of Ornamental Art, to violate design's laws was to transgress the social contract.[46]

Chapter Four

This moral charge went a long way toward validating the three principles enumerated in the museum's *Catalogue*. The first of these was the "geometry principle," which mandated that symmetry was "the basis of ornament." Second was the "stuck-on ornament principle," which argued that ornament should arise organically out of the object it adorned rather than appear as an insincere afterthought. This notion was critical in an era when carving, inlaying, gilding, and burnishing were dominant. Such decorative practices, the department held, valued superfluous glitter and wasteful adornment over truth. Related to the stuck-on principle of ornamentation was a third rule, which the *Catalogue* touted as the most important. This was the "direct imitation of nature principle." It warned against copying objects from the natural or material world onto decorative surfaces.[47] Time and again, the *Catalogue*'s authors criticized the replication of such motifs as roses, nosegays, and lily pads onto vases, pitchers, and candlesticks. The proper role of the designer, they explained, was not to "vie with nature" but to use it as a guide.[48] The line to tread here was tricky. The architectural critic Edward Lacy Garbett, a contemporary, may have maneuvered it best when he explained that the goal of ornament was not to copy "what nature presents" but to do "as nature does."[49]

In the *Catalogue*, Cole, Redgrave, and Jones appraised the museum's installations in accordance with their taste principles.[50] Like the *Journal of Design and Manufactures*, the *Catalogue* heaped praise on objects of French provenance. A silver snuffbox from Paris was notable for avoiding stuck-on ornamentation.[51] Indigenous productions such as a modest brass flower vase from Birmingham received laurels for their "sound principles," too.[52] Axminster and Kidderminster carpets demonstrated the "flat treatment of ornament."[53] Other wares stood out for their workmanship, if not their design.[54] Among these holdings were rare pieces of Sèvres porcelain, which had garnered high praise at the Great Exhibition. Commendable in their execution, these treasures tended to err in their excessively imitative styles.[55] A Chelsea porcelain vase, pictured here, received similarly mixed reviews (fig. 46). An eighteenth-century luxe object, it was of the utmost rarity. Its coloring was exemplary, but the shapes were "generally contorted and overloaded with details in relief." With its "birds, flowers and 'Watteau Subjects,'" it transgressed two cardinal rules—the direct imitation of nature principle and the stuck-on principle of ornamentation.[56]

Principled Disagreements

The print of the Chelsea vase appeared in the *Art Journal* in 1855 when this preeminent art publication ran a series of articles by the department's curator, John Charles Robinson, which featured the collections at Marlborough House. The appearance of this series is noteworthy, for it indicates a synergy between the burgeoning art press and the Museum of Ornamental Art. This is not to say that the *Journal* offered the museum uncritical acceptance. To the contrary, in the very year that it published the engraving it criticized the museum's selections, for they were too ornate and detailed to be carried out by the "ordinary processes employed in manufactures." For future purchases, it recommended that the leadership place a premium on "practical utility."[57] Still, the *Art Journal* aided the museum's broader mission. Thanks to its pictorial capacities, it assisted in the project of promoting visual literacy that had been so important to design reformers, and to the illustrated press, since the 1830s. When it featured Marlborough House's holdings, the *Journal* brought the manufactured treasures of the day beyond the walls of the museum, albeit to an elite segment of the reading public.[58] Others who exploited a growing arsenal of techniques of image reproduction also furthered this project. For example, Thomas Underwood, a Birmingham publisher, released a series of annotated lithographs that featured the museum's holdings. Sold for a shilling each, these lithographs brought the finest examples of pottery from Britain and the world into the homes of middle-class consumers (fig. 47).[59] Aided by these publications, those unable to travel to Marlborough House could thereby enjoy the benefits of its teachings and reap the wisdom of its laws.

INDIAN DESIGN, GOTHIC PASTS, AND IMPERIAL AMBIVALENCE

It was not, however, the European wares that best exemplified the principles of art enshrined at the museum. Those who studied the *Catalogue* would have discovered that the goods from the Indian subcontinent held this distinction. For this reason, the galleries at Marlborough House featured many of the very objects that had delighted visitors to the Great Exhibition's Indian Courts. The museum gave the saris, daggers, spice boxes, and rosewater bottles of the subcontinent pride of place (fig. 48).[60] Similarly, the *Catalogue* upheld the Indian productions as "the most important" for their adherence to the rules of design.[61] They dis-

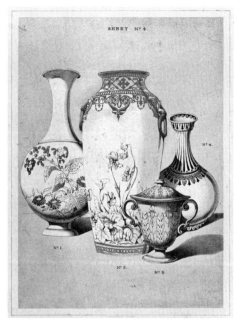

46 Chelsea vase. *Art Journal*, new ser., 1 (1855): 150. Reproduced courtesy of the Winterthur Library, Printed Book and Periodical Collection.

47 Museum of Ornamental Art holdings. Lithograph by Thomas Underwood in *Choice Examples of Art Manufacture*, plate 4 (185-). Yale Center for British Art, Paul Mellon Collection.

48 Rosewater bottle. *Art Journal*, new ser., 1 (1855): 118. Reproduced courtesy of the Winterthur Library, Printed Book and Periodical Collection.

played symmetry of ornament, they eschewed direct imitation of nature, and they avoided stuck-on designs, as a notice in the *Journal of Design and Manufactures* indicated.[62] For this last reason, they offered a welcome respite from European decorative practices. Writing of the Indian collection, Owen Jones claimed that "every ornament arises quietly and naturally from the object decorated, inspired by some true feeling, or embellishing some real want." He waxed lyrical as he boiled decorative practice down to the level of aphorism: "With them the construction is decorated; decoration is never, as with us, purposely constructed."[63]

Jones and his colleagues joined their veneration of the subcontinent's designs to a broader romantic portrayal of Indian society and craft production. According to Jones, Indian design arose from "instinct." It evinced the very faith that the people brought to their "religion, habits, and modes of thought." With such effusions, Jones echoed those Great Exhibition commentators who had meditated on Indian crafts. He also echoed their lyricism when he suggested that the Indian wares were the fruit of an organic, true society that was unmarred by Western modernity.[64] Elsewhere, Richard Redgrave expanded on this notion. More explicitly than Jones, he coupled the adulation of Indian wares with a critique of industrial capitalism, its machines, and its marketplaces.[65] In India, Redgrave found a romantic, preindustrial realm whose beautiful gems provided material testimony to "feelings of piety." In Britain, conversely, he saw a degraded, mechanized world where feckless wares exposed alienated labor. Its mechanics preoccupied themselves more with their molds, stamps, and dies than with the very goods they produced. Its fleeting rhythms proved antithetical to aesthetic devotion. "Who loves a labor that is so soon to pass away?" Redgrave asked, as he recalled the arguments propounded by design copyright's advocates. All told, industrial Britain offered a poor foil to artisanal India.[66]

For all the adulation it received, India did not provide the only idealized realm of labor in the nineteenth century. When they venerated Indian crafts, Redgrave and Jones followed on the writings of Augustus Welby Pugin, the designer of the Great Exhibition's Medieval Court. Pugin had worked with them in selecting the goods to be displayed at Marlborough House.[67] Just a few decades before, Pugin, an architect and revivalist, had offered modern Britons access to a romanticized past in his writings on Gothic, or "pointed," architecture. He claimed that Gothic art arose from sentiments of "faith," "zeal," and "unity." Accord-

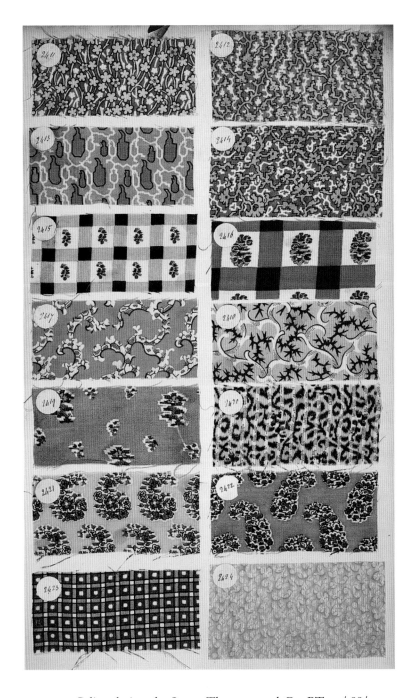

PLATE 1 Calico designs by James Thomson and Co. BT 43/188/2411–
2424, National Archives, Kew, United Kingdom.

PLATE 2 "Medieval Court." Hand-colored lithograph. Plate 40 in *Dickinson's Comprehensive Pictures of the Great Exhibition of 1851*. Yale Center for British Art, Paul Mellon Collection.

PLATE 3 "India, no. 4." Hand-colored lithograph. Plate 33 in *Dickinson's Comprehensive Pictures of the Great Exhibition of 1851*. Yale Center for British Art, Paul Mellon Collection.

PLATE 40

GROUP OF CRYSTAL VASES, AND INDIAN JEWELLERY.

LONDON PRINTED AND PUBLISHED FEB 1ST 1851 BY DAY & SON LITHOGRAPHERS TO THE QUEEN

PLATE 5 French paper hanging. *Journal of Design and Manufactures* 1 (2) (1849). Reproduced courtesy of the Huntington Library, San Marino, California.

(*opposite*) PLATE 4 Crystal vases and Indian jewelry. Chromolithograph. Plate XL in Digby Wyatt, *Industrial Arts of the Nineteenth Century*. Reproduced courtesy of the Winterthur Library, Printed Book and Periodical Collection.

Within the image:
FALSE PRINCIPLES. **31**
IMITATION OF ARCHITECTURE.

PLATE 7 Wallpaper with Gothic architecture, Gallery of False Principles, Museum of Ornamental Art (1852–53). V & A Images, Victoria and Albert Museum, London.

(*opposite*) PLATE 6 Crystal Palace wallpaper, no. 28, Gallery of False Principles, Museum of Ornamental Art (1852–53). V & A Images, Victoria and Albert Museum, London.

PLATE 8 Chintz fabric with toreador and flowers, a violation of the principles of design. BT 43/358/93111, National Archives, Kew, United Kingdom.

ing to Pugin, this organic relationship had manifested itself in the architectural practice of the Middle Ages. At that time, the "salutary and ennobling influence" of Catholicism had guided Gothic architecture. Because it followed the dictates of Catholicism, Gothic architecture displayed fitness, purpose, and honesty.[68] Pugin's words are remarkably similar to Jones's and Redgrave's effusions about Indian art. Like Jones, Pugin longed for an era free of the "glaring, showy, meretricious" ornament of the nineteenth century. Like Redgrave, he yearned for a time when "the mind which originated worked in perfect accordance with the hand which produced."[69] The art historian Tim Barringer has recently titled the fusion of these ideals "colonial gothic." By venerating the "medieval stonemason" and the "Indian craftsman," Barringer argues, its proponents offered a "devastating critique of modern society," its labor practices, and its aesthetic products.[70]

In contrast to Pugin's decisive embrace of medievalism, however, there were limits to Jones's endorsement of Indian art. His love of the subcontinent's design notwithstanding, Jones remained ambivalent about the relationship between the aesthetics of the subcontinent and the industry of the metropole.[71] In fact, Jones cautioned students against the imitation of Indian arts. He instructed them to learn the principles exemplified by the subcontinent's wares without copying its art. To do so posed dangerous possibilities. With considerable hyperbole, Jones suggested that slavish copying might transform Englishmen into the "poor, half-clad, rice-fed people" of the subcontinent.[72] Jones's warning epitomizes the ambivalence of mid-Victorian imperialism, which sought to venerate India while ruling its inhabitants and to display the subcontinent while containing its influence. The decorative arts more generally provide an excellent vantage point on this ambivalence. Even as they lauded Indian wares, midcentury critics consigned the subcontinent to stasis and even decline.[73] These concerns about the decline of Indian arts would lead to a number of reforming efforts on the subcontinent. Among these we can count the School of Arts at Madras and the *Indian Journal of Arts, Sciences, and Manufactures*, both of which sought to resuscitate native practices of production in the face of British rule.[74]

Given these contradictory currents, it is not surprising that the response to the Indian wares at the museum was mixed in character. On the one hand, daily and weekly newspapers embraced Jones's notions. While abstract, they averred, his ideas might improve English commercial life.

Through the Indian holdings, they imagined, manufacturers might learn valuable lessons about form, color, and harmony. They could also find a welcome antidote to European wares, claimed a writer to the *Leader*, who preferred India's exquisite designs to England's shoddy patterns.[75] There were several, however, who disagreed vehemently with this sentiment. The *Spectator* called the zeal for Indian art into question as it lashed out at the "vulgar" shawls showcased at the museum.[76] Even the *Art Journal* chided the infatuation with Asian design, which smacked of aristocratic privilege and despotism. On this score, the *Art Journal* foreshadowed a criticism that would come to be associated with the South Kensington Museum, its neighborhood, and its very collection policies. There, according to some critics, design reform would trade its concern with market improvement for an obsession with aristocratic collecting.[77]

These criticisms notwithstanding, the Museum of Ornamental Art played a foundational role in the making of the imperial metropolis and its spectacular displays. It also helped to consolidate a grammar for discussing Indian art and a criterion for collecting it that would persist throughout the century. The South Kensington Museum provides ample evidence of these continuities. There the Indian collection continued to expand, as the department acquired goods from numerous international exhibitions.[78] At the end of our historical epoch, South Kensington would become the repository for the East India Company's museum. This peripatetic collection, which had delighted museumgoers in various metropolitan locations throughout the century, relocated to South Kensington in 1879.[79] Moncure Daniel Conway would celebrate its opening in May 1880 as "an historic day in the annals" of the museum.[80] When he did so, he reprised the midcentury veneration of Indian design outlined above. Another American, a traveler from Maine who visited the museum in 1889, would do the same in his unpublished diary. Here the tourist pulled out all of the rhetorical stops. In phraseology reminiscent of the Great Exhibition's catalogues, he waxed lyrical about "the richness, the beauty, the prodigality, [and] the wonderful originality" of the Indian Collection. Like his predecessors, the American traveler participated in the twinned veneration and mystification of Indian labor. The goods in the Indian Collection, he meditated, were the work of "several lifetimes"; they seemed to have been "wrought by the hand of magic."[81] Ambivalence aside, the midcentury idealization of Indian art had considerable staying power.

If they were unable to apprehend the department's principles from the displays of Indian art and the *Catalogue*'s musings, visitors to Marlborough House had recourse to another installation during the museum's first year. In 1852 and 1853, consumers such as the fictional Crumpet could tour an infamous Gallery of False Principles. This ancillary collection took a pedagogical tack different from that of the principal displays. The main galleries showcased expensive and rare handicrafts from Europe and Asia. To succeed, they relied on the museumgoer's ability to extract taste principles from the displays and the accompanying *Catalogue*. The Gallery of False Principles, conversely, concerned itself with those "objects of daily use" that were affordable to the middle and working classes. It sought to communicate its message through "matter-of-fact" examples. Instead of nuance and abstraction, the gallery used stark "contrasts" and shocking "negatives" to convey strong lessons about bad design.[82] Colloquially, the gallery came to be known as the Chamber of Horrors. Presumably this moniker derived from the notorious exhibit of the same title at the London museum of Madame Tussaud, which was filled with the waxen heads of victims of the French Revolution. One contemporary visitor to London described Madame Tussaud's chamber as "bloody," "ghastly," and "enough to chill one's blood."[83] If the displays in the Chamber of Horrors at Marlborough House were blood-chilling, it was because they exhibited stark violations of the taste principles enshrined therein.

Incidentally, Cole had employed this very strategy of gibbeting transgressions in advance of the Chamber of Horrors' opening. Just a few years earlier, he had employed the pages of the *Journal of Design and Manufactures* to shame offenders before a jury of their peers. In a manner that would anticipate the chamber, the *Journal* repeatedly castigated manufacturers who relied on the direct imitation of nature. It derided flower vases adorned with birds and candlesticks decorated with dolphins. The *Journal* reserved special condemnation for the urn pictured here. Although it was "graceful" in its construction, it had erred tragically in its use of a serpent motif (fig. 49).[84]

As it played its part to effect the shift from training producers to educating consumers, the Chamber of Horrors brought such desecrations to a broader lay audience composed of potential buyers. The *Catalogue* allowed the museum's leadership to promulgate its views on the horrid wares. Here there were no illustrations, so Cole resorted to terse appraisals of the offending objects. Their most common error was the direct imitation of nature, epitomized by the resort to floral ornament. Carpet number 1, for example, exhibited "flowers out of scale" on which feet might fear to tread. Such errors marred chintzes and wallpapers, too. "Vulgar" and "erroneous" flowers plagued chintzes 10 through 13. Such ornamentation disturbed the folds of furniture and curtains. Branches of lilac bushes and rose trees, the *Catalogue* remonstrated, should not be "made to bend to the forms of sofa cushions and arms."[85] Finally, the proclivity toward floral ornament was all too evident in glasses shaped like anemones and lamps bursting with tulips such as the Winfield gas jet lamp pictured here (fig. 50). The lamp has had a notable career as a showpiece. Its unwitting exhibitor proudly showcased his masterpiece at the Great Exhibition of 1851.[86] It became an object of derision in the Chamber of Horrors just one year later. Subsequently, the museum consigned it to storage for over one hundred years. Today, when visitors have come to expect floral excess as a hallmark of the nineteenth century, it has regained its prominence in the new British galleries of the Victoria and Albert Museum as a beloved example of Victoriana.[87]

Victorian floral ornament proved to be just one of the many transgressions evident in the Chamber of Horrors. The museum unveiled shirt calicoes that sported "direct imitations" of "ballet girls, polka dancers, and race horses." Presumably, these were the sorts of goods that had led the fictional Crumpet to inform his friend Frippy that his very garment was a "hideous rag." After visiting the chamber, the clerk would have been equally offended by wallpapers such as number 23, which displayed "horses and ground floating in the air," or number 27, which showed "perspective representations of a railway station." In number 28, which pictured the Crystal Palace and the Serpentine Lake in Hyde Park, consumers could find a memento of the glories of the past year. This last was hardly the way to pay tribute to the Great Exhibition, the *Catalogue* suggested. Nor did wallpaper number 31, which demonstrated the direct imitation of Gothic architecture, portray Pugin's medieval aesthetic to its best advantage (plates 6 and 7). If they were to serve their proper function of providing a background for a room, the *Catalogue* explained,

49   Urn with snake handle pattern.
Journal of Design and Manufactures
1 (1849): 12. Reproduced courtesy of
the Huntington Library, San Marino,
California.

50   Gas jet lamp by R. W. Winfield (1848). V & A Images, Victoria and
Albert Museum, London.

paper hangings should not obtrude. Instead, they should be "flat," "con-
ventionalized," and "subdued."[88]

The harsh moralism and descriptive hyperbole of the *Catalogue* might
suggest that the goods ridiculed in the Chamber of Horrors were fanciful oddities that occupied the margins of the marketplace. But the goods
deposited at the Board of Trade's designs registry, established by an act
of Parliament in 1839, reveal otherwise. During the very years in which
the Museum of Ornamental Art propounded its principles of taste, carpet makers deposited samples overflowing with flowers. Calico printers
registered shirt patterns with renditions of the Crystal Palace (fig. 51).

Wallpaper designers, too, violated the strictures against the direct imitation of architecture with stocks that featured Palladian villas. But worst of all were the furniture chintzes produced in the museum's day. Surely the *Catalogue* would have admonished the creators of fabrics showing castles surrounded by verdant foliage, which managed to violate all of the museum's strictures (fig. 52). And we can only imagine the wrath that would have befallen a chintz showing toreadors flanked by floral wreaths (plate 8).[89]

Because of its didactic approach to the material culture of the day, the chamber received a broad measure of approval. Prince Albert, for one, believed the chamber would prove a "very useful" educational venture.[90] Such newspapers as the *Observer*, the *Daily News*, and the *Spectator* endorsed the chamber for its practical pedagogy. In the Gallery of False Principles, they claimed, many would gain their first opportunity to grapple with aesthetic questions. According to the *Daily News*, the Chamber of Horrors allowed the "man with poor to moderate means" to "make his home beautiful."[91] It was, therefore, no surprise that the gallery attracted the "greatest throng" at the museum during its short career. Despite its popularity, it would remain open for only a year. To the disappointment of many, spatial constraints forced its closure in 1853.[92]

MUSEUM CRITICS, THE TASTE DICTATORSHIP, AND THE FREEBORN ENGLISHMAN

Alongside its advocates, the museum—and its Chamber of Horrors especially—had its share of critics. One who would not have been sorry to see the chamber close was Henry Morley, who criticized the museum's didactic moralism through the fictional tale of poor Crumpet. Crumpet would meet his undoing after visiting the chamber. There papier-mâché tray number 79, which displayed a Landseer painting, had made an especially strong impression. According to the *Catalogue*, this offending object was "an example of popular but vulgar taste, of a very low character." As the *Catalogue* explained, hiding a picture with a teapot was simply and unequivocally "wrong."[93] Given the stringency of this stricture, it was especially unfortunate that Crumpet encountered this tea tray at his friend Frippy's home. The travesty was enough, in fact, to send him into an apoplectic fit, which left him unpresentable and unmanned. As

Chapter Four

51 Calico print showing the Crystal Palace. BT 43/248/76457.

52 Furniture chintz showing castles and foliage. BT 43/358/91343.

Both from the National Archives, Kew, United Kingdom.

Morley suggested in his comic tale, Crumpet's sojourn at the Chamber of Horrors compromised the clerk's controlled comportment and polite sociability. In the end, it destabilized the very hallmarks of his suburban lower-middle-class masculinity.[94]

Charles Dickens, the editor of *Household Words*, the very magazine that had printed Morley's tale, offered a similar critique of the museum. Readers of Dickens's *Hard Times*, published in 1854, may have recognized a caricature of Henry Cole in the character of Thomas Gradgrind. A "man of facts and calculations," Gradgrind played the fancy-quashing dullard who advised the whimsical Sissy Jupe that she was to "discard the word Fancy" from her vocabulary. He called Sissy to task for her assertion that she would carpet a room with "representations of flowers." This, we now know, was a violation of the direct imitation of nature principle—and one that was certainly evident in the carpet patterns that remain in the designs registry of the era (fig. 53). Just a year before Dickens published *Hard Times*, carpets bearing flowers had shamefully hung in the Chamber of Horrors. Pursuant to its strictures, Gradgrind remonstrated with Sissy, "You cannot be allowed to walk on flowers in carpets."[95]

In its early days, critiques of the museum went far beyond the pages of fiction. Provincial interests, notably, called the museum to task for its infringement on the free market. With his charges, radical member of Parliament John Bright, a celebrated reformer, echoed a set of provincial predecessors who had opposed the design copyright. He complained to Cole that Marlborough House threatened the very tenets of laissez-faire economics. "I think you are aiming at what is unnecessary and at much that is impossible," Bright wrote in a February 1853 letter, as he sought to defend a free market in labor. "I suspect all attempts to teach people their trades at the public expense, and don't see where your principle, if good at all, is to stop," he warned.[96]

A Manchester economist named F. J. Prouting would pick up and expand on this line of critique. Under the pseudonym Argus, Prouting launched the most thoroughgoing attack on the museum and its leadership. His weapon was a series of three pamphlets entitled *A Mild Remonstrance against the Taste-Censorship at Marlborough House*.[97] Prouting published the pamphlets during early 1853, just a few months after *Household Words* released Morley's tale. If Morley employed the burlesque to press his points, Argus's stock in trade was invective. Ferociously and tren-

53 Floral carpet design.
BT 53/115/91252, National
Archives, Kew, United
Kingdom.

chantly, Argus tore into the museum. As he saw it, the collection threatened the very pillars of the nation—Englishness, Protestantism, liberty,
and commerce.[98] At bottom, it compromised a particular version of provincial masculinity that venerated "John Bull" and the "beef-devouring
Briton." It is worth delving into Argus's critique. His harangues show, in
stark and entertaining form, that metropolitan aesthetics and provincial
liberalism were unquestionably at odds at midcentury.

Time and again, Argus lashed out against the museum's "Triumvirate"
for its foreign proclivities. Cole, Redgrave, and Jones had proceeded
under the assumption that "Englishmen know nothing of taste." This
very notion, not to mention the preoccupation with taste itself, smacked
of foreign sympathy. The department, Argus charged, only found fault
with British art because it was not *"foreign."* The pamphleteer lambasted
the triumvirate for its penchant for the "sunny south" over his native

land of "rain, fog, and semi-darkness." Linking the gastronomic and the aesthetic, as the sociologist Pierre Bourdieu later would, he criticized the fondness for "macaroni," "wine," and "frizzled frogs" so evident at the museum.[99] If the concern with taste recalled continental foppishness, the preoccupation with principles was, certainly, a sign of oriental sympathies. Of course, there was Owen Jones himself, who was allegedly "half a Moor, and more than half a Musslum." But the department, more generally, displayed a leaning toward "Moorish and Hindoo contrivance." These very sentiments and the aesthetic proclivities they enjoined were out of place in England. At the day's end, the result of the triumvirate's doings would be to impose India on England and even to insert "Pekin into Middlesex."[100]

The museum's foreign proclivities also threatened two sacrosanct pillars of the nation: Protestantism and liberty. According to Argus, the museum's strictures were tantamount to religious conspiracy. They compromised Protestantism in favor of Catholicism, and even Buddhism, Islam, and Hinduism.[101] Just as perilous was the endangerment of liberty. This was especially evident in the triumvirate's dictates, which suggested continental absolutism and oriental despotism. Argus found the principles of taste "arbitrary," "absurd," "pestilent," and "impractical"; he derogated the department that sought to enforce them as "tyrannical, unjust, and unconstitutional." At bottom, it was a "taste-censorship" and a "dictatorship."[102] There was no telling where the museum's encroachment on "John-Bull-justice" would stop.[103]

Finally, the museum threatened the continued progress and prosperity of the nation. Its plan for taste education constituted market interference, Argus held, as he looked to the tenets of Mancunian political economy. To begin, he punctured Cole's assumption that the museum could, and should, shape the "will of the consumer." According to Argus, it was the market, not the museum, that provided the real adjudicating ground for consumer preference. When he advanced such an argument, Argus hearkened back to the boisterous opponents of the design copyright, who had rallied around free trade. Like these predecessors, Argus showed that the department's principles were misdirected. It was "commerce," he argued, not "taste-dogmas," that assured the well-being of the nation. It was trade, not strictures on design, that guaranteed that the people would be "cared for, educated, refined, civilized, clothed, and fed." When all was said and done, Argus concluded, the department's strictures on design compromised the very growth that the triumvirate purported to promote.[104]

As Argus argued, the "Triumvirate of Taste" threatened a popular ideal of Englishness. Its principles weakened the very notions of Protestantism, liberty, and commerce that buttressed the national character. Ultimately, Argus hinted, the department undermined a particular brand of masculinity that was associated with these ideals. In suggesting as much, he held that the department's principles and preoccupations smacked of "effeminate taste and holiday habit." Aesthetic cultivation required "the vanity of the Frenchman, the swarthiness of the Spaniard, the idleness of the Italian, [or] the voluptuousness of the Turk." All were opposed to English manhood.[105] By proposing as much, Argus upheld a distinctly provincial masculine ideal in the face of metropolitan aesthetic intervention. The figures of John Bull and the beef-devouring Briton captured this notion in all of its boldness and vigor. To be sure, this ideal departed from Crumpet's polite sociability. Despite their differences, however, Argus's bulldog-fancier and Morley's Crumpet indicate together that masculinity—in its various forms—provided an effective rhetorical currency for critiquing the excesses of design reform. By marshaling the two figures, Argus and Morley called into question the ideals of Marlborough House, its pretensions, and the intrusions that it seemed to commit.

ARGUS'S TRACTS, HOUSEHOLD POLITICS, AND THE GENDERED CONSUMER

Like the Chamber of Horrors, Argus's tracts boiled down the department's abstract principles to the concrete and tangible. Given this commonality, it is hardly surprising that his writing received considerable attention in contemporary newspapers. In late February 1852, for instance, the *Morning Advertiser* responded to Argus's complaints. It imagined that Argus was an "honest Englishman" who was "anxious to prevent the importation of the Continental way of doing things" into Britain. Ultimately, however, it dismissed his concerns as parochial and paranoid. The *Morning Advertiser* doubted that Marlborough House posed a threat to the "independence" of the people. Accordingly, it urged its readers to dismiss Argus's "carping criticisms" and "sarcastic bitterness."[106] The elite *Court Journal* was more trenchant in its refutation of the provincial Argus. It charged that the tracts masked a distasteful "virulence . . . under a veil of humorous satire." Perhaps, it imagined, Argus was himself the "unfortunate designer" of a work that had been "cruelly gibbeted" at the museum—maybe even tea tray 79, the very "monstrosity" that Crumpet had spotted at Frippy's home. So as not to blow his cover, the *Journal* advised Argus to cease his publication immediately.[107]

Such criticisms notwithstanding, Argus also enjoyed considerable support. One grateful soul was a letter writer to the *Morning Advertiser*, who identified himself as a "manufacturer of an article of general consumption, in which pattern is everything." He expressed the utmost gratitude for the pamphleteer's efforts. In his trade, this manufacturer relied on floral designs based on the direct imitation of nature. The department, as we know, had condemned this category of productions "in toto." It had even gone so far as to identify his very patterns as "monstrosities." The museum's efforts to educate the "will of the consumer" had played havoc with this manufacturer's trade. With despair, he thus lamented, "My whole stock—my machinery—my capital—my all—is jeopardized."[108] His complaint, which employed a language of imperiled masculinity, is reminiscent of those advanced by the calico printers who decried design piracy in the early 1840s. For them, state intervention in the form of the copyright offered a way to shore up their livelihoods. It also provided a means for improving a marketplace composed of uneducated consumers who came largely from the working classes. Things were different for the manufacturer of floral patterns, however. He found in the government-sponsored museum the seeds of his undoing. Rather than taste principles, he urged that consumer demand drive the retail culture of the metropolis.[109]

Happily, Argus had provided a welcome buffer against the museum, the manufacturer explained in the pages of the *Morning Advertiser*. In the pamphleteer's writings, the manufacturer and his colleagues found a refutation of the despised principles that could ruin fortune and compromise reputations. In fact, Argus's tracts had protected one of the contributor's neighbors from losing a large sale to a notable customer who happened to be a member of Parliament. Recently, the member's wife had paid a visit to the museum. There the lady had made an unfortunate discovery about a new household purchase. From the Chamber of Horrors, she learned that everything she and her husband had ordered was "in the worst possible taste." She beseeched her husband, a

Chapter Four

man charged with the maintenance of the nation and empire, to cancel the order. A man of action, the MP did exactly as his wife directed. It was, of course, in his interest to "save his credit as a man of taste."[110] Happily for the purveyor, the member of Parliament was also a man of letters and a creature of reason. After he canceled the order, he stumbled on Argus's pamphlets, which exposed the museum's biases. Promptly, the MP renewed his order. Single-handedly, it seems, Argus saved the purveyor from financial ruin and rescued the MP. from the false influence of Marlborough House.[111]

The letter to the *Morning Advertiser* is instructive, for it shows us the effects of the museum in the marketplace. The letter is valuable, too, for what it reveals about the politics of consumption in mid-Victorian Britain. Who were the real and rhetorical consumers who visited the museum? When Cole spoke of the "will of the consumer," he drew on the discourse of liberal political economy that, as Regenia Gagnier has noted, was in transition from emphasizing production to spotlighting consumption during the mid–nineteenth century.[112] Inspired by its conception of a rational marketplace, Cole envisaged his theoretical consumers as calculable agents. They were statistical subjects unfettered by matters of gender, budget, or fancy. Teachable vessels, they were the keys to market reform. Once educated, Cole imagined, these consumers would demand the fruits of principled design.[113] Cole was not alone in understanding consumption in such a way. Those who followed in voicing concerns about demand-side practices similarly assessed consumers as an ungendered aggregate. They were, alternatively, "the millions," "the mass of the population," "the people," or the disembodied "public taste."[114] There were certainly exceptions to this rhetorical practice, such as the art critic Anna Jameson, who argued for the especial importance of educating women at midcentury.[115] Still, the pervasive tendency toward discursive homogenization leaves unclear the very matter of just who the consumers of domestic wares were in the growing mid-nineteenth-century marketplace.

More finely honed images of consumers emerge in journalistic discussions of the museum and especially its Chamber of Horrors. This is not surprising, for the chamber dealt with material goods not abstract principles. A notice in the *Observer* provides a case in point. It reported the fascination with which a "party of young ladies" studied the chamber.[116] We know from other vignettes and from images like this one found in

SEVRES CHINA FROM THE MUSEUM OF ART MANUFACTURES, AT MARLBOROUGH HOUSE.

54   Visitors to the Museum of Ornamental Art. *Illustrated London News*,
18 September 1852. Special and Area Studies Collection, George A. Smathers Library, University of Florida.

the *Illustrated London News* that women visited the Museum of Ornamental Art at a moment when they were just beginning to populate the
streets of the West End in unprecedented numbers (fig. 54).[117] Still, we
should not underestimate the significance of this mention because some
midcentury collections, such as the Hunterian Museum of Natural History, did not allow women to enter at all.[118] Like the *Observer*, the *Spectator*, too, enumerated the many benefits that the chamber would confer
on the homes of those who visited Marlborough House. Benefits were
sure to accrue to ladies who dressed in "huge gaudiness" and drank tea
out of cups bearing hideous landscapes. But it was not women alone to
whom the chamber appealed. The *Spectator* imagined that it might teach
lessons to all the members of "respectable families." There husbands,
wives, and children might find their "pet article of ornament" or their
"item of gentility" on display. Perhaps it would be "gibbeted for public
reprobation" in the Gallery of False Principles. The result of the visit

to the museum, the *Spectator* imagined, would be poignant but positive. On returning home, the family members would ponder, with regret, the question of what to do with the new discovery. And together they would decide to discard their offending object.[119]

With these speculations, the contributor to the *Spectator* suggested that the Chamber of Horrors proved an effective engine of aesthetic education for those who visited the museum. Conversely, the manufacturer who wrote to the *Morning Advertiser* held that it was Argus, not the museum, who offered the proper guidelines for domestic improvement. This important divergence notwithstanding, the two articles exhibit a striking commonality. Both revealed that domestic purchases and decor were the collective prerogative of the family. The story of the fictional Crumpet, who would drag his reluctant wife and daughter to Marlborough House, indicates the same.

These narratives suggest the complexities of negotiating household purchases at midcentury within "respectable families," to use the words of the *Spectator*.[120] If we look to the museum's audience—at least as it was portrayed in print—such families seemed to run the gamut from the lower-middle to the upper-middle classes. Representations such as the *Spectator*'s provide a cautionary note against reading the history of midcentury consumption through the late nineteenth century's recasting of the consumer as a woman. There is a vibrant and growing literature that discusses this process, which was enabled by such diverse forces as fashion plates and the feminization of London's West End.[121] However powerful, the findings of these works should not uncritically inform our precise notions of who the consumers for designed goods and furnishings in the mid–nineteenth century actually were.[122] To be sure, the home was middle-class women's sphere in the mid–nineteenth century. Even so, Leonore Davidoff and Catherine Hall suggest that, up to 1850, the process of furnishing and decorating the home was a household endeavor, involving both husband and wife. As such, it could reveal discord in the middle-class family.[123] Adrian Forty has shown, furthermore, that men were responsible for many of the items bought to furnish middle-class homes before 1860, when domestic decor became an "accepted and even expected activity for middle-class women."[124] After that date, middle-class and aristocratic women would become a more formidable presence as shoppers in London's West End, contributors to the aesthetic movement, and eventually pioneers in interior design.

My own investigations into the ledgers and account books of decorators, furniture makers, and upholsterers support the notion that the 1850s marked a moment when both men and women participated in household consumption. This was certainly the case for elite customers. Holland and Sons, the eminent decorating firm, listed among its clients men who were heads of households, married ladies, and single women. Often, though not always, it was men who were listed as clients for the larger jobs of decorating entire households. Women, on the other hand, made more modest purchases of carpets and damasks.[125] The furniture maker Gillow, who had a shop in Oxford Street, dealt in more limited terms to a clientele that bought oak tables, mahogany bookcases, and satinwood commodes. His estimate book shows a preponderance of male purchasers, although the firm also purveyed to married and single women.[126] Finally, Thomas Handyside and Son, Upholsterers, had a mixed client list for its services, which included polishing, furnishing, and repairs.[127]

These sources render a measure of specificity to conjectures about consumption. Men certainly did participate in furnishing households at midcentury. Women played a role, too, especially when it came to buying the decorative wares with which the museum concerned itself. The changing place of the male consumer, however, is noteworthy — especially when we compare the ledgers listed above to the later records of such firms as Cowtan and Sons, which show a preponderance of ladies among the customers during the 1880s.[128]

It appears, regardless, that the position of the male consumer — and the man of taste more generally — was characterized in the 1850s by ambivalence and transition. With this in mind, it follows nicely that masculinity provided the rhetorical currency of critique at Marlborough House, which sought to turn principles of design into matters of state. In the face of these aspirations, contemporary critics conveyed their discomfort by marshaling a range of male figures. Models of imperiled masculinity, they all found themselves endangered by the museum and its endeavors. For Crumpet, the museum posed a threat to the sociability and rationality that were the very hallmarks of his lower-middle-class masculinity. The beef-devouring Briton of Argus's tracts argued that, with its foreign and cosmopolitan proclivities, the museum compromised John Bull justice in favor of oriental despotism and continental foppishness. The manufacturer for whom pattern was "everything"

Chapter Four

found that Marlborough House put his business, not to mention his very livelihood, at risk. And the MP found his credit as a man of taste in question.

Pieces from the collection at Marlborough House remain on display in London today, where they attest to the ornamental excess, grand collecting, and imperial splendor of the Victorian era, if not to the charged meanings of masculinity during the nineteenth century. They hold a place of prominence at the Victoria and Albert Museum, the successor to the South Kensington Museum. The South Kensington Museum debuted in 1857 with the Museum of Ornamental Art as its centerpiece. In that year, Cole moved his museum to a roomy estate in Brompton, a suburb located southwest of central London. There it would become the hub of a network of collections devoted not only to manufacture but also to art, science, and education.

With this westward move, design reform became more elastic in its purpose and its audience.[129] Rather than educating consumers from the middling ranks, Cole promoted the moral uplift of the nation's artisans, particularly the skilled laboring men of London. As many critics pointed out, this was an ironic, perhaps even deceitful shift given that South Kensington was an aristocratic—or at least a faux-aristocratic—locality. This fissure between rhetoric and geography proved contentious. If matters of principle were the subject of debate at Marlborough House, location and its connotations became the focus of dispute at South Kensington. There advocates and critics debated the merits of ministering to laborers at a site that stood so far from their places of habitation and work. This contest hearkens back to the early days of design reform chronicled in this book. At South Kensington, labor assumed renewed prominence, albeit in unanticipated ways. As the debates that circulated around the South Kensington Museum in its first few decades will show, labor supplied the language, criteria, and priorities for waging the culture wars of the mid-Victorian era.

CHAPTER FIVE

Cultural Locations

SOUTH KENSINGTON, BETHNAL GREEN, AND

THE WORKING MAN, 1857–1872

On a November evening in 1857, hundreds of artisans, connoisseurs, and suburbanites filled a lecture hall in West London.[1] They had gathered to hear a talk by the director of the Department of Science and Art, Henry Cole.[2] For Cole, the lecture was an opportunity to introduce his latest triumph, a new institution called the South Kensington Museum, the predecessor to the Victoria and Albert Museum. Opened in June 1857, this addition to the metropolis offered its visitors collections of an unparalleled range. At its center stood the ever expanding Museum of Ornamental Art, which Cole had transported from Marlborough House a few miles southwest to a bucolic suburban neighborhood. There it was flanked by architectural models, patented designs, and British paintings.[3] Along with its roomier accommodations and its broader collections, Cole's design reform enterprise attained a larger purpose at South Kensington. It was no longer concerned simply with the economic exigencies of edifying producers and reforming consumers. Instead, design reform had become an expressly moral pursuit for an increasingly democratic age. Despite its remote location, Cole promised that the new, state-sponsored South Kensington Museum would minister to "everyone in the kingdom" and especially to the working man.[4]

In his November 1857 lecture, Henry Cole suggested a correlation between the rise of liberal government and the growth of public collections. By the 1850s, when South Kensington debuted, museums had become well-established engines of liberal political reform, as institutional, architectural, and political historians have noted.[5] More recently, scholars in cultural studies and museum history have reconsidered the relationship between civic collections and liberal governance thanks in large part to the work of Michel Foucault. His notion of governmentality framed nineteenth-century liberal reforms as efforts to manage populations that were increasingly reaping the spoils of democracy. Building on Foucault and Gramsci too, the cultural critic Tony Bennett argued that museums provided especially effective mechanisms for governance and rule during the second half of the nineteenth century. As they ministered to growing populations, museums cannily recast dazzling spectacle as consensual surveillance. To encapsulate this understanding, Bennett introduced the notion of the "exhibitionary complex" in an influential 1988 essay. He defined the exhibitionary complex as "a set of cultural technologies concerned to organize a voluntary self-regulating citizenry." With its collections designed to edify and delight the working man, Bennett deemed Cole's South Kensington Museum the very epitome of the exhibitionary complex.[6]

Bennett's notion has carried considerable influence and enjoyed enviable staying power. It has, in fact, become a veritable shorthand for the South Kensington Museum.[7] The term is attractive because it provides a unifying logic for a hodgepodge of collections that nineteenth-century critics derided as a "curious jumble of odds and ends."[8] Of late, museum studies scholars have criticized Bennett's totalizing notion. But even these detractors have not mounted a sustained challenge to two assumptions embedded in Bennett's understanding. First, the exhibitionary complex implies that museums were utopian locations that existed outside of spatial realities and geographical politics. Second, the framework suggests that museums were regulatory agents that constructed a passive and monolithic audience of working men from above.[9]

This final chapter of our design reform story calls these assumptions into question by analyzing the debates that bedeviled South Kensington during its first fifteen years. Mid-nineteenth-century museological contests revolved around several issues, ranging from opening hours to collections policies to admissions costs. But by far the most volatile set of questions for these fundamentally urban institutions considered the

55 Map of London showing Brompton (quadrant A'fg) and Bethnal Green (quadrant F'c) (1841). Chromolithograph. Yale Center for British Art, Paul Mellon Collection.

"geography of art."[10] At midcentury, museum professionals, politicians, and gallery visitors from all classes engaged in fierce discussions over where to house the nation's expanding collections of art, antiquities, and natural science artifacts. One possible location was South Kensington, formerly called Brompton and located in the southwest corner of Bauerkeller's map from earlier in the century (fig. 55). On several occasions, Cole attempted to lure the nation's collections of art, science, and design there. His most notable attempt involved Trafalgar Square's National Gallery. In this episode and others, critics including skilled laborers and benevolent reformers would point out that Cole's bucolic western suburb stood far from the habitations of the working classes. Their challenges to Cole's grand designs attest to the political nature of place in the mid-nineteenth-century metropolis. They bear out the understandings of cultural geographers and urban historians who have shown geography to be an "active agent in the processes of modern historical change."[11]

In the end, these discussions would lead to a remapping of London's museums. This project culminated in 1872, when a crosstown outpost of South Kensington debuted in the East End neighborhood of Bethnal Green, which is located right of center on Bauerkeller's map. Opened to great ceremony, this institution promised to minister to the working poor who resided nearby.[12]

In the debates over location, members of Parliament, design reformers, benevolent ministers, and civic leaders spoke on behalf of a working man whom they portrayed in a paternalistic guise. In his ideal form, this resolutely male figure was a skilled artisan.[13] Yet he could at times be a member of the toiling poor. Regardless of their range, these putative workers were no mere vessels for museological regulation. Instead, they were agents in the making of South Kensington and its Bethnal Green satellite. Laborers themselves joined the campaign for access, advocating evening openings, free days, and especially neighborhood collections. They staked out their positions in lecture halls, local newspapers, and even those public houses for which museums were to be an antidote in an era of rational recreation.[14]

Ultimately, in these venues working men engaged in a complex process of self-fashioning. Most notably, London's laborers looked to their positions as skilled producers to gain cultural capital. To do so, they recalled the concerns about artisanship brought before the Select Committee on Arts and Manufactures; they also exploited the perorations on toil popularized at the Great Exhibition of 1851. But they enlarged on these understandings, too. The self-proclaimed working men who joined in the debates about culture and its locations echoed liberal reformers when they framed themselves as imperiled domestic subjects. Moreover, in portraying themselves as urban wayfarers, they joined those male flaneurs, shopping ladies, and imperial subjects recently studied by cultural historians and historical geographers.[15] Finally, they associated themselves with contemporary debates over suffrage and so added to the museological enterprise a measure of urgency as the contest over the Second Reform Act (1867) drew near. By fashioning themselves in these ways, London's working men gained entry into a national debate about cultural institutions and their very locations. In the process, they would become aesthetic arbiters, urban interlocutors, and the subjects of cultural history.

Like the preceding reforms chronicled in this book, the South Kensington Museum had its roots in the *Report of the Select Committee on Arts and Manufactures*. It grew more immediately, however, out of the Great Exhibition of 1851, which provided the aesthetic preoccupations, surplus funds, ceremonial traditions, and ideal audience for the new museum.[16] As chapter four demonstrated, the exhibition fueled the concerns about British aesthetic inferiority that galvanized the original collection at Marlborough House. The hallowed spectacle also left a sizable surplus of 186,000 pounds. Together Henry Cole, Prince Albert, and the exhibition's royal commissioners used the funds to consolidate the South Kensington estate. Aided by Parliament, they purchased lands in a neighborhood called Brompton, which was located in Kensington Parish, just south of where the Crystal Palace had stood until its 1852 dismantling.[17] By 1857, the commissioners had managed to amass an eighty-seven-acre estate in the bucolic suburb, which was on the cusp of a monumental transformation. In the eighteenth century, Brompton had gained fame for its market gardens, rusticity, and salubrious air. By the mid–nineteenth century, it had become the modest preserve of the middle classes, not to mention a bohemian sampling of actors and artists. It was also on its way to becoming a hub of museological London. Henry Cole, who rechristened Brompton as South Kensington, was the most instrumental figure in this transformation. He found on the estate a roomy home for his growing Museum of Ornamental Art, not to mention a fertile ground for his own vision. In a striking deployment of mid-Victorian melodrama, he declared of the endeavor of bringing museums and institutes to South Kensington, "If I were to die for it, I would do so rather than should the plan fail."[18] For twenty-five years, he remained true to the project, opening educational institutes, purchasing coveted treasures, and luring existing collections to West London.[19] By century's end, South Kensington would be home to myriad collections and institutes, among them the Victoria and Albert Museum, the Natural History Museum, Imperial College, the Royal Albert Hall, and the Albert Memorial.[20]

This was no foreordained success in 1857, when the South Kensington Museum debuted. As if to spite Cole's grand designs, the museum opened in a temporary expedient, a corrugated iron shed with a green and white striped roof. The *Builder*, the leading architectural journal of the day, bestowed an unfortunate and enduring nickname on the structure in advance of the museum's opening: the "Brompton Boilers."[21] Several other organs of the press followed with their own contemptuous assessments. The *Daily News* delivered the most damning description when it castigated the structure as the work of an architect suffering from indigestion wrought by a supper of pork pies.[22] In the face of this architectural travesty, the deflated Cole lamented, "The public laugh at its outside ugliness and [at] us."[23] The bucolic surroundings rendered in the *Illustrated London News* were not enough to compensate for the stark functionality of the structure. Indeed, in photographs it took on a proto-modernist aspect that recalled the Crystal Palace (figs. 56 and 57). But the structure lacked the glass and grandeur of its magical predecessor in Hyde Park. In the end, the reception of the building could not have differed more from the rapture that had greeted the Crystal Palace. In the face of this embarrassment, the Department of Science and Art sought to compensate at the South Kensington Museum's opening with a level of pomp and circumstance redolent of 1851. At the height of the London season in June 1857, the department opened its museum to the queen, the court, members of Parliament, and the nation's scientific elite at a series of inaugural soirées. And, with pageantry reminiscent of the Great Exhibition, red-coated military sappers guided the visitors through the building, just as they had done at the Crystal Palace.[24]

Collections, funds, and ceremonies linked the Great Exhibition to South Kensington, but the ideal audience was the most important continuity between the exhibition and the museum. In 1851, orators and writers had celebrated the first world's fair, which showcased the fruits of industrial and artisanal toil, as a "festival of the working man."[25] Henry Cole similarly placed the laborer on center stage at South Kensington. He promised that the new museum would build on the exhibition's spirit of democratic accessibility. The collection was, he explained, "a book with its pages always open, and not shut." Thanks to its suburban location and its commodious halls, South Kensington offered plenteous space to showcase those national treasures "packed away" in London's crowded cellars. Along with this improvement, Cole promised clear dis-

56   The Brompton Boilers in their bucolic setting. *Illustrated London News*, 27 June 1857, 635. Special and Area Studies Collections, George A. Smathers Library, University of Florida.

57   Photograph of the Museum of Science and Art built by Young and Son (1855–56). V & A Images, Victoria and Albert Museum, London.

plays and instructive labeling as part of his efforts to advance a modern museology.[26] When all was done, these innovations would render the nation's riches accessible to the respectable laborer.

This sentiment was luminously clear in Cole's 1857 speech. There he had vowed to make his new museum available to the upstanding artisan and even to the "poor man."[27] With this promise, Cole echoed those Great Exhibition commentators who had imagined workers as figures both worthy of celebration and needful of education. But in an important shift, Cole also refined the formulations of exhibition writers, who had rendered English laborers primarily as economic men. Exhibition commentators had portrayed workers as valiant producers, but Cole depicted laborers as spiritually impoverished, morally imperiled subjects. Rather than the heroes of industry, they had become its victims. According to Cole, midcentury workers were enslaved to a "dreary treadmill of labor."[28] They lived in a "murky atmosphere of toil."[29] The gin palace provided the only respite from work's vicissitudes for these poor men, who were vulnerable to the "vice and debauchery" of the metropolis.[30] Taking a cue from the contemporary critic John Ruskin, Cole envisioned that art might serve as a salve on the spiritual and moral brutalities of the "work-day-world."[31]

With the shift from portraying laborers as producers to framing them as imperiled subjects came another important change. When they discussed working men, Cole and his contemporaries imagined them as domestic figures attached to women and children in equal, if not greater, need of uplift. The South Kensington Museum promised to rescue these families. In his inaugural lecture, Cole imagined a "working man" passing a pleasurable evening at the museum with his bonneted wife, baby, and children. Freed from the constrictions of its dim, cheerless, and crowded dwelling, the family might enjoy the museum's new British picture galleries.[32] At South Kensington, the landscapes and portraits in the British picture galleries donated by John Sheepshanks provided the ideal vehicle for this sort of uplift. In his own inaugural lecture, Cole crony and art superintendent Richard Redgrave expanded on this point. He held that the British picture galleries would offer to working families lessons in those "home feelings" that were so markedly English.[33]

It is important to recognize that these rhapsodies were essentially "idealized projections" of what reformers hoped the "museum public"

THE TURNER AND VERNON ROOMS AT THE SOUTH KENSINGTON MUSEUM.

58 Purpose-built galleries exemplifying modern museology and showing an artisanal visitor. *Illustrated London News*, 4 February 1860. Special and Area Studies Collections, George A. Smathers Library, University of Florida.

would become.[34] This said, Cole and his staff went to great lengths to turn their utopian projections into legitimate possibilities. The Department of Science and Art made the introductory addresses accessible to workmen who attended in great numbers by providing penny seats in its lecture hall. South Kensington also offered more long-standing commitments to the education of laborers. It opened its doors gratis several days each week, not to mention during the Christmas and Easter holidays.[35] If this image from the *Illustrated London News* is any indication, workmen like the one pictured on the left did indeed join their more elevated brethren in viewing the museum's British paintings in the Turner and Vernon Galleries. There they could reap the benefits of the progressive museological ideal of uncluttered display. In the purpose-built galleries, they could see paintings far more clearly than the cluttered apartments of the National Gallery and the Royal Academy, with their more traditional hanging practices, had allowed (fig. 58).[36] Moreover, in order to serve urban wayfarers of all classes, the museum was the first to provide refreshment rooms for its visitors. First- and second-class facilities served coffee, sandwiches, and beer to visitors who had made the trek to West London. Finally, the museum was pathbreaking for its evening openings. Thanks to its use of gaslight, the department enabled those who worked during the day to take advantage of its collections at night. Three times a week visitors could survey the treasures between seven and nine. This seems to be how a great many saw the collections. Notably, by 1861 two million had passed through the museum's doors, a large number of them in the evenings.[37]

Because of its novelty and efficacy, this last innovation sparked the imagination of the press more than any other, as an article from the populist periodical *Lloyd's* indicates. The aptly titled "A Light in the Dark" heralded the museum's use of gas as the triumph of freedom. This breakthrough sounded the death knell to the "dark ages," it marked the decisive termination of aristocratic corruption, and it spread the light of liberalism on the people.[38] Even more striking than this measure of approval is the rhetorical means that *Lloyd's* deployed to register it. Like the museum's staff, *Lloyd's* imagined the benefits that evening openings might bestow by marshaling the laboring man in his sentimental guise. This was an endangered figure caught on a precipice between art and drink. Evening openings, *Lloyd's* imagined, promised to lead workers from temptation. Instead of going to bed inebriated, "the artisan" might "close his eyes with some refining work of art dwelling joyfully on his mind." Moreover, the museum promised to confer benefits on the working man's distressed wife. Saved from the agonizing process of searching for her husband in neighborhood taprooms, she could find him instead in "rapt contemplation" of an Old Master or a British landscape at the museum. The subject of speeches and journalistic musing in 1857, gaslight would receive governmental affirmation three years later when a select committee applauded the well-lit museum and its reassuring domestic glow as an antidote to the "beer house."[39]

When they highlighted the potential of museums to cure these ailments, Cole, Redgrave, and their colleagues tapped into a contemporary refrain that extended well beyond South Kensington. By midcentury, liberal reformers had picked up on the early Victorian radical understanding that museums were ideal vehicles for rescuing "weary workmen."[40] In the face of this pervasive belief, the working man himself became an organizing figure for broader discussions about museum hours, admission costs, and Sunday openings.[41] In fact, by the 1850s the perceived needs of labor supplied the very rationale for extending the reach of cultural institutions in public debate. This was evident, of course, at

Cultural Locations   **169**

South Kensington. But it also informed the writings of eminent Victorians such as Ruskin. Given these tendencies, it was not long before skilled working men recognized the power of their subject positions. In their capacity as laborers, they found an authority that allowed them entry to a restrictive, if democratizing, public sphere. Indeed, Jordanna Bailkin has recently shown that working men took recourse to their status as laborers to claim access to the national patrimony.[42] This development would become markedly evident at South Kensington in May 1861. At that time, a self-proclaimed "Working Man" proposed to Cole that the South Kensington Museum be opened free of charge on the queen's birthday. This date, he explained, was customarily a holiday for "the working classes." If the leadership opened the museum, metropolitan laborers were sure to "rejoice." The author's strategy of appeal proved effective, as a note on the back of the missive attests.[43]

By framing themselves as laborers, working men gained entry not only to the museum but also to print, as an 1859 letter to the radical *Star* indicates. Its author, "Pimlico," was an advocate of Sunday openings who turned middle-class understandings of rational recreation to his advantage. He portrayed himself as an "industrious and sober mechanic" who sought to be dutiful to his master. The author was also a quintessential domestic figure, a husband and father who sought to live righteously and steer clear of the "gin shop." According to Pimlico, museums provided an attractive alternative to the perils that he and other working men faced. To press his case, Pimlico evoked a touching story of a working man who visited the museum on six consecutive evenings to behold a painting that reminded him of his childhood. "All men, no matter how rough or ignorant, enjoy looking at a picture," he rhapsodized, as he beseeched the museum to open its doors on Sundays to glovers, masons, and other laborers, too.[44]

SOUTH KENSINGTON, TRAFALGAR SQUARE, AND THE FINEST SITE IN EUROPE

Pimlico echoed Cole and other reformers who regarded museums as instruments of rescue, but he stood apart in a crucial regard. When Cole lyricized about the artisan, he invoked an ideal figure who hovered above the geography of the metropolis. If his name is any indication, Pimlico dwelt, conversely, on the spatial realities and urban politics of the metropolitan laborer's existence. Located on the north bank of the Thames approximately two and a half miles southeast of Brompton, Pimlico was itself a London neighborhood undergoing rapid transition from a shabby district to well-heeled entrepôt during the third quarter of the nineteenth century.[45] A likely resident of Pimlico, the eponymous author claimed that he lived a "great distance" from South Kensington. Granted, the letter writer had the advantage of dwelling far closer to the museum than his East End brethren. He did, in fact, manage the occasional evening visit to Cole's museum. Still, the vicissitudes of London geography made the journey to South Kensington far more difficult than he would have liked.[46]

Pimlico joined countless laborers and their advocates when he pointed to the difficulties—and even the injustices—posed by London's geography of art and especially by the South Kensington Museum. Collectively, they bemoaned the long distance that separated Brompton, which lay on the western edge of the metropolis, from the habitations of working men dotting the East End and, increasingly, the northern and southern suburbs. One man to join Pimlico in these laments was the Rev. William Rogers, who organized parish excursions to South Kensington. Regrettably, these expeditions had to wait for holidays when his poor parishioners who could not afford the omnibus could make the long trek from the East End. South Kensington was, after all, "a long way to walk" at the end of a day's work.[47] Others similarly attested to the difficulties of urban mobility for the working poor. Traveling to South Kensington was a toilsome undertaking, which involved "the labor of wading through a stream of human beings miles in length."[48] As they decried these difficulties, critics exposed the fissures between Cole's rhetoric and geographical reality. All told, it was toilsome, expensive, and at times even impossible for skilled and unskilled laborers to visit the museum.[49]

Such concerns were more than the stuff of personal anecdote at mid-century. At that time, the metropolitan geography of art preoccupied numerous parliamentary commissions.[50] One of the most notable, the National Gallery Site Commission, met in 1857, the very year that the South Kensington Museum opened its doors.[51] Its task was to determine whether the nation's paintings should remain in Trafalgar Square, a central London site, or move elsewhere, most likely South Kensington. Cole, Prince Albert, and the royal commissioners of 1851 had advocated

NATIONAL GALLERY.

H. R. H. F. M. P. A. AT IT AGAIN!

Policeman. "ONLY MOVING THE PICTURES TO KENSINGTON GORE! SUPPOSE YOU LEAVE 'EM WHERE THEY ARE, EH?"

59   The site question.
Punch 31 (1856): 15.
Reproduced courtesy of the
Huntington Library, San
Marino, California.

this relocation earlier in the decade. Their machinations had met the criticisms of radical, liberal, and bohemian interests, including the National Gallery Reform Association and *Punch*, which lampooned Albert's ardent desire to relocate the paintings to South Kensington in the 1856 cartoon pictured here (fig. 59).[52] As the debate reached its denouement in 1857, the Site Commission interrogated curators, aesthetes, and critics such as Ruskin to ascertain their opinions one final time. To gauge the feelings of working men, it sent a survey to manufactories around the metropolis, including haberdasheries, coach makers, and silk weavers.[53] Its proceedings show us that London's laborers did indeed attend museums. Moreover, they link museums to other reforming initiatives in the nineteenth-century liberal city, including lighting, sanitation, and mobility.[54] And, finally, they provide a clear record of the distinct meanings of a popular Trafalgar Square and a privileged South Kensington in the public imagination.

In 1857 and well before, Trafalgar Square had its share of critics, who dismissed the gallery as "shabby" and its location "unmanageable."[55] Dilapidated and run down, the site was far too shoddy for a national museum.[56] Naysayers decried the "maze of mean and squalid streets" that surrounded the gallery. When they traversed these roads, visitors encountered workhouses, washhouses, barracks, and railway lines.[57] Such surroundings made the National Gallery all too accessible to undesirable characters wearing "filthy dress." The esteemed German critic Gustav Waagen told the committee that the gallery had devolved of late into a "large nursery" filled with babies and wet nurses. Together they "stained the atmosphere with a most disagreeable smell." Despite his "love" for the paintings, Waagen confessed, he had left the building in sheer disgust on more than one occasion.[58] Of even greater concern than the stench was the dirt that these masses tracked in. Subscribing to the miasmatic theories that held such great sway at midcentury, witnesses suggested that the national treasures were themselves at great risk from this effluvia.[59] Concerns about the filth of the metropolis—all too evident in the "blacks" that polluted the snow and the smoke that accrued on the coats of sheep—pervaded the testimony of a nascent cadre of curators. The keeper of the National Gallery, John Nieuwenhuys, complained that he was "constantly wiping" the pictures to clear them of dirt. Some used breadcrumbs for the purpose. The curator of the Dulwich Picture Gallery, S. P. Denning, put things dramatically when he warned that "great evil" had arisen in the paintings at Charing Cross.[60] Whether quaint or theatrical, such concerns bear out Brandon Taylor's assertion that public health and curatorial practice developed coevally in mid-nineteenth-century Britain.[61]

In the face of these challenges, South Kensington appeared to offer a welcome solution to the intertwined problems of population and pollution that plagued Trafalgar Square. One witness who advocated the South Kensington estate was a Royal Academy associate, Edward William Cooke, the very man who had informed the commission of the purifying powers of breadcrumbs. Cooke was no stranger to the dirt of the metropolis, having spent much of his life in Hackney. In that borough's murky environs, paintings and plants were especially vulnerable to the London smoke and soot, which the winds carried to the northeast. To escape these dangers, Cooke had moved to Kensington, where the bright atmosphere and clean air proved restorative. Such accounts were common at midcentury. With its space and salubriousness, Kensington had become a "vast locality for artists." What better home was there for the national treasures? Given these attributes, several other witnesses joined Cooke in a bid for South Kensington.[62]

For all the advantages it bestowed on plants and paintings, however, South Kensington lay off the beaten track in 1857. "It is a sort of exertion for a man to go there," the architect James Fergusson alleged. At mid-century, Kensington remained the privileged retreat of omnibuses and cabs, the preserve of the "rich, the idle, and the holiday-maker." It stood well out of reach of the "poor, the industrious, and the studious," who comprised the ideal museumgoing public.[63] In light of London's social geography, Fergusson thus beseeched Parliament to maintain the paintings at Trafalgar Square.[64] Others, too, pled on behalf of the "very heart of the population"—a group whose ranks extended well beyond Tony Bennett's ideal exhibitionary audience, the respectable working men of the metropolis. Their numbers included the "sight-seeing million," the "mass whose means merely suffice to procure the ordinary necessaries of life," and even "the many who may be said to dwell beyond the confines of civilization." In the end, Trafalgar Square was the preferred site for tradesmen, day laborers, and those who "carried their lunches in their pockets," that is, everyone save the "upper ten thousand."[65] In an age when accessibility, rather than purity, was the order of the day for art, such pleas held great sway. Armed with such evidence, the National Gallery Site Commission declared that Trafalgar Square was "incontestably" more convenient than South Kensington. When it chose in favor of Trafalgar Square, the commission elevated it as the "very heart of London" and the "finest site in Europe."[66]

URBAN ACCESS, METROPOLITAN REFASHIONING, AND MUSEUM POLITICS

The opposition between a popular, accessible Trafalgar Square and an elite, remote South Kensington left Cole with two challenges. The first had to do with the physical geography of London. To make South Kensington an appealing location, Cole had to render it convenient to the respectable London public. From the outset, Cole held no illusions about the challenges that South Kensington might pose to urban wayfarers. In an 1853 address, even he admitted that it lay "a little out of the way of civilization."[67] A relentless reformer, Cole therefore joined in the contemporary campaign to enhance mobility and access to labyrinthine London.[68] Nowhere, in fact, was this taken up with more fervor than in the sprawling western suburbs, where building bridges, constructing boulevards, securing walking paths, and clearing turnpike gates became subjects of intense concern during the museum's early years.[69] Cole was an instrumental collaborator in these efforts. He advocated a road-building project that brought such majestic thoroughfares as Prince Albert's Road, Exhibition Road, Cromwell Road, and Gore Road to the commissioners' estate.[70] He built the museum near several omnibus routes. Finally, he ensured that the museum was accessible to the burgeoning Underground's Metropolitan District Railway, whose construction had begun in 1854. To Cole's delight, South Kensington's station would open on this very loop in 1864.[71] A little more than a decade later, one commentator noted that this last innovation had decisively solved that "most formidable" problem of access faced by South Kensington.[72] During his two decades as museum director, Cole would ultimately succeed in making South Kensington more available to the freeborn—and increasingly mobile—Englishman.

Cole faced a more overwhelming task when it came to the imagined geography of the metropolis. Here, it turned out, the fearless innovator would meet his match. The very name of the South Kensington Museum derived from a geographical neologism coined by Cole, who had consolidated his estate in suburban Brompton. His perorations for the working man notwithstanding, Cole was dissatisfied with the humble connotations of Brompton, which was known for its market gardens and, more recently, for its middle-class residences. Filled with grand ambitions, Cole decided to rechristen the district.[73] Through a linguistic amendment, Cole sought to attach his museum to lofty Kensington. A parish, borough, and village, Kensington had long been associated with royalty, aristocracy, and fashion.[74] During the museum's early years, the link between Kensington and royalty remained strong enough to manifest itself even in the records of the Poor Law Guardians, which documented the "pauper lunatics" of the district. One claimed to be "worth much money," another promised that she would "lay in state" upon her death, and a third proclaimed that she was the queen.[75]

For all of its storied history, however, Kensington was itself a location in transition at midcentury, as a slew of trade journals, neighborhood newspapers, and local histories suggests. The birth of Cole's museum coincided with a transformation of West London and especially of Kensington, whose built environment and population were in great flux.[76] Long a polite Georgian paradise, Kensington was traditionally famed for its rustic air.[77] During the mid–nineteenth century, chroniclers repeatedly made note of Kensington's metamorphosis from a "small country town" into a vibrant metropolitan hub filled with thriving retail centers, small-scale manufactures, and new residential enclaves.[78] Its growth was the most notable manifestation of what the urban chronicler Edward Bowring described as the "constant tendency of society to travel westward."[79] Indeed, by midcentury, Kensington stood as the self-designated "center" of London's burgeoning western suburbs.[80] The day would not be long, another urban interlocutor noted, before Kensington might be a "truer center of London than Trafalgar Square or Bloomsbury."[81]

New populations had come to live within this dynamic parish. Although Kensington retained its affluent, aristocratic aura, by midcentury, this "old court suburb" was not solely the preserve of the court. It had instead become home to businessmen, artists, and statesmen who were, perhaps, lured by the parish's "aristocratic pretension." The budding local press celebrated this constituency as it welcomed the emergence of a prosperous and vibrant "Westurbia." In its inaugural year of 1859, for instance, the *Kensington Chronicle* declared that the parish boasted "more than the usual proportion of those who enjoy wealth and station."[82] At midcentury, then, Kensington remained one of the richest districts in all of Europe, but it was also home to several constituencies who subsisted beyond the purview of privilege.[83] As London expanded westward, comparatively humble middling professionals, including "clerks, schoolmasters, and government officials," dotted Kensington's streets.[84] The parish also had its share of laborers, who possessed a "Working Men's Club."[85] It even boasted a quotient of republicans. Most infamous of the blights on Kensington, however, was the colony of Irish poor who lived in a dirty and disease-ridden slum called Jennings Buildings.[86] Cole himself was well aware of the slum with its pungent smells and discordant yells.[87] He was just one of several mid-Victorian chroniclers to bring a level of prurient fascination to bear on its shoeless children, dissolute men, and ragged women, who presented a "painful contrast to the general decency" of the area.[88] A "skeleton" in Kensington's closet, they were a strata that existed well outside of the ideal museumgoing public, however expansively constructed.[89]

Kensington was unquestionably a protean locale at midcentury. It was at once a rural oasis and an urban frontier; it was a capital of wealth and a locus of poverty; it was the preserve of royalty and the home of republicans.[90] Refashioning and containing the associations carried by Kensington thus proved a formidable undertaking even for so enterprising a man as Cole. Because he could not circumscribe the moniker, Cole used its indeterminacy to his advantage in the effort to draw the national collections westward. Although he had not prevailed with the National Gallery's Trafalgar Square collections, he would triumph when it came to such prizes as the Natural History Museum and the India Museum, whose treasures remain in South Kensington today.[91]

These victories were hard won. During the museum's first few decades, adversaries both liberal and radical sought to thwart Cole and his grand designs to move the national collections to South Kensington.[92] In their copious assaults, they ignored the parish's transformations or noted them grudgingly at best.[93] As part of their strategy, opponents reified the oppositions between a populist urban center and an exclusive suburban preserve that had been so evident in the National Gallery site report.[94] They dismissed South Kensington as a "Royal Wasteland" and an outpost of "Court Favor."[95] They castigated it as a "distant suburb" or "a low, flat, humid site, peculiar for being out of the way even to people who live close by."[96] Moreover, they deemed Kensington anathema to gentlemanly trade and manly toil.[97] This objection arose in strikingly clear terms when it came to collections such as the Patent Museum and the India Museum, which had an avowedly commercial purpose.[98] When the removal of these collections to South Kensington was in question, opponents did not hesitate to mention that Cole's museum stood a long distance from hubs of commerce and hives of labor, that is, "three miles from Temple Bar, four from the Bank, and five or six from Spitalfields or Whitechapel."[99] When all was said and done, design reform's purpose, however broadly understood, was ill-suited to "far-away South Kensington."[100]

Building on these assessments, many critics insinuated that the neighborhood of South Kensington smacked of effeteness and effeminacy. When they made such charges, adversaries pointed out the museum's proximity to London's West End, which was just beginning to burst with boutiques, department stores, and ladies' clubs. As Erika Rappaport has so well demonstrated, that nearby preserve of female pleasure and consumption was expanding in scope and complexity during South Kensington's early years.[101] It was also assuming a more prominent place in the metropolitan and national imagination. In the minds of critics, the museum had come to resemble the West End all too closely. Ultimately, South Kensington connoted "frothy syllabubs" rather than "substantial roast beef."[102] By 1865, even the establishment *Art Journal* took South Kensington to task as it denounced the silver, china, and bronzes that filled the museum's ornate galleries. The *Journal* longed, instead, to find sturdy Wedgwood pottery on South Kensington's shelves. In contrast to the current holdings, such exemplars of English manufacture would offer useful lessons to Cole's ideal artisanal visitors. At South Kensington, the *Art Journal* concluded, the enterprise of design reform had strayed far from the "true interests of the genuine workman," whether these be aesthetic or geographic.[103]

BENJAMIN LUCRAFT, BETHNAL GREEN, AND THE HONEST HIVE

In the very year that the *Art Journal* advanced this charge, Henry Cole made one final effort to minister to laboring men. He announced a plan for branch museums in greater London's working neighborhoods in an 1865 speech delivered in South Kensington's lecture theater. There he unveiled a scheme to form a series of neighborhood museums throughout greater London to an audience of local worthies, benevolent ministers, and working men. Satellites of South Kensington, these institutions would serve the laborers of the metropolis by providing them with collections in their own neighborhoods. The collections would be drawn from South Kensington in more ways than one. The neighborhood museums would showcase the overflow from South Kensington. More significantly, the structures of these satellites would be comprised of the Boilers themselves, which were to be removed from Brompton to make way for the elegant buildings already filling the estate, including the Italianate South Court. Designed by the architect Francis Fowke and ornamented by the decorator Godfrey Sykes, this construction would soon become an exemplar of the South Kensington style (fig. 60).[104] With its intricate veneer and elaborate interior, it proved a far grander stage for Cole's ambitions than the homely Boilers had.

Like his inaugural address delivered nearly eight years before, Cole's 1865 speech met a hearty welcome. It was certainly timely in the face of contemporary developments that brought increased prominence to working men as cultural consumers and political subjects. For example,

Chapter Five

NEW BUILDINGS OF THE SOUTH KENSINGTON MUSEUM.

60   New construction at South Kensington by Francis Fowke and Godfrey
Sykes. *Illustrated London News*, 29 September 1866, 304. Special and Area
Studies Collections, George A. Smathers Library, University of Florida.

the 1860s witnessed the efflorescence of working men's exhibitions.
These shows broke with earlier traditions of display by crediting handi-
craftsmen rather than employers for the goods that they showed. Held
in such hives of labor as Lambeth and Islington, the exhibitions themselves provided a platform for advocating branch museums.[105] In the
mid-1860s, access to art also preoccupied the National Sunday League,
whose meetings and pleadings played their part to raise the debate about
the proper use of the artisan's day of rest to fever pitch.[106] Even imperial
fault lines gave the English working man greater political currency. Most
notably, Jamaica's Governor Eyre Controversy of 1865, which pitted
harsh colonial justice against expansive British liberty, brought renewed
attention to the social and political condition of the English working
classes.[107] At home, it would help to fuel the heady contest over the Reform Act of 1867, in which the working man was the "axial figure."[108]
Ultimately, these developments would make Cole's project of rendering

his collections accessible to the respectable artisan evermore urgent. In fact, although the *Saturday Review* dismissed the notion that "Jamaica could have anything whatever to do with South Kensington," the many possible connections were not lost on at least one participant in the debate over Sunday openings.[109] And, though he may not have figured the equation in these terms, Cole himself was well aware of the interrelationships between culture and politics. In fact, as the *Art Journal* noted, Cole recorded the numbers of visitors to South Kensington as assiduously as a politician might count "voters at an election."[110]

In the face of these developments, it should come as no surprise that the most effective speaker at the May 1865 meeting was Benjamin Lucraft, a cabinetmaker from the East London neighborhood of Hoxton, an erstwhile Chartist, and the editor of the *Bee-Hive*, a newspaper at the vanguard of electoral reform.[111] When he rose to address those assembled at the museum, Lucraft announced that he spoke in the interests of his own class. Like preceding petitioners, he sketched the working pilgrim's progress from the East End to South Kensington. He pulled out all of the rhetorical stops as he showed the journey to be a challenging one. On several occasions Lucraft had worked "very hard" so that he might take a Saturday half-holiday at the museum, where he could learn to be a "better workman." However, the realities of urban topography made this laudable aspiration difficult to achieve, even for a skilled artisan like himself. The ninety-minute omnibus ride from Hoxton was itself hard work. When the cabinetmaker reached South Kensington, he inevitably had to rest before studying the collections. Moreover, the arduous journey was also replete with temptation, requiring museumgoers to pass hundreds of gin palaces, which threatened to ensnare even the most "sober" of men.[112]

Like his contemporaries, Lucraft framed the working man as an endangered moral subject. Yet he also broke with recent practices as he drew on the legacies of design reform. His rhetoric hearkened back to those reformers who had pressed to open schools of design during the 1830s and 1840s. They had cast artisans expressly as skilled producers engaged in competition with French and German rivals. Lucraft's words also recalled those enterprising forbears who had campaigned for the design copyright. They had based their claims to political capital on the notion of property of skill. By placing himself within these trajectories, Lucraft fashioned himself as a venerable producer. In the process, he complicated the logic of his reforming contemporaries. They had argued that access to collections would produce better workmen. Lucraft, on the other hand, declared that his very status as a workman allowed him to make claims on the collections. In the process, he railed against the "injustice" presented by the museological topography of London.[113] No longer could an elite cultural arena and a circumscribed political sphere continue to justify one another.[114]

In the wake of the 1865 meeting, civic leaders and working men in the East End sought to rectify the injustice that Lucraft had decried. There three local leaders, Rev. Septimus Hansard, Sir Antonio Brady, and Dr. Andrew Millar, spearheaded a campaign to build a branch museum. For the site, they found a parcel of land on Bethnal Green that was both undeveloped and accessible. Gifted to the poor in the reign of James I, it had at one time provided pasturage for cattle with the proceeds benefiting the indigent, who received ten shillings and a parcel of coal each Christmas. By the 1860s, this land stood at the center of a "network of railways and omnibuses"; a million artisans lived within a few miles.[115] A number of these workers joined in the campaign for the Bethnal Green Museum. With verve, they organized meetings, raised funds, and collected signatures on behalf of the putative collection.[116] There is no telling whether the neighborhood's residents embraced Cole's directives about art edification for the masses, but the enthusiasm with which they campaigned certainly suggests that a neighborhood museum was a rallying point for civic pride in London's East End.[117] The working men of the East End wished for more than the "beef, beer, warm clothing, and good wages" that radical critics of South Kensington claimed they required. They wanted a museum, too.[118]

Its passion notwithstanding, the coalition that toiled in favor of the East London Museum would have to wait a good seven years to gain its share of the national treasures.[119] In June 1872, Cole conveyed the Boilers to Bethnal Green at long last. There laborers covered the peripatetic Boilers with a brick exterior. Back at South Kensington, ladies crafted mosaics intended to decorate the structure. The museum boasted yet another monument to its crosstown progenitor in Minton's famed majolica fountain, which had debuted at South Kensington's International Exhibition of 1862. As it charted the eastward movement of the infant museum's constituent parts, the *East London Observer* proclaimed with optimism that the structure would long be a symbol of pride for Bethnal

Green.[120] But if Cole had been generous with the physical furnishings, he proved far less so with the installations, offering meager collections of unwanted animal products and wax models that gave Bethnal Green a reputation as an "asylum for South Kensington refuse."[121] Unaware of—or perhaps indifferent to—design reform's grander intentions, the residents of the East End tried to help out with modest donations of animal specimens, musical diagrams, and, especially, handmade flowers. One prospective contributor was G. W. Halfpenny of Lower Shadwell, who kindly offered his daughter's wax flowers for show at the museum. For potential donors such as Halfpenny, these acts of largesse may have seemed the ideal opportunity to combine civic generosity with personal or family pride. But this was not to be the case, for they were told by the museum's officials that such goods "scarcely c[a]me within the scope of the collections." It was of no consequence that their offerings bore a disconcertingly close approximation to the surplus collections that Cole had sent from South Kensington.[122] Happily for the progenitors, Sir Richard Wallace, MP, saved the museum from ignominy with his re-markable collection and lustrous name. In a celebrated act of philan-thropy, Wallace deposited his impressive cache of paintings, porcelain, and furniture at Bethnal Green on extended loan, where it would remain as the centerpiece of the museum until 1875.[123]

The actual holdings, however, concerned few on the museum's open-ing day in June 1872. All eyes instead were on the royal visit of the Prince and Princess of Wales (fig. 61).[124] Their sojourn marked the first time in two hundred years that royalty had entered Bethnal Green.[125] There they presided over a "resplendent assemblage," including uniformed men, elegant ladies, exotic dignitaries, and, of course, Henry Cole. These luminaries had convened for an opening ceremony that evoked the spirit of 1851. In particular, the prince's speech recalled the ethos of the Great Exhibition, as it linked aesthetic acumen, individual im-provement, and national strength. The prince placed "the English work-man"—and especially the laborer of the East End—at the center of the decades-long project of design reform, whose mantle he duly passed to Bethnal Green.[126] The time had come for design reform from below. If the working man could not go to South Kensington, South Kensington would come to the working man.[127]

Many contemporaries noted the irony of these pronouncements. For all the talk of Bethnal Green at the museum's opening, the neighbor-

ARRIVAL OF THE PRINCE OF WALES AT THE BETHNAL-GREEN MUSEUM.

61 The Prince and Princess of Wales at the Bethnal Green Museum with Minton's majolica fountain in front. *Illustrated London News*, 29 June 1872, 620. Special and Area Studies Collection, George A. Smathers Library, University of Florida.

hood's residents had no part in the ceremony itself.[128] Excluded from the official proceedings, its denizens made their own celebration instead. They thronged the neighborhood's byways as they greeted the royals in the streets. There the parishioners made a spectacle of themselves, receiving the royals with a picturesque array of colored paper, calicoes, and tea trays. Banners announced, "Welcome to Bethnal Green." Cries of "Long live the Prince and Princess of Wales" filled the streets. For a day, the resounding display of affection assuaged pervasive concerns about the East End as a hotbed of republicanism.[129] According to the fashionable *Morning Post*, the occasion presented the "most striking" display of "national loyalty" in recent memory.[130]

In such renderings, Bethnal Green appears as the abode of a humble, industrious, and loyal people. These characterizations resonate with a long-standing literary rendition of the parish. A legend of indeterminate origin, "The Blind Beggar of Bethnal Green" recounted the trials of an Elizabethan knight who had been injured in battle. Consigned to a life of penury, he settled in the bucolic parish, where he lived as a pauper and sought to defend the honor of his beautiful daughter. The prevalence of burlesques, farces, nursery ballads, and melodramas based on the legend indicates that the tale resonated with a transatlantic public during the nineteenth century.[131] It also offered a rallying point for civic pride in the neighborhood.[132] Indeed, the image of a loyal Bethnal Green conveyed through the tale of the "Blind Beggar" seems to have influenced several accounts of the museum's opening.[133]

However, the "Blind Beggar" was not the only narrative associated with the parish. By the 1870s, newer representational practices of novelistic realism, urban ethnography, and sensational journalism had combined to make Bethnal Green, and London's East End more generally, infamous as dens of poverty and vice that stood beyond the pale of civilized society.[134] At the museum's opening, the *Daily Telegraph* and the *Daily News* capitalized most strikingly on these representational strategies. They cast the royals' visit as a journey to a faraway land, a terra incognita as alien as Dr. Livingstone's Africa.[135] The East Enders were a distinct race that consumed "viands not dreamt of in the philosophy of the West End." Decrepit foils to Argus's "beef-devouring" Briton, the denizens of the East End had their own particular taste. They consumed "cowpoke," "staggering bob," and "doubtful 'pieces'" swarming with flies.[136] According to the *Telegraph* and the *News*, Bethnal Green's inhabitants literally embodied penury. Among their ranks, the *Daily News* counted "gaunt, ragged men" who were "stunted, narrow-chested, and spider-limbed." They stood alongside "lean, wan-faced women" who wore "limp, dingy prints."[137] The *Telegraph*, too, portrayed poverty as synonymous with deformity and homeliness in its accounts of the crowd of dwarfs, hunchbacks, and "crooked and bandy and rickety babes." The privation of the East End took a particular toll on the district's women, as the *Telegraph* vividly showed.

> Here yesterday, female ugliness of face and form, in blank monotonous, unvarying typification, was predominant. Sickly mothers nursing sickly

babies; sickly girls toying in a sickly manner with sickly weaver boys; listless emaciated middle-aged women; dreadful old women, as ugly as sin, who looked as though they supported nature on a diet of lucifer matches and gin—these made up a considerable proportion of the vast course which lined the kerb, and was easily kept in order by the police while waiting for the Royal procession.[138]

The whole spectacle was stunning in its degeneracy. With such renderings, the *Telegraph* and the *News* cast the people of Bethnal Green outside of the respectable, museumgoing public. They were too dirty, deformed, and decrepit to be the subjects of aesthetic improvement and liberal reform.

Such portrayals kindled "indignation" in Bethnal Green. The voice of the parish, the *East London Observer*, decried the offending papers. Granted, Bethnal Green was a humble region. But to cast it as the den of "misery, profligacy, vice, and crime" was to engage in the most flagrant abuses of English journalism. The *East London Observer* called, therefore, for a boycott of the offending papers.[139] Bethnal Green's parishioners followed the directive and then some. They decried the papers on street corners and in coffee shops, they denounced them in ballads, and they hung placards opposing them in shop windows. Finally, drawing on a tradition of radical dissent, the working men held a series of "indignation meetings" in town halls and public houses. Congregating in the thousands, tradesmen, artisans, and laborers charged the offending papers with "libel" and adopted resolutions against them. One, of course, repudiated the horrid rags; another defended the beautiful women of the parish; and a third championed Bethnal Green itself as "one of the largest hives of honest industry in the metropolis of the world."[140]

It is telling that Bethnal Green's parishioners sought to vindicate the neighborhood by framing it as a "hive of honest industry."[141] By defending the neighborhood in such terms, they challenged the insinuation that they belonged to a notorious residuum comprised of "cadaverous weavers" who worked "eighteen hours a day," "half-bloodless" seamstresses who lived off tea and bread," and "weak-kneed" match sellers who trekked "in a forlorn and shiftless manner."[142] Decrepit and degraded, these figures shared little with respectable working men such as Pimlico, who had skillfully inserted himself into the era's museological debates to gain access to the South Kensington Museum, or Lucraft,

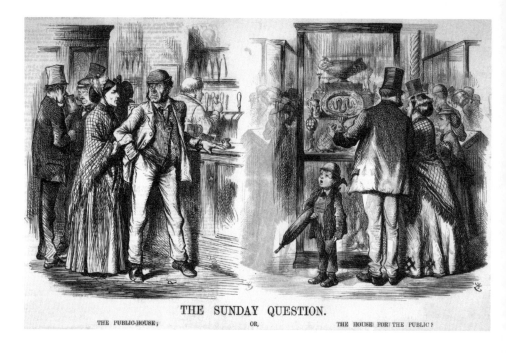

THE SUNDAY QUESTION.

THE PUBLIC-HOUSE; OR, THE HOUSE FOR THE PUBLIC?

62   Roughness, respectability, and the Sunday question. *Punch* 56 (1869): 160.
Reproduced courtesy of the Huntington Library, San Marino, California.

who had cannily deployed the lineage of design reform to press for a
neighborhood collection.

   When they separated themselves from the residuum, Bethnal Green's
residents appealed, unquestionably, to middle-class notions of respectability. But they also defended themselves on their own terms—and on
their own turf, too. It is telling that Bethnal Green's residents launched
their defense of the neighborhood in a public house—that perennial
locale of working-class protest, not to mention the supposed antithe-
sis to the museum. This juxtaposition certainly held great sway in the
middle-class reforming imagination. In fact, just three years before the
opening of the Bethnal Green outpost, *Punch* had lampooned the earnest assumption that museums could turn rough characters into respectable families (fig. 62). When they protested, Bethnal Green's residents
called into question the presumed dichotomy of public house and public gallery. In the process, they defied the middle-class distinction be-

tween rough and respectable. Indeed, their very actions lend credence to Peter Bailey's assertion that working men consumed culture on their own terms in the middle of the nineteenth century. They attended those establishments that provided the rational recreation valued by the bourgeoisie while still patronizing the institutions that offered the traditional pleasures associated with the poor—oftentimes on the very same day.[143]

This phenomenon of adaptive use begs the question of exactly what the residents of the East End might have sought from the Bethnal Green Museum and the broader project of design reform. Long after the protests quieted, the museum attracted its share of visitors from near and far. In fact, the museum recorded over two million patrons between June of 1872 and March of 1875. These numbers can be attributed, at least in part, to the museum's evening openings and free days, which were certainly popular among the working classes.[144] This was especially the case on holidays such as Easter, as an 1873 illustration from the *Graphic* suggests (fig. 63). Its artist demonstrated that the laborers of the East End were certainly an important constituency within the mixed-class audience that visited the museum. In fact, the contributor to the *Graphic* took pains to press this point by placing two working men wearing fustian jackets at the center of the image. But if the *Graphic* substantiates our understandings of the museum's audience, it also challenges orthodoxies about museum behavior. It appears that the museum provided a space for sociability, not simply a mechanism for governmentality. As such, the *Graphic*'s image bears out an assertion made recently by Kate Hill. "Rather than disciplining," Hill argued, "the space of the gallery . . . could encourage self-display."[145]

The museum offered the residents of the East End a rallying ground for civic pride. It also provided a welcome forum for social display. To be sure, the many alternative uses for the museum help us to challenge received notions of the exhibitionary complex. However, this is not to say that neighborhood residents rejected the aims of design reform and its undergirding assumptions wholesale. Lucraft, for example, had emphasized the economic advantages that the Bethnal Green Museum would bestow on trade in the continuing contest with the Continent. And at least some of his brethren approached the museum as the very schoolroom of the sort that design reform's progenitors had hoped it would be. This is evident in the tale of a working man unskilled in museum eti-

ART CONNOISSEURS AT THE EAST END

63 Working men and other visitors at the Bethnal Green Museum. *Graphic*, 19 April 1873, 177. General Research Division, New York Public Library, Astor, Lenox, and Tilden Foundations.

quette who visited the museum on its opening day. Inspired by the marvelous furniture in Wallace's collection, he reached out to touch an inlaid bureau. Before a guard could remonstrate, another visitor explained that this humble guest just so happened to be a "cabinet maker by trade." The heir of Haydon's awed artisan and Dyce's competent craftsman, there could not have been a more fitting vessel for design reform nearly forty years on.

CONCLUSION

It appears that Tony Bennett's exhibitionary complex does not account for the many contests that plagued South Kensington in its early years. Nor does Bennett's theory illuminate the prominent role of location and its politics in shaping the cultural geography of art. But, while this chapter has exposed the limits of Bennett's schema, it might also indicate his acuity. When he defined the exhibitionary complex, Bennett argued that its primary audience was the working man. This point deserves repetition; it also warrants expansion—and not simply for the purpose of vindicating Bennett but rather for writing labor's cultural history. Just as histories of politics and production were once reconfigured by attention to working-class subjects, now matters of culture, urban geography, and aesthetics deserve the same.

The working man, construed as skilled artisan and sometimes even as poor toiler, was, indeed, the ideal target for South Kensington and its satellites. But, as we have seen, this figure in his many incarnations was no passive recipient of the museum's efforts. During the middle years of the nineteenth century, working men played an active role in the making of museological London. To do so, they fashioned themselves as valiant producers. But they also showed themselves to be domestic figures and political subjects. Moreover, labor supplied the language and criteria for waging the cultural battles of the day. With this in mind, we can see how working men left their imprints on the collections of metropolitan London, their logics, and their very locations. We can also discover how they reinterpreted design reform and its institutions for their own uses.

For our purposes, interrogating the exhibitionary complex has been no mere theoretical exercise. Such an endeavor allows us to bring our story of mid-nineteenth-century design reform to its conclusion. It is now commonplace to assume that design reform lapsed into bourgeois complacency at South Kensington, as Henry Cole traded the project of market reform for the loftier ambitions of building his estate, collecting art treasures, and currying aristocratic favor. Moreover, South Kensington's project would become ever more diffuse after Cole's retirement in 1873. To be sure, design reform's priorities shifted with the westward move from Marlborough House. Regardless of Cole's proclivities, however, design reform's original preoccupation with labor and trade did not disintegrate at South Kensington. Nowhere is this continuity more evident than in the site debates, which reconfigured the preoccupations about production and commerce that had been so prevalent at the School of Design, the Great Exhibition, and the Museum of Ornamental Art, not to mention in the copyright debates. The concerns expressed before the Select Committee on Arts and Manufactures in the 1830s did not disappear from view at South Kensington. Instead, they would persist through midcentury, even as the movement's express priorities shifted from training artisans to consolidating collections, from elevating production to managing consumption, and from improving patterns to designing men.

Travels in South Kensington

Ten years after the Bethnal Green Museum opened its doors, Moncure Daniel Conway penned *Travels in South Kensington*, his tribute to Henry Cole's collection. In these pages, Conway offered a vision of a vigorous institution that was bursting with the "cream of the East and West." In a familiar Victorian conceit that aligned museums with conquest and exploration, Conway argued that there was no need to settle for the "'skim milk' of travel" in his day.[1] London's museums—and Henry Cole's collection especially—offered all the wonders that the adventurer could desire. For the American visitor in London, promenading through the South Kensington Museum was every bit as tantalizing as making a "pilgrimage" across the earth.[2]

This was especially the case after the South Kensington Museum's Indian section debuted on 17 May 1880 (fig. 64). Indian designs had occupied pride of place at the Great Exhibition and in the Museum of Ornamental Art, but this new section consolidated a far more comprehensive collection from the subcontinent. At its core stood the treasures of the East India Company.[3] Goods purchased by Cole and his circle from exhibitions and world's fairs across Europe flanked the East India Company's trove. Armor donated by Queen Victoria headlined a long list of gifts, which also included Buddhist sculptures and ethnographic watercolors. It all amounted to a magnificent whole. In *Travels in South Kensington*, Conway declared that there was "no university in the world

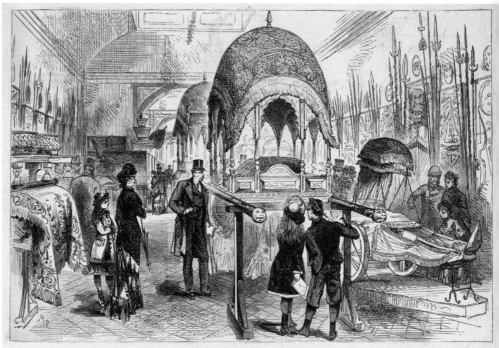

THE NEW INDIAN SECTION, SOUTH KENSINGTON MUSEUM.

64   India at South Kensington. *Illustrated London News*, 22 May 1880, 501. Special and Area Studies Collection, George A. Smathers Library, University of Florida.

where one [could] learn so much about India."[4] At a time when Britain was ascending to the height of its global power, South Kensington had become the imperial archive par excellence.[5]

Conway recommended the new installation to anyone interested in India, "its pantheon, its mythology, or its relation to the evolution of humanity." Such counsel attested to the American visitor's long-standing interests in orientalism and ethnology, two scholarly endeavors that would reinvigorate the museum enterprise in late Victorian London.[6] South Kensington's Indian Court put the ethnographic turn on display in all of its material and metaphysical richness.[7] Its Muslim temple photographs, Hindu jewelry, and Buddhist gates provided a "spiritual biography" of the subcontinent while offering transcendent lessons that surpassed the particularity of place. In the Indian Court, and through-

192   *Afterword*

out the South Kensington Museum, Conway explained, visitors could behold nothing less than a "museum of civilization."[8]

Like the museum to which it paid homage, Conway's narrative consigned imperialism to the realm of the aesthetic. If we are to judge by Conway's account, or even by the South Kensington Museum's very displays, Britain's incursions into the subcontinent over the foregoing century had, by and large, been triumphant, peaceful, and bloodless.[9] Violence was a glaring omission from this account, but it was not the sole exclusion from Conway's text, which offers a retrospective assessment of many of the reforming efforts chronicled in *Grand Designs*. Notably, the concerns about trade that had guided midcentury design reform and its attendant displays were nowhere evident in the American voyager's discussions of the Indian Court. In Conway's South Kensington Museum, we find a marked contrast to the Great Exhibition of 1851. Although the East India Company had assembled a lavish showcase in the Crystal Palace, it had done so with the express aim of convincing the British populace of the worthiness of imperial trade. It had seemed in 1851 that India might provide fertile ground for cultivating such commodities as cotton, tea, and flax. Admittedly, the art manufactures of the subcontinent left the greatest and most enduring impression on the public and the press. Many of the treasures from the subcontinent would, of course, reappear in 1852 at the Museum of Ornamental Art, located nearby at Marlborough House. Yet Henry Cole and his circle had expressly commercial aims in mind for this museum, which aspired to engineer market improvement by elevating the taste of consumers. At Conway's South Kensington, conversely, spectacle had become an end in itself, associated with ethical practice and oriental knowledge.

To be sure, Henry Cole and his circle eschewed market improvement in favor of magisterial collecting at the South Kensington Museum. However, design reform's preoccupation with skilled labor did not disappear with the westward move to Brompton. Not only did the working man become the ideal audience for Cole's museum; labor also became a part of South Kensington's aesthetic. The museum's very walls paid tribute to artisanship, as Tim Barringer has shown in his analysis of the South Court. Ornamented by Godfrey Sykes, a onetime student at the Sheffield School of Design, the South Court's interior featured allegorical figures of spinners, smiths, and sculptors.[10] Labor was also a decorative flourish in the museum's Ceramic Courts, discussed by Conway in his *Travels*. For these courts, William B. Scott had designed a series of fifteen etched windows that chronicled the development of the manufacture. These windows transported beholders from the birthplace of the art in China to Egypt, India, and Italy. Ultimately, they brought viewers to England, where the famed Josiah Wedgwood had given the trade renewed vigor. Particularly notable were the first two windows, which commemorated the ancient Chinese art of porcelain. The first pictured half-naked natives transporting kaolin from caves; the second featured dextrous potters working their rude wheels and sending their productions to the kiln (fig. 65). These craftsmen, Conway noted, had distinguished themselves by means of their patient study and toil. Perhaps they inspired the students at the South Kensington Art School, heir to the once struggling School of Design.[11] Not incidentally, these very students would do their part to build and decorate the museum along with contractors, sappers, and even chain gang convicts. Cole's tributes to the working man notwithstanding, very few London artisans participated in this endeavor.[12]

The campaign for design reform chronicled in this book unquestionably changed its character as the South Kensington Museum matured, especially after Cole retired in 1873. Conway's South Kensington Museum endeavored to elevate collecting to a spiritual practice worthy of an age of high imperialism. In stark contrast stood the infant School of Design, which had sought to improve British trade by teaching artisans how to produce better patterns. According to one select committee witness, England's artisans were the keys to "national greatness."[13] For all of its spectacular aspirations, the Great Exhibition sustained this commitment in its displays and texts, which sought to venerate the English artisan and his craft. These understandings were not lost on the laborers of mid-Victorian London. They used their positions as reputable producers to make claims to both political agency and museum collections. Their strategy met certain success with the opening of the Bethnal Green Museum. Despite the fanfare at its opening, however, the institution's triumph would turn out to be short-lived. Ten years after the collection debuted, the Bethnal Green Museum was languishing, having suffered a "heavy blow" when Sir Richard Wallace removed his riches from the East End.[14] No longer was the museum or its audience an object of concern at South Kensington. The particularly "mid-Victorian symbiosis of

65 Window in the Ceramic Courts depicting
Chinese potters at work. Engraving in Conway, *Travels
in South Kensington* (1882). Yale Center for British Art,
Paul Mellon Collection.

SIR HENRY COLE, K.C.B.

66   A distinguished Henry Cole
in his later years. Engraving
in Conway, *Travels in South
Kensington* (1882). Yale Center
for British Art, Paul Mellon
Collection.

labor and art" identified by Tim Barringer had, unquestionably, dissipated by the time Conway published his *Travels*.[15]

The shifting fortunes of the Bethnal Green Museum suggest that mid-century design reform was a more uneven and complicated process than Conway had indicated. He portrayed South Kensington's rise as a triumph over adversity and indifference. Thanks to the perspicacity and perseverance of a few men, Conway explained, the museum had grown out of the culturally barren soil of the early nineteenth century. It was an unlikely development for an era consumed by "Peterloo massacres, bread riots and corn laws," but against all odds a few pioneers had successfully established the School of Design. The Great Exhibition revealed the limitations of this school all too glaringly. There, the "laughter of cultivated foreigners" had shamed the host nation, which set to work to effect a "great revolution" in English art under the helm of Henry Cole, portrayed here in venerable old age (fig. 66). The result, in the words of a contemporary article in the *Times*, was a "transition from darkness to light." Its greatest achievement was the South Kensington Museum.[16]

Here I have offered a different set of conclusions about the transition from the School of Design to South Kensington. Rather than sprouting from barren soil, I have argued that the museum evolved out of a culture concerned with market reform and artisanal education. The *Report of the Select Committee on Arts and Manufactures* expressed these preoccupations methodically; publications such as the *Penny Magazine* gave voice to them in less systematic ways. As the first official response to these concerns, the School of Design sought to elevate artisans by teaching them to draw. Building on these efforts, proponents of copyright extension aimed to dignify trade and enhance patterns by providing longer periods of protection. Conway, notably, omitted the matter of copyright, which remained an issue of contention in his day, from his *Travels*.[17] In so doing, he differed little from contemporary journalists or subsequent chroniclers of the Victoria and Albert Museum. By redressing this omission, I have sought to refine our understandings of midcentury design reform, its preoccupations, its geography, and its chronology. This book has placed the supply-side concerns that preceded the Great Exhibition front and center, it has highlighted the attempts to redress ailments plaguing specific trades, and it has illuminated a provincial component to this crusade that is so often overlooked.

My analysis also differs from Conway's in its positioning of the Great Exhibition. Like many of his contemporaries and ours, Conway portrayed the Great Exhibition as the turning point for design reform's upward march.[18] Of course, the exhibition brought industrial design to an audience of unprecedented proportions through its displays and texts. But if these innovations represented a break with the past in terms of scale and strategy, there were important continuities as well. For all of its dependence on spectacular display, the exhibition sustained the interest in artisanal skill that had been so central to preceding efforts at design reform. Notably, 1851's catalogues popularized the ideal of the skilled laborer in his various national manifestations as they promoted the exhibition among a cross-class readership.

Following the exhibition, design reform's express strategies shifted, by and large, to training consumers, cultivating connoisseurs, and collecting worldly goods. Under Cole and the curator John Charles Robinson, this last endeavor proceeded with an intensity that inspired Conway's reverie about the world contained at South Kensington. Yet even in Conway's day, labor retained a place of prominence, whether as decorative object, rhetorical flourish, or reforming concern. In fact, the American traveler's very account was peppered with mentions of the museum crowd, which included a sampling of "rough-looking youths" who were every bit as decorous as the more elevated patrons. The museum's orderly visitors offered reassurance at a moment of heightening militancy and class tension. In the institution's first quarter century, Conway noted, sightseers at South Kensington had comported themselves in a fashion worthy of London's "best drawing-rooms." During the museum's twenty-five-year history, in fact, only two visitors had borne the indignity of ejection, and this because of "tipsiness." If the crowds were orderly, they were also honest. As Conway reported, nothing of value had ever gone missing from the collection.[19] The current Victoria and Albert Museum, it turns out, has not been so fortunate.[20]

Finally, *Grand Designs* proffers a more dynamic analysis of labor than did Conway. Here I have tried to illuminate the enduring, albeit vexed, place of artisanal values within mid-nineteenth-century design reform. At South Kensington, connoisseurship often took priority over commerce. However, artisans enjoyed a notable degree of cultural capital at the museum and its Bethnal Green satellite. To gain access to the collections, men such as Pimlico and Lucraft hearkened back to the supply-side concerns that were so important during the early phase of the campaign for design reform. Conway's museumgoing masses, notable for their tractability, thus differed from Lucraft and his ilk. They recall the obedient subjects of Tony Bennett's exhibitionary complex, not the heroic producers who fill the historical record unearthed in these pages.

Despite its shortcomings, *Travels in South Kensington* offers a perceptive assessment of the aesthetic culture of the 1870s and 1880s and especially of South Kensington's place within it. In keeping with his laudatory narrative, Conway announced that South Kensington had "awakened a higher taste throughout the nation, and especially in London."[21] There are a number of broader indications of this success. First, South Kensington enjoyed growing acceptance as an institution, idea, and destination following Henry Cole's 1873 retirement when it settled into a more complacent, if sometimes uncertain, middle age.[22] Notably, critics no longer derided the museum's neighborhood as "a dreary cabbage garden in a deserted suburb."[23] Attendance figures also attest to the museum's increasing popularity and accessibility. In fact, by the time that Conway published *Travels in South Kensington*, the museum was boasting a million visitors per year.[24]

In Conway's day, the South Kensington Museum was on its way to

Afterword

becoming a model for museums of ornamental art in the United States, Mexico, Germany, and even France. This last was certainly an indication of triumph.[25] Perhaps ironically, Britain seemed to be assuming the mantle as "one of the world's leading suppliers" of "design ideas."[26] But the most important measure of success was the fact that "English and ugly" were no longer synonyms in the public imagination by the 1870s and 1880s.[27] There were still plenty of naysayers who remained skeptical about South Kensington's direct impact on design, but many aesthetes and journalists joined Conway in attributing a marked improvement in the material culture of everyday life at least in part to South Kensington and its predecessors.[28] This is a difficult matter to judge, but the pattern books in the designs registry provide what Cole and his circle would have deemed palpable evidence of improvement. By the 1880s, the calicoes deposited there did not display the garish coloring and shoddy workmanship of their predecessors from the 1840s. Moreover, the books showed none of the violations of taste principles that had yielded wallpapers with gothic cathedrals, chintzes with chariot racers, and carpets with garish flowers. In their place were more refined and less obtrusive samples with smaller patterns and subtler coloring.

In the face of these trends, Conway was hopeful about South Kensington's future. He envisioned that the millions would continue to throng the museum, especially if it were to open its doors on Sundays. The chronicler was equally sanguine about the network of art training schools that had grown out of the forlorn School of Design. By the 1880s, over 150 branch academies had mushroomed throughout the nation, counting in excess of 30,000 pupils. In 1880, the South Kensington Art School, the successor to the once embattled Somerset House, enrolled 824 students, both male and female.[29] For Conway, even more encouraging than the numbers themselves were the designs that the students produced for household goods, which were "universally recognized as results of South Kensington." Only one shortcoming persisted. For designs featuring the human figure, manufacturers had still to look to the Continent even as late as the 1880s.[30]

Despite his optimism, however, Conway suggested that the mantle of improving design had moved elsewhere at a moment when Cole's taste principles seemed to be increasingly outdated and individual consumer preferences were becoming ever more important.[31] In the 1880s, Conway noted, countless academies outside of South Kensington's network beckoned to pupils. These institutions held out their own attractions. The Royal Academy and the Slade School of Art had far more liberal policies for life drawing, especially when it came to lady students. Established nearby, the fledgling Royal School of Art Needlework promised practical training to respectable ladies in need of employment. According to Conway, this expansion of aesthetic training for women was part of "a quiet revolution" whose rumblings were evident across London.[32] Women had studied at the schools of design from the outset. Yet, thanks to new educational ventures, the burgeoning women's press, and best-selling manuals such as Charles Eastlake's 1868 *Hints on Household Taste*, the fairer sex was taking an ever greater interest in decorative art.[33] Women, for instance, were at the helm of the "latest craze" of home decoration.[34] Along with several contemporaries, Conway agreed that this line of work promised a "beautiful and congenial employment" for those looking to secure a modicum of fame or fortune in flower painting, home decor, or the art of dress.[35]

Finally, as he assessed the art culture of the day, Conway pointed his readers' attention to new luminaries: "named designers" such as William Morris, who fashioned exquisite tiles; Walter Crane, who designed gorgeous paper hangings; and Lawrence Alma-Tadema, who made fine candelabra.[36] These men were the vanguard of the fledgling—and still un-named—arts and crafts movement, which has since received scholarly, popular, and museological acclaim.[37] At the very moment when Conway published *Travels in South Kensington*, works by these artist-craftsmen were gracing West End clubs and wealthy London homes inhabited by "middle-class millionaires."[38] Thanks to the partnership forged between these artists and the metropolitan bourgeoisie, England's aesthetic future appeared to be in good hands. It was a marriage that promised to strike yet another blow to the "barbaric element in English taste" that had persisted into the late nineteenth century, especially among the aristocracy.[39] Even so, Conway noted the limits of improving the national taste by "beautifying London households." In the early 1880s, the works of the artists he so praised were affordable only to those able to make a "liberal, if not a lavish" expenditure on their homes. Arts and crafts productions had not yet attained the wider popularity that they would enjoy in the following decades, when some became more affordable to a broader market.[40] Of the elite productions, Conway therefore observed,

"They do not readily adapt themselves to a commonplace house adopted by commonplace people."[41]

A complicated relationship exists between the midcentury design reform crusade and the better-known arts and crafts movement that followed on its heels. Both sought to redress the plague of "shoddy wares," and both were utopian in their designs. In fact, there is a good deal of institutional and personal overlap between these two movements. To give just a few examples, in 1867, Morris and Company designed the Green Dining Room at the South Kensington Museum, and in 1893 a Morris disciple, Walter Crane, became principal of the Royal College of Art, which grew out of the School of Design.[42] But midcentury design reform is more often remembered as a foil to the arts and crafts movement than as a precondition for its development and success.[43] In this formulation, the midcentury movement, with its earnest and didactic leaders such as Henry Cole, has long appeared as the limited forerunner to William Morris or the doctrinaire counterpart to John Ruskin.[44] Nowhere is this clearer than in Nikolas Pevsner's *Pioneers of Modern Design*, which proclaimed Morris to be a designing genius and brilliant critic whose teachings contrasted sharply to those of Cole and his circle.[45] Scholars have continued to find Morris and his followers appealing for their far-reaching socioeconomic critique. On the whole, the arts and crafts movement has offered compelling assessments of industrialization, mechanization, alienation, and capitalism, though experts now recognize its protagonists' positions as more paradoxical and equivocal than we once understood them to be. The arts and crafts movement has also proved intriguing for its socialist vision, which sought to reform the arts and redesign the world for all, not just those who were able to purchase its works.[46]

In contrast to the arts and crafts movement, and to Morris especially, Cole and his circle did not seek to rehabilitate industrial society in the same thoroughgoing ways. Although they embraced artisanal labor, especially of an Indian variety, they did not offer a wholesale critique of machinery, capitalism, or the marketplace. But if they lacked a far-reaching social vision, their program had its own foresight. Cole and his circle sought to reform production and consumption on a national level by reworking aesthetics. To do so, they allowed market relations to intrude on aesthetic practice in the hopes of embarking on a progressive refashioning of the nation's goods.[47] Cole's midcentury movement aspired to bring its reforms to a broader segment of the British consuming and producing public than the arts and crafts movement later would. In its early days, for instance, the School of Design sought to elevate the productive habits of artisans throughout the nation, not simply to venerate craft as an ethical practice. This, incidentally, stands in contrast to the arts and crafts movement, and to Morris especially. He tended to employ middle-class artists rather than revolutionary working men in his firm.[48] Together, design copyright legislation and the Museum of Ornamental Art aspired to bring the tangible products of aesthetic reform—that is, affordable, tasteful household goods—to a far more inclusive range of consumers from the working and middle classes than the arts and crafts movement would address, especially in its early years. And, even if it did not seek to redesign the world, the South Kensington Museum strove to minister to the whole nation. We need only visit the Victoria and Albert Museum and the surrounding institutions to see the enduring imprint of Henry Cole's circle.

With its grand designs, midcentury reform embraced a notably wide range of figures: those forlorn boys who attended the School of Design, and especially its branch institutions, during its early years; the embattled provincial printers who sought protection under a strengthened industrial copyright; the exhibitiongoing millions who visited the Crystal Palace and read about it in its catalogues; those lower-middle-class consumers who learned new principles of taste at Marlborough House; and, of course, the working men of the metropolis who made a claim on South Kensington's collections. Often the protagonists of social history, these figures were also leading cultural actors of their day. As such, they vied to ascend aesthetic hierarchies, engaged in processes of self-fashioning, and transformed London's art collections. Together with the larger reforming movement in which they played a part, their story allows us to challenge the boundaries between aesthetics and economics, between art and industry, between consumption and production, and, finally, between culture and society.

Introduction

1 South Kensington Museum, *Local Metropolitan Museums*, 24–25.

2 *Report from the Select Committee on Arts and Manufactures* (1835), 13–21, esp. 14.

3 Ibid., 3, 28–29; *Report from the Select Committee on Arts and Their Connection with Manufactures* (1836), iii–xi.

4 *Report from the Select Committee on Arts and Manufactures* (1835), 5.

5 Barringer, *Men at Work*, 227.

6 Conway, *Travels in South Kensington*. Barbara Black provides a canny analysis of Conway in *On Exhibit*, introduction, chap. 1, chap. 4, chap. 6.

7 For a critical reading of Conway, see Barlow and Wilson, "Consuming Empire?" 156–71, esp. 162.

8 See, for example, Altick, *The Shows of London*; Apter, "On Imperial Spectacle," 564–96; Burton, "Making a Spectacle of Empire"; Clark, *The Painting of Modern Life*; Coombes, *Reinventing Africa*; Crary, *Techniques of the Observer*; Gilbert, "London in All Its Glory; or, How to Enjoy London"; McClintock, *Imperial Leather*; Mitchell, *Colonising Egypt*; Schwartz, *Spectacular Realities*; and Walkowitz, "The Indian Woman, the Flower Girl, and the Jew."

9 See, notably, Gagnier, *The Insatiability of Human Wants*, esp. the introduction, chap. 1, and chap. 4.

10 This literature is vast. See notes 8 and 36. See also Crossick and Jaumain, *Cathedrals of Consumption*; Nead, *Victorian Babylon*; Rappaport, *Shopping for Pleasure*; and Walkowitz, "Going Public." For an account of the rise of this historiography, see Eley, *A Crooked Line*, 167. For a critical review of this literature, see Finn, "Sex and the City."

11 As such, this work builds on the arguments about design as a lens through which to view society advanced by Adrian Forty in his groundbreaking *Objects of Desire*. See especially the introduction. Louise Purbrick presciently addresses capitalism and the museum in "South Kensington Museum," 69–86.

12 Barringer, *Men at Work*, 1.

13 Rogers, "Victorian Studies in the United Kingdom," 244–59, esp. 249; Hoock, "Reforming Culture," 254–270; Corrigan and Sayer, *The Great Arch*.

14 Bell, *The Schools of Design*; Burton, *Vision and Accident*; Lubbock, *The Tyranny of Taste*; Minihan, *The Nationalization of Culture*; Pevsner, *Academies of Art, Past and Present*; Physick, *The Victoria and Albert Museum*; Port, *Imperial London*. On Minihan and an earlier mode of cultural history, see Mandler, "Cultural Histories Old and New."

15 Duncan and Wallach's "The Universal Survey Museum" was a seminal text here. For a more sustained analysis, consult Duncan's *Civilizing Rituals*. Important works that have taken up and critiqued these formulations include Bailkin, *The Culture of Property*; McClellan, *Inventing the Louvre*; Pointon, *Art Apart*; Sherman and Rogoff, *Museum Culture*; and Vergo, *The New Museology*.

16 Foucault, "Governmentality."

17 Bennett, "The Exhibitionary Complex"; *The Birth of the Museum*, esp. 61–88; *Culture*, chap. 5.

18 See, for example, Hooper-Greenhill, *Museums and the Shaping of Knowledge*; and Taylor, *Art for the Nation*. Recent critiques can be found in Bennett, *Pasts beyond Memory*; Conn, *Museums and American Intellectual Life, 1876–1926*, 11–12; Kriegel, "After the Exhibitionary Complex"; Luke, *Museum Politics*; and Starn, "A Historian's Brief Guide to New Museum Studies," 68–98, esp. 74. See also Arnold, *Culture and Anarchy*, in which the author asserts that "culture suggests the idea of the state" (79).

19 Felix Driver and David Gilbert consider South Kensington as a heart of empire in their "Heart of Empire?"

20 Antoinette Burton offers a comprehensive overview and analysis of this literature in "Introduction"; she addresses the relationships between cultural and social history in "Thinking beyond the Boundaries."

21 See, for example, Barringer, "The South Kensington Museum and the Colonial Project"; Pagani, "Chinese Material Culture and British Perceptions of China in the Mid–Nineteenth Century"; Clunas, "China in Britain"; and Mitter and Clunas, "The Empire of Things."

22 Richards, *The Imperial Archive*.

23 See, for instance, Barringer and Flynn, *Colonialism and the Object*; Baker and Richardson, *A Grand Design*; and the critique by Saumarez Smith, Waterfield, Barringer, and Baker, "The Victoria and Albert Museum."

24 *Report of the Select Committee on Arts and Manufactures* (1835), iii.

25 Barringer has called for an examination of the museum in this light in "Re-presenting the Imperial Archive," 357–73.

26 Bizup's *Manufacturing Culture* reconsiders culture as a defense of industry.

27 Agnew, *Worlds Apart*, 12.

28 Ibid. See also Gagnier, *The Insatiability of Human Wants*; Haskell,

"Capitalism and the Origins of the Humanitarian Sensibility, Parts I and II"; and Poovey, *Making a Social Body*.

29 Haskell and Teichgraeber, *The Culture of the Market*, introduction, esp. 2.

30 Notable exceptions include Finn, *The Character of Credit*; and Reddy, *The Rise of Market Culture*.

31 Rule, "The Property of Skill in the Period of Manufacture," 99–118; McClelland, "Some Thoughts on Masculinity and the 'Representative Artisan' in Britain, 1850–1880," 165–77.

32 This notion is often associated with Bourdieu's *Distinction* (1984), but he developed the understanding in his earlier writings on education published in the 1960s, as Calhoun's "Habitus, Field, and Capital," Harker's "Bourdieu: Education and Reproduction," and Robbins's *The Work of Pierre Bourdieu* show.

33 Pevsner, *High Victorian Design*. For another classic study that portrays 1851 as a turning point, if not a beginning, see Steegman, *Victorian Taste*. Paul Greenhalgh has argued that 1851 should be considered the starting point for the history of design criticism (*Ephemeral Vistas*, 143). Deborah Cohen offers a different trajectory in her recent *Household Gods*. See esp. the introduction and chapter 1.

34 Weiner, *English Culture and the Decline of the Industrial Spirit, 1850–1980*.

35 Debord, *The Society of the Spectacle*; Richards, *The Commodity Culture of Victorian England*, chap. 1. For a critical approach to spectacle and labor, see Hoffenberg, "Equipoise and Its Discontents," 40, 51, 55, 59.

36 Prominent works that take 1851 as their beginning include Auerbach, *The Great Exhibition of 1851*; Greenhalgh, *Ephemeral Vistas*; Hoffenberg, *An Empire on Display*; and Richards, *The Commodity Culture of Victorian England*. In *English Culture and the Decline of the Industrial Spirit*, Wiener argues, conversely, that the exhibition was an end, not a beginning. For a more general history that foregrounds 1851, consult Best, *Mid-Victorian Britain, 1851–1875*.

37 Purbrick, "Introduction," esp. 4–5; Barringer, *Men at Work*, 13–14.

38 This literature is vast. See, for instance, the works listed in note 35. Similarly, in *On Exhibit*, her study of Victorian museums, Black notes the "intense visuality of Victorian London" (24).

39 Hewitt, "Victorian Studies," 137–61. See also Finn, "When Was the Nineteenth Century Where?"; Hewitt, "Why the Notion of Victorian Britain *Does* Make Sense"; McWilliam, "What is Interdisciplinary about Victorian History Today?"

40 Taylor, "Introduction," esp. 3–7; Burton, "The Revival of Interest in Victorian Decorative Art and the Victoria and Albert Museum"; Briggs, *Victorian Things*; Schmiechen, "The Victorians, the Historians, and the Idea of Modernism."

41 Barlow and Wilson, "Consuming Empire?" 156–71, esp. 157; Black, *On*

Exhibit, 7; Conforti, "The Idealist Enterprise and the Applied Arts," 23–47, esp. 27.

42 Hewitt, "Victorian Studies," 141–42; Taylor and Wolff, *The Victorians since 1901*; Rieger and Daunton, "Introduction," esp. 2–3, 7.

43 See, notably, the debate in *Social History* from the early 1990s, including Mayfield and Thorne, "Social History and Its Discontents," 165–88; Taylor, "The Poverty of Protest," 1–15; Joyce, "The Imaginary Discontents of Social History," 81–86; Mayfield and Thorne, "Reply to 'The Poverty of Protest' and 'Imaginary Discontents,'" 219–33; and Vernon, "Who's Afraid of the 'Linguistic Turn'?" 81–97; as well as Epstein's recent reappraisal, *In Practice*, 3–4. See also Burton, "Thinking beyond the Boundaries," 65; and Kent, "Victorian Social History," 97–134.

44 See, notably, Stedman Jones, *Languages of Class*; Joyce, *Visions of the People*; and Joyce, *Democratic Subjects*. On Stedman Jones and Joyce, see Epstein, *In Practice*, chaps. 1 and 2.

45 Jones, "Peter Mandler's 'Problem with Cultural History'; or, Is Playtime Over?" 209–15, esp. 210–11. French scholarship includes Reddy, *The Rise of Market Culture*; Scott, *Gender and the Politics of History*; and Sewell, *Work and Revolution in France*.

46 Williams, *Culture and Society, 1780–1950*; Thompson, *The Making of the English Working Class*. On Thompson and this earlier moment in cultural history, see Dworkin, *Cultural Marxism in Postwar Britain*; and Epstein, *In Practice*, introduction. See also Burke, *What Is Cultural History?* 24, 40; and Eley, *A Crooked Line*, 19, 31, 49, 57, 194.

47 Burke, *What Is Cultural History?* 81; Eley, *A Crooked Line*, 196.

48 Eley, *A Crooked Line*, 185. On the turn in the social sciences more generally, see Suny, "Back and Beyond"; and Ray and Sayer, "Introduction," 1–24.

49 Epstein, *In Practice*, 7.

50 Scott, *Gender and the Politics of History*; Steedman, *Landscape for a Good Woman*; Walkowitz, *City of Dreadful Delight*. For works that address the stakes of this historiography more generally, see Maza, "Stories in History," 1493–1515; Eley, *A Crooked Line*, 157, 171–81; and Joyce, "Introduction," esp. 3.

51 Rogers, "Victorian Studies in the United Kingdom," 246.

52 Hewitt, "Victorian Studies," 142.

53 Epstein, *In Practice*, 12. See also Eley, *A Crooked Line*, 11.

54 Burn, *The Age of Equipoise*. Hewitt offers a reappraisal in "Prologue," esp. 7–11, 26. See also Barringer, "Equipoise and the Object," 68–83.

55 A sampling of important new work on liberalism and reform includes Bailkin, *The Culture of Property*; Bailkin, "The Place of Liberalism"; Durbach, *Bodily Matters*, chap. 3; and Kahan, *Liberalism in Nineteenth-Century Europe*.

56 Burke, *What Is Cultural History?* 114; Eley, *A Crooked Line*, 197–203.

57 Bonnell and Hunt, *Beyond the Cultural Turn*, 11, 26. Other new directions are offered in Walkowitz, "The Cultural Turn and a New Social History"; and Mandler, "The Problem with Cultural History."

58 Conway, *Travels in South Kensington*, 34, 60.

59 By employing an institutional narrative that represents an older variety of cultural history, I do not mean to limit the concerns that this book entertains. Instead, I aim to redress those criticisms of the new cultural history that question its representativeness and emphasize its eccentricities. For this line of critique, see Mandler, "The Problem with Cultural History."

60 Curtis, *Visual Words*.

61 Gagnier, *The Insatiability of Human Wants*, esp. introduction, chap. 1, chap. 4.

Chapter One CONFIGURING DESIGN

1 Bell, *Schools of Design*, 72–73.

2 Physick, "The Government School of Design," 14–19, esp. 14.

3 On the committee and its composition, see Gretton, "Art Is Cheaper and Goes Lower in France"; Rifkin, "Success Disavowed"; and Bell, *Schools of Design*, chap. 4.

4 *Report from the Select Committee on Arts and Their Connection with Manufactures* (1836), iii–v.

5 Northcote, "Schools of Design," 475.

6 "South Kensington Museum," *Post*, 22 June 1857, Press Cuttings, Archive of Art and Design, London (hereafter AAD PC) (March 1856—February 1859, vol. 1), 27.

7 Conway, *Travels in South Kensington*, 3.

8 Cardoso Denis, "Drawing or Design," 20–24, esp. 23.

9 Bermingham, *Learning to Draw*, 6, 230–35, 246; Cardoso Denis, "The Educated Eye and the Industrial Hand."

10 See Rifkin, "Success Disavowed"; and Frayling and Catterall, *Design of the Times*. Leading histories of art institutions include Barlow and Trodd, *Governing Cultures*; Hemingway and Vaughan, *Art in Bourgeois Society, 1790–1850*; Hoock, *The King's Artists*; Pointon, *Art Apart*; and Taylor, *Art for the Nation*.

11 Bell, *Schools of Design*, 1–2.

12 Brown, *South Kensington and Its Art Training*, 4.

13 Bermingham, *Learning to Draw*, x.

14 Goldstein, *Teaching Art*, 12, chap. 8. See also Pevsner, *Academies of Art, Past and Present*.

15 Bell, *Schools of Design*, 1–2.

16 Haydon, *The Diary of Benjamin Robert Haydon*, 5:447.

17 My thanks go to Tim Barringer for this phrasing.

18 Altick, *The Shows of London*; *Report from the Select Committee on National Monuments and Works of Art*; Crary, *Techniques of the Observer*.

19 Bermingham, *Learning to Draw*, 134–41, esp. 134.

20 Crossick, "Past Masters," 26–28.

21 For Haydon's debtor history and his dramatic rendering of debt, see Finn, *The Character of Credit*.

22 Haydon, *The Diary of Benjamin Robert Haydon*, 4:355.

23 Ibid., 5:96–97.

24 Sandby, *The History of the Royal Academy of Arts*, 1:87; see also Leslie, *The Inner Life of the Royal Academy*, 270.

25 Hoock, *The King's Artists*; "Reforming Culture," 254–55.

26 Barrell, "Benjamin Robert Haydon," 253–90; *The Political Theory of Painting from Reynolds to Hazlitt*, 313.

27 Bell, *Schools of Design*, 43.

28 "Epitaph of a Great Man," Huntington MS 45445, Huntington Library, San Marino, California.

29 Bell, *Schools of Design*, 43.

30 Taylor, *Life of Benjamin Robert Haydon*, 1:171; Symonds, *Little Memoirs of the Nineteenth Century*, 58–60; Haydon, *Lectures on Painting and Design*, 2:144.

31 Munford, *William Ewart, MP*.

32 Haydon, *The Diary of Benjamin Robert Haydon*, 4:356, 600.

33 Gretton, "Art Is Cheaper and Goes Lower in France," 84.

34 *Report of the Select Committee on Arts and Manufactures* (1836), 88–92; *Report of the Select Committee on Arts and Manufactures* (1835), 7–8; Letter from Benjamin Robert Haydon to Robert Southey, 28 July 1835, MS2529, National Library of Scotland, Edinburgh. For the countervailing argument, see Shee, *A Letter to Joseph Hume*.

35 *Report of the Select Committee on Arts and Manufactures* (1836), 93–95.

36 Haydon, *Lectures on Painting and Design*, 1:x.

37 Haydon, *The Diary of Benjamin Robert Haydon*, 4:404.

38 Haydon, *Lectures on Painting and Design*, 1:34–35.

39 Haydon, *The Diary of Benjamin Robert Haydon*, 5:207.

40 Haydon, "The School of Design," manuscript, 88.JJ.10, National Art Library (NAL).

41 Haydon, *Lectures on Painting and Design*, 1:34–35.

42 *Report of the Select Committee of the House of Commons on the Earl of Elgin's Collection of Sculptured Marbles*, 70–71.

43 Haydon, "The School of Design."

44 Hance, *An Address to the Leading Men of Manchester*, 4, 8.

45 Nicholls, *National Drawing Master*, 25; Hay, *Geometric Beauty of the Human Figure*; Howard, *Imitative Art; or, the Means of Representing the Pictorial Appearances of Objects*; Cheesman, *Rudiments of Drawing the Human Figure*; Bartolozzi, *Thirty-Four Lessons for Drawing the Human Figure*. For the latter part of the century, see Fowler, *Portrait and Figure Painting*, 1; Hicks, *A Guide to Figure-Drawing*; Warren, *An Artistic Treatise on the Human Figure*, 11; and Warren, *Artistic Anatomy of the Human Figure*.

46 Philips, *Rudiments of Curvilinear Design*. For a later discussion, see Warren, *An Artistic Treatise on the Human Figure*, 11.

47 *Select Committee on Arts and Manufactures* (1836), 52.

48 Haydon, *Lectures on Painting and Design*, 1:2.

49 Kriz, *The Idea of the English Landscape Painter*, chaps. 3 and 4 (see also 7, 141).

50 Grant, *Drawing for Young Children* (1848); Hicks, *Guide to Figure Drawing*, 6, 8; Howard, *Imitative Art*; *The School of Arts Improv'd*, 1.

51 Haydon, *Lectures on Painting and Design*, 1:2-3.

52 Haydon, *The Diary of Benjamin Robert Haydon*, 1:532; Haydon, *Lectures on Painting and Design*, 1:21.

53 Haydon, *The Diary of Benjamin Robert Haydon*, 5:81-82.

54 Ibid., 447.

55 Clark, *The Struggle for the Breeches*, chaps. 9, 11-12; Epstein, *Radical Expression*.

56 Lewis, *An Address on the Subject of Education*, 3-4.

57 Behagg, *Politics and Production in the Early Nineteenth Century*, 4, 45, 49, 64, 223; Crossick, "Past Masters," 1-40; Prothero, *Radical Artisans in England and France*, chaps. 1, 4, 8, 11.

58 Hannigan, *The Artisan of Lyons; or, Love's Traces*, esp. 2, 4.

59 "The Sketcher" [John Eagles], "Schools of Design," 584-85.

60 "Drawing from Models," *Punch* 4 (1843): 104; "High Art," *Punch* 12 (1847): 25. See also "Art as Applied to Twelfth-Cakes," *Punch* 14 (1848): 15.

61 *Minutes of the Council of the Government School of Design*, 1:1, 10; "School of Design," *Art Union*, no. 6 (1839): 106.

62 Gretton, "Art Is Cheaper and Goes Lower in France," 98.

63 *Minutes of the Council of the Government School of Design*, 1:11. See also Bell, *Schools of Design*, 67, 72.

64 Haydon, *Correspondence and Table Talk*, 2:234.

65 *Minutes of the Council of the Government School of Design*, 1:3, 7, 11, 14-16, 68; Letter from C. R. Cockerell to Charles Poulett Thompson, 14 July 1837, British Library Add. Ms. 31218, ff. 51-52; f. 59.

66 *Mechanics' Magazine*, 1837, AAD PC (1837-1852), f. 1.

67 On the acerbic contest between Joseph Hume and the Royal Academy, see Shee, *A Letter to Joseph Hume*; and Letter from Charles Poulett Thompson to William Ewart, 1 November 1836, British Library Add. Ms. 31218, f. 10.

68 Altick, *The Shows of London*, 132; McCalman, *Radical Underworld*, chap. 10; Sheppard, *London*, 359.

69 On the rooms for the School of Design, see Board of Trade Letters, 30 June 1837, 24 July 1837, BT 3/27, National Archives, Kew, London (hereafter

NA); Minutes of the Committee of Trade, Board of Trade, 14 February 1837 and 7 March 1837, NA BT5/44, f. 201, ff. 232-33. See also "Somerset House," *Penny Magazine of the Society for the Diffusion of Useful Knowledge* 1 (3) (14 April 1832): 17; and Charles Knight, *Pictorial Half-Hours of London Topography*, 30.

70 Smith, *The Victorian Nude*, 25-28, 48-51; Nead, *The Female Nude*, 3, 46-55; Smith, *Exposed*.

71 See Haydon, *Correspondence and Table-Talk*, 198-200; Letter from William Dyce to Charles Poulett Thompson, 20 February 1839, British Library Add. Mss. 31218, ff. 87-88; *Minutes of the Council of the Government School of Design*, 1:41, 46, 51.

72 Pointon, *William Dyce*.

73 Dyce, *Report Made to the Rt. Hon. C. Poulett Thompson on Foreign Schools of Design for Manufacture*, 38-40. See also "Life, Correspondence, and Writings of William Dyce," Aberdeen Art Gallery (hereafter "Life of William Dyce), 1:193-94.

74 Haydon, *The Diary of Benjamin Robert Haydon*, 5:217, 333, 433.

75 Dyce, *Introduction to the Drawing-Book of the School of Design*, viii.

76 Dyce, *Report Made to the Rt. Hon. C. Poulett Thompson on Foreign Schools of Design for Manufacture*, 8.

77 Cardoso Denis, "The Educated Eye and the Industrial Hand."

78 Dyce and Wilson, *Letter to Lord Meadowbank*, 3.

79 Ibid., 23-29. See also Wilson, *Address Delivered in the Government Branch School of Design at Spitalfields*, 4-5.

80 Dyce and Wilson, *Letter to Lord Meadowbank*, 50-53, 31-32. See also Dyce, *Report Made to the Rt. Hon. C. Poulett Thompson on Foreign Schools of Design for Manufacture*, 11, 32.

81 Hay, cited in Edwards, *The Fine Arts in England*, 102.

82 Crossick, *An Artisan Elite in Victorian Society*, 135.

83 "Artistic Ambition," *Decorator's Assistant* 3 (16 September 1848): 201.

84 Dyce, *Report Made to the Rt. Hon. C. Poulett Thompson on Foreign Schools of Design for Manufacture*, 21, 28-29, 40. See also Richards, "A True Siberia."

85 Frayling, *The Royal College of Art*, 17; *Minutes of the Council of the Government School of Design*, 1:62.

86 Mackenzie, *General Observations on the Principles of Education for the Use of Mechanics' Institutions*, 94.

87 Haydon, *The Diary of Benjamin Robert Haydon*, 5:81, 217, 433. On the German example in high art, and especially fresco painting, see Winter, "German Fresco Painting and the New Houses of Parliament."

88 "School of Design," *Illustrated London News* 2 (56) (1843): 375-76.

89 "Life of William Dyce," 1:210-12, 217-18.

90 *Report of the Council of the School of Design, 1842-43*, 3-4.

91 "Life of William Dyce," 1:217-19, 262.

92 Dyce, *Introduction to the Drawing-Book of the School of Design*.

93 Grant, *Drawing for Young Children*; *A Catechism of Drawing, with the Necessary Explanations of the Principal Terms in the Art*, 4.

94 *Handbook of Pencil Drawing Intended as Key to All Drawing Books Which Have No Written Instruction*, iii–iv, 7; Wallis, "Lecture on the Cultivation of a Popular Taste in the Fine Arts of Painting and Sculpture," 74.

95 On the class and disciplinary aspects of midcentury drawing books, see Cardoso Denis, "An Industrial Vision"; Grant, *Drawing for Young Children* (1862 ed.), 21; Harding, *Elementary Art*, 1, 5, 4; Howard, *Imitative Art*, iv; Smith, *The Art of Drawing in Its Various Branches*, iii; and Taylor, *A Familiar Treatise on Drawing for Youth*. See also Wallis, "Art Education for the People, No. 1"; and "Publications Committee: Copy of Minutes and Extracts of Correspondence, 1830–1834," Papers of the Society for the Diffusion of Useful Knowledge, University College, London, 1.

96 Dyce, *Introduction to the Drawing-Book of the School of Design*, 34, 38–40, 46–47.

97 Cardoso Denis, "The Educated Eye and the Industrial Hand," introduction, 42, 103.

98 Dyce, *Introduction to the Drawing-Book of the School of Design*, x–xi, xx, xxii.

99 Ibid., x.

100 On the drawing book's future, see Bell, *The Schools of Design*, 88; Cardoso Denis, "The Educated Eye and the Industrial Hand"; and Macdonald, *History and Philosophy of Art Education*, 122.

101 Pointon, *William Dyce*, 52.

102 Dyce, *Introduction to the Drawing-Book of the School of Design*, 31.

103 Haydon, *The Diary of Benjamin Robert Haydon*, 4:416–17.

104 See, for example, Letters from Haydon, 1 September 1837 and 21 September 1837, Papers of the Royal Manchester Institution, Central Library, Manchester (hereafter RMI), M6/1/51/162 and M6/1/51/163; and Haydon, "Syllabus of Six Lectures on the History of Art and Design to Be Delivered in the Hall of the Society," 10 December 1839, RMI M6/1/170/17. On the RMI, see Reilly, *People's History of Manchester*; and Sutherland, *The Royal Manchester Institution, Its Origin, Its Character, and Its Aims*. On cultural capital in this Victorian city, see Seed, "'Commerce and the Liberal Arts'"; Gunn, *The Public Culture of the Victorian Middle Class*; MacLeod, *Art and the Victorian Middle Class*; and Hill, *Culture and Class in English Public Museums*.

105 Haydon in the *Manchester Guardian*, 13 September 1837, excerpted in Hance, *An Address to the 'Leading Men of Manchester*,' 3–4, 8.

106 Jackson, *On the Means of Improving Public Taste*, 6–8, 17, 28–29.

107 Letter from James Thomson to Charles Poulett Thompson, 8 June 1838, British Library Add. Ms. 31218, ff. 75–76; Crozier, "Recollections of the

Manchester School of Design," Central Library, Manchester; Murgatroyd, *Remarks Concerning the Manchester School of Art and Schools of Art Generally*, 1–3; Macdonald, *History of Art Education*, 84–88.

108 *Minutes of the Council of the Government School of Design*, 190–99; "Life of William Dyce," 1:294–96.

109 Crozier, "Recollections of the Manchester School of Design."

110 Haydon, *Correspondence and Table-Talk*, 1:446–47.

111 See Bell, *The Schools of Design*, chap. 9; Macdonald, *The History and Philosophy of Art Education*, 96–98; and Physick, "The Government School of Design," 17.

112 See Wilson, *Letter to Lord Meadowbank*, 23–26; and Wilson, *Address Delivered in the Government Branch School of Design at Spitalfields*, 8–9.

113 Richardson, *A Letter Addressed to the Council of the Head Government School of Design*, 7.

114 Northcote, "Schools of Design," 492.

115 "The School of Design," *Punch* 9 (1845): 21; "The School of Bad Designs," *Punch* 9 (1845): 70; "The School of Bad Designs," *Punch* 9 (1845): 117. See also "The Chinese Exhibition at Knightsbridge," *Punch* 3 (1842): 185.

116 Richardson, *A Letter Addressed to the Council of the Head Government School of Design*, 4–5, 7.

117 *Minutes of the Council of the Government School of Design*, 1:248.

118 Alpha, *Times of London*, 30 May 1845; Alpha, "Schools of Design," *Times of London*, 14 May 1845; Bell, *The Schools of Design*, chap. 9, esp. 156, 160.

119 Rifkin, "Success Disavowed," 89–102, esp. 100.

120 Bell, *Schools of Design*, 168.

121 Alpha, "School of Design," *Times of London*, 13 May 1845; Alpha, *Times of London*, 30 May 1845. On the authorship of these pieces, see Bell, *The Schools of Design*, 155.

122 Haydon, *The Diary of Benjamin Robert Haydon*, 5:447.

123 See, for example, Wallis, *A Letter to the Council of the Manchester School of Design*, 25–27; and *Fifth Report of the Council of the School of Design for the Year 1845–46*, 20, 22.

124 *Minutes of the Council of the Government School of Design*, 1:69, 377.

125 *Fourth Report of the Council of the School of Design*, 10; *Report of the Council of the School of Design, 1842–43*, 4.

126 *Report of the Select Committee on the School of Design*, 99.

127 Chancellor, *Master and Artisan in Victorian England*, 2, 13–20.

128 Miller, *The Training of a Craftsman*, 8–9.

129 On these points, see also Bermingham, *The Consumption of Culture*; and Taylor, *Art for the Nation*, chap. 2.

130 For a canny analysis of the *Penny Magazine*, see Anderson, *The Printed Image and the Transformation of Popular Culture*, introduction, chap. 2. On the execution of these developments, see Beegan, "The Mechanization of the Image."

131 *Report of the Select Committee on Arts and Manufactures* (1836), vi, 49–51.

132 "The Commercial History of a *Penny Magazine*, No. 2," *Penny Magazine* 2 (101) (30 September 1833–31 October 1833): 420–21; Benjamin, "The Work of Art in the Age of Mechanical Reproduction." On the democracy of print and image in the nineteenth century, see Altick, *The English Common Reader*; and Curtis, *Visual Words*.

133 "National Gallery," *Penny Magazine* 2 (58) (31 January 1833–28 February 1833): 73–75, esp. 73; "British Museum," *Penny Magazine* 5 (290) (8 October 1836): 395.

134 Fox, *Graphic Journalism in England during the 1830s and 1840s*, 12–13. For a later discussion of these developments, see Barringer, *Men at Work*, 148.

135 "Leonardo da Vinci," *Penny Magazine* 3 (124) (8 March 1834): 92–94.

136 "Gratuitous Exhibition of Pictures," *Penny Magazine* 10 (570) (20 February 1841): 68–69; "Bernard Palissy," *Penny Magazine* 13 (773) (20 April 1844): 151–52, and 13 (774) (27 April 1844): 155–56; Morley, *Palissy the Potter*.

137 "Small Things," *Penny Magazine* 4 (234) (28 November 1835): 462–63.

138 "West's Pictures in the National Gallery," *Penny Magazine* 7 (399) (1837): 236–37.

139 "A Poor Student's Literary Ways and Means," *Penny Magazine* 4 (204) (7 June 1835): 218–19. On sign painting and aesthetic hierarchy, see Conlin, "'At the Expense of the Public.'"

140 See, for example, Crossick, *An Artisan Elite in Victorian Society*, 135.

141 Viollet-le-Duc, *Learning to Draw*. See also "Drawing," *Saturday Review*, 4 September 1880, AAD PC (September 1880–January 1882): 202.

142 *Report from the Select Committee on the School of Design*, 149, 308.

143 B., "On the Government Schools of Design," *Art Journal* 11 (September 1849): 270–71, esp. 270. See also Pearson, *The State and the Visual Arts*, 16; and Minihan, *The Nationalization of Culture*, 49–50, 103.

144 *Report from the Select Committee on the School of Design*, 89, 115, 175, 223.

145 Sparkes, *Schools of Art*, 53.

146 *Report from the Select Committee on the School of Design*, iii; B., "On the Government Schools of Design."

147 *Report from the Select Committee on the School of Design*, 12, 90, 173, 195, 322.

Chapter Two ORIGINALITY AND SIN

1 *Report from the Select Committee on Copyright of Designs* (hereafter SCCD), 20–36, 82–99, esp. 20, 92, 94.

2 Cooke Taylor, "Copyright in Design," 59–60.

3 Ibid., 59.

4 Greysmith, "Patterns, Piracy, and Protection in the Textile Printing Industry." See also "A Day at a Lancashire Print-Work," *Penny Magazine* 12 (727) (July 1843): 289–96.

5 Appadurai, "Commodities and the Politics of Value."

6 Berg, "From Imitation to Invention"; Burke, *Lifebuoy Men, Lux Women*, 3, 116; Mukerji, *From Graven Images*, chaps. 1, 5, and 6.

7 Berg, "New Commodities, Luxuries, and Their Consumers in Eighteenth-Century England"; Berg, "In Pursuit of Luxury"; Cox, *The Complete Tradesman*; Kowaleski-Wallace, *Consuming Subjects*; Wills, "European Consumption and Asian Production in the Seventeenth and Eighteenth Centuries," 133–47.

8 Lemire, *Dress, Culture, and Commerce*, 6–7; *Fashion's Favourite*, chaps. 1 and 3.

9 On this and other luxuries, see Agnew, "Coming up for Air," 19–39; Berg, *Luxury and Pleasure in Eighteenth-Century England*; Berg and Clifford, "Introduction"; Berg, "New Commodities, Luxuries, and Their Consumers"; Campbell, *The Romantic Ethic and the Spirit of Modern Consumerism*; Fine and Leopold, "Consumerism and the Industrial Revolution"; Kwass, "Big Hair"; and McKendrick, Brewer, and Plumb, *Birth of a Consumer Society*.

10 Berg, "New Commodities, Luxuries, and Their Consumers," 64, 68; Cox, *The Complete Tradesman*, chap. 7, esp. 198–202.

11 See McKendrick, "The Consumer Revolution of Eighteenth-Century England," 9–33; and "The Commercialization of Fashion," 34–99.

12 Mackie, *Market à la Mode*, 4, 13, 15, 41, 45. On luxury more generally, see Berg, *Luxury and Pleasure in Eighteenth-Century Britain*.

13 J. Roberts, *The Spinster*, quoted in Turnbull, *A History of the Calico Printing Industry of Great Britain*, 21.

14 Defoe, *Weekly Review*, quoted in Wood and Wilmore, *The Romance of the Cotton Industry in England*, 46.

15 David Greysmith, "Patterns, Piracy, and Protection," 165. See also Styles, "Manufacturing, Consumption, and Design in Eighteenth-Century England," 527–54.

16 Lemire, *Fashion's Favourite*, chaps. 1 and 2. On similar duties imposed to protect the silk trade, see Calico Printer, *Letter to the Rt. Hon. Lord Althorp*, 11.

17 On the inefficacy of the laws, see Wills, "European Consumption and Asian Production," 137.

18 Wood and Wilmore, *Romance of the Cotton Industry*, 48.

19 Potter, *Calico Printing as an Art Manufacture*, 7; Chapman, *The Lancashire Cotton Industry*, 49–52; Greysmith, "Patterns, Piracy, and Protection"; Lemire, *Fashion's Favourite*, chaps. 1 and 2; Wood and Wilmore, *Romance of the Cotton Industry*, 48.

20 Turnbull, *History of the Calico Printing Industry*, 21. See also Berg, "New Commodities, Luxuries, and Their Consumers," 77–78.

21 "The Calico Printer," *The Book of English Trades and Library of the Useful Arts*, 65–69.

22 O'Brien, *The British Manufacturer's Companion and Callico Printer's Assistant*; A Person Concerned in Trade, *A Complete History of the Cotton Trade*, 100.

23 On the cylinder, see A Person Concerned in Trade, *A Complete History of the Cotton Trade*, 162–65. For a sense of the inventive activity around the printing trade, see the notices of patents in *London Journal of Arts and Sciences; and Repertory of Patent Inventions* (1839–1843). See also Styles, "What Was New?" 301.

24 Potter, *Calico Printing as an Art Manufacture*, 13–14; Thomson, *A Letter to the Rt. Hon. Sir Richard Lalor Sheil*, 6. On mechanical developments, see also Chapman, "Quantity versus Quality in the British Industrial Revolution," 175–92; Chapman, *The Cotton Industry in the Industrial Revolution*; Clark, "The Design and Designing of Lancashire Printed Calicoes during the First Half of the Nineteenth Century," 101–18; Forty, *Objects of Desire*, chap. 3; Greysmith, "Patterns, Piracy, and Protection"; and Turnbull, *History of the Calico Printing Industry*.

25 "A Day at a Lancashire Print-Work," 295.

26 Chapman and Chassagne, *European Textile Printers of the Eighteenth Century*, 78.

27 Farnie, *The English Cotton Industry and the World Market*, 97. See also Potter, *Calico Printing as an Art Manufacture*, 24, 38; and Wills, "European Consumption and Asian Production," 139–40.

28 See Lemire, *Fashion's Favourite*, 29–42; Clark, "Design and Designing of Lancashire Printed Calicoes"; and Turnbull, *A History of the Calico Printing Industry*, chap. 5.

29 Potter, *Calico Printing as an Art Manufacture*, 24.

30 Thomson, *Notes on the Present State of Calico Printing in Belgium*, 21.

31 On the pervasiveness of this practice, see Berg, "From Imitation to Invention," 24; and Greysmith, "Patterns, Piracy, and Protection," 166.

32 O'Brien, *British Manufacturer's Companion*; Thomson, *Letter to the Rt. Hon. Sir Robert Peel*, 6–7.

33 Thomson, *Letter to Sheil*, 1, 4–5; SCCD, 168; see also Farnie, *The English Cotton Industry and the World Market*, chap. 2.

34 Snodin, "Who Led Taste?" 369.

35 "Copyright of Designs," *Art Journal* 12 (January 1850): 14–16, esp. 14; *Report from the Select Committee on Arts and Manufactures* (1835), 16, 28.

36 *Report from the Select Committee on Arts and Manufactures* (1835), 11, 16, 27–28, 66, 92. Attempts to extend the copyright in 1821 and 1837–38 had failed. See Greysmith, "Patterns, Piracy, and Protection," 166.

37 Tennent, *A Treatise on the Copyright of Designs for Printed Fabrics*, 18. For a detailed description of the 1839 act, see *London Journal of Arts and Sciences and Patent Register* 15 (92) (1840): 106–16; and *London Journal of Arts and Sciences and Patent Register* 16 (99) (1840): 95–98. See also Trade Letters, Board of Trade, 3 May 1838, BT 3/27, National Archives, Kew, London (hereafter NA).

38 *Hansard Parliamentary Debates*, 3d ser., vol. 61 (1842), col. 675.

39 Forty, *Objects of Desire*, chap. 3.

40 Babbage, *On the Economy of Machinery and Manufactures*, 69. See also Forty, *Objects of Desire*, 55. On Babbage, see Purbrick, "The Dream Machine."

41 Benjamin, "The Work of Art in the Age of Mechanical Reproduction."

42 *Hansard Parliamentary Debates*, 3d ser., vol. 51 (1839), col. 1263.

43 Albisetti, "The 'Inevitable Schwabes.'"

44 SCCD, 6, 12–13.

45 *Report from the Select Committee on Arts and Manufactures* (1835), 121–22; "Original Designs for Manufactures," *Journal of Design and Manufactures* 3 (13) (March 1850): 32.

46 SCCD, 361–62; Tennent, *Treatise on the Copyright of Designs*, xiv–xv, 1–17, chap. 5.

47 Ibid., 518. On duration, fashion, and industrialization, see Perot, *Fashioning the Bourgeoisie*, 24–25, 183.

48 SCCD, 100, 108.

49 Ibid., 114, 116, 518.

50 Snodin, "Who Led Taste?: Georgian Britain, 1714–1837," 217–46; Clifford, "The Printed Illustrated Catalogue"; Kusamitsu, "British Industrialization and Design before the Great Exhibition," 77–95, esp. 85.

51 On the development of visual practices of display in the eighteenth century and before, see Cox with Walsh, *The Complete Tradesman*, chap. 3. See also Walsh's "Shop Design and the Display of Goods in Eighteenth-Century London." Two notable works for the later period, when the department store epitomized consuming modernity, are Rappaport, *Shopping for Pleasure*; and Walkowitz, "Going Public." The testimony produced in the design copyright debate suggests that this middle period was one of both continuities and changes in retail culture. On this historiography and its effects, see Finn, "Sex and the City."

52 SCCD, 9, 32, 41, 290, 399.

53 James Thomson, *Letter to Peel*, 12; "Copyright," *Art Union* no. 40 (May 1842): 95–97, esp. 95.

54 SCCD, 120–21.

55 SCCD, 39–41, 49, 290, 399, "Speech of James Emerson Tennent," *Morning Post*, 30 January 1843, James Emerson Tennent Papers, Public Record Office of Northern Ireland (hereafter PRONI), Belfast, D2922/C/9/5. On calico and the wish to compete in the international marketplace, see Greg, *Not Overproduction but Deficient Consumption, the Source of Our Sufferings*, 26.

56 Thomson, *Letter to Peel*, 10.

57 *Report from the Select Committee on Arts and Manufactures* (1835), 65.

58 "Speech of James Emerson Tennent," *Morning Post*. For discussions of the formation of French national definition around the category of taste, see Auslander, *Taste and Power*; and Walton, *France at the Crystal Palace*.

59 Brace, *Observations on Extension of Protection of Copyright of Designs*, 3.

60 Greysmith, "Patterns, Piracy, and Protection," 167; "Obituaries of Eminent Manufacturers: Memoir of the Late James Thomson, Esq., F.R.S., of Clitheroe," *Journal of Design and Manufactures* 4 (November 1850): 65–72, esp. 65.

61 Thomson, *Letter to Peel*, 4–5, 15, 52–53; *Letter to Sheil*, 21–23. See also Senior et al., *From the Report of the Commissioners of Hand-Loom Weaving on Improvement of Designs and Patterns and Extension of Copyright*.

62 Scott, "Art and Industry."

63 Colley, *Britons*.

64 Stephen Greenblatt developed this notion at length in *Renaissance Self-Fashioning*, 1, 6, 9.

65 SCCD, 161–67, 356.

66 Potter, *A Letter to Mark Philips, Esq.*, 18.

67 Letter from Augustus Applegath to James Emerson Tennent, 26 January 1843, James Emerson Tennent Papers, PRONI D2922/C/9/4; SCCD, 106, 161–63, 184–87.

68 Ibid.

69 Ditz, "Shipwrecked"; Kuchta, *The Three-Piece Suit and Modern Masculinity*. On masculinity and craft production, see McClelland, "Some Thoughts on Masculinity and the 'Representative Artisan' in Britain."

70 Although Thomson and Potter sought to correlate artisanal structure and good design, they did not necessarily oppose industrial labor regimes and their labor politics. Later in his career, Thomson would lead a campaign to extend the hours of children laboring in print works. See "Obituaries of Eminent Manufacturers," 67.

71 This line of argument on Potter's behalf is puzzling, or perhaps disingenuous, for, according to David Greysmith, Potter was among the first printers to dispense with blocks. See Greysmith, "Patterns, Piracy, and Protection," 183.

72 Potter's life and affiliations are well documented in Hurst, *Edmund Potter and Dinting Vale* (see esp. chaps. 3 and 5).

73 SCCD, 20–23, 33, 493–94. On the persistence of hand labor, see Samuel, "The Workshop of the World."

74 These phrases are taken from Poovey, "Figures of Arithmetic, Figures of Speech." See also Poovey, *Making a Social Body*, esp. chaps. 1, 3, and 6.

75 SCCD, 20–23, 33, 493–94.

76 Ibid., 204–5.

77 SCCD, 21–22, 493–94, 458–68, 496–97. A statistician for the opposition called Potter's findings into question.

78 Thomson, *Letter to Sheil*, 20.

79 Rule, "The Property of Skill in the Period of Manufacture," 99–118.

80 Coulter, *Property in Ideas*; Macleod, *Inventing the Industrial Revolution*; Purbrick, "Knowledge Is Property."

81 Foucault, "What Is an Author?"; Poovey, "The Man-of-Letters Hero"; Rose, *Authors and Owners*; Ross, "Copyright and the Invention of Tradition"; Saunders and Hunter, "Lessons from the 'Literatory'"; Woodmansee, "The Genius and the Copyright."

82 See "Copyright of Designs," *London Journal and Repertory of Arts, Sciences, and Manufactures* 21 (1843): 132; and Vanden Bossche, "The Value of Literature."

83 Spedding, "Dickens' *American Notes*," 497, 500.

84 For an example of Tennent's publications, see *Ceylon*.

85 Tennent, *A Treatise on the Copyright of Designs*, 20–21. See also *Hansard Parliamentary Debates*, 3d ser., vol. 61 (1842), cols. 667–70, 683–84.

86 SCCD, 161–63.

87 "Copyright," *Art Union* 4 (40) (May 1842): 95–97; Cooke Taylor, "Copyright in Design," 59–60; Bizup, *Manufacturing Culture*, chaps. 1 and 4.

88 See Hurst, *Edmund Potter of Dinting Vale*.

89 Thomson, *Letter to Peel*, 13. See also Cooke Taylor, "Copyright in Design."

90 Greenblatt, *Renaissance Self-Fashioning*, 9.

91 Thomson, *Letter to Sheil*, 1; *Manchester Guardian*, 6 March 1841; Brace, *Observations on the Extension of Protection of Copyright of Designs*, 11. See also SCCD, 113–15, 185, 399, 482.

92 Thomson, *Letter to Sheil*, i. See also *Manchester Guardian*, 6 March 1841; and SCCD, 113–15, 185, 399, 482.

93 SCCD, 123.

94 *Hansard Parliamentary Debates*, 3d ser., vol. 51 (1840), cols. 1262, 1265, and vol. 56 (1841), col. 490; SCCD, 20–23, 31, 33; Thomson, *Letter to Peel*, 20–21.

95 Cooke Taylor, "Copyright in Design," 59–60; see also "Copyright," *Art Union* 4 (40) (May 1842): 95–97.

96 SCCD, 161–63.

97 Cooke Taylor, "Copyright in Design," 59.

98 Hill, "Radical Pirates"; Ritchie, *Captain Kidd and the War against the Pirates*, chaps. 1 and 10; Turley, *Rum, Sodomy, and the Lash*, introduction, chaps. 1 and 2.

99 Hill, *Radical Politics, Religion, and Literature in Seventeenth-Century England*, chap. 1; Senior, *A Nation of Pirates*.

100 "Social Piracy; or, the Rovings, Roamings, Motions, Locomotions, Peregrinations, Pouncings, Maneuvers, and Maraudings, Great Larcenies, and

Petty Larcenies of Mr. and Mrs. Hawke," *New Monthly Magazine* 72 (September 1844): 1–17.

101 Potter, *Letter to Philips*, 14, 17, 22. See also SCCD, 14, 63, 102.

102 SCCD, 119–20.

103 Ibid., 167.

104 Ibid., 63–67.

105 See Baines, *History of the Cotton Manufacture of Great Britain*, 284–85.

106 This understanding is enabled by Martin Daunton's "The Material Politics of Natural Monopoly," 69–88, esp. 73.

107 *Manchester Guardian*, 6 March 1841; "On the Multitude of New Patterns," *Journal of Design and Manufactures* 1 (1) (March 1849): 3–4.

108 Greysmith, "Patterns, Piracy, and Protection," 174. See also "Copyright of Designs," *Art Journal* 12 (1 February 1850): 14–16, esp. 14.

109 [Tennent], *Argument Made Easy* and *The Policy of Piracy*.

110 Greysmith, "Patterns, Piracy, and Protection," 173.

111 SCCD, 213, 223, 257, 368.

112 SCCD, 229, 233, 266–68, 289, 332, 348; Brace, *Observations on the Extension of Protection of Copyright of Designs*, 44–45. See also Greysmith, "Patterns, Piracy, and Protection," 168–74.

113 SCCD, 350–60.

114 Ibid., 333.

115 *Hansard Parliamentary Debates*, 3d. ser., vol. 56 (1841), col. 495.

116 SCCD, 310–11, 317, 374–88.

117 Ibid., 334.

118 Ibid., 284, 390, 398. See also Cooke Taylor, "Copyright in Designs," 59–60.

119 SCCD, 208, 228, 289, 333, 351, 361, 365.

120 See, for example, Ornamental Design Act 1842 Representations Submitted to the Patents, Designs and Trade Marks Office and Its Predecessor, NA BT 43/188, nos. 1874–88.

121 Thomson, *Letter to Sheil*, 20.

122 SCCD, 351.

123 SCCD, 19, 264; Senior et al., *From the Report of the Commissioners of Hand-Loom Weaving*, 33; Thomson, *Letter to Sheil*, 7.

124 SCCD, 263.

125 Schwartz, *The Culture of the Copy*, 229.

126 SCCD, 39. For an earlier view on the necessities of copying, see Boardman, *Museum Etruriae*.

127 Perot, *Fashioning the Bourgeoisie*, 179–80. On the internal economy of the fashion system, see Barthes, *The Fashion System*, chap. 20, esp. 277–80.

128 *Report from the Select Committee on Arts and Manufactures* (1835), 59.

129 Speech of Mark Philips as printed in Potter, *Letter to Philips*, 3–4. See also SCCD, 208.

130 *Hansard Parliamentary Debates*, 3d ser., vol. 65 (1842), col. 965.

131 SCCD, 257–58.

132 Schwartz, *Culture of the Copy*, 218–19.

133 [Tennent], *Argument Made Easy*, 6.

134 On Reynolds, see Schwartz, *Culture of the Copy*, 249.

135 Berg, "From Imitation to Invention," 9–12. See also Coltman, "Sir William Hamilton's Vase Publications."

136 *Report from the Select Committee on Arts and Manufactures*, 73.

137 SCCD, 258.

138 Ibid., 49. See also Thomson, *Letter to Sheil*, 119.

139 Thomson, *Letter to Peel*, 19; SCCD, 172.

140 Thomson, *Letter to Sheil*, 16–17, 119–20.

141 Thomson, *Letter to Peel*, 19; SCCD, 172.

142 Cooke Taylor, "Copyright in Design," 59.

143 See Bizup, *Manufacturing Culture*, 4, chap. 1.

144 Baines, *History of the Cotton Manufacture of Great Britain*, 7–9. For use of organic metaphors in the course of the copyright debate, see Thomson, *Letter to Sheil*, 11; and Potter, *Calico Printing as an Art Manufacture*, 6–7. For an earlier discussion, see Young, *Conjectures on Original Composition*, 7.

145 SCCD, 99; Thomson, *Letter to Peel*, 18–21; Thomson, *Letter to Sheil*, ii, 8, 17; Potter, *Letter to Philips*, 12.

146 *Hansard Parliamentary Debates*, 3d ser., vol. 56 (1841), col. 500.

147 See, for example, Hay, *An Essay on Ornamental Design*, 2, 4.

148 SCCD, 153–54, 158, 326; Adas, *Machines as the Measure of Men*.

149 Potter, *Calico Printing as an Art Manufacture*, 34–37. See also Potter, *A Letter to One of the Commissioners for the Exhibition of 1851*; and Thomson, *Letter to Sheil*, 11.

150 "Speech of James Emerson Tennent," *Morning Post*, 30 January 1843.

151 For a thorough and suggestive examination of these books, see Grey-smith, "Patterns, Piracy, and Protection." For early rates of registration, see "Designs Registration," *Art Union* 8 (August 1846): 239.

152 See, for example, *Journal of Design and Manufactures* 5 (25) (March 1851): 24; and *Journal of Design and Manufactures* 6 (34) (December 1851): 127.

153 "Correspondence," *Journal of Design and Manufactures* 3 (14) (April 1850): 63.

154 Ornamentor, "Correspondence: Copyright in Designs," *Art Journal* 12 (February 1850): 63.

155 "Copyright in Silks," *Journal of Design and Manufactures* 1 (2) (April 1849): 72.

156 "Report of the Registrar of Designs on the Memorial from the Damask Manufacturers of Halifax, Praying for an Extension of the Period of Copyright of Designs for Their Manufactures" and "Alterations in the Copyright of Designs Act" (1850), Papers of the Board of Trade, NA BT1/476/40 and

BT1/478/1985; "Miscellaneous," *Journal of Design and Manufactures* 2 (12) (February 1850): 214–15; "Copyright in Silks," *Journal of Design and Manufactures* 1 (5) (July 1849): 172; "Correspondence," *Journal of Design and Manufactures* 3 (13) (March 1850): 32.

157 "Occasional Chapters on Copyright in Designs," *Journal of Design and Manufactures* 3 (15) (May 1850): 74–77, esp. 74. On the local reception in Manchester, see Papers Relating to the Great Exhibition, Papers of the Royal Manchester Institution, Central Library, Manchester, M6/3/8/119, M6/3/8/126–27.

158 "Amended Act for the Copyright of Design," *Journal of Design and Manufactures* 3 (18) (August 1850): 177–79; "Mutilation of the Amended Act for the Copyright of Design," *Journal of Design and Manufactures* 4 (190) (September 1850): 7–8; "Designs Act of 1850," *Journal of Design and Manufactures* 4 (22) (December 1850): 102–5; "Copyright of Design Amendment Act," *Art Journal* 12 (September 1850): 283–84; "Copyright of Designs at the Exhibition" (1851), Board of Trade Papers, NA BT 1/484/1210.

Chapter Three COMMODIFICATION AND ITS DISCONTENTS

1 Walton, *France at the Crystal Palace*, chap. 7, esp. 199–201.

2 *Tallis's History and Description of the Crystal Palace*, 1:67; Blanqui, "Letters on the Great Exhibition," *Illustrated Exhibitor* 11 (16 August 1851): 187–88; Blanqui, "Letters on the Great Exhibition," *Illustrated Exhibitor* 13 (30 August 1851): 231.

3 *Tallis's History and Description of the Crystal Palace*, 1:67; Blanqui, "Letters on the Great Exhibition," *Illustrated Exhibitor* 11 (16 August 1851): 187–88; Blanqui, "Letters on the Great Exhibition," *Illustrated Exhibitor* 13 (30 August 1851): 231.

4 *Tallis's History and Description of the Crystal Palace*, 1:67; Blanqui, "Letters on the Great Exhibition," *Illustrated Exhibitor* 11 (16 August 1851): 187–88; Blanqui, "Letters on the Great Exhibition," *Illustrated Exhibitor* 13 (30 August 1851): 231.

5 Auerbach, *The Great Exhibition of 1851*, chaps. 1 and 4.

6 For both endorsements and challenges to this view, see Auerbach, *The Great Exhibition of 1851*, chaps. 5 and 6; Barringer, *Men at Work*, introduction; Richards, *The Commodity Culture of Victorian England*, chap. 1; Purbrick, "Introduction"; and Gurney, "An Appropriated Space."

7 *Tallis's History and Description of the Crystal Palace*, 1:258; see also 14, 23, 84, 100, 207. Such assessments were legion. See, for example, Lush, "Teachings of the Exhibition," 432; "Three May Days in London," *Household Words* 3 (53) (3 May 1851): 121–24.

8 Nowell-Smith, *The House of Cassell, 1848–1958*, 31–32. On the relationship between text and image in the nineteenth-century press, see Anderson, *The Printed Image and the Transformation of Popular Culture, 1790–1860*; Beegan, "The Mechanization of the Image"; and Curtis, *Visual Words*.

9 *Gems of the Great Exhibition: London, 1851; New York, 1853*.

10 Ellis, *Official Descriptive and Illustrated Catalogue of the Great Exhibition*, 1:v–viii; "The Exhibition Jury Reports," *Fraser's Magazine of Town and Country* 46 (74) (1852): 491–502, esp. 491–92. See also "The Catalogue's Account of Itself," *Household Words* 3 (74) (23 August 1851): 519–23.

11 Digby Wyatt, *The Industrial Arts of the Nineteenth Century*; *Art Journal Illustrated Catalogue of the Industry of All Nations*.

12 *Gems of the Great Exhibition: London, 1851; New York, 1853*.

13 Kriegel, "Narrating the Subcontinent in 1851," 146–78, esp. 147–49.

14 Greenhalgh, *Ephemeral Vistas*, 27.

15 See Auerbach, *The Great Exhibition of 1851*, esp. chaps. 1, 3, 4, and 6; Purbrick, "Introduction"; and Kahan, *Liberalism in Nineteenth-Century Europe*, 156–57.

16 "Porcelain Works in the Great Exhibition," *Illustrated Exhibitor* 24 (15 November 1851): 433–45, esp. 439.

17 Richards, *Commodity Culture of Victorian England*, chap. 1. See also Allen, "Culinary Exhibition"; Debord, *The Society of the Spectacle*; McClintock, *Imperial Leather*; and Miller, *Novels behind Glass*, introduction.

18 Maidment, "Entrepreneurship and the Artisans," 79–113, esp. 109. On the object in the disciplines, see also Barringer and Flynn, *Colonialism and the Object*; Conn, *Museums and American Intellectual Life, 1876–1926*; Miller, "Why Some Things Matter," 3–21; and Starn, "A Historian's Brief Guide to New Museum Studies." On spectacle and print in France, see Schwartz, *Spectacular Realities*, introduction and chap. 1.

19 Maidment, "Entrepreneurship and the Artisans," 93. On commodity fetishism, consult Marx, "The Fetishism of Commodities and the Secret Thereof," esp. 328. For another account of the challenge to fetishism in the exhibition's texts, see Kriegel, "The Pudding and the Palace."

20 See Hoffenberg, *An Empire on Display*, 21, 179; and "Equipoise and Its Discontents," 44, 52, 55, 57.

21 On "nationalism" and "internationalism" in 1851, see Auerbach, *The Great Exhibition of 1851*, chap. 6. William A. Drew offers one exemplar of this problematic in *Glimpses and Gatherings during a Voyage and Visit to London and the Great Exhibition*, 195, 320–23.

22 *Tallis's History and Description of the Crystal Palace*, 1:67–68, 160.

23 Blanqui, "Letters on the Great Exhibition," *Illustrated Exhibitor* 23 (8 November 1851): 428–30, esp. 429; *Tallis's History and Description of the Crystal Palace*, 1:67–68.

24 "Machinery in the Crystal Palace," *Illustrated Exhibitor* 3 (21 June 1851): 42.

25 See Klingender, *Art and the Industrial Revolution*; *Tallis's History and Description of the Crystal Palace*, 1,159; Steegman, *Victorian Taste*, 224–27; *Official Descriptive and Illustrated Catalogue of the Great Exhibition*, 1:479.

26 "The Cotton Machinery of the Exhibition," *Illustrated Exhibitor* 16 (20 September 1851): 279–85, esp. 279.

27 "Machinery in the Crystal Palace," *Illustrated Exhibitor* 3 (21 June 1851): 42; "Great Coalbrookdale Dome and Eagle Slayer," *Illustrated Exhibitor* 1 (7 June 1851): 15.

28 See Rule, "The Property of Skill in the Period of Manufacture."

29 Maidment, "Entrepreneurship and the Artisans," 94. On the domestication of machinery, see Hoffenberg, *An Empire on Display*, 197. On mechanical illustration at midcentury, see Purbrick, "Machines and the Mechanism of Representation."

30 See, for example, Giedion, *Mechanization Takes Command*, 344–47; Pevsner, *High Victorian Design*, 31–44; and Steegman, *Victorian Taste*, 224–28.

31 Auerbach, *The Great Exhibition of 1851*, 114, 120–21, 135; Wiener, *English Culture and the Decline of the Industrial Spirit, 1850–1980*, 27–30; Hoffenberg, "Equipoise and Its Discontents."

32 Smith, "Voltaire in the Crystal Palace," esp. 143.

33 On this image, see Pearson, "Thackeray and *Punch* at the Great Exhibition," 182.

34 "Specimens from Mr. Punch's Industrial Exhibition of 1850," *Punch* 17 (1850): 145. See also "The Industry of All Nations," *Punch* 18 (1850): 137; "Exhibition of Idleness," *Punch* 18 (1850): 137; "Articles Intended for the Exhibition of Industry," *Punch* 19 (1850); and "South Staffordshire and the Exhibition of 1851," *Punch* 19 (1850): 265. On "Mr. Punch's Industrial Exhibition," see also Auerbach, *The Great Exhibition of 1851*, 133–34.

35 Wiener, *English Culture and the Decline of the Industrial Spirit*, 27–30.

36 See also Barringer, *Men at Work*, 258.

37 Samuel, "The Workshop of the World."

38 Digby Wyatt, *Industrial Arts of the Nineteenth Century*, vol. 1, plate XXIII. See also Gaginer, *The Insatiability of Human Wants*, 13.

39 *Art Journal Illustrated Catalogue*, 222.

40 *Official Descriptive and Illustrated Catalogue*, 1:671; "Silver Plate in the Crystal Palace," *Illustrated Exhibitor* 5 (5 July 1851): 87–89, esp. 87; *Tallis's History and Description of the Crystal Palace*, 1:144; Digby Wyatt, *Industrial Arts of the Nineteenth Century*, vol. 1, plate XLVI.

41 Steegman, *Victorian Taste*, 226.

42 Pevsner, *High Victorian Design*, esp. 49, 114–15.

43 For a similar line of argument across the English Channel, see Walton, *France at the Crystal Palace*.

44 On exhibitions and equipoise, see Hoffenberg, "Equipoise and Its Discontents."

45 Stansky, *William Morris*, 8; Pevsner, *Pioneers of Modern Design*; Pevsner, *High Victorian Design*.

46 Wiener, *English Culture and the Decline of the Industrial Spirit*, 30.

47 Berg, *The Age of Manufactures, 1700–1820*, 255–56, 258.

48 "Great Coalbrookdale Dome and Eagle Slayer," *Illustrated Exhibitor* 1 (7 June 1851): 15.

49 Digby Wyatt, *Industrial Arts of the Nineteenth Century*, vol. 1, plate XIX.

50 Berg, *The Age of Manufactures*, 255–56.

51 "Electro-Plate," *Illustrated Exhibitor* 3 (21 June 1851): 57–59, esp. 59.

52 *Tallis's History and Description of the Crystal Palace*, 2:1.

53 "Ornamental Articles in Glass," *Illustrated Exhibitor* 17 (27 September 1851): 312–13, esp. 312.

54 Pevsner, *High Victorian Design*, 20, 49.

55 *Art Journal Illustrated Catalogue*, 193.

56 "Electro-Plate," *Illustrated Exhibitor* 3 (21 June 1851): 58–59.

57 On this process, see Auerbach, *The Great Exhibition of 1851*, chap. 3.

58 "Sheffield Contributions to the World's Fair," *Illustrated Exhibitor* 12 (23 August 1851): 201–12, esp. 202, 204.

59 Ibid., 207–8.

60 Blanqui, "Letters on the Great Exhibition," *Illustrated Exhibitor* 11 (16 August 1851): 187–90, esp. 189.

61 Barringer, *Men at Work*, chap. 4, esp. 190–92, 210–15.

62 "Sheffield Contributions to the World's Fair," *Illustrated Exhibitor* 12 (23 August 1851): 207–9; Barringer, *Men at Work*, 194–99.

63 *Art Journal Illustrated Catalogue*, 93, 311. See also Pevsner, *High Victorian Design*, 96.

64 *Art Journal Illustrated Catalogue*, 222.

65 "Ireland in the Exhibition," *Illustrated London News* 19 (4 October 1851): 417–18. For the Irish at turn-of-the-century exhibitions, see Coombes, *Reinventing Africa*, 208–10.

66 See ibid. See also, for example, *Tallis's History and Description of the Crystal Palace* 1:175–82; "The Highlands in the Exhibition," *Illustrated London News* 19 (20 September 1851): 353–54; and Sproule, *The Resources and Manufacturing Industry of Ireland*. According to Bailkin, such understandings of Ireland's relationship to material culture persisted through the century. See Bailkin, *The Culture of Property*, chap. 1, esp. 36–55.

67 Greeley, *Glances at Europe in a Series of Letters during the Summer of 1851*, 92, 317.

68 *Mr. Goggleye's Visit to the Exhibition of National Industry to Be Held in London on the 1st of April 1851*. In a similar vein, see also [Sala], *The Great Exhibition Wot Is to Be*.

69 *The World's Fair; or, Children's Prize Gift Book of the Great Exhibition of 1851*.

70 "Ireland's Contributions to the World's Fair," *Illustrated Exhibitor* 9 (2 August 1851): 142.

71 "Carvings in Irish Bog Wood," *Illustrated Exhibitor* 9 (2 August 1851): 143–44.

72 "Ireland's Contributions to the World's Fair, No. 2," *Illustrated Exhibitor* 10 (9 August 1851): 166–67; "Ireland's Contributions to the World's Fair," *Illustrated Exhibitor* 9 (2 August 1851): 142–43.

73 "The Belgian Lace-Makers," *Household Words* 1 (14) (29 June 1850): 320–23, esp. 322; *Art Journal Illustrated Catalogue*, 203; *Tallis's History and Description of the Crystal Palace* 3:40.

74 "Ladies' Carpet," *Illustrated Exhibitor* 4 (28 June 1851): 73; "Ladies' Department," *Illustrated Exhibitor* 12 (23 August 1851): 218–20.

75 "Limerick Lace," *Illustrated Exhibitor* 10 (9 August 1851): 169–75; "Ladies' Department," *Illustrated Exhibitor* 12 (23 August 1851): 218–20, esp. 219; "Nottingham Lace Machinery in the Crystal Palace," *Illustrated Exhibitor* 15 (13 September 1851): 260–62; "Needlework in the Great Exhibition," *Illustrated Exhibitor* 15 (13 September 1851): 274–76; "Needlework in the Crystal Palace," *Illustrated Exhibitor* 19 (11 October 1851): 354–56; *Tallis's History and Description of the Crystal Palace*, 3:40–43; "A Lady's Glance at the Great Exhibition," *Illustrated London News* 19 (19 July 1851): 98; "Needlework in the Crystal Palace," *Illustrated Exhibitor* 16 (20 September 1851): 293–95, esp. 294.

76 Cunningham, "Gender and Design in the Victorian Period," 175–92, esp. 175–80. See also Greenhalgh, *Ephemeral Vistas*, chap. 7; and Grever and Waaldijk, *Transforming the Public Sphere*.

77 Digby Wyatt, *Industrial Arts of the Nineteenth Century*, vol. 2, plates CXLVI, CLIV.

78 Cole, "Introduction," *Official Descriptive and Illustrated Catalogue*, 1:3.

79 Blanqui, "Letters on the Exhibition," *Illustrated Exhibitor* 11 (16 August 1851): 187–88, 196; Blanqui, "Letters on the Exhibition," *Illustrated Exhibitor* 14 (6 September 1851): 251–53, esp. 252.

80 Blanqui, "Letters on the Great Exhibition," *Illustrated Exhibitor* 23 (8 November 1851): 428–30, esp. 429.

81 *Tallis's History and Description of the Crystal Palace*, 2:67–69.

82 Dyce, *Report Made to the Rt. Hon. C. Poulett Thompson, MP, President of the Board of Trade, on Foreign Schools of Design*, 75, 79.

83 Digby Wyatt, *Report on the Eleventh French Exhibition of the Products of Industry*, 3; *Industrial Arts of the Nineteenth Century*, plate CXIX.

84 Digby Wyatt, *Industrial Arts of the Nineteenth Century*, vi.

85 Digby Wyatt, *Report on the Eleventh French Exhibition of the Products of Industry*, 8.

86 Auslander, *Taste and Power*, chap. 5.

87 "Gobelins and Beauvais Tapestries in the Great Exhibition," *Illustrated Exhibitor* 22 (1 November 1851): 395–400, esp. 400; "France: The Gobelins—

French Contributions Reviewed by a Frenchman," *Illustrated Exhibitor* 13 (30 August 1851): 221–24, 235–36.

88 Blanqui, "Letters on the Great Exhibition," *Illustrated Exhibitor* 15 (13 September 1851): 263–65, esp. 263; *Tallis's History and Description of the Crystal Palace*, 2:62, 67, 259; *Official Descriptive and Illustrated Catalogue*, 3:1169.

89 "Tea Urn," *Illustrated Exhibitor* 13 (30 August 1851): 227.

90 *Tallis's History and Description of the Crystal Palace*, 1:62.

91 "London in 1851," *Fraser's Magazine of Town and Country* 44 (254) (February 1851): 127–36, esp. 133, 136. On fear of disease, see *The Philosopher's Mite to the Great Exhibition of 1851*. See also Steegman, *Victorian Taste*, 215–18; and Auerbach, *The Great Exhibition of 1851*, chap. 6.

92 Blanqui, "Letters on the Great Exhibition," *Illustrated Exhibitor* 13 (30 August 1851): 231–34, esp. 233.

93 Auslander, *Taste and Power*, 148, 197–98; Walton, *France at the Crystal Palace*, 211. See also Cooke Taylor, "On the Cultivation of Taste in the Operative Classes," 3–5.

94 Digby Wyatt, *Industrial Arts of the Nineteenth Century*, vol. 2, plate XCIII.

95 "French Contributions to the World's Fair," *Illustrated Exhibitor* 27 (6 December 1851): 493–96, esp. 496. For a more critical assessment of the relationship between revolution and artisanship, see Auslander, *France at the Crystal Palace*, 152–53.

96 Digby Wyatt, *Industrial Arts of the Nineteenth Century*, vol. 1, plate XXVI.

97 "France: The Gobelins," *Illustrated Exhibitor* 13 (30 August 1851): 221–24, esp. 224.

98 *Tallis's History and Description of the Crystal Palace*, 1:158.

99 Digby Wyatt, *Industrial Arts of the Nineteenth Century*, vol. 1, plate XIV.

100 "Gobelins and Beauvais Tapestry Shown at the Great Exhibition," *Illustrated Exhibitor* 22 (1 November 1851): 395–400, esp. 396; "France: The Gobelins," *Illustrated Exhibitor* 13 (30 August 1851): 221–24, esp. 223.

101 Auslander, *Taste and Power*, 142.

102 Cooke Taylor, "On the Cultivation of Taste in the Operative Classes," 3–5.

103 Digby Wyatt, *Industrial Arts of the Nineteenth Century*, vol. 1, plates XXVI, LX; vol. 2, plates XCI, XCII, CXVI.

104 "French Bronzes," *Illustrated Exhibitor* 13 (30 August 1851): 227; Walton, *France at the Crystal Palace*, 199.

105 *Tallis's History and Description of the Crystal Palace*, 2:72.

106 Ibid., 1:31; Breckenridge, "The Aesthetics and Politics of Colonial Collecting"; *Official Descriptive and Illustrated Catalogue*, 1:17.

107 E. A. Moriarty, "The Official Catalogue of the Great Exhibition," *Edinburgh Review* 94 (October 1851): 557–98, esp. 590. The landmark study

of British imperial exhibitions is Hoffenberg, *An Empire on Display*. See also Mitchell, *Colonising Egypt*; and Coombes, *Reinventing Africa*. For the American case, see Rydell, *All the World's a Fair*; and Kramer, "Making Concessions." On France, see, for example, Morton, *Hybrid Modernities*.

108 Hoffenberg, *An Empire on Display*, 101, 110–17. On the East India Company and the real and ideal marketplace, see Sen, *Empire of Free Trade*, introduction. On the persuasive imperial work of exhibitions, see Auerbach, *The Great Exhibition*, chap. 6; Greenhalgh, *Ephemeral Vistas*, chap. 3; Mitchell, "Orientalism and the Exhibitionary Order"; Morton, *Hybrid Modernities*; and Rydell, *All the World's a Fair*. On public opinion and the East India Company, see Alborn, *Conceiving Companies*, chap. 2; Lawson, *The East India Company*, chaps. 6–8, esp. 145, 159, 162; Metcalf, *Ideologies of the Raj*, chap. 2, esp. 28–43, 49; and Walvin, *Fruits of Empire*, 31. For mid-nineteenth-century critiques of Britain in India, see "The Peasants of British India," *Household Words* 4 (95) (17 January 1852): 389–93; "Modern India," *Bentley's Miscellany* 31 (April 1852): 465–73; W. R. Greg, "Shall We Retain Our Colonies?" *Edinburgh Review* 93 (190) (April 1851): 475–98; and Knight, *The Imperial Cyclopaedia*. See also *Official Descriptive and Illustrated Catalogue*, 2:858–60.

109 "A Guide to the Great Exhibition of Industry," *Illustrated London News* 18 (3 May 1851): 359; *Tallis's History and Description of the Crystal Palace*, 1:239–40; "India and the Indian Contributions to the Industrial Bazaar," *Illustrated Exhibitor* 18 (4 October 1851): 319–29, esp. 319. On crafts at Indian exhibitions more generally, see Hoffenberg, *An Empire on Display*, 158–62.

110 Digby Wyatt, *Industrial Arts of the Nineteenth Century*, vol. 1, plates XXIV, XL, XLIV.

111 "A Lady's Glance at the Great Exhibition, no. 5," *Illustrated London News* 19 (4 October 1851): 431.

112 Ibid. See also "A Lady's Glance at the Great Exhibition, no. 3," *Illustrated London News* 19 (23 August 1851): 242; Digby Wyatt, *Industrial Arts of the Nineteenth Century*, vol. 1, plate LXVIII; and *Tallis's History and Description of the Crystal Palace*, 1:23, 33, 158, 239–40. On the production and circulation of the *Arabian Nights* in the West, see Kabbani, *Europe's Myths of Orient*, introduction, chaps. 2 and 3.

113 "India and Indian Contributions," *Illustrated Exhibitor* (4 October 1851): 317–18.

114 On labor as an expressly colonial category, see Kale, *Fragments of Empire*; and Wolfe, "Land, Labor, and Difference."

115 "Indian Ivory Carvings for the Great Exhibition," *Illustrated London News* 18 (26 April 1851). On the iconography of Indian labor, see Barringer, *Men at Work*.

116 Digby Wyatt, *Industrial Arts of the Nineteenth Century*, vol. 1, plate XXIV.

117 McClintock, *Imperial Leather*.

118 "India and the Indian Contributions to the Industrial Bazaar," *Illustrated Exhibitor* 18 (4 October 1851): 317–18.

119 For similar treatments of India's artisans, see *Tallis's History and Description of the Crystal Palace*, 1:201, 238–39, 2:67–71, 128, 3:39–44; "The Hindoo Cotton Manufacture," *Illustrated Exhibitor* 18 (4 October 1851): 322–23; "Silk from the Punjab," *Household Words* 5 (146) (8 January 1853): 388–90; Royle, "The Arts and Manufactures of India"; and *Official Descriptive and Illustrated Catalogue*, 2:479, 483–84, 933–35.

120 Digby Wyatt, *Industrial Arts of the Nineteenth Century*, vol. 1, plate XII; McClintock, *Imperial Leather*, 40, 56–59.

121 *Official Descriptive and Illustrated Catalogue*, 2:881; "Shawls," *Household Words* 5 (127) (28 August 1852): 552–56. On shawls, see also Digby Wyatt, *Industrial Arts of the Nineteenth Century*, vol. 1, plate XLIV; and "British India," *Illustrated London News* 19 (2 August 1851): 163–64.

122 *Tallis's History and Description of the Crystal Palace*, 2:67.

123 Digby Wyatt, *Industrial Arts of the Nineteenth Century*, vol. 1, plate XII. See also "The Belgian Lace-Makers," *Household Words* 1 (14) (29 June 1850): 320–23.

124 Digby Wyatt, *Industrial Arts of the Nineteenth Century*, vol. 1, plates XXIV, XLVIII; "The Hindoo Cotton Manufacture," *Illustrated Exhibitor* 18 (4 October 1851): 322–23.

125 Digby Wyatt, *Industrial Arts of the Nineteenth Century*, vol. 1, plate XXIV.

126 "Indian Ivory Carvings for the Great Exhibition," *Illustrated London News* 18 (26 April 1851): 355. See also *Official Descriptive and Illustrated Catalogue*, vol. 2:932–33; *Tallis's History and Description of the Crystal Palace*, 1:33–34; and Royle, "Arts and Manufactures of India," 333–34.

127 Digby Wyatt, *Industrial Arts of the Nineteenth Century*, vol. 1, plate XL.

128 See Royle, "Arts and Manufactures of India," 366–67, 394–96; "A Guide to the Great Exhibition of Industry: Textile Fabrics," *Illustrated London News* 18 (3 May 1851): 369; "India," *Illustrated London News* 18 (10 May 1851): 392; and *Tallis's History and Description of the Crystal Palace*, 1:193, 2:71–72.

129 *The World's Fair; or, Children's Prize Gift Book of the Great Exhibition of 1851*, 9.

130 See, for example, Mathur, "Living Ethnological Exhibits"; Coombes, *Reinventing Africa*; and Greenhalgh, *Ephemeral Vistas*, chap. 4.

131 *Tallis's History and Description of the Crystal Palace*, 2:192–93. See also *Official Descriptive and Illustrated Catalogue*, 2:930–31.

132 *Tallis's History and Description of the Crystal Palace*, 1:239–40; Blanqui, "Letters on the Great Exhibition, no. 5," *Illustrated Exhibitor* 17 (27 September 1851): 301–2. On the miniature, labor, and nostalgia, see Stewart, *On Longing*, chap. 2.

133 *Tallis's History and Description of the Crystal Palace*, 2:71–72; Blanqui,

"Letters on the Great Exhibition, No. 4," *Illustrated Exhibitor* 15 (13 September 1851): 263–65, esp. 264.

134 "India and Indian Contributions to the Industrial Bazaar," *Illustrated Exhibitor* 18 (4 October 1851): 318.

135 Concannen, *Remembrances of the Great Exhibition Complete in Twenty Views*. The foundational discussion of the production of the categories of the manly Englishman and the effeminate Bengali as a strategy of rule is found in Sinha, *Colonial Masculinities* (see especially the introduction).

136 *Tallis's History and Description of the Crystal Palace*, 1:37.

137 J. Roberts, *The Spinster*, quoted in Turnbull, *A History of the Calico Printing Industry of Great Britain*, 21.

138 "East India Contributions," *Illustrated Exhibitor* 17 (27 September 1851): 301; Blanqui, "Letters on the Great Exhibition, No. 4," *Illustrated Exhibitor* 15 (13 September 1851): 263–65, esp. 264.

139 Helix [Adams], "The Great Exhibition of 1851," *Westminster Review* 53 (April 1850): 85–100; Helix [Adams], *Westminster Review* 55 (July 1851): 346–94. See also *Tallis's History and Description of the Crystal Palace*, 1:238; Digby Wyatt, *Industrial Arts of the Nineteenth Century*, vol. 2, plate CXXIII; Royle, "Arts and Manufactures of India," 352; and "The East Indian Courts," *Illustrated London News* 18 (4 June 1851): 563.

140 Whewell, "The General Bearing of the Great Exhibition on the Progress of Art and Science," 1:18–19.

141 *Tallis's History and Description of the Crystal Palace*, 1:31. Such admonitions of wasteful production were not restricted to India. See, for example, "Silver Plate in the Crystal Palace," *Illustrated Exhibitor* 11 (16 August 1851): 193–94; and "The Queen of Spain's Jewellery," *Illustrated Exhibitor* 13 (30 August 1851): 228–29.

142 Digby Wyatt, *Industrial Arts of the Nineteenth Century*, vol. 1, plate LIV. On the visibility of China in the metropolis, see Altick, *The Shows of London*, chap. 21. For an earlier discussion of China in England, see Fang, "Empire, Coleridge, and Charles Lamb's Consumer Imagination." See also Clunas, "China in Britain"; Hevia, *English Lessons*; Pagani, "Chinese Material Culture and British Perceptions of China in the Mid-Nineteenth Century"; and Pagani, "Objects and the Press."

143 Digby Wyatt, *Industrial Arts of the Nineteenth Century*, vol. 2, plate CXVIII.

144 *Tallis's History and Description of the Crystal Palace*, 1:118; see also 14. On Chinese labor, see "How Chinese Workmen Built an English House," *Builder*, no. 456 (1 November 1851): 688; "Pottery and Porcelain," *Household Words* 4 (80) (4 October 1851): 32–37; and Dickens and Horne, "The Great Exhibition and the Little One." See also Dolin, "Cranford and the Victorian Collection." For representations of China at midcentury more generally, see Corner, *China*; and Edwards, *Authentic Account of the Chinese Commission*.

145 *Tallis's History and Description of the Crystal Palace*, 3:48.

146 "The Ladies' Carpet," *Illustrated Exhibitor* 4 (28 June 1851): 73; "Ladies' Needlework," *Illustrated Exhibitor* 11 (16 August 1851): 198; "Needlework in the Crystal Palace," *Illustrated Exhibitor* 16 (20 September 1851): 294–95.

147 [Cole], *A Short Statement of the Nature and Objects of the Proposed Great Exhibition of the Works of Industry of All Nations*, 2–3, as found in Henry Cole Miscellanies, 9, 55.AA.53, National Art Library, London.

148 "Austrian Contributions to the Great Exhibition," *Illustrated Exhibitor* 17 (27 September 1851): 306–7; Digby Wyatt, *Industrial Arts of the Nineteenth Century*, vol. 2, plate CLVII; Whewell, "On the General Bearing of the Great Exhibition," 19.

149 "Cabinet Work in the Crystal Palace," *Illustrated Exhibitor* 5 (5 July 1851): 102–5.

150 For yet another example of this optimism, see *The Exhibition in 1851 of the Products and Industry of All Nations, Its Probable Influence upon Labor and Commerce*, 18.

151 See, for example, Digby Wyatt, "Form in the Decorative Arts"; and Jones, "Colour in the Decorative Arts." See also Wornum, "The Exhibition as a Lesson in Taste."

152 *Tallis's History and Description of the Crystal Palace*, 2:260.

153 *Official Descriptive and Illustrated Catalogue of the Great Exhibition*, 2:729.

154 Digby Wyatt, *Industrial Arts of the Nineteenth Century*, vol. 1, plate LX.

155 Blanqui, "Letters on the Great Exhibition, No. 10," *Illustrated Exhibitor* 23 (8 November 1851): 428–30.

156 Whewell, "On the General Bearing of the Great Exhibition," 19.

Chapter Four PRINCIPLED DISAGREEMENTS

1 On the lower middle class, see Crossick, *The Lower Middle Class in Britain, 1870–1914*; Bailey, "White Collars, Gray Lives?"; Hammerton, "Pooterism or Partnership?"; and Hosgood, "Mercantile Monasteries."

2 Morley, "A House Full of Horrors."

3 Ibid., 265–66; Breward, *Fashioning London*.

4 Department of Practical Art, *Catalogue of the Articles of Ornamental Art*, iii.

5 Gagnier, *The Insatiability of Human Wants*, 3–4, 11, 20, 41, 123.

6 On the distinction between the eighteenth and nineteenth centuries on this point, see Steegman, *Victorian Taste*, 62.

7 Jules Lubbock identifies Morley as the author of the story in his *Tyranny of Taste*. For a helpful discussion of Morley and other opponents, see part 6, chapter 5 of Lubbock's book.

8 Morley, "A House Full of Horrors," 267–70.

9   Important works on masculinity include Burton, *At the Heart of the Empire*; Deslandes, *Oxbridge Men*; Friedman, *Masculinity, Autocracy, and the Russian University*; Hall, *White, Male, and Middle-Class*; Hall, *Civilising Subjects*; and Sinha, *Colonial Masculinities*.

10   See, for example, Redgrave, *Manual of Design*, 7.

11   "Artizans and Industrial Education," *Home Companion* 2 (19) (5 March 1853): 299.

12   For secondary works on France and design, see Auslander, *Taste and Power*, esp. 19–25; Silverman, *Art Nouveau in Fin-de-Siècle France*; and Walton, *France at the Crystal Palace*, esp. introduction and chaps. 1, 6, and 7. On Britain's national formation in opposition to France, see Colley, *Britons*.

13   See, for example, Lloyd, *Papers Relating to Proposals for Establishing Colleges of Arts and Manufactures for the Better Instruction of the Industrial Classes*, 10; *Morning Chronicle*, 18 November 1852, "Great Exhibition of 1851: Extracts from Newspapers," vol. 5, National Art Library (hereafter NAL); *London Weekly Paper*, 2 April 1853, Archive of Art and Design Press Cuttings (hereafter AAD PC) (November 1852 to October 1853 [vol. 2]), f. 57; and "Fine Arts: Practical Art," *Athenaeum*, no. 1310 (4 December 1852): 1333–34.

14   *Morning Chronicle*, 18 November 1852. See also "Suburban Artisan Schools: The North London School of Drawing and Modeling," *Art Journal* 12 (June 1850): 197; Wornum, "The Government Schools of Design," 16; and "Art Education: A Knowledge of Practical Art," *Home Companion* 2 (20) (12 March 1853): 310–12.

15   *Daily News*, 19 May 1852, and N.n., n.d., AAD PC (1837–52 [vol. 2]), f. 2 and f. 13; Wornum, "The Exhibition as a Lesson in Taste."

16   "Reopening of the Museum of Ornamental Manufactures," *Daily News*, 3 October 1853, AAD PC, vol. 2, f. 103; "Schools of Design: Their Management," *Birmingham Journal*, 5 April 1852, AAD PC, vol. 1, f. 3.

17   Henry Cole Miscellanies, NAL, London, vol. 1, 55.AA.45, f. 1c; vol. 8b, 55AA53 f. 40.

18   See Henry Cole Diary, NAL 55.AA.14, 31 October 1851.

19   Letter from Harry Chester to George Grove, Secretary of the Society of Arts, 28 November 1851, NAL EX.1851.153; Lloyd, *Papers Relating to Proposals for Establishing Colleges of Arts and Manufactures for the Better Instruction of the Industrial Classes*, 14; Twining, *Notes on the Organization of an Industrial College for Artisans*; Thomas, *Suggestions for a Crystal College, or New Palace of Glass, for Combining the Intellectual Talent of All Nations; or, a Sketch of a Practical Philosophy of Education*. See also *The Crystal Palace*, 11.

20   The committee received 5,000 pounds from the surfeit of 186,000. Of these funds, it spent 2,076 pounds on articles from the "foreign side" of the exhibition, 866 on articles from the "British side," and 1,276 on articles exhibited by the East India Company. See Department of Practical Art, *Catalogue*, iii. See also Letters from Gen. Charles Grey to Henry Cole, 27 April 1852, 10

May 1852, 14 May 1852, and 15 May 1852, NAL 55.BB.2, ff. 113–17; Papers of the Board of Trade, National Archives, London (hereafter NA), BT 1/488/144 and BT 1/502/327; *Morning Chronicle*, 24 October 1851 and 27 October 1851; "Great Exhibition of 1851: Extracts from Newspapers," vol. 5, NAL; *Morning Chronicle*, 19 May 1852, and *Daily News*, 19 May 1852, both in AAD PC, vol. 1, ff. 2–3; and Henry Cole Diary, 31 August, 3 September, 7–8 October, and 13 October, 1851, NAL 55.AA.14. On the collection, see Wainwright with Gere, "The Making of the South Kensington Museum I and II."

21 Henry Cole Diary, 19 February 1852 and 21 February 1852, NAL 55.AA.15. See also "Office of Works and Successors: Art and Science Buildings," NA WORK 17/26/11/ff. 40–41. Cole and the department officials were fortunate to enjoy the support of the prince consort from the museum's inception, and the museum hosted him and the queen for a visit on 17 May 1852, the day before it opened. Letter from General Charles Grey to Sir Henry Cole, 28 June 1852, Henry Cole Correspondence, NA 55.BB.2. On Marlborough House, see Physick, *The Victoria and Albert Museum*, 13–18.

22 On the Department of Practical Art, see Henry Cole Diary, 31 October 1851, NAL 55.AA.14; Henry Cole Diary, 26 January 1852, NAL 55.AA.15; Letter from Henry Cole to Lord Granville, 1 November 1851, Henry Cole Correspondence, NAL 55.BB.4; "Draft, Memorandum on Estimates for 1852–1853 (with notes after reading to Prince Albert)," Henry Cole Miscellanies, vol. 11, NAL 55.AA.55, f. 16; Department of Practical Art, *First Report of the Department of Practical Art*, 2; Cole and Redgrave, *Letter to the Rt. Hon. J. W. Henley, MP, President of the Board of Trade*; Henry Cole and Alan Summerly Cole, *Fifty Years of Public Work of Sir Henry Cole, KCB*, 28–86. For a detailed bureaucratic history of the department, see Levine, "The Politics of Taste."

23 Cole, "On the Facilities Afforded to All Classes of the Community for Obtaining Education in Art," 10–13; Cole, "Address at the Opening of an Elementary Drawing School," 4; Redgrave, "An Introductory Address on the Methods Adopted by the Department of Practical Art to Impart Instruction in Art to All Classes of the Community"; *Times*, 14 April 1852, 13 May 1852, 19 May 1852, AAD PC, vol.1, f. 2, f. 4; Wornum, "The Government Schools of Design," 37–40.

24 Cole, "On the Facilities Afforded to All Classes of the Community for Obtaining Education in Art," 4, 9–13; Redgrave, "On the Methods Employed for Imparting Education in Art to All Classes," 72–73, 79–80; Department of Practical Art, *First Report*, 3, 30; *Morning Chronicle*, 22 January 1853, AAD PC, vol. 2, f. 34.

25 *People's Illustrated Journal*, 12 June 1852, AAD PC, vol. 1, f. 5; N.n., n.d., AAD PC, vol. 1, f. 13; Jones, "An Attempt to Define the Principles Which Should Regulate the Employment of Colour in the Decorative Arts," esp. 293.

26 "Mixture of Styles," *Journal of Design and Manufactures*, 1 (1) (March 1849): 21.

27 *Morning Chronicle*, 22 January 1853, AAD PC, vol. 2, f. 34; N.n., nd., AAD PC, vol. 1, f. 13; Wornum, "The Government School of Design," 102; Jameson, "Some Thoughts on Art Addressed to the Uninitiated," 69–70.

28 For discussions of nineteenth-century British museums and education, see, for example, Bennett, *The Birth of the Museum*, chap. 7; Bennett, *Pasts beyond Memory*; Coombes, *Reinventing Africa*; Koven, "The Whitechapel Picture Exhibitions and the Politics of Seeing"; Hooper-Greenhill, *Museums and the Shaping of Knowledge*; and Trodd, "Culture, Class, City."

29 On the museum's strategies of display, see Whitehead, *The Public Art Museum in Nineteenth Century Britain*, 44–45, 53.

30 Department of Practical Art, *First Report of the Department*, 30–34; *Prospectus, Department of Practical Art, Marlborough House, Pall Mall, under the Authority of the Board of Trade*, November 1852; "Department of Practical Art and Science and Art Department, Minutes," 8 July 1854, NA ED 28/2 f. 176, 23 July 1855, NA ED 28/4 f. 77.

31 *Observer*, 9 January 1853, AAD PC, vol. 2, f. 31; "The British Museum" and "Our Weekly Gossip" *Athenaeum*, no. 1281 (15 May 1852): 542–43; "Fine Art Gossip," *Athenaeum*, no. 1282 (22 May 1852): 584; Cole; "On the Facilities Afforded to All Classes of the Community for Obtaining Education in Art," 24. See also Department of Practical Art, *First Report of the Department of Practical Art*, 35; "Department of Practical Art, and Science and Art Department, Minutes," 24 May 1853 and 4 June 1853, NA ED 28/1, ff. 137–38, 188; and "Minutes, Office of Works and Successors," NA ED 28/4, f. 65.

32 By 1855, the museum was open five days per week—Monday through Thursday and Saturday, too. It was recommended that Friday be added as well to provide three free and three paid days for visitors. See "Minutes, Office of Works and Successors," 23 July 1855, NA ED 28/4, f. 77.

33 "Department of Practical Art and Science and Art Department, Minutes," 2 November 1852, 6 October 1853, NA ED 28/1, ff. 106–7, 269; 11 February 1856, NA ED 28/5, f. 101, 11.

34 "Traveling Museum," 3 March 1855, "Department of Practical Art and Science and Art Department, Minutes," NA ED 28/4, f. 11. Robinson, *Catalogue of a Collection of Works of Decorative Art*; *Daily News*, 4 January 1855, AAD PC (December 1853–February 1857): 103.

35 "Department of Practical Art and Science and Art Department, Minutes," 4 March 1854, NA ED 28/2, f. 66.

36 *Morning Post*, 6 September 1852, AAD PC, vol. 1, f. 10. On the *Catalogue*'s pedagogy and the museum's more generally, see Burton, "The Uses of the South Kensington Art Collections," 83–84.

37 These words are Richard Redgrave's. See his *On the Necessity of Principles in Teaching Design*, 11. Redgrave spent considerable energy and effort enumerating these principles. See also his *Report on Design*; and *Morning Post*, 6 September 1852, AAD PC, vol. 1, f. 10.

38 See Henry Cole Miscellanies, NAL 55.AA.53, vol. 9.

39 These included [Cole], *Felix Summerly's Catalogue of the Pictures in the British Museum*; *Handbook for Holidays Spent in and Near London*; *Handbook for the Pictures in the Soane Museum, the Society of Arts, and the British Museum*; and *Handbook for the Dulwich Picture Gallery*.

40 Cole, *First Exercises for Children in Light, Shade, and Color*, vii.

41 See Owen Jones's masterpiece of the same title, *The Grammar of Ornament*.

42 Hay, *The Laws of Harmonious Coloring*, 3. Hay's corpus included *Proportion; or, the Geometrical Principle of Beauty Analysed*; *An Essay on Ornamental Design*; *The Principles of Beauty in Colouring Systematized*; *A Nomenclature of Colours*; and *Letter to the Council of the Society of Arts on Elementary Education in the Arts of Design*. For another contemporary assertion of the laws of design, see Pictor, *The Hand-Book of Taste*. On color especially, see Rafael Cardoso Denis, "The Educated Eye and the Industrial Hand"; Wilkinson, *On Colour*; and Jones, "An Attempt to Define the Principles Which Should Regulate the Employment of Colour in the Decorative Arts." On form, consult Digby Wyatt, "Form in the Decorative Arts."

43 Hay, *An Essay on Ornamental Design*, 5-6; *The Laws of Harmonious Coloring*, vi. See also his *The Principles of Beauty in Colouring Systematized*; and *Proportion; or, the Geometrical Principle of Beauty Analysed*, 20.

44 "Paper Hangings," *Journal of Design and Manufactures* 1 (2) (April 1849): 50; "Original Designs for Manufacture," *Journal of Design and Manufactures* 1 (3) (May 1849): 80.

45 Wornum, "The Exhibition as a Lesson in Taste," i–xxii, esp. xxii. See also Society of Arts, Manufactures, and Commerce, *Lectures on the Results of the Great Exhibition of 1851 Delivered before the Society of Arts, Manufactures and Commerce*.

46 Cohen, *Household Gods*, chap. 1; Cohen, "Material Good"; Snodin, "Who Led Taste?: Victorian Britain," esp. 369; Wilk, "Foreword."

47 Department of Practical Art, *Catalogue*, iv-v, app. A: "Principles of Practical Art," 63; Prouting [Argus], *A Mild Remonstrance*, no. 1, 27; Department of Practical Art, *Catalogue of the Articles of Ornamental Art in the Museum of the Department with Appendix*, 2nd ed., 74.

48 Redgrave, *On the Necessity of Principles*, 21. See also Keyser, "Ornament as Idea."

49 Garbett, *Rudimentary Treatise on the Principles of Design in Architecture*, 109.

50 Department of Practical Art, *Catalogue*, iii–iv; Department of Practical Art, *Catalogue*, 4th ed., 3–4; Department of Practical Art, *Principles of Decorative Art*. On taste and authority, see Bourdieu, *Distinction*, esp. 91.

51 Department of Practical Art, *Catalogue*, 42.

52 Ibid., 53.

53 Ibid, 55–56.

54 Ibid., 46.

55 Department of Practical Art, *Catalogue*, 4th ed., 47.

56 Robinson, "Museum of Ornamental Art," 150.

57 "The Experimental Traveling Museum," *Art Journal*, new ser., 1 (April 1855): 125.

58 Robinson, "The Museum of Ornamental Art at Marlborough House."

59 Underwood, *Choice Examples of Art Manufactures from the Marlborough House and Other Valuable Collections*, No. 4. Customers could buy a set of four lithographs for two shillings sixpence.

60 Robinson, "The Museum of Ornamental Art at Marlborough House," 118.

61 Department of Practical Art, *Catalogue*, 6–8.

62 "Gleanings from the Great Exhibition of 1851," *Journal of Design and Manufactures* 5 (30) (1851): 177.

63 Ibid.; Department of Practical Art, *Catalogue*, 6–8. On Indian art in the nineteenth century, see, for example, Mitter, *Much Maligned Monsters*, 229–33. On the reception of Indian design in the West, see Barringer, *Men at Work*; Barringer and Flynn, *Colonialism and the Object*; Mackenzie, *Orientalism*, chap. 5; and Sweetman, *The Oriental Obsession*, esp. chap. 5.

64 Department of Practical Art, *Catalogue*, 6–8.

65 Wiener, *English Culture and the Decline of the Industrial Spirit, 1850–1980*. For a counterargument, see Bizup, *Manufacturing Culture*, chaps. 4–5.

66 Redgrave, *Manual of Design*, 61–63, 130, 135.

67 On Pugin's relationship to the museum, see Wainwright, "Principles True and False." For examples of Pugin's writing, see *Contrasts* and *The True Principles of Pointed or Christian Architecture*. For an examination of Pugin's philosophy, see Lubbock, *Tyranny of Taste*, part 5, chap. 3.

68 Pugin, *The True Principles of Pointed or Christian Architecture*, 1–4, 23, 30; *Contrasts*, 1–3, 8, 15, 27, 30–31, 35.

69 Redgrave, "On the Methods Employed for Imparting Education in Art to All Classes," 68.

70 Barringer, *Men at Work*, chap. 5, esp. 249, 258, 261.

71 On this ambivalence, see Mitter and Clunas, "The Empire of Things," 222; Cohn, "Cloth, Clothes, and Colonialism," 303–53, esp. 337; and Said, *Orientalism*, introduction.

72 Department of Practical Art, *Catalogue*, 8–9.

73 For some representative writings on Indian art at midcentury, see "The Useful Arts in Other Nations and Times," *Home Companion* 2 (16) (16 February 1853): 244–47; "How to Receive Knowledge," *Home Companion* 2 (22) (26 March 1853): 347; and "The Duty of Our Manufacturers at the Present Crisis," *Art Journal*, new ser., 2 (October 1850): 304–6.

74 Barringer, *Men at Work*, 289; "Dr. Hunter's School of Design at

Madras," *Art Journal*, new ser., 5 (1853): 280–82; "Dr. Hunter's School of Arts and Industrial School at Madras," *Art Journal*, new ser., 5 (1853): 310–11. See also Guha-Thakurta, *The Making of a New "Indian" Art*. For a discussion of an Indian art revival that occurred later in the century, see Birdwood, *The Industrial Arts of India*; and *Two Letters on the Industrial Arts of India*.

75 *Leader*, 22 May 1852, AAD PC, vol. 1, f. 2.

76 "The Museum of Ornamental Art," *Spectator*, 22 October 1853, 1021–22, AAD PC, vol. 2, f. 111.

77 "The School of Ornamental Art: Department of Practical Art, Marlborough House," *Art Journal*, new ser., 4 (July 1852): 227–28.

78 See, for example, "Department of Practical Art and Science and Art Department: Minutes," 20 April 1855, NA ED 28/4, f. 49. See also Barringer, "The South Kensington Museum and the Colonial Project."

79 See Desmond, *The India Museum*.

80 Conway, *Travels in South Kensington*, 86.

81 Document 983, Travel Diary, 1889, Winterthur Museum, Library, and Gardens, Winterthur, Delaware.

82 "The Museum of Ornamental Art," *Spectator*, 22 October 1853, AAD PC, vol. 2, f. 111.

83 For a recent, especially astute analysis of the chamber, its aesthetic lessons, its moral connections, see Cohen, *Household Gods*, 14–24. On Madame Tussaud's, see Bartlett, *London by Day and Night*, 51.

84 "Original Designs for Manufactures," *Journal of Design and Manufactures* 1 (2) (April 1849): 51; "A Couple of Mistakes in Candlesticks," *Journal of Design and Manufactures* 5 (27) (May 1851): 80–81; "Original Designs for Manufactures," *Journal of Design and Manufactures* 1 (1) (March 1849): 12.

85 Department of Practical Art, *Catalogue*, 2nd ed., 75–84.

86 Ibid., 74–75. For a contemporary novelistic description of such works, see Collins, *Basil*, 2, 31, 35, 61, 348.

87 Turner, "Gas Jet," 123–24.

88 Department of Practical Art, *Catalogue*, 2nd ed., 74–84.

89 See, for example, Ornamental Design Act 1842 Representations Submitted to the Patents, Designs and Trade Marks Office and Its Predecessor, NA BT 43/93/111; 43/115/91252; BT 43/248/76457; BT 43/90/85627; BT 43/358/91343; BT 43/358/82874.

90 Letter from Colonel Phipps to Henry Cole, 10 September 1852, Henry Cole Correspondence, NAL 55.BB.1, ff. 47–48.

91 *Daily News*, 3 October 1853, AAD PC, vol. 2, f. 103.

92 "The People at Marlborough House," *Observer*, 9 January 1854, AAD PC, vol. 2, f. 31; "The Museum of Ornamental Art," *Spectator*, 22 October 1853, AAD PC, vol. 2, f. 111.

93 Department of Practical Art, *Catalogue*, 2nd ed., 75–84.

94 Morley, "A House Full of Horrors," 270.

95 Dickens, *Hard Times*, 3, 8–9.

96 Letter from John Bright to Henry Cole, 14 February 1853, Henry Cole Correspondence, NAL 55.BB.8.

97 Prouting [Argus], *A Mild Remonstrance against the Taste-Censorship at Marlborough House in Reference to Manufacturing Ornamentation and Decorative Design*, 3 nos. Lubbock names F. J. Prouting as the author of these pamphlets in *The Tyranny of Taste*, 273.

98 These are issues that many scholars, including Linda Colley, have identified as central to the production of British national identity in the eighteenth century and the early nineteenth. See her *Britons*, introduction, chaps. 1, 2, and 7. For an earlier period, see Armitage, *Ideological Origins of the British Empire*.

99 Bourdieu, *Distinction*, 1, 79–80, 99.

100 Prouting [Argus], *A Mild Remonstrance*, no. 1, 3–4, 10, 16; no. 2, 7, 11, 13; no. 3, 14–15, 23.

101 Ibid., no. 1, 1, 10–11, 15; no. 2, 3–4, 7–9, 11–12; no. 3, 25.

102 Ibid., no. 3, 8–9, 35.

103 Ibid., no. 1, 8–9; no. 2, 13, 19, 22, 31, 33; no. 3, 8–9, 21, 35.

104 Ibid., no. 1, 6, 12, 27; no. 2, 22–24, 31–32; no. 3, 16–18, 23, 34.

105 Ibid., no. 1, 3–5.

106 *Morning Advertiser*, 24–25 February 1853, AAD PC, vol. 2, ff. 41–42.

107 "The Museum of Practical Art," *Court Journal*, 19 February 1853, as found in AAD PC, vol. 2, f. 42.

108 "The Taste Censorship," *Morning Advertiser*, 2 March 1853, AAD PC, vol. 2, f. 42.

109 On the retail culture of the 1850s, see, notably, Rappaport, *Shopping for Pleasure*, chap. 1.

110 "Credit" was a charged notion, morally, legally, and financially. See Finn, *The Character of Credit*. On the particularly gendered dynamics of the credit economy for the middle classes, see Rappaport, "A Husband and His Wife's Dresses," 163–87; Rappaport, *Shopping for Pleasure*, chap. 2; and Ross, *Love and Toil*. On working-class legal conflict, see Finn, "Working-Class Women and the Contest for Consumer Control in Victorian County Courts." On credit and gender in the sphere of empire, see Rappaport, "The Bombay Debt."

111 "The Taste Censorship," *Morning Advertiser*, 2 March 1853, AAD PC, vol. 2, f. 42; Campbell, "Consumption and the Rhetorics of Need and Want."

112 Gagnier, *The Insatiability of Human Wants*, 2–4, 20, 41, 123.

113 Cole, "On the Facilities Afforded to All Classes of the Community for Obtaining Education in Art," 12–13.

114 See N.n., n.d., AAD PC, vol. 1, f. 13; *Morning Chronicle*, 22 January 1853, AAD PC, vol. 2, f. 34; *Morning Advertiser*, 24 February 1853, AAD PC, vol. 2, f. 41; Wornum, "The Government School of Design," 102.

115 Jameson, "Some Thoughts on Art."

116 "The People at Marlborough House," *Observer*, 9 January 1853, AAD PC, vol. 2, f. 31.

117 "Sèvres and Other Porcelains at the Exhibition of Art Manufactures," *Illustrated London News* 21 (579) (18 September 1852): 221. On women and the West End, see Rappaport, *Shopping for Pleasure*, introduction.

118 "The Hunterian Museum," *Home Companion* 1 (48) (27 November 1852): 760–61.

119 "The Museum of Ornamental Art," *Spectator*, 22 October 1853, AAD PC, vol. 2, f. 111.

120 Ibid.

121 See, notably, Auerbach, "What They Read"; Breward, "Femininity and Consumption"; Rappaport, *Shopping for Pleasure*; and Walkowitz, "Going Public." For an African example, see Burke, "Fork up and Smile."

122 For important work in this vein, see Breward, *The Hidden Consumer*; Breward, "Femininity and Consumption"; Finn, "Men's Things"; Finn, "Sex and the City"; Kwass, "Big Hair"; and Shannon, "ReFashioning Men," 597–630. For the twentieth century, see Mort, *Cultures of Consumption*.

123 See Tosh, *A Man's House*. Davidoff and Hall write that "Women were mainly responsible for creating and maintaining the house, its contents and its human constituents." However, their discussion of the politics and processes of furnishing the home suggests that this was often a familial endeavor or one that revealed discord within the middle-class family (*Family Fortunes*, 360, see also 375–80). See also Rappaport, "A Husband and His Wife's Dresses." For a recent, dynamic analysis of these matters, see Cohen, *Household Gods*, chap. 4.

124 Forty, *Objects of Desire*, 105. Christopher Breward, coincidentally, has pointed out that home furnishing assumed greater importance after 1860. See his "Victorian Britain," 401–29, esp. 406.

125 Ledger, Holland and Sons (1852–1853), AAD 13/29/1983.

126 Estimate Book, Waring and Gillow Furniture Maker (1849–1855), City of Westminster Archives Centre, London, 0344/105.

127 Ledger, Thomas Handyside and Son, Upholsterers (1842–53), Guildhall Library, London, MS 10833/2.

128 Ledger, Cowtan and Sons, Decorators, Upholsters, Cabinet Makers, and Electrical Engineers (1881–1888), London Metropolitan Archives, B/CWT/1.

129 Whitehead, *The Public Art Museum in Nineteenth Century Britain*, 79, 163.

Chapter Five CULTURAL LOCATIONS

1 "Science and Art," *Post*, 17 November 1857, Press Cuttings, Archive of Art and Design, London (hereafter AAD PC) (March 1856–February 1859 [vol. 6]), 69.

2 *Civil Service Gazette*, 21 November 1857, AAD PC, vol. 6, 72.

3 At the time of its opening, South Kensington featured eight distinct collections: the Museum of Ornamental Art, an Educational Museum, the Commissioners of Patents Museum, an Architectural Museum, the Sculpture of the United Kingdom, the Gallery of British Fine Arts, a Trade Museum, and an Economic Museum. For a description of these, see "South Kensington Museum: First Notice," *Post*, 22 June 1857, AAD PC, vol. 6, 27. See also "South Kensington Museum," ED 23/629/42/a, National Archives, London (hereafter NA).

4 Cole, "The Functions of the Science and Art Department," 8, 11, 13. On Cole's notion of museological duty, see Black, *On Exhibit*, 32. On midcentury liberalism, see Kahan, *Liberalism in Nineteenth-Century Europe*.

5 See, for example, Baker and Richardson, *A Grand Design*; Bonython and Burton, *The Great Exhibitor*; Burton, *Vision and Accident*; Minihan, *The Nationalization of Culture*; and Physick, *The Victoria and Albert Museum*. For a prescient analysis of the contests over commerce, see Purbrick, "South Kensington Museum."

6 Bennett, "The Exhibitionary Complex"; *The Birth of the Museum*, introduction, part 1, esp. 6, 63. See also Duncan, *Civilizing Rituals*; and Hooper-Greenhill, *Museums and the Shaping of Knowledge*, chap. 7. For broader considerations of these ideas that take them beyond the museum, see Gilbert, *Mapping the Victorian Social Body*; Joyce, *The Rule of Freedom*; and Poovey, *Making a Social Body*.

7 Taylor, *Art for the Nation*, chaps. 2 and 3, esp. 29, 70. See also McClellan, "A Brief History of the Art Museum Public," 1–50; and Fyfe, *Art, Power, and Modernity*.

8 "The South Kensington Museum," *Chambers' Journal of Popular Literature, Science, and Arts*, 5 September 1857, AAD PC, vol. 6, 53; Barlow and Wilson, "Consuming Empire?" 156–71, esp. 162; Whitehead, *The Public Art Museum in Nineteenth Century Britain*, 83.

9 Conn, *Museums and American Intellectual Life, 1876–1926*, 11; Barlow and Trodd, "Introduction," 1–29, esp. 1; Kriegel, "After the Exhibitionary Complex"; McClellan, "A Brief History of the Art Museum Public," 8. For a critique of Barlow and Trodd, see Barringer, "Vision and Re-vision in Histories of Victorian Art." For Bennett's own reconsideration, see, for example, *Pasts beyond Memory*, esp. 8, 27–28.

10 Taylor, *Art for the Nation*, 40. On the museum as an urban institution, see Sherman, *Worthy Monuments*; and Hill, *Culture and Class in English Public Museums*.

11 Mort and Ogborn, "Transforming Metropolitan London, 1750–1960," 1–14; Driver, *Geography Militant*; Driver and Gilbert, "Heart of Empire?"; Driver and Gilbert, *Imperial Cities*; Feldman and Stedman Jones, *Metropolis London*; Gilbert, *Mapping the Victorian Social Body*; Rappaport, "Art, Commerce

or Empire?"; Rappaport, *Shopping for Pleasure*; Walkowitz, *City of Dreadful Delight*; Walkowitz, "Going Public"; Walkowitz, "The Indian Woman, the Flower Girl, and the Jew"; Walkowitz, "The 'Vision of Salome.'" For an earlier period, see Ogborn, *Spaces of Modernity*.

12 The Whitechapel Art Gallery is the prototype here. See Koven, "The Whitechapel Picture Exhibitions and the Politics of Seeing"; Steyn, "Inside-Out"; and Wilson, "The Highest Art for the Lowest People." See also Waterfield, *Art for the People*.

13 On this point, see also Barringer, "Equipoise and the Object." For larger discussions of the labor aristocracy, see Gray, *The Aristocracy of Labor in Victorian Edinburgh*; and Crossick, *An Artisan Elite in Victorian Society*.

14 On rational recreation, see Bailey, *Leisure and Class in Victorian England*.

15 For a contemporary discussion of the flaneur and his historiography, see Mort and Ogborn, "Transforming Metropolitan London," 12. See also note 11, as well as Burton, *At the Heart of the Empire*; Burton, "Making a Spectacle of Empire"; Nord, *Walking the Victorian Streets*; Ross, *Love and Toil*; and Schneer, *London 1900*.

16 Robinson, "The Museum of Art," 3.

17 Auerbach, *The Great Exhibition of 1851*, chap. 7; Hassam, "Portable Iron Structures and Uncertain Colonial Spaces at the Sydenham Crystal Palace," 174–93; Twining, *Notes on the Organization of an Industrial College for Artisans*.

18 Letters from Henry Cole to Charles Grey, 6 January 1855 and 19 October 1858, Henry Cole Correspondence, National Art Library, London (hereafter NAL), vol. 1, 55.BB.1, ff. 113–15, ff. 128–29; Wainwright, "Shopping for South Kensington"; Wainwright and Gere, "The Making of the South Kensington Museum III."

19 Bonython and Burton, *The Great Exhibitor*, part 4; Cole, *Observations by Mr. Cole on the Means of Carrying out the Plans Proposed for Kensington Gore*. See also "Prince Albert's Views on Buildings at Kensington in 1855," Henry Cole Miscellanies, vol. 12, NAL 55.AA.57, f. 188.

20 On this history, see, for example, Burton, *Vision and Accident*, chap. 3; Cole, *Observations on the Expediency of Carrying out the Proposals of the Commissioners for the Exhibition of 1851*; Minihan, *The Nationalization of Culture*, 121–24; Sheppard, *Survey of London: The Museums Area of South Kensington and Westminster* vol. 38, 49–53, 72–73; *Survey of London: Southern Kensington: Brompton*, vol. 41.

21 Papers of the Board of Trade, NA BT1/526/1332; Physick, *The Victoria and Albert Museum*, 23; Cole, *Introductory Address*, 20. On the career of the "Boilers," see also Cardoso Denis, "The Brompton Barracks."

22 *Daily News*, 29 June 1861, AAD PC (March 1859–June 1861), 403.

23 Letter from Henry Cole to Charles Grey, August 1856, Henry Cole Correspondence, vol. 1, 55.BB.1, ff. 118–19; Sheppard, *Survey of London* 38, 98.

24 "South Kensington Museum," *Post*, 22 June 1857, and "The South Kensington Museum," *Observer*, 28 June 1857, AAD PC, vol. 6, 27, 31.

25 See, for example, Cole, *A Short Statement of the Nature and Objects of the Proposed Great Exhibition of the Works of Industry of All Nations*, 6, as found in Henry Cole Miscellanies, vol. 8b, NAL 55.AA.53, f. 166.

26 See Whitehead, *The Public Art Museum in Nineteenth Century Britain*, introduction.

27 Cole, "The Functions of the Science and Art Department," 21–22, 27–28.

28 Playfair, "On Scientific Institutions in Connection with the Department of Science and Art," 15–16. See also Robinson, "The Museum of Art," 13.

29 "Letter," *Daily News*, 8 February 1856, AAD PC (January 1855–April 1856 [vol. 5]), 234.

30 Redgrave, *An Address on the Gift of the Sheepshanks Collection*, 29.

31 "Popular Art Education," *Meliora* 1 (2) (July 1858): 165–76, esp. 165.

32 Cole, "The Functions of the Science and Art Department," 25–26.

33 Redgrave, *An Address on the Gift of the Sheepshanks Collection*, 28–29.

34 See McClellan, "A Brief History of the Art Museum Public," 7.

35 "Specifications of Works Relating to the South Kensington Museum," 26 June 1851, AAD ED 84/215/4127/57.

36 Whitehead, *The Public Art Museum in Nineteenth-Century Britain*, 166–72.

37 "South Kensington Museum," *Morning Star*, 23 June 1857, "South Kensington Museum," *Times*, 28 June 1857, and "A Visit to the South Kensington Museum," *Brighton Herald*, 8 January 1859, AAD PC, vol. 6, 28, 32, 220; *Bayswater Chronicle*, 6 March 1861, AAD PC (March 1859–June 1861), 276. See also Physick, *The Victoria and Albert Museum*, 30–31; "Lighting the Museum," 14 July 1856, NA ED28/6, f. 9; "Lighting up of the Museum," 26 June 1857, f. 203; and "Removal of Science and Art Department to Kensington Gore," NA WORK 17/24/4, ff. 14–15, ff. 19–22, f. 27. By the end of December 1878, nearly eighteen million visitors had passed through the museum's doors according to South Kensington Museum, *Memorandum upon the Formation, Arrangement, and Administration of the South Kensington Museum*, 17.

38 Joyce, *The Rule of Freedom*; Otter, "Cleansing and Clarifying."

39 *Report from the Select Committee on the South Kensington Museum Together with the Proceedings of the Committee, Minutes of Evidence, and Appendix*, 30, 115. On gaslight, see Otter, "Cleansing and Clarifying," 40–64, esp. 56.

40 See, for example, *Report from the Select Committee on National Monuments and Works of Art, with the Minutes of Evidence and Appendix*; Wilson, "The Relation of Ornamental to Industrial Art," 33; Forbes, *On the Educational Uses of Museums*; and Philostrate, "Sincerity versus Fashion," 91.

41 See, for example, Letter from National Sunday League, 29 August 1860, Home Office: Registered Papers, HO 45/6884; and "Sunday Openings: South Kensington Museum and Bethnal Green Museum," AAD ED 84/234. The latter file demonstrates that the opinions of the working classes were, in truth, split on the matter.

42 Bailkin, *The Culture of Property*, 10.

43 Letter from "A Working Man," 15 May 1861, AAD ED 84/216.

44 Pimlico, in *Star*, 1 June 1859, AAD PC (March 1859–June 1861), 22; "The British Museum Shut against Working Men," *Daily News*, 9 July 1855, AAD PC, vol. 5, 71.

45 "A Collection of Newspaper Cuttings Relating to Pimlico, 1849–85," British Library, London; Liddell, *Pastoral Letter to the Parishioners of St. Paul's, Knightsbridge, and St. Barnabas, Pimlico*.

46 "Pimlico," *Star*, 1 June 1859, AAD PC (March 1859–June 1861, vol. 1), 22.

47 *Report from the Select Committee on the South Kensington Museum*, 110–12.

48 "The South Kensington Museum," *Chambers' Journal of Popular Literature, Science, and the Arts*, 5 September 1857, AAD PC, vol. 6, 53.

49 See "South Kensington Museum," *Morning Star*, 23 June 1857; "The South Kensington Museum," *Observer*, 28 June 1857; *Morning Star*, 20 June 1857; and "Opening the South Kensington Museum on Sundays," *Morning Star*, 22 August 1857, AAD PC, vol. 6, 28, 31, 40, 47.

50 See Whitehead, *The Public Art Museum in Nineteenth Century Britain*, chaps. 6 and 7.

51 *Report of the National Gallery Site Commission*. See also *Report of the Select Committee on the National Gallery* (1853). On the National Gallery, see Trodd, "Culture, Class, City"; Trodd, "The Paths to the National Gallery"; and MacGregor, "A Pentecost in Trafalgar Square."

52 On the intricacies of these coalitions, see Whitehead, *The Public Art Museum in Nineteenth Century Britain*, chap. 7, esp. 158–71.

53 *Report of the National Gallery Site Commission*, 168–69.

54 Taylor, *Art for the Nation*, chap. 2; Joyce, *Rule of Freedom*; Otter, "Cleansing and Clarifying."

55 See Taylor, *Art for the Nation*, chap. 2.

56 On London's inadequacy as an imperial capital, see Gilbert, "'London in All Its Glory.'"

57 Excerpt from Edward Everett Papers, Massachusetts Historical Society, Boston, 9 August 1842, "History of the National Gallery," National Gallery Archives, London. See also Eastlake, *The National Gallery*. Such assessments would persist into the 1860s. See, for example, *Telegraph*, 14 June 1864, and "A National Palace for Art," *Builder*, 9 July 1864, AAD PC (January–August 1864, vol. 2), 255, 295; and Robinson, *The National Gallery Considered in Reference to Other Public Collections and to the Proposed New Building in Trafalgar Square*, 3.

58 Waagen, "Thoughts on the New Building to Be Erected for the National Gallery of England," 101–3, 121–25.

59 Eastlake, *The National Gallery*; Wornum, "The National Gallery," 37–39.

60 *Report of the National Gallery Site Commission*, 1–2, 43, 45–46.

61 Ibid., 10–11, 21–23, 52–53. See also Taylor, *Art for the Nation*, 61.

62 *Report of the National Gallery Site Commission*, 21–23, 137.

63 Ibid., 129, 157–58.

64 Ibid., 69, 95, 137.

65 Ibid., 95, 103, 157–58, 167; *Morning Star*, 20 June 1857; "The South Kensington Museum," *Observer*, 28 June 1857, AAD PC vol. 6, 40, 31; *Star*, 8 June 1864, AAD PC (January–August 1864, vol. 2).

66 Excerpt from Waagen, *Works of Arts and Artists in England*, vol. 1; and *Times*, 27 March 1857, both in History of the National Gallery Building: Related Written Information File I: Publications, 1818–1880, National Gallery Archives. For reactions to the decision in the press in 1857, see History of the National Gallery Building, File I, National Gallery Archives. See also *Telegraph*, 14 June 1864, AAD PC (January–August 1864, vol. 2), 255.

67 Cole, "On Public Taste in Kensington," unpublished lecture, 5 April 1853, Henry Cole Miscellanies, vol. II, NAL 55.AA.56, ff. 8–42, esp. f. 15.

68 Nead, *Victorian Babylon*.

69 See, for example, "Leader Comment," *Notting Hill and Bayswater Times and West-End Family Journal*, 7 February 1863, 4; "Possible Boulevards," *Kensington News and West-London Times*, 27 March 1869, 2; *Belgravia and South Kensington New Road, 31 and 32 Vict., Session, 1867 to 1868: An Act Amended in Committee to Extend and Amend the Borrowing Powers of the Belgravia Road Company and for Other Purposes*, n.p. See also "The Encroachments in Kensington Gardens," *West End Advertiser*, 21 and 28 July, 18 August, and 8 September 1860, n.p.; *Chelsea, Pimlico, and Brompton Advertiser*, 12 January 1861, 2; and "The Albert Bridge," *Chelsea News and Central Advertiser*, 18 November 1865, 6. These discussions were long-standing ones, particularly when it came to Kensington Gardens, which technically lay outside of the parish. See, for instance, *Times*, 2 and 4 November, 1840; and "A Resident in Brompton," *Morning Chronicle*, 4 November 1840, as found in *History and Antiquities of Kensington*, Faulkner III, ff. 209–11, Kensington Local Studies Library, London.

70 Bowring, "South Kensington," 563–83, esp. 570. See also "Book of Plans for Kensington Road Improvements," London Metropolitan Archive, MBW 2475. These plans were just as contested as Cole's collecting efforts. See, for example, "Letter to the Editor," *Times*, 25 May 1865; "Nature of a Boulevard from Sloane Street to South Kensington Museum, *Builder*, 27 May 1865, AAD PC (October 1864–July 1865), 284, 287.

71 *Report of the Select Committee on the South Kensington Museum*, 39; Metropolitan District Railway, *Opening of the Line from Blackfriars Bridge to* the *Mansion House Station, Queen Victoria Street, of the Enlarged Station at South Kensington, and of the Northern Junction between Kensington High Street Station and the West London Railway* (London, 1871). On Cole's attempts to build a subway between the museum and the station, see "Subway Proposals," AAD ED 84/78; "Proposed Subway Railways," AAD ED 84/79; "Subway from South Kensington Station to Museum," AAD ED 84/80; and Cole, *A Special Report on the Annual International Exhibitions of the Years 1871, 1872, 1873, and 1874.*

72 Bowring, "South Kensington, Part 2," 62–81, esp. 70, 79. See also "Plan for South Kensington Railway," Metropolitan London Archive, MBW2629. The Underground displeased some of the residents of Kensington, who feared that it would allow the "lowest and most degraded" elements of the metropolis into the parish. See, for example, Bayly, "Westurbia," 3.

73 See, for example, "Old Kensington," *All the Year Round*, 2 March 1889, 197–201, esp. 197, as found in Local Studies Files, Kensington and Chelsea Library, H914.213 (1889).

74 See, for example, "The Exhibition Buildings," *Saturday Review*, 30 May 1863, 681–83, as found in AAD PC (1862 Exhibition: October 1862–March 1865), 143; Burt, *Historical Notices of Chelsea, Kensington, Fulham, and Hammersmith*, 56; "Kensington, Ancient and Modern," *Kensington Argus and West London Guardian*, 14 September 1878, 2; and *Bayswater Chronicle*, 31 August 1871, 4.

75 "Kensington Board of Guardians: Copies of Orders for the Reception of Pauper Lunatics into Asylums," KBG 200/1.0011, 2 December 1871; KBG 200/1.002, 18 October 1870; KBG 200/1.004, 9 December 1874, London Metropolitan Archives.

76 Bowring, "South Kensington," 565. On the transformations of this era, see, for example, Davis, "Modern London"; Olsen, *The Growth of Victorian London*; Port, *Imperial London*; Sheppard, *London, 1808–1870*; Summerson, *The Architecture of Victorian London*; and Summerson, *The London Building World of the Eighteen-Sixties*. See also Sheppard, *Survey of London*.

77 *Bayswater Chronicle and West-London Journal*, 21 June 1873, 5; "Rustic Adornments," *Kensington News and West London Times*, 10 April 1869, 4; "A West End Nuisance," *Bayswater Chronicle and West-London Journal*, 5 July 1873, 5.

78 "Kensington, Ancient and Modern," *Kensington Argus and West London Guardian*, 14 September 1878, 2; Rappaport, *Shopping for Pleasure*, chap. 1.

79 Bowring, "South Kensington," 565.

80 "Address," *Kensington Chronicle and Bayswater, Notting Hill, and Hammersmith Advertiser*, 1 October 1859, 3.

81 Robinson, *The National Gallery*, 11. One commentator had remarked in 1857 that "London is growing so fast, that it could not be said with certainty, that London would not be round [South Kensington] in twenty-five years" (*Report of the National Gallery Site Commission*, 84).

82 Leigh Hunt, *The Old Court Suburb*, 1:4; *Bayswater Chronicle and West-*

London Journal, 2 August 1873, 4; "Address," *Kensington Chronicle*, 22 October 1859, 3; "Kensington, Ancient and Modern," *Kensington Argus and West London Guardian*, 14 September 1878, 2.

83 See, for example, *Simpson's Chelsea, Pimlico, Brompton, and Knightsbridge Directory and Court Guide, Including Lists of Vestry, Parish Officers, Post Office Intelligence, and Chelsea Charities*; "Kensington, Ancient and Modern," *Kensington Argus and West London Guardian*, 14 September 1878, 2. See also *Notting Hill and Bayswater Times and West-End Family Journal*, 7 February 1863, 4; Sherwell, *Life in West London*, 8; and Rappaport, *Shopping for Pleasure*, chap. 4.

84 "Leader Comment," *Kensington Argus and West London Guardian*, 30 November 1878, 2.

85 "Leader Comment," *Bayswater Chronicle and West-London Journal*, 5 April 1873, 2.

86 *Bayswater Chronicle*, 31 August 1871, 4. See also Davis, "Jennings Buildings and the Royal Borough."

87 Cole, "On Public Taste in Kensington," ff. 8–11.

88 Hunt, *The Old Court Suburb*, 1:6, 130–33.

89 *Bayswater Chronicle*, 31 August 1871, 4.

90 "Kensington Gardens," *Illustrated London News*, 14 July 1855; "Kensington," *Household Words* 7, 11 February 1854, Kensington Local Studies Files, Kensington and Chelsea Library; "A West End Nuisance," *Bayswater Chronicle and West-London Journal*, 5 July 1873, 5; "Kensington, Ancient and Modern," *Kensington Argus and West London Guardian*; Burt, *Historical Notices of Chelsea, Kensington, Fulham, and Hammersmith*, 46; Hunt, *The Old Court Suburb*, 1:1–2.

91 See, for example, Whitehead, *The Public Art Gallery in Nineteenth Century Britain*; and Yanni, *Nature's Museums*.

92 *Daily News*, 30 August 1860, AAD PC (March 1859–June 1861, vol. 2), 191.

93 "South Kensington Again," *Saturday Review*, 14 May 1864, AAD PC (January–August 1864), 199. See also *Report of the National Gallery Site Commission*, 83. By the later 1860s, an internal commission at South Kensington pointed out that a greater variation in temperature and higher level of moisture made it a more perilous site for paintings than Trafalgar Square. See South Kensington Museum, *Report of the Commission on Heating, Lighting, and Ventilation of the South Kensington Museum*.

94 "The South Kensington Job," *Spectator*, 13 June 1863, 2109–10, AAD PC (1862 Exhibition: October 1862–March 1865), 158. See also "South or East Kensington?" *West Middlesex Advertiser*, January 1857, AAD PC, vol. 6, 246; and *Saturday Review*, 18 September 1858, 279–80, AAD PC vol. 6, 155.

95 *Times*, 21 June 1856; "History of the National Gallery Building," National Gallery Archives; *Daily News*, 30 August 1860, AAD PC (March 1859–June 1861), 191. See also Driver and Gilbert, "Heart of Empire?"

96 "The Threatened Removal of the National Gallery to Kensington,"

Daily News, 17 January 1859, AAD PC (March 1856–February 1859, vol. 2), 222; "South Kensington Again," *Saturday Review*, 3 March 1866, AAD PC (August 1865–March 1866), 239; *Daily News*, 29 June 1861, AAD PC (March 1859–June 1861), 403. See also "The Vagaries of the South Kensington Clique," *Scientific Review and Journal of the Inventors Institute*, 1 April 1866, AAD PC (March–August 1866), 24.

97 Barlow and Wilson, *Governing Cultures*, 164.

98 *Building News*, 14 October 1864, 761, AAD PC (October 1864–July 1865), 8; Watson, *The Imperial Museum for India and the Colonies*, 1, 34, 36.

99 "The South Kensington Museum," *Chambers' Journal of Popular Literature, Science, and the Arts*, 5 September 1857, AAD PC vol. 6, 53.

100 "The India Museum," *Chambers Journal*, 24 July 1857, Museums, Box 1, John Johnson Collection, Oxford; "Pickings by the Way," *Design and Work: A Home and Shop Companion* (19 August 1876): 238. On the India Museum, see also *The East India Museum*; *Inventory of the Collection of Examples of Indian Art and Manufactures Transferred to the South Kensington Museum*; Desmond, *The India Museum*; Barringer, "The South Kensington Museum and the Colonial Project"; and Barlow and Wilson, *Governing Cultures*, 164.

101 See, for example, *Daily News*, 8 June 1864, AAD PC (January–August 1864, vol. 2), 240; "Art and Science," *Spectator*, 18 August 1860, AAD PC (March 1859–June 1861), 169; Rappaport, *Shopping for Pleasure*; Walkowitz, "Going Public"; and Barringer, "Leighton in Albertopolis."

102 *Times*, 15 April 1864, AAD PC (January–August 1864), n.p.; *Daily Telegraph*, 1 April 1865, AAD PC (October 1864–July 1865), 207.

103 "Rival Museums: The British Museum and the Museum at South Kensington," *Art Journal*, new ser., 6 (September 1865): 281–83; "The South Kensington Museum," *Art Journal*, new ser., 8 (January 1869): 17–19. On this period in South Kensington's history, see Burton, *Vision and Accident*, chaps. 4–6.

104 South Kensington Museum, *Local Metropolitan Museums*, 4–6, 15, 19, 30. See also Official Correspondence on the East London Museum, AAD ED84/244; "New Buildings of the South Kensington Museum," *Illustrated London News* 40 (1301) (29 September 1866): 304–6; Barringer, *Men at Work*, chap. 4; and Whitehead, *The Public Art Museum in Nineteenth Century Britain*, chap. 2. On the infatuation with a romantic, aesthetic Italy, see O'Connor, *The Romance of Italy and The English Political Imagination*; and Siegel, *Haunted Museum*.

105 *Lloyd's*, 6 March 1864, and *Illustrated Times*, 12 March 1864, AAD PC (January–August 1864), n.p. and 95; Wallis, "Art and Handicraft, no. 2," *The Working Man*, 13 January 1866, as found in Wallis, *Records of Art and Industry*, vol. 4, NAL PP.34.G; "Exhibition of Arts and Manufactures for Northeast London," *Art Journal*, new ser., 6 (October 1865): 301–2.

106 "Sunday Openings: Bethnal Green Museum and South Kensington Museum," AAD ED 84/234.

107 See Hall, *Civilising Subjects*.

108 McClelland, "England's Greatness, the Working Man," 71–118, esp. 72; McClelland, "Rational and Respectable Men"; McClelland, "Some Thoughts on Masculinity and the 'Representative Artisan' in Britain, 1850–1880."

109 This was Mr. Baxter Langley, an erstwhile supporter of Sunday openings, who changed his position in the interests of the working man. See "The Artisan and His Day of Rest," *Saturday Review*, 9 December 1865, as found in AAD ED 84/234.

110 "Rival Museums: The British Museum and the Museum at South Kensington," *Art Journal*, new ser., 6 (1865): 281–83.

111 McClelland, "England's Greatness, the Working Man," 73.

112 South Kensington Museum, *Local Metropolitan Museums*, 24–25.

113 Ibid.

114 For such arguments as they applied to the eighteenth century, see Barrell, *The Birth of Pandora and the Division of Knowledge*, esp. chap. 3.

115 Black, *Catalogue of the Collection of Paintings, Porcelain, Bronzes, Decorative Furniture, and Other Works of Art*, vii–xi. See also *Report of Proceedings at a Deputation to his Grace the Duke of Marlborough*, AAD ED84/46; "Bethnal Green Museum," *Civil Service Gazette*, 29 June 1982, Alan Summerly Cole Newspaper Cuttings, vol. I, NAL 55.CC.32, 53; and *Daily News*, 22 June 1872, 5.

116 "Justitia Fiat," *East London Observer*, 22 June 1872, 6; South Kensington Museum, *Memorandum upon the Formation, Arrangement, and Administration of the South Kensington Museum*, 17.

117 For an American iteration of art as uplift, see James, "The Wallace Collection in Bethnal Green," 67. Thanks to Morna O'Neill.

118 "The Museum at South Kensington," *Art Journal*, new ser., 6 (October 1860): 317–18; "Speech of William Conningham," *Post*, 16 September 1860; "Is There a Liberal Party?" *Star* 17 February 1860, AAD PC (March 1859–June 1861), 206.

119 *East London Observer*, 26 October 1872, Alan Summerly Cole Newspaper Cuttings, vol. I, NAL 55.CC. 32, 61; *East London Observer*, 13 April 1872, 5; *East London Observer*, 4 May 1872, 5; "East London Museum," *East London Observer*, 25 May 1872, 7; "Royal Opening of the East London Museum," *East London Observer*, 8 June 1872, 4; "Bethnal Green Museum," *Athenaeum*, 22 June 1872, AAD PC (1870–1875), 97; "Bethnal Green Museum," *Art Journal*, new ser., 11 (December 1872): 301; Greenwood, *Museums and Art Galleries*; Taylor, *Art for the Nation*, 82.

120 *Daily News*, 22 June 1872, 5; "The East London Museum," *East London Observer*, 20 April 20, 1872, 5. The *Observer* reported that a mosaic made by female prisoners at Woking covered the museum's floors.

121 *Fun*, 6 July 1872, Alan Summerly Cole Newspaper Cuttings, vol. 1, NAL 55.CC. 32, 58–59.

122 "Bethnal Green Museum Correspondence: Out Letters," 61, 90–92, 321, 327, AAD ED 84/23.

123 Black, *On Exhibit*, 33; Physick, *The Victoria and Albert Museum*, 56, 97, 143–46; *History of the Victoria and Albert Museum*, 34–35, and "Memorandum on the Historical Purpose of the Art Museum," January 1903, 5–6, both in AAD ED 84/215; "On the Opening of the Bethnal Green Museum," Henry Cole Miscellanies, vol. 16, NAL 55.AA.61, ff. 203–4.

124 "Royal Visit," *East London Observer*, 22 June 1872, 4; "Ceremonial of the Opening of the Bethnal Green Museum by His Royal Highness the Prince of Wales, on Behalf of Her Majesty the Queen," Henry Cole Miscellanies, vol. 16, NAL 55.AA.61, ff. 205–8.

125 *East London Observer*, 26 October 1872, Alan Summerly Cole Newspaper Cuttings, vol. 1, NAL 55.CC. 32, 61.

126 *Daily Telegraph*, June 25, 1872, 5; "Opening of the East London Museum," *Daily News*, June 25, 1872, 5–6.

127 My thanks go to Tim Barringer for this phrasing.

128 "Opening of the East London Museum," *Daily News*, 25 June 1872, 5–6.

129 "Opening of the East London Museum, *Daily News*, 25 June 1872, 5–6; *Daily Telegraph* 25 June 1872, 5.

130 The *Post*'s words were quoted in neighborhood papers, for example, in "Bethnal Green and the Telegraph," *East London Observer*, 29 June 1872, 4–5. See also *Tower Hamlets Express*, 28 June 1872.

131 The American writer Henry James also recalled the legend in "The Wallace Collection in Bethnal Green," 67.

132 Chancellor, *Walks among London's Pictures*, 464; "Museum in East London," Henry Cole Miscellanies, vol. 16, NAL 55.AA.59, ff. 52–53; *History of the Blind Beggar of Bethnal Green*.

133 See, for example, "Bethnal Green's Welcome to the Prince of Wales," *East London Observer*, 6 July 1872, 3; "Leader Comment," *Bethnal Green Chronicle*, 6 December 1872, 4.

134 "Opening of the East London Museum," *Daily News*, 25 June 1872, 5. See also Mayhew, *London Labor and the London Poor*. For a later characterization of Bethnal Green along these lines, see "Bethnal Green," *Saturday Review*, 1 July 1882, 11–12, AAD PC (April 1882–June 1883), 20. Such coverage predates the new journalism of the 1880s studied by Walkowitz in *City of Dreadful Delight*.

135 See, for example, Driver, *Geography Militant*, esp. chap. 8; Koven, *Slumming*; and Herbert, "Mayhew's Cockney Polynesia" in his *Culture and Anomie*.

136 "Opening of the East London Museum, *Daily News*, 25 June 1872, 5; *Daily Telegraph*, 25 June 1872, 5–6.

137 "Opening of the East London Museum," *Daily News*, 25 June 1872, 5.

138 *Daily Telegraph*, 25 June 1872, 5.

139 "Bethnal Green and the Telegraph," *East London Observer*, 29 June 1872, 4-5; "Leader Comment," *East London Observer*, 6 July 1872, 4.

140 "The Slanders on Bethnal Green," *East London Observer*, 6 July 1872, 5. See also "Leader Comment," *East London Observer*, 6 July 1872, 4; Letter from Septimus Hansard, *East London Observer*, 13 July 1872, 5; G. W., *East London Observer*, 29 June 1872, 3; and "Amicus," *East London Observer*, 6 July 1872, 6.

141 "The Slanders on Bethnal Green," *East London Observer*, 6 July 1872, 5; "A Museum for East London," *Daily News*, 22 September 1879, AAD PC (July 1879-July 1880), 22.

142 "Opening of the East London Museum, *Daily News*, 25 June 1872, 5; *Daily Telegraph*, 25 June 1872, 5-6.

143 See Bailey, "Will the Real Bill Banks Please Stand Up?"; Kate Hill's discussion of Bailey in *Culture and Class in English Public Museums*, 133; and Bailey, *Popular Culture and Performance in the Victorian City*, chap. 2.

144 Black, *Catalogue of the Wallace Collection*, xv; "Correspondence, Reports, and Specifications Relating to Works at the Bethnal Green Museum," ED 84/46. By the end of 1878, the museum had counted nearly 4.8 million visitors according to South Kensington Museum, *Memorandum upon the Formation, Arrangement, and Administration of the South Kensington Museum*, 18.

145 Hill, *Culture and Class in English Public Museums*, 135.

Afterword TRAVELS IN SOUTH KENSINGTON

1 Conway, *Travels in South Kensington*, 25, 27, 29-30, 33-35; *Times*, 20 and 21 April 1882, Press Cuttings, Archive of Art and Design, London (hereafter AAD PC) (April 1882-June 1883): 4; Kirschenblatt-Gimblett, *Destination Culture*, 133; Clifford, *The Predicament of Culture*, chap. 10.

2 Conway, *Travels in South Kensington*, 24-25; Fitzgerald, "The Romance of the Museum," Museums, Box 2, John Johnson Collection, Oxford.

3 *Daily News*, 13 May 1880, AAD PC (July 1879-July 1880, vol. 2): 199. On the India Museum, see Desmond, *The India Museum*. On the "interlocking practices of empire building and collecting," see Black, *On Exhibit*, 65; Aguirre, *Informal Empire*; Bailkin, *The Culture of Property*; Coombes, *Reinventing Africa*; and Jasanoff, *Edge of Empire*.

4 Conway, *Travels in South Kensington*, 86-93, esp. 86-87.

5 For recent work on the collections from far-reaching sites of formal and informal empire, see n. 3; and Hevia, *English Lessons*.

6 Conway, *Autobiography, Memories, and Experiences*, vol. 2. On ethnography and collections, see Bennett, *Pasts beyond Memory*; Coombes, *Reinventing*

Africa, introduction, chaps. 6 and 7; and Yanni, *Nature's Museums*. See also Dirks, "Introduction"; Mitchell, "Orientalism and the Exhibitionary Order"; Stocking, "Introduction"; and Chapman, "Arranging Ethnology."

7 See note 6. See also Herbert, *Culture and Anomie*; Penny, *Objects of Culture*; and Baudrillard, "The System of Collecting."

8 Conway, *Travels in South Kensington*, 25, 61.

9 The display of Tipoo's Tiger offers an important exception. See Jasanoff, *Edge of Empire*.

10 Barringer, *Men at Work*, 227–28.

11 Conway, *Travels in South Kensington*, 25, 49–50.

12 Thanks go to Tim Barringer for this point. See also his *Men at Work*, 228–29.

13 *Report from the Select Committee on Arts and Manufactures* (1835), 116–17.

14 *Daily News*, 19 September 1872, AAD PC (July 1879–July 1880): 22.

15 Barringer, *Men at Work*, 2, 321.

16 Conway, *Travels in South Kensington*, 25, 27, 29–30, 33–35; *Times*, 20–21 April 1882, AAD PC (April 1882–June 1883): 4.

17 See, for example, Woodward, *A Handbook to the Law of Copyright in Registered Designs*.

18 Conway, *Travels in South Kensington*, 101.

19 Ibid., 102.

20 See, for example, Sean O'Neill, "Robbers Are Turning Theft into a Fine Art at the V & A," *Times of London* 31 December 2004.

21 Conway, *Travels in South Kensington*, 101.

22 Burton, *Vision and Accident*, chaps. 5–8; Stuart Macdonald, *History and Philosophy of Art Education*, 222, 263–64.

23 *Times*, 9 July 1878, AAD PC (October 1877–June 1879), 5.

24 See, for example, AAD ED 84/238.

25 "Ghosts at South Kensington," *Saturday Review*, 14 June 1879, AAD PC (October 1877–June 1879), 160. See also Conn, *Museums and American Intellectual Life*.

26 Wilk, "Foreword," vii.

27 This had become a common refrain in publications for decorators and art workmen even as early as the later 1850s. See, for example, such periodicals as *Universal Decorator: A Complete Guide to Ornamental Design*; *Decorator: An Illustrated Practical Magazine and Advertiser for the Furnishing Trades*; *Art Workman: A Monthly Journal of Design for the Artist, Artificer, and Manufacturer*; and *Journal of Decorative Art*.

28 *Echo*, 19 November 1873, AAD PC (1870–1875): 182; *Telegraph*, 30 July 1879, AAD PC (July 1879–July 1880): 82; *Daily News*, 7 September 1878, AAD PC (October 1877–June 1879): 31. See also Greenwood, *Museums and Art Galleries*, chap. 15; and Brown, *South Kensington and Its Art Training*.

29 On the growth of the schools, see Cole, *What Is Art Culture?* 11.

30 Conway, *Travels in South Kensington*, 104–6, 110.

31 Cohen, "Why Did *The House* Fail?" 35–42; Cohen, *Household Gods*, chap. 5.

32 See "South Kensington Museum," *Chambers' Journal*, 4 October 1873, 628–30, John Johnson Collection, Museums, Box 1. On women's art education, see, for example, Dodd, "Art Education for Women in the 1860s," 187–200; Chalmers, *Women in the Nineteenth-Century Art World*; and Israel, *Names and Stories*.

33 On these developments, see also Snodin, "Victorian Britain?" 369–97, esp. 387–89; and Rappaport, *Shopping for Pleasure*, chap. 4.

34 *Daily News*, 7 September 1878, AAD PC (October 1877–June 1879): 31; Eastlake, *Hints on Household Taste*; "The Scope of Art," *House Decorator and School of Design* 5 (7 January 1881): 53. On house decoration and domestic interiors, see Ferry, "Decorators May Be Compared to Doctors"; Sparke, "Historical Revivals, Commercial Enterprise, and Public Confusion"; Rich, "Designing the Dinner Party"; and Kinchin, "Designer as Critic."

35 Conway, *Travels in South Kensington*, 166, 170–71. For a discussion of women, craft, and exhibitions at the turn of the century, see Grever and Waaldijk, *Transforming the Public Sphere*.

36 See Snodin, "Who Led Taste?: Victorian Britain," 390–95.

37 For museum exhibitions especially, see Kaplan, *The Art That Is Life*; Kaplan, *The Arts and Crafts Movement in Europe and America*; Parry, *William Morris*; and Waggoner, *The Beauty of Life*.

38 "Travels in South Kensington," *Saturday Review*, 18 November 1882, AAD PC (April 1882–June 1883): 212.

39 On aristocrats as barbaric in taste, see Mandler, *The Fall and Rise of the Stately Home*, chap. 3.

40 See, for example, MacCarthy, "The Designer," 32; and Harvey and Press, "The Businessman," 52.

41 Conway, *Travels in South Kensington*, 137, 146, 202, 206.

42 Thompson, *William Morris*, 96.

43 Ibid.; Stansky, *Redesigning the World*, 23–29; Crawford, "United Kingdom," 26.

44 On Ruskin's critique of Cole and his circle, see Lubbock, *The Tyranny of Taste*, part 5, chap. 6. See also Barringer, *Men at Work*, 143, 246, 265.

45 Pevsner, *Pioneers of Modern Design*, 42.

46 Stansky, *From William Morris to Sergeant Pepper*, 65, 88; Stansky, *Redesigning the World*, 23–24, 32, 38, 49; Stansky, *William Morris*, 89; Thompson, *William Morris*, 643–49; Pevsner, *Pioneers of Modern Design*, 14–17; Kaplan, "Design for the Modern World," 11–12. "Redesign the world" is Stansk's phrasing.

47 On Cole's prescience, see Francastel, *Art and Technology in the Nine-*

teenth and Twentieth Centuries, 37–45; and Giedion, *Mechanization Takes Command*, 348, 365–66.

48 Admittedly, Morris did try, as his work advanced, to market more widely to the middle classes, but this was a gradual process. See Harvey and Press, *William Morris*, chaps. 3, 4, and 6; Stansky, "Recent Work on William Morris"; Stansky, *From William Morris to Sergeant Pepper*, 57; and Thompson, *William Morris*, 666.

BIBLIOGRAPHY

Archival Sources

Aberdeen Art Gallery, Aberdeen

"Life, Correspondence, and Writings of William Dyce, RA, 1806–1964, by his Son, James Stirling Dyce," Multivolume typescript.

Archive of Art and Design, Olympia, London

ED 84, History of the Victoria and Albert Museum.
Ledger, Holland and Sons (1852–1853), AAD 13/29/1983.
Press Cuttings, 1837–1882. Multiple vols.

British Library, London

Collection of newspaper-cuttings, handbills, advertisements, etc., relating to Pimlico, 1849–1885.
School of Design Correspondence, Add. MS 31218.

Central Library, Manchester

Papers of the Royal Manchester Institution, M6/1, M6/3.
Crozier, "Recollections of the Manchester School of Design," September 1879. Manuscript.

Huntington Library, San Marino, California

Benjamin Robert Haydon, "Epitaph of a Great Man," Huntington MS 45445.

John Johnson Collection, Oxford

Museums, Boxes 1 and 2.

Kensington Local Studies Archives, Kensington and Chelsea Public Library

History and Antiquities of Kensington, Faulkner III.
Local Studies Files.

London Guildhall Library

Ledger, Thomas Handyside and Son, Upholsterers (1842–53), MS 10833/2.

London Metropolitan Archives

Kensington Board of Guardians: Copies of Orders for the Reception of Pauper Lunatics into Asylums.

Ledger, Cowtan and Sons, Decorators, Upholsters, Cabinet Makers, and Electrical Engineers (1881–1888), B/CWT/1.

MWB2475, Book of Plans for Kensington Road Improvements.

MBW2629, Plan for South Kensington Railway.

National Archives, Kew, London

BT 1, Papers of the Board of Trade.

BT 3, Letters from the Board of Trade.

BT 43, Ornamental Design Act 1842 Representations Submitted to the Patents, Designs, and Trade Marks Office and Its Predecessor.

ED 9, Correspondence, Minute Books, and Reports of the Committee of the Privy Council on Education and Associated Departments.

ED 23, Establishment Files of the Department of Education and Science and Predecessors.

ED 28, Department of Science and Art Minute Books.

HO 45, Home Office Registered Papers.

WORK 17, Metropolitan Board of Works Papers.

National Art Library, Victoria and Albert Museum, London

Alan Summerly Cole Press Cuttings, 55.CC.32.

Benjamin Robert Haydon, "The School of Design," 88.JJ.10. Manuscript.

George Wallis, Records of Art and Industry, PP34G. Multiple vols.

Great Exhibition of 1851: Extracts from Newspapers, 5 vols.

Henry Cole Correspondence. Multiple vols.

Henry Cole Diaries. Multiple vols.

Henry Cole Miscellanies. Multiple vols.

National Gallery Archives, London

History of the National Gallery.

History of the National Gallery Building: Related Written Information, File I: Publications, 1818–1880.

National Library of Scotland, Edinburgh

Letter from Benjamin Robert Haydon to Robert Southey, MS 2529.

Public Record Office of Northern Ireland, Belfast

James Emerson Tennent Papers, D2922/C/9/5.

University College, London

Publications Committee: Copy of Minutes and Extracts of Correspondence, 1830–34, Papers of the Society for the Diffusion of Useful Knowledge.

Westminster City Archives, London

Estimate Book, Gillow Furniture Maker, 344/105.

Winterthur Library, Museum, and Gardens, Winterthur, Delaware

Document 983, Travel Diary, 1889.

Government Documents, Museum Catalogues, and Official Reports

Department of Practical Art. *Catalogue of the Articles of Ornamental Art in the Museum of the Department, with Appendix.* 2nd ed. London: Eyre and Spottiswoode, 1853.

————. *A Catalogue of the Articles of Ornamental Art in the Museum of the Department for the Use of Students and Manufacturers and the Consultation of the Public, with Appendices.* 4th ed. London: Eyre and Spottiswoode, 1853.

————. *Catalogue of the Articles of Ornamental Art Selected from the Exhibition of the Works of All Nations in 1851 and Purchased by the Government.* 1st ed. London: Chapman and Hall, 1852.

————. *First Report of the Department of Practical Art Presented to Both Houses of Parliament by Command of Her Majesty.* London: Eyre and Spottiswoode, 1853.

————. *Principles of Decorative Art Published by Authority of the Department of Science and Art.* London: Chapman and Hall, 1853.

————. *Prospectus: Department of Practical Art, Marlborough House, Pall Mall, under the Authority of the Board of Trade.* London: N.p., 1852.

Government School of Design. *Fifth Report of the Council of the School of Design for the Year 1845–46.* London: William Clowes and Sons, 1846.

————. *Fourth Report of the Council of the School of Design for the Year 1844–45.* London: William Clowes and Sons, 1845.

————. *Minutes of the Council of the Government School of Design.* 3 vols. London: William Clowes and Sons, 1849.

————. *Report of the Council of the School of Design for the Year 1842–43.* London: William Clowes and Sons, 1843.

House of Commons. *Report from the Select Committee on Arts and Manufactures Together with the Minutes of Evidence and Appendix.* London: His Majesty's Stationery Office, 1835.

————. *Report from the Select Committee on Arts and Their Connections with*

Manufactures, with the Minutes of Evidence, Appendix, and Index. London: His Majesty's Stationery Office, 1836.

———. *Report from the Select Committee on Copyright of Designs Together with the Minutes of Evidence Taken before Them*. 1840. Rpt.; Shannon: Irish University Press, 1968.

———. *Report of the Select Committee of the House of Commons on the Earl of Elgin's Collection of Sculptured Marbles*. London: John Murray, 1816.

———. *Report from the Select Committee on National Monuments and Works of Art, with the Minutes of Evidence and Appendix*. London: Her Majesty's Stationery Office, 1841.

———. *Report from the Select Committee on the School of Design Together with the Proceedings of the Committee, Minutes of Evidence, Appendix, and Index*. London: Her Majesty's Stationery Office, 1849.

———. *Report from the Select Committee on the South Kensington Museum Together with the Proceedings of the Committee, Minutes of Evidence, and Appendix*. London: House of Commons, 1860.

National Gallery Site Commission. *Report of the National Gallery Site Commission, Together with the Minutes, Evidence, Appendix and Index, Presented to both Houses of Parliament by Command of Her Majesty*. London: Harrison and Sons, 1857.

Parliament of Great Britain. *Hansard Parliamentary Debates*, 3rd ser., vols. 51, 56, 61.

South Kensington Museum. *Inventory of the Collection of Examples of Indian Art and Manufactures Transferred to the South Kensington Museum*. London: Eyre and Spottiswoode, 1880.

———. *Local Metropolitan Museums: Report of the Proceedings Held in the Lecture Theater, South Kensington, on Saturday, 6 May 1865*. London: Eyre and Spottiswoode, 1865.

———. *Memorandum upon the Formation, Arrangement, and Administration of the South Kensington Museum*. London: Science and Art Department, 1879.

———. *Report of the Commission on Heating, Lighting, and Ventilation of the South Kensington Museum Together with Minutes of Evidence and Appendix*. London: Eyre and Spottiswoode, 1869.

Journals, Newspapers, and Serials

Art Union
Art Journal
Art Workman
Athenaeum

Bayswater Chronicle and West London Journal
Bentley's Miscellany
Blackwood's Edinburgh Magazine
Builder
Chelsea News and Central Advertiser
Chelsea, Pimlico, and Brompton Advertiser
Daily News
Daily Telegraph
Decorator: An Illustrated Practical Magazine and Advertiser for the Furnishing Trades
Decorator's Assistant
Design and Work: A Home and Shop Companion
East London Observer
Edinburgh Review
Fraser's Magazine of Town and Country
Home Companion
House Decorator and School of Design
Household Words
John Cassell's Illustrated Exhibitor
Journal of Decorative Art
Journal of Design and Manufactures
Kensington Argus and West London Guardian
Kensington Chronicle and Bayswater, Notting Hill, and Hammersmith Advertiser
Kensington News and West-London Times
London Journal of Arts and Sciences and Patent Register
Magazine of Art
Manchester Guardian
Morning Advertiser
Morning Chronicle
Morning Post
Morning Star
New Monthly Magazine
Nineteenth Century
Notting Hill and Bayswater Times and West-End Family Journal
Penny Magazine of the Society of the Diffusion of Useful Knowledge
Punch; or, the London Charivari
Saturday Review
Times of London
Universal Decorator: A Complete Guide to Ornamental Design
West End Advertiser

Arnold, Matthew. *Culture and Anarchy*. 1869. 3rd ed.; London: Smith, Elder, 1882.

The *Art Journal Illustrated Catalogue: The Industry of All Nations, 1851*. London: G. Virtue [1851].

Crystal Palace Exhibition Illustrated Catalogue, London 1851: An Unabridged Republication of the Art Journal Special Issue, ed. John Gloag, 1851. Rpt.; New York: Dover, 1970.

Babbage, Charles. *On the Economy of Machinery and Manufactures*. 1835. Rpt.; London: Routledge, 1993.

Baines, Edward. *History of the Cotton Manufacture of Great Britain*. 1835. Rpt.; New York: Augustus M. Kelley, 1966.

Bartlett, David W. *London by Day and Night; or, Men and Things in the Great Metropolis*. New York: Hurst, [1852?].

Bartolozzi, Francesco. *Thirty-Four Lessons for Drawing the Human Figure Engraved from the Original Drawings of Bartolozzi and Adapted to the Use of Students in the Polite Arts*. London: John Walker, 1828.

Bayly, Mary. "Westurbia." *Notting Hill and Bayswater Times and West-End Family Journal* 4 (July 1865).

Birdwood, George. *The Industrial Arts of India*. London: Chapman and Hall, 1880.

———. *Two Letters on the Industrial Arts of India*. London: W. B. Whittingham, 1871.

Black, C. C. *Catalogue of the Collection of Paintings, Porcelain, Bronzes, Decorative Furniture, and Other Works of Art Lent for Exhibition in the Bethnal Green Branch of the South Kensington Museum by Sir Richard Wallace*. 9th ed. London: Eyre and Spottiswoode, 1875.

Boardman, James. *Museum Etruriae; or, a Catalogue of Cameos, Intaglios, Metals, Busts, and Bas Reliefs, Chiefly after the Antique, by the Late Josiah Wedgwood*. Liverpool: G. F. Harris' Widow and Brothers, 1817.

The Book of English Trades and Library of the Useful Arts, with Seventy Engravings. London: F. C. and J. Rivington, 1821.

Bowring, Edgar A. "South Kensington," *Nineteenth Century* 1 (4) (June 1877): 563–83.

———. "South Kensington, Part 2," *Nineteenth Century* 2 (1) (August 1877): 62–81.

Brace, George. *Observations on Extension of Protection of Copyright of Designs*. London: Smith and Elder, 1842.

Brown, Frank P. *South Kensington and Its Art Training*. London: Longmans, Green, 1912.

Burt, Isabella. *Historical Notices of Chelsea, Kensington, Fulham, and Hammersmith*. London: J. Saunders, 1871.

Calico Printer. *Letter to the Rt. Hon. Lord Althorp*. London: James Ridgway, 1831.

Chancellor, E. Beresford. *Walks among London's Pictures*. London: Kegan Paul, Trench, Trübner, 1910.

Chapman, Sydney J. *The Lancashire Cotton Industry: A Study in Economic Development*. Manchester: Manchester University Press, 1904.

Cheesman, Thomas. *Rudiments of Drawing the Human Figure from Cipriani, Guido, Poussin, Rubens*. London: R. Ackermann, 1816.

Cole, Henry. "Address at the Opening of an Elementary Drawing School at Westminster." In *Department of Practical Art: Elementary Drawing Schools*. London: Eyre and Spottiswoode, 1853.

———. *First Exercises for Children in Light, Shade, and Color*. London: Charles Knight, 1840.

———. *The Functions of the Science and Art Department: Introductory Addresses on the Science and Art Department and the South Kensington Museum*. No. 1. London: Chapman and Hall, 1857.

———. "Introduction." In *Official Descriptive and Illustrated Catalogue of the Great Exhibition of 1851*, (1) 1–35. London: William Clowes and Sons, 1851.

———. *Observations on the Expediency of Carrying out the Proposals of the Commissioners for the Exhibition of 1851*. London: Chapman and Hall, [1854?].

———. *Observations by Mr. Cole on the Means of Carrying out the Plans Proposed for Kensington Gore*. N.p., 1853.

———. "On the Facilities Afforded to All Classes of the Community for Obtaining Education in Art." In *Addresses of the Superintendents of the Department of Practical Art Delivered in the Theatre at Marlborough House*, 5–38. London: Chapman and Hall, 1853.

———. *A Special Report on the Annual International Exhibitions of the Years 1871, 1872, 1873, and 1874*. London: Eyre and Spottiswoode, 1879.

———. *What Is Art Culture? An Address Delivered to the Manchester School of Art*. Manchester: N.p., 1877.

———. *A Short Statement on the Nature and Objects of the Proposed Great Exhibition of the Works of Industry of All Nations*. London: Harrison and Son, [1850].

[Cole, Henry]. *Felix Summerly's Catalogue of the Pictures in the British Museum*. London: George Bell, 1842.

———. *Handbook for the Dulwich Picture Gallery*. London: George Bell, 1842.

———. *Handbook for Holidays Spent in and Near London*. London: George Bell, 1842.

———. *Handbook for the Pictures in the Soane Museum, the Society of Arts, and the British Museum*. London: Bell and Wood, 1842.

Cole, Henry, and Alan Summerly Cole. *Fifty Years of Public Work of Sir Henry Cole, KCB*. 2 vols. London: George Bell and Sons, 1884.

Cole, Henry, and Richard Redgrave. *Letter to the Rt. Hon. J. W. Henley, MP, President of the Board of Trade, by the Superintendents of the Department of Practical Art.* London: Foreign Office, 1852.

Collins, Wilkie. *Basil.* 1852. Rpt.; New York: Oxford, 1990.

Concannen, Edward. *Remembrances of the Great Exhibition Complete in Twenty Views.* London: Ackerman, [1852?].

Conway, Moncure Daniel. *Autobiography, Memories, and Experiences.* 2 vols. Boston: Houghton Mifflin, 1904.

———. *Travels in South Kensington with Notes on Decorative Art and Architecture in England.* New York: Harper and Brothers, 1882.

Cooke Taylor, William. "Copyright in Design." *Art Union*, no. 27 (April 1841): 59–60.

———. "On the Cultivation of Taste in the Operative Classes." *Art Journal* 11 (1849): 3–5.

Corner, Mrs. *China: Pictorial, Descriptive, and Historical.* London: H. G. Bohn, 1853.

The Crystal Palace: Report of the Meeting at Mr. Oliviera's, March 29, 1852. London: James Ridgway, 1852.

Dickens, Charles. *Hard Times.* 1854. Rpt.; New York: Oxford University Press, 1989.

Dickens Charles, and R. H. Horne. "The Great Exhibition and the Little One." *Household Words* 3 (68) (12 July 1851): 356–60.

Dickinson's Comprehensive Pictures of the Great Exhibition of 1851. London: Dickinson Brothers, 1854.

Digby Wyatt, Matthew. "An Attempt to Define the Principles Which Should Determine Form in the Decorative Arts." In *Lectures on the Results of the Great Exhibition of 1851 Delivered before the Society of Arts, Manufactures, and Commerce,* 2:213–52. 3 vols. London: David Bogue, 1852.

———. *The Industrial Arts of the Nineteenth Century, a Series of Illustrations of the Choicest Specimens Produced by Every Nation at the Great Exhibition of Works of Industry, 1851.* 2 vols. London: Day and Son, 1851–53.

———. *Report on the Eleventh French Exhibition of the Products of Industry.* London: J. Cundall, 1849.

Drew, William A. *Glimpses and Gatherings during a Voyage and Visit to London and the Great Exhibition.* Augusta, Maine: Homan and Manley, 1852.

Dyce, William. *Introduction to the Drawing-Book of the School of Design Published in the Years 1842–1843.* London: Chapman and Hall, 1854.

———. *Report Made to the Rt. Hon. C. Poulett Thompson on Foreign Schools of Design for Manufacture.* London: House of Commons, 1840.

Dyce, William, and Charles Heath Wilson. *Letter to Lord Meadowbank and the Committee of the Honorable Board of Trustees for Encouragement of Arts and Manufactures on the Best Means of Ameliorating the Arts and Manufactures of Scotland in Point of Taste.* Edinburgh: Thomas Constable, 1837.

East India Company. *The East India Museum: A Description of the Museum and Library of the Honorable East India Company, Leadenhall Street*. London: H. G. Clarke, 1851.

Eastlake, Charles Locke. *Hints on Household Taste*. 1868. Rpt.; New York: Dover, 1969.

Eastlake, Charles Lock. *The National Gallery: Observations on the Unfitness of the Present Building for Its Purpose*. London: W. Clowes and Sons, 1845.

Edwards, Edward. *The Fine Arts in England: Their State and Prospects Considered Relatively to National Education*. London: Saunders and Ottley, 1840.

Edwards, Henry Sunderland. *Authentic Account of the Chinese Commission*. London: Vizetelly, 1852.

Ellis, Robert. "Preface." In *Official and Descriptive Illustrated Catalogue of the Great Exhibition of the Works of Industry of All Nations*. (1) v–viii. London: William Clowes and Sons, 1851.

The Exhibition in 1851 of the Products and Industry of All Nations, Its Probable Influence upon Labor and Commerce. London: Arthur Hall, 1851.

Fitzgerald, William. "The Romance of the Museum." *Strand* 11 (1896): 62.

Forbes, Edward. *On the Educational Uses of Museums*. London: Eyre and Spottiswoode, 1853.

Fowler, Frank. *Portrait and Figure Painting*. New York: Cassell, 1894.

Garbett, Edward Lacy. *Rudimentary Treatise on the Principles of Design in Architecture as Deducible from Nature and Exemplified in the Works of the Greek and Gothic Architects*. London: John Weale, 1850.

Gems of the Great Exhibition: London, 1851, New York, 1853. [N.p., 1853?].

Grant, Horace. *Drawing for Young Children*. London: Houlston and Wright, 1862.

———. *Drawing for Young Children Containing One Hundred and Fifty Drawing Copies and Numerous Exercises*. London: Society for the Diffusion of Useful Knowledge 1848.

Greeley, Horace. *Glances at Europe in a Series of Letters during the Summer of 1851, Including Notices of the Great Exhibition or World's Fair*. New York: Dewitt and Deavenport, 1851.

Greenwood, Thomas. *Museums and Art Galleries*. London: Simpkin and Marshall, 1888.

Greg, W. R. *Not Over-production but Deficient Consumption, the Source of Our Sufferings*. London: N.p., 1842.

Hance, I. W. *An Address to the Leading Men of Manchester Suggested by a Letter on Establishing a School of Design by R. B. Haydon, Esq*. Rpt. Manchester: Manchester Courier, 1837.

Handbook of Pencil Drawing Intended as Key to All Drawing Books Which Have No Written Instruction. London: David Bogue, 1843.

Hannigan, Dennis. *The Artisan of Lyons; or, Love's Traces*. New York: W. H. Graham, 1846.

Harding, J. D. *Elementary Art; or, the Use of the Lead Pencil Advocated and Explained*. London: Charles Tilt, 1834.

Hay, David Ramsay. *An Essay on Ornamental Design with an Attempt to Develop Its Principles and to Point Out an Easy Method of Acquiring Facility in Its Practice*. London: David Bogue, 1844.

———. *Geometric Beauty of the Human Figure*. Edinburgh: William Blackwood and Sons, 1851.

———. *The Laws of Harmonious Coloring Adapted to Interior Decorations, Manufactures, and Other Useful Purposes*. London: Orr and Smith, 1836.

———. *Letter to the Council of the Society of Arts on Elementary Education in the Arts of Design*. London: Blackwood, 1852.

———. *A Nomenclature of Colours Applicable to the Arts and Natural Sciences to Manufacturers and Other Purposes of General Utility*. 2nd ed. Edinburgh: Blackwood and Sons, 1846.

———. *The Principles of Beauty in Colouring Systematized*. London: Blackwood and Sons, 1845.

———. *Proportion; or, the Geometrical Principle of Beauty Analysed*. London: Blackwood and Sons, 1843.

Haydon, Benjamin Robert. *Correspondence and Table Talk*. Ed. Frederic Wordsworth Haydon. 2 vols. London: Chatto and Windus, 1876.

———. *The Diary of Benjamin Robert Haydon*. Ed. Willard Bissell Pope. 5 vols. Cambridge: Harvard University Press, 1963.

———. *Lectures on Painting and Design*. 2 vols. London: Longman, Brown, Green, and Longmans, 1844.

Hicks, G. E. *A Guide to Figure Drawing*. London: George Rowney, 186-.

History of the Blind Beggar of Bethnal Green. Newcastle: George Angus, [1815?].

Howard, Frank. *Imitative Art; or, the Means of Representing the Pictorial Appearances of Objects as Governed by Aerial and Linear Perspective*. London: Darnton and Clark, [1840].

Hunt, Leigh. *The Old Court Suburb; or, Memorials of Kensington, Regal, Critical, and Anecdotal*. 2 vols. London: Hurst and Blackett, 1855.

Jackson, George. *On the Means of Improving Public Taste*. Manchester: Council of the School of Design, 1844.

James, Henry. "The Wallace Collection in Bethnal Green" (1873). In *The Painter's Eye: Notes and Essays on the Pictorial Arts by Henry James, Selected and Edited with an Introduction by John L. Sweeney*, 67–78. London: Rupert Hart-Davis, 1956.

Jameson, Anna. "Some Thoughts on Art Addressed to the Uninitiated." *Art Journal*, new ser., 1 (March 1849): 69–70.

Jones, Owen. "An Attempt to Define the Principles Which Should Regulate the Employment of Colour in the Decorative Arts." In *Lectures on the*

Results of the Great Exhibition of 1851, 263–300. 2nd ser. 3 vols. London: David Bogue, 1852.

———. *The Grammar of Ornament*. 1856. Rpt.; New York: Van Nostrand Reinhold, 1972.

Knight, Charles. *The Imperial Cyclopaedia*. London: Charles Knight, [1852].

———. *Pictorial Half Hours of London Topography*. London: Charles Knight, 1851.

Leslie, George Dunlop. *The Inner Life of the Royal Academy*. London: John Murray, 1914.

Lewis, George R. *An Address on the Subject of Education, as Connected with Design, in Every Department of British Manufacture Together with Hints on the Education of the Poor Generally*. London: Simpkin, Marshall, 1838.

Liddell, Robert. *Pastoral Letter to the Parishioners of St. Paul's, Knightsbridge, and St. Barnabas, Pimlico*. London: J. T. Hayes, 1858.

Lloyd, J. A. *Papers Relating to Proposals for Establishing Colleges of Arts and Manufactures for the Better Instruction of the Industrial Classes*. London: W. Clowes, 1851.

Lush, Frederick. "Teachings of the Exhibition." *Builder* 10 (440) (July 12, 1851): 432.

Mackenzie, George S. *General Observations on the Principles of Education for the Use of Mechanics' Institutions*. Edinburgh: John Anderson, 1836.

Marx, Karl. "The Fetishism of Commodities and the Secret Thereof." In *The Marx-Engels Reader*, ed. Robert C. Tucker, 319–29. New York: Norton, 1978.

Mayhew, Henry. *London Labor and the London Poor*. 4 vols. Rpt.; New York: Dover, 1970.

Miller, Fred. *The Training of a Craftsman*. London: Virtue, 1898.

Morley, Henry. "A House Full of Horrors." *Household Words* 4 (141) (December 4, 1852): 265–70.

———. *Palissy the Potter: The Life of Bernard Palissy*. London: Chapman and Hall, 1852.

Mr. Goggleye's Visit to the Exhibition of National Industry to Be Held in London on the 1st of April, 1851. London: Timy Takem'in, 1851.

Murgatroyd, J. *Remarks concerning the Manchester School of Art and Schools of Art Generally*. Manchester: John Heywood, 1881.

Nicholls, W. A. *National Drawing Master*. London: Ackermann, 1854.

Northcote, Stafford H. "Schools of Design." *Edinburgh Review* 90 (October 1849): 473–96.

O'Brien, George. *The British Manufacturer's Companion and Callico Printer's Assistant*. London: Hamilton, 1795.

Official Descriptive and Illustrated Catalogue of the Great Exhibition of the Works of Industry of All Nations. 4 vols. London: William Clowes and Sons, 1851.

[Person Concerned in the Trade]. *A Complete History of the Cotton Trade*. Manchester: C. W. Leake, 1823.

Philips, George. *Rudiments of Curvilinear Design*. London: Shaw and Sons, 1839.

The Philosopher's Mite to the Great Exhibition of 1851. London: Houston and Stoneman, [1851?].

Philostrate. "Sincerity versus Fashion." *Magazine of Art* 1 (4) (1878): 91.

Pictor, Fabius. *The Hand-Book of Taste; or, How to Observe Works of Art*. London: Longman, Brown, Green, and Longmans, 1843.

Pinnock, William. *A Catechism of Drawing with the Necessary Explanations of the Principal Terms in the Art*. London: Whittaker, Treacher, 1829.

Playfair, Lyon. *On Scientific Institutions in Connection with the Department of Science and Art: Introductory Addresses on the Science and Art Department and the South Kensington Museum*. No. 3. London: Chapman and Hall, 1857.

Potter, Edmund. *Calico Printing as an Art Manufacture*. London: John Chapman, 1852.

———. *A Letter to Mark Philips, Esq., in Reply to his Speech in the House of Commons on the Design Copyright Bill*. Manchester: Thomas Forrest, 1841.

———. *A Letter to One of the Commissioners for the Exhibition of 1851*. London: John Chapman, 1853.

Prouting, F. J. [Argus]. *A Mild Remonstrance against the Taste-Censorship at Marlborough House in Reference to Manufacturing Ornamentation and Decorative Design*. 3 nos. London: Houlston and Stoneman, 1853.

Pugin, Augustus Welby. *Contrasts; or, a Parallel between the Noble Edifices of the Fourteenth and Fifteenth Centuries and Similar Buildings of the Present Day Shewing the Present Decay of Taste*. London: St. Marie's Grange, 1836.

———. *The True Principles of Pointed or Christian Architecture*. London: John Weale, 1841.

Redgrave, Gilbert R., ed. *Manual of Design Compiled from the Writings and Addresses of Richard Redgrave*. London: Chapman and Hall, 1876.

Redgrave, Richard. *An Address on the Gift of the Sheepshanks Collection with a View to the Foundation of a National Gallery of British Art*. London: Chapman and Hall, 1857.

———. *An Elementary Manual of Colour with a Catechism*. London: Chapman and Hall, 1853.

———. "An Introductory Address on the Methods Adopted by the Department of Practical Art to Impart Instruction in Art to All Classes of the Community." In *Addresses of the Superintendents of the Department of Practical Art Delivered in the Theatre at Marlborough House*, 41–81. London: Chapman and Hall, 1852.

———. *On the Necessity of Principles in Teaching Design, Being an Address at the*

Opening Session of the Department of Science and Art. London: Chapman and Hall, 1853.

————. *Report on Design Prepared as a Supplement to the Report of the Jury of Class XXX of the Exhibition of 1851*. London: William Clowes and Sons, 1852.

Reilly, John. *The People's History of Manchester*. London: Simpkin, 1859–60.

Richardson, Charles James. *A Letter Addressed to the Council of the Head Government School of Design*. London: J. and H. Cox, 1846.

Robinson, J. C. *Catalogue of a Collection of Works of Decorative Art, Being a Selection from the Museum at Marlborough House Circulated for Exhibition in Provincial Schools of Art*. London: Eyre and Spottiswoode, 1855.

————. *The Museum of Art: Introductory Addresses on the Science and Art Department and the South Kensington Museum*. No. 5. London: Chapman and Hall, 1857.

————. "Museum of Ornamental Art," *Art Journal*, new ser., 1 (May 1855): 150–52.

————. "The Museum of Ornamental Art at Marlborough House," *Art Journal*, new ser., 1 (January 1855): 15–16.

————. *The National Gallery Considered in Reference to Other Public Collections and to the Proposed New Building in Trafalgar Square*. London: James Toovey, 1867.

Royle, J. Forbes. "The Arts and Manufactures of India." In *Lectures on the Results of the Great Exhibition Delivered before the Society of Arts, Manufactures, and Commerce*, 2:333–400. 3 vols. London: David Bogue, 1852.

[Sala, G. A.] *The Great Exhibition Wot Is to Be: Probable Results of the Industry of All Nations by Vates Secundus*. London: Committee of the Society for Keeping Things in Their Places, 1850.

Sandby, William. *The History of the Royal Academy of Arts*. 2 vols. London: Longman, Green, Longman, Roberts, and Green, 1862.

School of Arts Improv'd; or, Companion for the Ingenious. Gainsbrough: John Mozley, 1780.

Senior, Nassau William, Samuel Jones Lloyd, William E. Jackson, and John Leslie. *From the Report of the Commissioners of Hand-Loom Weaving on Improvement of Designs and Patterns and Extension of Copyright*. London: Stewart and Murray, 1841.

Shee, Martin Archer. *A Letter to Joseph Hume, Esq., MP, in Reply to His Aspersions on the Character and Proceedings of the Royal Academy*. London: Ridgway, 1838.

Sherwell, Arthur. *Life in West London: A Study and a Contrast*. 2nd ed. London: Methuen, 1897.

Simpson's Chelsea, Pimlico, Brompton, and Knightsbridge Directory and Court Guide, Including Lists of Vestry, Parish Officers, Post Office Intelligence, and Chelsea Charities. Kensington: Tomkies and Son, 1863.

The Sketcher [John Eagles]. "Schools of Design: Remarks on a Letter in the *Morning Chronicle.*" *Blackwood's Edinburgh Magazine* 49 (May 1841): 583–88.

Smith, Thomas. *The Art of Drawing in Its Various Branches Exemplified in a Course of 28 Progressive Lessons.* London: Sherwood, Jones, 1825.

Smith, W. H. "Voltaire in the Crystal Palace." *Blackwood's Edinburgh Magazine* (70) 430 (August 1851): 142–53.

Society of Arts, Manufactures, and Commerce. *Lectures on the Results of the Great Exhibition of 1851 Delivered before the Society of Arts, Manufactures, and Commerce.* 3 vols. London: David Bogue, 1852.

Sparkes, John C. L. *Schools of Art: Their Origin, History, Work, and Influence.* London: William Clowes and Sons, 1884.

Spedding, James. "Dickens' *American Notes,*" *Edinburgh Review* 76 (January 1843): 497–522.

Sproule, John. *The Resources and Manufacturing Industry of Ireland.* Dublin: John Sproule, 1854.

Symonds, Emily Morse. *Little Memoirs of the Nineteenth Century.* 1902. Rpt.; Freeport, N.Y.: Books for Libraries Press, 1969.

Tallis, John. *Tallis's History and Description of the Crystal Palace and the Exhibition of the World's Industry in 1851.* 3 vols. London: John Tallis, 1851.

Taylor, Charles. *A Familiar Treatise on Drawing for Youth, Being an Elementary Introduction to the Fine Arts Designed for the Instruction of Young Persons Whose Genius Leads Them to Study This Elegant and Useful Branch of Education.* London: C. Taylor, 1815.

Taylor, Tom. *Life of Benjamin Robert Haydon, Historical Painter, from His Autobiography and Journals.* 2 vols. New York: Harper and Brothers, 1853.

Tennent, James Emerson. *Ceylon: An Account of the Island, Physical, Historical, and Topographical.* London, 1859.

———. *A Treatise on the Copyright of Designs for Printed Fabrics.* London: Smith, Elder, 1841.

[Tennent, James Emerson.] *Argument Made Easy; or, the Whole Art of Answering Yourself Expounded and Illustrated in the Evidence of James Kershaw.* London: George Bell, 1840.

———. *The Policy of Piracy as a Branch of National Industry and a Source of Commercial Wealth Expounded in the Evidence of Daniel Lee.* London: George Bell, 1840.

Thomas, W. Cave. *Suggestions for a Crystal College, or New Palace of Glass, for Combining the Intellectual Talent of All Nations; or, a Sketch of a Practical Philosophy of Education.* London: Dickinson Brothers, 1851.

Thomson, James. *A Letter to the Rt. Hon. Sir Richard Lalor Sheil on Copyright in Original Designs and Patterns for Printing.* Clitheroe: H. Whalley, 1841.

————. *A Letter to the Rt. Hon. Sir Robert Peel, Bart., on Copyright in Original Designs and Patterns for Printing*. Clitheroe: H. Whalley, 1841.

————. *Notes on the Present State of Calico Printing in Belgium*. Clitheroe: H. Whalley, 1841.

Twining, Thomas. *Notes on the Organization of an Industrial College for Artisans*. London: G. Barclay, 1851.

Underwood, Thomas. *Choice Examples of Art Manufactures from the Marlborough House and Other Valuable Collections*. Birmingham: Underwood, 185-.

Viollet-le-Duc, Emmanuel. *Learning to Draw; or, the Story of a Young Designer*. Trans. Virginia Champlin. New York: G. P. Putnam's Sons, 1881.

Waagen, Gustav. "Thoughts on the New Building to Be Erected for the National Gallery of England." *Art Journal*, new ser., 5 (April–May 1853): 101–25.

Wallis, George. *A Letter to the Council of the Manchester School of Design*. Manchester: School of Design, 1845.

Warren, Henry. *Artistic Anatomy of the Human Figure*. London: Windsor and Newton, 1874.

————. *An Artistic Treatise on the Human Figure*. New York: G. P. Putnam's Sons, 1881.

Watson, J. Forbes. *The Imperial Museum for India and the Colonies*. London: W. H. Allen, 1876.

Whewell, William. "The General Bearing of the Great Exhibition on the Progress of Art and Science." In *Lectures on the Results of the Great Exhibition of 1851 Delivered before the Society of Arts, Manufactures, and Commerce*, 3–34. London: David Bogue, 1852.

Wilkinson, J. Gardner. *On Colour and on the Necessity for a General Diffusion of Taste among All Classes*. London: John Murray, 1858.

Wilson, Charles Heath. *Address Delivered on the Sixteenth Day of May, 1844, in the Government Branch School of Design at Spitalfields*. London: W. Clowes and Sons, 1844.

Wilson, George. "The Relation of Ornamental to Industrial Art." In *Lectures Delivered in the National Galleries*. Edinburgh: Edmonston and Douglas, 1857.

Woodward, Parker. *A Handbook to the Law of Copyright in Registered Designs*. Nottingham: Express, 1891.

The World's Fair; or, Children's Prize Gift Book of the Great Exhibition of 1851. London: Thomas Dean and Son, [1851?].

Wornum, Ralph Nicholson. "The Exhibition as a Lesson in Taste." In *Crystal Palace Exhibition Illustrated Catalogue, London 1851: An Unabridged Republication of the Art Journal Special Issue*. i–xxii. 1851. Rpt.; New York: Dover, 1970.

———. "The Government School of Design." *Art Journal*, new ser., 3 (April 1851): 102.

———. "The Government School of Design." *Art Journal*, new ser., 5 (January 1852): 16.

———. "The National Gallery." *Art Journal*, new ser., 2 (February 1851): 37–39.

Yapp, George. *Art-Education at Home and Abroad: The British Museum, the National Gallery, and the Proposed Industrial University*. 2nd ed. London: Chapman and Hall, 1853.

Young, James. *Conjectures on Original Composition*. 1759. Rpt.; London: Longmans, 1918.

Secondary Sources

Adas, Michael. *Machines as the Measure of Men*. Ithaca: Cornell University Press, 1989.

Agnew, Jean-Christophe. "Coming up for Air: Consumer Culture in Historical Perspective." In *Consumption and the World of Goods*, ed. John Brewer and Roy Porter, New York: Routledge, 1993. 19–39.

———. *Worlds Apart: The Market and the Theater in Anglo-American Thought, 1550–1750*. Cambridge: Cambridge University Press, 1986.

Aguirre, Robert. *Informal Empire: Mexico and Central America in Victorian Culture*. Minneapolis: University of Minnesota Press, 2005.

Albisetti, James C. "The 'Inevitable Schwabes': An Introduction." *Transactions of the Lancashire and Cheshire Antiquarian Society* 90 (2002): 91–112.

Alborn, Timothy. *Conceiving Companies: Joint-Stock Politics in Victorian England*. London: Routledge, 1998.

Allen, Emily. "Culinary Exhibition: Victorian Wedding Cakes and Royal Spectacle." *Victorian Studies* 45 (3) (spring 2003): 457–84.

Altick, Richard. *The English Common Reader: A Social History of the Mass Reading Public, 1800–1900*. Chicago: University of Chicago Press, 1957.

———. *The Shows of London*. Cambridge: Harvard University Press, 1978.

Anderson, Patricia. *The Printed Image and the Transformation of Popular Culture, 1790–1870*. Oxford: Clarendon, 1991.

Appadurai, Arjun. "Commodities and the Politics of Value." In *The Social Life of Things*, ed. Arjun Appadurai, 3–63. Cambridge: Cambridge University Press, 1986.

Apter, Andrew. "On Imperial Spectacle: The Dialectics of Seeing in Colonial Nigeria." *Comparative Studies in Society and History* 44 (3) (2002): 564–96.

268   *Bibliography*

Armitage, David. *Ideological Origins of the British Empire*. Cambridge: Cambridge University Press, 2000.

Auerbach, Jeffrey. *The Great Exhibition of 1851: A Nation on Display*. New Haven: Yale University Press, 1999.

———. "What They Read: Mid-Nineteenth-Century English Women's Magazines and the Emergence of a Consumer Culture." *Victorian Periodicals Review* 30 (2) (1997): 121–40.

Auslander, Leora. *Taste and Power: Furnishing Modern France*. Berkeley: University of California Press, 1996.

Bailey, Peter. *Leisure and Class in Victorian England: Rational Recreation and the Contest for Control, 1830–1885*. London: Routledge and Kegan Paul, 1978.

———. *Popular Culture and Performance in the Victorian City*. Cambridge: Cambridge University Press, 2003.

———. "White Collars, Gray Lives? The Lower Middle Class Revisited." *Journal of British Studies* 38 (3) (July 1999): 273–90.

———. "'Will the Real Bill Banks Stand Up?' Towards a Role Analysis of Mid-Victorian Working-Class Respectability." *Journal of Social History* 12 (1978): 336–53.

Bailkin, Jordanna. *The Culture of Property: The Crisis of Liberalism in Modern Britain*. Chicago: University of Chicago Press, 2004.

———. "The Place of Liberalism." *Victorian Studies* 48 (1) (Autumn 2005): 83–91.

Baker, Malcolm, and Brenda Richardson. *A Grand Design: The Art of the Victoria and Albert Museum*. New York: Harry N. Abrams, 1997.

Barlow, Paul, and Shelagh Wilson. "Consuming Empire? The South Kensington Museum and Its Spectacles." In *Governing Cultures: Art Institutions in Victorian London*, ed. Paul Barlow and Colin Trodd, 156–71. Aldershot: Ashgate, 2000.

———. "Introduction: Constituting the Public—Art and Its Institutions in Nineteenth-Century London." In *Governing Cultures: Art Institutions in Victorian London*, ed. Paul Barlow and Colin Trodd, 1–29. Aldershot: Ashgate, 2000.

Barlow, Paul, and Colin Trodd, eds. *Governing Cultures: Art Institutions in Victorian London*. Aldershot: Ashgate, 2000.

Barrell, John. "Benjamin Robert Haydon: The Curtius of Kyber Pass." In *Painting and the Politics of Culture: New Essays on British Art, 1700–1850*, 235–90. Oxford: Oxford University Press, 1992.

———. *The Birth of Pandora and the Division of Knowledge*. Philadelphia: University of Pennsylvania Press, 1992.

———. *The Political Theory of Painting from Reynolds to Hazlitt*. New Haven: Yale University Press, 1986.

Barringer, Tim. "Equipoise and the Object: The South Kensington Museum." In *An Age of Equipoise? Reassessing Mid-Victorian Britain*, ed. Martin Hewitt, 68–83. Aldershot: Ashgate, 2000.

———. "Leighton in Albertopolis: Monumental Art and Objects of Desire." In *Frederic Leighton: Antiquity, Renaissance, Modernity*, ed. Tim Barringer and Elizabeth Prettejohn, New Haven: Yale University Press, 1999, 135–68.

———. *Men at Work: Art and Labour in Victorian Britain*. New Haven: Yale University Press, 2005.

———. "Re-presenting the Imperial Archive: South Kensington and Its Museums." *Journal of Victorian Culture* 3 (1998): 357–73.

———. "The South Kensington Museum and the Colonial Project." In *Colonialism and the Object: Empire, Material Culture, and the Museum*, ed. Tim Barringer and Flynn, 11–27. London: Routledge, 1998.

Barringer, Tim, and Tom Flynn, eds. *Colonialism and the Object: Empire, Material Culture, and the Museum*. London: Routledge, 1998.

Barthes, Roland. *The Fashion System*. Trans. Matthew Ward and Richard Howard. 1967. Rpt.; Berkeley: University of California Press, 1990.

Baudrillard, Jean. "The System of Collecting." In *The Cultures of Collecting*, ed. John Elsner and Roger Cardinal, 7–24. Cambridge: Harvard University Press, 1994.

Beegan, Gerry. "The Mechanization of the Image: Facsimile, Photography, and Fragmentation in Nineteenth-Century Wood Engraving." *Journal of Design History* 8 (4) (1995): 257–74.

Behagg, Clive. *Politics and Production in the Early Nineteenth Century*. London: Routledge, 1990.

Bell, Quentin. *The Schools of Design*. London: Routledge, 1963.

Benjamin, Walter. "The Work of Art in the Age of Mechanical Reproduction." In *Illuminations*, 217–52. Trans. Harry Zohn. New York: Schocken, 1968.

Bennett, Tony. *The Birth of the Museum: History, Theory, Politics*. London: Routledge, 1995.

———. *Culture: A Reformer's Science*. London: Sagae, 1998.

———. "The Exhibitionary Complex." *New Formations* 4 (1988): 73–102.

———. *Pasts beyond Memory: Evolution, Museums, Colonialism*. London: Routledge, 2004.

Berg, Maxine. *The Age of Manufactures, 1700–1820: Industry, Innovation, and Work in Britain*. 2nd ed. New York: Routledge, 1994.

———. "From Imitation to Invention: Creating Commodities in Eighteenth-Century Britain." *Economic History Review* 55 (1) (2002): 1–30.

———. "In Pursuit of Luxury: Global History and British Consumer Goods in the Eighteenth Century." *Past and Present* 182 (February 2004): 85–142.

———. *Luxury and Pleasure in Eighteenth-Century Britain*. Oxford: Oxford University Press, 2005.

———. "New Commodities, Luxuries, and Their Consumers in Eighteenth-Century England." In *Consumers and Luxury: Consumer Culture in Europe, 1650–1850*, ed. Maxine Berg and Helen Clifford, 63–85. Manchester: Manchester University Press, 1999.

Berg, Maxine, and Helen Clifford. "Introduction." In *Consumers and Luxury: Consumer Culture in Europe, 1650–1850*, ed. Maxine Berg and Helen Clifford, 1–16. Manchester: Manchester University Press, 1999.

Berg, Maxine, and Helen Clifford, eds. *Consumers and Luxury: Consumer Culture in Europe, 1650–1850*. Manchester: Manchester University Press, 1999.

Bermingham, Ann. *Learning to Draw: Studies in the Cultural History of a Polite and Useful Art*. New Haven: Yale University Press, 2000.

Bermingham, Ann, ed. *The Consumption of Culture, 1600–1800: Image, Object, Text*. New York: Routledge, 1995.

Best, Geoffrey. *Mid-Victorian Britain, 1851–1875*. London: Weidenfeld and Nicholson, 1971.

Bizup, Joseph. *Manufacturing Culture: Vindications of Early Victorian Industry*. Charlottesville: University of Virginia Press, 2003.

Black, Barbara. *On Exhibit: Victorians and Their Museums*. Charlottesville: University Press of Virginia, 2000.

Bonnell, Victoria E., and Lynn Hunt, eds. *Beyond the Cultural Turn: New Directions in the Study of Society and Culture*. Berkeley: University of California Press, 1999.

Bonython, Elizabeth, and Anthony Burton. *The Great Exhibitor: The Life and Work of Henry Cole*. London: V & A Publications, 2003.

Bourdieu, Pierre. *Distinction: A Social Critique of the Judgement of Taste*. Cambridge: Harvard University Press, 1984.

Breckenridge, Carol. "The Aesthetics and Politics of Colonial Collecting: India at World's Fairs." *Comparative Studies in Society and History* 31 (1989): 195–216.

Breward, Christopher. *Fashioning London: Clothing and the Modern Metropolis*. Oxford: Berg, 2004.

———. "Femininity and Consumption: The Problem of the Late-Nineteenth-Century Fashion Journal." *Journal of Design History* 7 (2) (1994): 71–89.

———. *The Hidden Consumer: Masculinities, Fashion, and City Life, 1860–1914*. Manchester: Manchester University Press, 1999.

———. "Victorian Britain: Fashionable Living." In *Design and the Decorative Arts*, ed. Michael Snodin and John Styles, 401–29. London: V & A Publications, 2001.

Briggs, Asa. *Victorian Things*. Chicago: University of Chicago Press, 1989.

Burke, Peter, *What Is Cultural History?* Cambridge: Polity, 2004.

Burke, Timothy. "'Fork Up and Smile': Marketing, Colonial Knowledge, and the Female Subject in Zimbabwe." *Gender and History* 8 (3) (November 1996): 440–56.

———. *Lifebuoy Men, Lux Women: Commodification and Cleanliness in Modern Zimbabwe*. Durham: Duke University Press, 1996.

Burton, Anthony. "The Revival of Interest in Victorian Decorative Art and the Victoria and Albert Museum." In *The Victorians since 1901: Histories, Representations, and Revisions*, ed. Miles Taylor and Michael Wolff, 121–37. Manchester: Manchester University Press, 2004.

———. "The Uses of the South Kensington Art Collections," *Journal of the History of Collections* 14 (1) (2002): 79–95.

———. *Vision and Accident: the Story of the Victoria and Albert Museum*. London: Victoria and Albert Museum, 1999.

Burton, Antoinette. *At the Heart of the Empire: Indians and the Colonial Encounter in Late-Victorian England*. Berkeley: University of California Press, 1998.

———. "Introduction: On the Inadequacy and the Indispensability of the Nation." In *After the Imperial Turn: Thinking with and through the Nation*, ed. Antoinette Burton, 1–23. Durham: Duke University Press, 2003.

———. "Making a Spectacle of Empire: Indian Travellers in Fin-de-Siècle London." *History Workshop Journal* 42 (1996): 127–46.

———. "Thinking beyond the Boundaries: Empire, Feminism, and the Domains of History." *Social History* 26 (1) (January 2001): 60–71.

Burton, Antoinette, ed. *After the Imperial Turn: Thinking with and through the Nation*. Durham: Duke University Press, 2003.

Calhoun, Craig. "Habitus, Field, and Capital: The Question of Historical Specificity." In *Bourdieu: Critical Perspectives*, ed. Craig Calhoun, Edward LiPuma, and Moishe Postone, 61–88. Chicago: University of Chicago Press, 1993.

Campbell, Colin. "Consumption and the Rhetorics of Need and Want." *Journal of Design History* 11 (3) (1998): 235–46.

———. *The Romantic Ethic and the Spirit of Modern Consumerism*. Oxford: Basil Blackwell, 1987.

Cardoso Denis, Rafael. "The Brompton Barracks: War, Peace, and the Rise of Victorian Art and Design Education." *Journal of Design History* 8 (1) (1995): 11–25.

———. "Drawing or Design? The Development of the National Art Training School." In *Design of the Times: One Hundred Years of the Royal College of Art*, ed. by Christopher Frayling and Claire Catterall, 20–24. London: Royal College of Art, 1996.

———. "The Educated Eye and the Industrial Hand: Art and Design Instruction for the Working Classes in Mid-Victorian Britain." Ph.D. diss., Courtauld Institute of Art, London, 1995.

———. "An Industrial Vision: The Promotion of Technical Drawing in Mid-Victorian Britain." In *The Great Exhibition of 1851: New Interdisciplinary Essays*, ed. Louise Purbrick, 53–78. Manchester: Manchester University Press, 2001.

Chalmers, Graeme. *Women in the Nineteenth-Century Art World: Schools of Art and Design for Women in London and Philadelphia*. Westport, Conn.: Greenwood, 1998.

Chancellor, Valerie E., ed. *Master and Artisan in Victorian England: The Diary of William Andrews and the Autobiography of Joseph Gutteridge*. London: Evelyn, Adams, and Mackay, 1969.

Chapman, Stanley D. *The Cotton Industry in the Industrial Revolution*. 2nd ed. London: Macmillan, 1987.

———. "Quantity versus Quality in the British Industrial Revolution: The Case of Printed Textiles." *Northern History* 21 (1985): 175–92.

Chapman, Stanley D., and Serge Chassagne. *European Textile Printers of the Eighteenth Century: A Study of Peel and Oberkampf*. London: Heinemann, 1981.

Chapman, William Ryan. "Arranging Ethnology: Pitt Rivers and the Typological Tradition." In *Objects and Others: Essays on Museums and Material Culture*, ed. George Stocking Jr., 16–43. Madison: University of Wisconsin Press, 1985.

Clark, Anna. *The Struggle for the Breeches: Gender and the Making of the British Working Class*. Berkeley: University of California Press, 1995.

Clark, Hazel. "The Design and Designing of Lancashire Printed Calicoes during the First Half of the Nineteenth Century." *Textile History* 15 (1984): 101–18.

Clark, T. J. *The Painting of Modern Life: Paris in the Art of Manet and His Followers*. Princeton: Princeton University Press, 1984.

Clifford, Helen. "The Printed Illustrated Catalogue." In *Design and the Decorative Arts, Britain, 1500–1900*, ed. Michael Snodin and John Styles, 288–89. London: V & A Publications, 2001.

Clifford, James. *The Predicament of Culture: Twentieth-Century Ethnography, Literature, and Art*. Cambridge: Harvard University Press, 1988.

Clunas, Craig. "China in Britain: The Imperial Collections." In *Colonialism and the Object: Empire, Material Culture, and the Museum*, ed. Tim Barringer and Tom Flynn. 41–51. London: Routledge, 1998.

Cohen, Deborah. *Household Gods: The British and their Possessions*. New Haven: Yale University Press, 2006.

———. "Material Good: Consumerism in the Age of Atonement." Manuscript, October 2003.

———. "Why Did *The House* Fail? Demand and Supply before the Modern

Home Magazine, 1880s–1900s." *Journal of Design History* 18 (1) (2005): 35–42.

Cohn, Bernard. "Cloth, Clothes, and Colonialism: India in the Nineteenth Century." In *Cloth and the Human Experience*, ed. Annette B. Weiner and Jane Schneider, 303–53. Washington, D.C.: Smithsonian Institution Press, 1989.

Colley, Linda. *Britons: Forging the Nation, 1707–1837*. New Haven: Yale University Press, 1992.

Coltman, Viccy. "Sir William Hamilton's Vase Publications (1766–1776): A Case Study in the Reproduction and Dissemination of Antiquity." *Journal of Design History* 14 (1) (2001): 1–16.

Conforti, Michael. "The Idealist Enterprise and the Applied Arts." In *A Grand Design: The Art of the Victoria and Albert Museum*, ed. Malcolm Baker and Brenda Richardson, 23–47. New York: Abrams, 1997.

Conlin, Jonathan. "'At the Expense of the Public': The Sign Painters' Exhibition of 1762 and the Public Sphere." *Eighteenth-Century Studies* 36 (1) (2002): 1–21.

Conn, Stephen. *Museums and American Intellectual Life, 1876–1926*. Chicago: University of Chicago Press, 1998.

Coombes, Annie. *Reinventing Africa: Museums, Material Culture, and Popular Imagination in Late Victorian and Edwardian England*. New Haven: Yale University Press, 1994.

Corrigan, Philip, and Derek Sayer. *The Great Arch: English State Formation as Cultural Revolution*. Oxford: Blackwell, 1985.

Coulter, Moureen. *Property in Ideas: The Patent Question in Mid-Victorian Britain*. Kirksville, Mo.: Thomas Jefferson University Press, 1991.

Cox, Nancy. *The Complete Tradesman: A Study of Retailing*. Aldershot: Ashgate, 2000.

Cunningham, Colin. "Gender and Design in the Victorian Period." In *Gender and Art*, ed. Gill Perry, 175–92. London: Yale University Press, 1999.

Crary, Jonathan. *Techniques of the Observer: On Vision and Modernity in the Nineteenth Century*. Cambridge: MIT Press, 1990.

Crawford, Alan. "United Kingdom: Origins and First Flowering." In *The Arts and Crafts Movement in Europe and America: Design for the Modern World*, ed. Wendy Kaplan, 20–67. New York: Thames and Hudson, 2004.

Crossick, Geoffrey. *An Artisan Elite in Victorian Society: Kentish London, 1840–1880*. London: Croom Helm, 1978.

———. "Past Masters: In Search of the Artisan in European History." In *The Artisan and the European Town, 1500–1900*, ed. Geoffrey Crossick, 1–40. Aldershot: Scholar, 1997.

Crossick, Geoffrey, ed. *The Lower Middle Class in Britain, 1870–1914*. New York: St. Martin's, 1977.

Crossick, Geoffrey, and Serge Jaumain, eds. *Cathedrals of Consumption: The European Department Store, 1850–1939*. Brookfield, Vt.: Ashgate, 1999.

Curtis, Gerard. *Visual Words: Art and the Material Book in Victorian England*. Brookfield, Vt.: Ashgate, 2002.

Daunton, Martin. "The Material Politics of Natural Monopoly: Consuming Gas in Victorian Britain." In *The Politics of Consumption: Material Culture and Citizenship in Europe and America*, ed. Martin Daunton and Matthew Hilton, 69–88. Oxford: Oxford University Press, 2001.

Davidoff, Leonore, and Catherine Hall. *Family Fortunes: Men and Women of the English Middle Class, 1780–1850*. London: Hutchinson, 1987.

Davis, Jennifer. "Jennings Buildings and Royal Borough: The Construction of the Underclass in Mid-Victorian England." In *Metropolis London: Histories and Representations since 1800*, ed. David Feldman and Gareth Stedman Jones, 13–32. London: Routledge, 1989.

Davis, John. "Modern London." In *The English Urban Landscape*, ed. Philip Waller, 125–50. New York: Oxford University Press, 2000.

Debord, Guy. *The Society of the Spectacle*. Trans. Donald Nicholson Smith. New York: Zone, 1995.

Deslandes, Paul. *Oxbridge Men: British Masculinity and the Undergraduate Experience, 1850–1920*. Bloomington: Indiana University Press, 2005.

Desmond, Adrian. *The India Museum*. London: Her Majesty's Stationery Office, 1982.

Dirks, Nicholas. "Introduction." In *Colonialism and Culture*, ed. Nicholas Dirks, 2–13. Ann Arbor: University of Michigan Press, 1992.

Dirks, Nicholas, ed. *Colonialism and Culture*. Ann Arbor: University of Michigan Press, 1992.

Ditz, Toby L. "Shipwrecked; or, Masculinity Imperiled: Mercantile Representations of Failure and the Gendered Self in Eighteenth-Century Philadelphia." *Journal of American History* 81 (1) (1994): 51–80.

Dodd, Sara M. "Art Education for Women in the 1860s: A Decade of Debate." In *Women in the Victorian Art World*, ed. Clarissa Campbell Orr, 187–200. New York: Manchester University Press, 1995.

Dolin, Tim. "Cranford and the Victorian Collection." *Victorian Studies* 36 (2) (winter 1993): 179–206.

Driver, Felix. *Geography Militant: Cultures of Exploration and Empire*. Oxford: Blackwell, 2001.

Driver, Felix, and David Gilbert. "Heart of Empire? Landscape, Space, and Performance in Imperial London." *Environment and Planning D: Society and Space* 16 (1998): 11–28.

Driver, Felix, and David Gilbert, eds. *Imperial Cities: Landscape, Display, and Identity*. New York: Manchester University Press, 1999.

Duncan, Carol. *Civilizing Rituals: Inside Public Art Museums*. London: Routledge, 1995.

Duncan, Carol, and Allan Wallach. "The Universal Survey Museum." *Art History* 3 (4) (1980): 448–96.

Durbach, Nadja. *Bodily Matters: The Anti-vaccination Movement in England, 1854–1907*. Durham: Duke University Press, 2005.

Dworkin, Dennis. *Cultural Marxism in Postwar Britain: History, the New Left, and the Origins of Cultural Studies*. Durham: Duke University Press, 1997.

Edwards, Steve. "The Accumulation of Knowledge; or, William Whewell's Eye." In *The Great Exhibition of 1851: New Interdisciplinary Essays*, ed. Louise Purbrick, 26–52. Manchester: Manchester University Press, 2001.

Eley, Geoff. *A Crooked Line: From Cultural History to the History of Society*. Ann Arbor: University of Michigan Press, 2005.

Epstein, James. *In Practice: Studies in the Language and Culture of Popular Politics in Modern Britain*. Stanford: Stanford University Press, 2003.

———. *Radical Expression: Political Language, Ritual, and Symbol in England, 1790–1850*. New York: Oxford University Press, 1994.

Fang, Karen. "Empire, Coleridge, and Charles Lamb's Consumer Imagination." *Studies in English Literature* 43 (4) (autumn 2003): 815–43.

Farnie, D. A. *The English Cotton Industry and the World Market, 1815–1896*. Oxford: Clarendon, 1979.

Feldman, David, and Gareth Stedman Jones, eds. *Metropolis London: Histories and Representations since 1800*. New York: Routledge, 1989.

Ferry, Emma. "'Decorators May Be Compared to Doctors': An Analysis of Rhoda and Agnes Garrett's *Suggestions for House Painting, Woodwork, and Furniture*." *Journal of Design History* 16 (1) (2003): 15–33.

Fine, Ben, and Ellen Leopold. "Consumerism and the Industrial Revolution." *Social History* 15 (2) (1990): 151–79.

Finn, Margot. *The Character of Credit: Personal Debt in English Culture, 1740–1914*. Cambridge: Cambridge University Press, 2003.

———. "Men's Things: Masculine Possession in the Consumer Revolution." *Social History* 25 (2) (May 2000): 133–55.

———. "Sex and the City: Metropolitan Modernities in English History." *Victorian Studies* 44 (1) (2001): 25–32.

———. "When Was the Nineteenth Century Where? Whither Victorian Studies?" *19. Interdisciplinary studies in the Long Nineteenth Century* (2) (Spring 2006): http://www.19.bbk.ac.uk.

———. "Working-Class Women and the Contest for Consumer Control in Victorian County Courts." *Past and Present* 161 (November 1998): 116–54.

Forty, Adrian. *Objects of Desire: Design and Society since 1750*. London: Thames and Hudson, 1986.

Foucault, Michel. "Governmentality." In *The Foucault Effect: Studies in Gov-*

ernmentality, ed. Graham Burchell, Colin Gordon, and Peter Miller, 87–104. Chicago: University of Chicago Press, 1991.

———. "What Is an Author?" In *Rethinking Popular Culture: Contemporary Perspectives in Cultural Studies*, ed. Chandra Mukerji and Michael Schudson, 446–64. Berkeley: University of California Press, 1991.

Fox, Celina. *Graphic Journalism in England during the 1830s and 1840s*. New York: Garland, 1974.

Francastel, Pierre. *Art and Technology in the Nineteenth and Twentieth Centuries*. New York: Zone, 2000.

Frayling, Christopher, and Claire Catterall, eds. *Design of the Times: One Hundred Years of the Royal College of Art*. London: Royal College of Art, 1996.

———. *The Royal College of Art: One Hundred and Fifty Years of Art and Design*. London: Barrie and Jenkins, 1987.

Friedman, Rebecca. *Masculinity, Autocracy, and the Russian University, 1804–1863*. London: Palgrave, 2005.

Fyfe, Gordon. *Art, Power, and Modernity: English Art Institutions, 1750–1950*. London: Leicester University Press, 2000.

Gagnier, Regenia. *The Insatiability of Human Wants: Economics and Aesthetics in Market Society*. Chicago: University of Chicago Press, 2000.

Giedion, Siegfried. *Mechanization Takes Command: A Contribution to Anonymous History*. 1940. Rpt.; New York: Oxford University Press, 1970.

Gilbert, David. "'London in All Its Glory; or, How to Enjoy London': Guidebook Representations of Imperial London." *Journal of Historical Geography* 25 (3) (1999): 279–97.

Gilbert, Pamela K. *Mapping the Victorian Social Body*. Albany: State University of New York Press, 2004.

Goldstein, Carl. *Teaching Art: Academies and Schools from Vasari to Albers*. Cambridge: Cambridge University Press, 1996.

Gray, Robert Q. *The Aristocracy of Labor in Victorian Edinburgh*. Oxford: Oxford University Press, 1976.

Greenblatt, Stephen. *Renaissance Self-Fashioning: From More to Shakespeare*. Chicago: University of Chicago Press, 1980.

Greenhalgh, Paul. *Ephemeral Vistas: The Expositions Universelles, Great Exhibitions, and World's Fairs, 1851–1939*. Manchester: Manchester University Press, 1988.

Gretton, Thomas. "'Art Is Cheaper and Goes Lower in France': The Language of the Parliamentary Select Committee on the Arts and Principles of Design of 1835–36." In *Art in Bourgeois Society, 1790–1850*, ed. Andrew Hemingway and William Vaughan, 84–100. Cambridge: Cambridge University Press, 1998.

Grever, Maria, and Berteke Waaldijk. *Transforming the Public Sphere: The*

Dutch National Exhibition of Women's Labor in 1898. Trans. Mischa F. C. Hoyinck and Robert Chesal. Durham: Duke University Press, 2004.

Greysmith, David. "Patterns, Piracy, and Protection in the Textile Printing Industry, 1787–1850." *Textile History* 14 (2) (1983): 165–94.

Guha-Thakurta, Tapati. *The Making of a New 'Indian' Art: Artists, Aesthetics, and Nationalism in Bengal, c. 1850–1920.* Cambridge: Cambridge University Press, 1992.

Gunn, Simon. *The Public Culture of the Victorian Middle Class: Ritual and Authority in the English Industrial City, 1840–1914.* Manchester: Manchester University Press, 2000.

Gurney, Peter. "An Appropriated Space: The Great Exhibition, the Crystal Palace, and the Working Class." In *The Great Exhibition of 1851: New Interdisciplinary Essays,* ed. Louise Purbrick, 114–45. Manchester: Manchester University Press, 2001.

Hall, Catherine. *Civilising Subjects: Metropole and Colony in the English Imagination.* Chicago: University of Chicago Press, 2002.

——. *White, Male, and Middle-Class: Explorations in Feminism and History.* New York, 1992.

Hammerton, A. James. "Pooterism or Partnership? Marriage and Masculine Identity in the Lower Middle Class, 1870–1920." *Journal of British Studies* 38 (3) (July 1999): 291–321.

Harker, Richard. "Bourdieu: Education and Reproduction." In *An Introduction to the Work of Pierre Bourdieu,* ed. Richard Harker, Cheleen Mahar, and Chris Wilkes, 86–108. New York: St. Martin's, 1990.

Harvey, Charles, and Jon Press. "The Businessman." In *William Morris,* ed. Linda Parry, 49–57. New York: Abrams, 1996.

——. *William Morris: Design and Enterprise in Victorian Britain.* Manchester: Manchester University Press, 1991.

Haskell, Thomas. "Capitalism and the Origins of the Humanitarian Sensibility, Parts I and II." *American Historical Review* 90 (2–3) (1985): 339–61, 547–66.

Haskell, Thomas, and Richard Teichgraeber, eds. *The Culture of the Market: Historical Essays.* New York: Cambridge University Press, 1993.

Hassam, Andrew. "Portable Iron Structures and Uncertain Colonial Spaces at the Sydenham Crystal Palace." In *Imperial Cities: Landscape, Display, and Identity,* ed. Felix Driver and David Gilbert, 174–93. New York: Manchester University Press, 1999.

Herbert, Christopher. *Culture and Anomie.* Chicago: University of Chicago Press, 1991.

Hevia, James. *English Lessons: The Pedagogy of Imperialism in Nineteenth-Century China.* Durham: Duke University Press, 2003.

Hewitt, Martin. "Prologue." In *An Age of Equipoise? Reassessing Mid-Victorian Britain,* ed. Martin Hewitt, 1–38. Aldershot: Ashgate, 2000.

————. "Victorian Studies: Problems and Prospects?" *Journal of Victorian Culture* 6 (2001): 137–61.

————. "Why the Notion of Victorian Britain *Does* Make Sense." *Victorian Studies* 48 (3) (Spring 2006): 395–438.

Hewitt, Martin, ed. *An Age of Equipoise? Reassessing Mid-Victorian Britain.* Aldershot: Ashgate, 2000.

Hill, Christopher. "Radical Pirates." In *Collected Essays of Christopher Hill.* Vol. 3: *People and Ideas in Seventeenth-Century England*, 161–87. Amherst: University of Massachusetts Press, 1986.

————. *Radical Pirates, Religion, and Literature in Seventeenth-Century England.* London: Routledge, 1990.

Hill, Kate. *Culture and Class in English Public Museums, 1845–1914.* Aldershot: Ashgate, 2005.

Hoffenberg, Peter Henry. *An Empire on Display: English, Indian, and Australian Exhibitions from the Crystal Palace to the Great War.* Berkeley: University of California Press, 2001.

————. "Equipoise and Its Discontents: Voices of Dissent during the International Exhibitions." In *An Age of Equipoise? Reassessing Mid-Victorian Britain*, ed. Martin Hewitt, 39–67. Aldershot: Ashgate, 2000.

Hoock, Holger. *The King's Artists: The Royal Academy of Arts and the Politics of British Culture, 1760–1840.* New York : Oxford University Press, 2003.

————. "Reforming Culture: National Art Institutions in the Age of Reform." In *Rethinking the Age of Reform: Britain, 1780–1850*, ed. Arthur Burns and Joanna Innes, 254–70. Cambridge: Cambridge University Press, 2003.

Hooper-Greenhill, Eilean. *Museums and the Shaping of Knowledge.* New York: Routledge, 1992.

Hosgood, Christopher P. "'Mercantile Monasteries': Shops, Shop Assistants, and Shop Life in Late-Victorian and Edwardian Britain." *Journal of British Studies* 38 (3) (1999): 322–52.

Hurst, J. G. *Edmund Potter and Dinting Vale.* Manchester: Edmund Potter, 1948.

Israel, Kali. *Names and Stories: Emilia Dilke and Victorian Culture.* New York: Oxford University Press, 1999.

Jasanoff, Maya. *Edge of Empire: Lives, Culture, and Conquest in the East, 1750–1850.* New York: Knopf, 2005.

Jones, Colin. "Peter Mandler's 'Problem with Cultural History'; or, Is Playtime Over?" *Cultural and Social History* 1 (2) (2004): 209–15.

Jones, Gareth Stedman. *Languages of Class: Studies in English Working Class History, 1832–1982.* Cambridge: Cambridge University Press, 1983.

Joyce, Patrick. *Democratic Subjects: The Self and the Social in Nineteenth-Century England.* Cambridge: Cambridge University Press, 1994.

————. "The Imaginary Discontents of Social History: A Note of Response to Mayfield and Thorne and Lawrence and Taylor." *Social History* 18 (1993): 81–86.

———. "Introduction." In *The Social in Question: New Bearings in History and the Social Sciences*, ed. Patrick Joyce, 1–18. London: Routledge, 2002.

———. *The Rule of Freedom: Liberalism and the Modern City*. London: Verso, 2003.

———. *Visions of the People: Industrial England and the Question of Class, 1840–1914*. Cambridge: Cambridge University Press, 1991.

Kabbani, Rana. *Europe's Myths of Orient: Devise and Rule*. London: Macmillan, 1986.

Kahan, Alan S. *Liberalism in Nineteenth-Century Europe: The Political Culture of Limited Suffrage*. New York: Palgrave, 2003.

Kale, Madhavi. *Fragments of Empire: Capital, Slavery, and Indentured Labor Migration in the British Caribbean*. Philadelphia: University of Pennsylvania Press, 1998.

Kaplan, Wendy. "Design for the Modern World." In *The Arts and Crafts Movement in Europe and America: Design for the Modern World, 1875–1920*, ed. Wendy Kaplan, 10–19. New York: Thames and Hudson, 2004.

Kaplan, Wendy, ed. *"The Art That Is Life": The Arts and Crafts Movement in America, 1875–1920*. Boston: Little, Brown, 1998.

———. *The Arts and Crafts Movement in Europe and America: Design for the Modern World*. New York: Thames and Hudson, 2004.

Kent, Christopher. "Victorian Social History: Post-Thompson, Post-Foucault, Postmodern." *Victorian Studies* 40 (1) (1996): 97–134.

Keyser, Barbara Whitney. "Ornament as Idea: Indirect Imitation of Nature in the Design Reform Movement." *Journal of Design History* 11 (2) (1998): 127–44.

Kinchin, Juliet. "Designer as Critic: E. W. Godwin and the Aesthetic Home." *Journal of Design History* 18 (1) (2005): 21–34.

Kirschenblatt-Gimblett, Barbara. *Destination Culture: Tourism, Museums, and Heritage*. Berkeley: University of California Press, 1998.

Klingender, *Art and the Industrial Revolution*. 1948. Rpt.; Chatham: Evelyn, Adams and Mackay, 1968.

Koven, Seth. *Slumming: Sexual and Social Politics in Victorian London*. Princeton: Princeton University Press, 2004.

———. "The Whitechapel Picture Exhibitions and the Politics of Seeing." In *Museum Culture: Histories, Discourses, Spectacles*, ed. Daniel J. Sherman and Irit Rogoff, 22–48. Minneapolis: University of Minnesota Press, 1994.

Kowaleski-Wallace, Elizabeth. *Consuming Subjects: Women, Shopping, and Business in the Eighteenth Century*. New York: Columbia University Press, 1997.

Kramer, Paul. "Making Concessions: Race and Empire Revisited at the Philippine Exposition, St. Louis, 1901-1905." *Radical History Review* 73 (1999): 71-114.

Kriegel, Lara. "After the Exhibitionary Complex: Museum Histories and the Future of the Victorian Past." *Victorian Studies* 48 (4) (Summer 2006): 681-704.

——. "Narrating the Subcontinent in 1851: India at the Crystal Palace." In *The Great Exhibition of 1851: New Interdisciplinary Essays*, ed. Louise Purbrick, 146-78. Manchester: Manchester University Press, 2001.

——. "The Pudding and the Palace: Labor, Print Culture, and Imperial Britain in 1851." In *After the Imperial Turn: Thinking with and through the Nation*, ed. Antoinette Burton, 230-45. Durham: Duke University Press, 2003.

Kriz, K. Dian. *The Idea of the English Landscape Painter: Genius as Alibi in the Early Nineteenth Century*. New Haven: Yale University Press, 1997.

Kuchta, David. *The Three-Piece Suit and Modern Masculinity: England, 1550-1850*. Berkeley: University of California Press, 2002.

Kusamitsu, Toshio. "British Industrialization and Design before the Great Exhibition." *Textile History* 12 (1981): 77-95.

Kwass, Michael. "Big Hair: A Wig History of Consumption in Eighteenth-Century France." *American Historical Review* 111 (3) (June 2006): 631-59.

Lawrence, John, and Miles Taylor. "The Poverty of Protest: Gareth Stedman Jones and the Politics of Language—a Reply." *Social History* 18 (1993): 1-15.

Lawson, Philip. *The East India Company: A History*. New York: Longman, 1993.

Lemire, Beverly. *Dress, Culture, and Commerce: The English Clothing Trade before the Factory, 1600-1800*. New York: St. Martin's, 1997.

——. *Fashion's Favourite: The Cotton Trade and the Consumer in Britain*. Oxford: Oxford University Press, 1991.

Levine, Arnold Sydney. "The Politics of Taste: The Science and Art Department of Great Britain, 1852-1873." Ph.D. diss., University of Wisconsin, 1972.

Lubbock, Jules. *The Tyranny of Taste: The Politics of Architecture and Design in Britain, 1550-1960*. New Haven: Yale University Press, 1995.

Luke, Timothy. *Museum Politics: Power Plays at the Exhibition*. Minneapolis: University of Minnesota Press, 2002.

MacCarthy, Fiona. "The Designer." In *William Morris*, ed. Linda Parry, 32-48. New York: Abrams, 1996.

Macdonald, Stuart. *History and Philosophy of Art Education*. London: University of London Press, 1970.

MacGregor, Neil. "A Pentecost in Trafalgar Square." In *Whose Muse? Art*

Museums and the Public Trust, ed. James Cuno, 27–48. Princeton: Princeton University Press, 2004.

Mackenzie, John. *Orientalism: History, Theory, and the Arts*. New York: Manchester University Press, 1995.

Mackie, Erin. *Market à la Mode: Fashion, Commodity, and Gender in the* Tatler *and the* Spectator. Baltimore: Johns Hopkins University Press, 1997.

Macleod, Christine. *Inventing the Industrial Revolution: The English Patent System, 1660–1800*. Cambridge: Cambridge University Press, 1988.

MacLeod, Dianne Sachko. *Art and the Victorian Middle Class: Money and the Making of Cultural Identity*. New York: Cambridge University Press, 1996.

Maidment, Brian. "Entrepreneurship and the Artisans: John Cassell, the Great Exhibition, and the Periodical Idea." In *The Great Exhibition of 1851: New Interdisciplinary Essays*, ed. Louise Purbrick, 79–113. Manchester: Manchester University Press, 2001.

Mandler, Peter. *The Fall and Rise of the Stately Home*. New Haven: Yale University Press, 1997.

———. "The Problem with Cultural History." *Cultural and Social History* 1 (1) (2004): 94–117.

Mandler, Peter, Alex Owen, Seth Koven, and Susan Pedersen. "Cultural Histories Old and New: Rereading the Work of Janet Oppenheim." *Victorian Studies* 41 (1) (1997–98): 69–105.

Mathur, Saloni. "Living Ethnological Exhibits: The Case of 1886." *Cultural Anthropology* 15 (4) (2000): 492–524.

Mayfield, David, and Susan Thorne. "Reply to 'The Poverty of Protest' and 'Imaginary Discontents.'" *Social History* 18 (May 1993): 219–33.

———. "Social History and Its Discontents: Gareth Stedman Jones and the Politics of Language." *Social History* 17 (1992): 165–88.

Maza, Sarah. "Stories in History: Cultural Narratives in Recent Works in European History." *American Historical Review* 101 (5) (1996): 1493–1515.

McCalman, Iain. *Radical Underworld: Prophets, Revolutionaries, and Pornographers in London, 1795–1840*. New York: Cambridge University Press, 1988.

McCarthy, Fiona. "The Designer." In *William Morris*, ed. Linda Parry, 32–48. New York: Abrams, 1996.

McClellan, Andrew. "A Brief History of the Art Museum Public." In *Art and Its Publics: Museum Studies at the Millennium*, ed. Andrew McClellan, 1–50. New York: Blackwell, 2003.

———. *Inventing the Louvre: Art, Politics, and the Origins of the Modern Museum in Eighteenth-Century Paris*. Berkeley: University of California Press, 1999.

McClelland, Keith. "England's Greatness, the Working Man." In *Defining the Victorian Nation: Class, Race, Gender, and the Reform Act of 1867*, ed.

Catherine Hall, Keith McClelland, and Jane Rendall, 71–118. Cambridge: Cambridge University Press, 2002.

———. "Rational and Respectable Men: Gender, the Working Class, and Citizenship in Britain, 1850–1867." In *Gender and Class in Modern Europe*, ed. Laura L. Frader and Sonya O. Rose, 280–93. Ithaca: Cornell University Press, 1996.

———. "Some Thoughts on Masculinity and the 'Representative Artisan' in Britain, 1850–1880." *Gender and History* 1 (2) (1989): 165–77.

McClintock, Anne. *Imperial Leather: Race, Gender, and Sexuality in the Colonial Contest*. London: Routledge, 1995.

McKendrick, Neil. "The Commercialization of Fashion." In *Birth of a Consumer Society: The Commercialization of Eighteenth-Century England*, ed. Neil McKendrick, John Brewer, and J. H. Plumb, 34–99. Bloomington: Indiana University Press, 1982.

———. "The Consumer Revolution of Eighteenth-Century England." In *Birth of a Consumer Society: The Commercialization of Eighteenth-Century England*, ed. Neil McKendrick, John Brewer, and J. H. Plumb, 9–33. Bloomington: Indiana University Press, 1982.

McKendrick, Neil, John Brewer, and J. H. Plumb, eds. *Birth of a Consumer Society: The Commercialization of Eighteenth-Century England*. Bloomington: Indiana University Press, 1982.

McWilliam, Rohan. "What is Interdisciplinary about Victorian History Today?" *19. Interdisciplinary Studies in the Long Nineteenth Century* 48 (1) (Autumn 2005): http://www.19.bbk.ac.uk.

Metcalf, Thomas. *Ideologies of the Raj*. New York: Cambridge University Press, 1994.

Miller, Andrew. *Novels behind Glass: Commodity Culture and Victorian Narrative*. Bloomington: Indiana University Press, 1995.

Miller, Daniel. "Why Some Things Matter." In *Material Cultures: Why Some Things Matter*, ed. Daniel Miller, 3–21. Chicago: University of Chicago Press, 1998.

Minihan, Janet. *The Nationalization of Culture*. London: Hamish Hamilton, 1977.

Mitchell, Timothy. *Colonising Egypt*. Cambridge: Cambridge University Press, 1988.

———. "Orientalism and the Exhibitionary Order." In *Colonialism and Culture*, ed. Nicholas Dirks, 289–318. Ann Arbor: University of Michigan Press, 1992.

Mitter, Partha. *Much Maligned Monsters: A History of European Reactions to Indian Art*. Oxford: Oxford University Press, 1977.

Mitter, Partha, and Craig Clunas. "The Empire of Things: The Engagement with the Orient." In *A Grand Design: The Art of the Victoria and*

Albert Museum, ed. Malcolm Baker and Brenda Richardson, 221–37. New York: Harry N. Abrams, 1997.

Mort, Frank. *Cultures of Consumption: Masculinities and Social Space in Late Twentieth-Century Britain*. Routledge: London, 1996.

Mort, Frank, and Miles Ogborn. "Transforming Metropolitan London, 1750–1960." *Journal of British Studies* 43 (January 2004): 1–14.

Morton, Patricia. *Hybrid Modernities: Architecture and Representation at the 1931 Colonial Expo, Paris*. Cambridge: MIT Press, 2000.

Mukerji, Chandra. *From Graven Images: Patterns of Modern Materialism*. New York: Columbia University Press, 1983.

Munford, W. A. *William Ewart, MP, 1789–1869: Portrait of a Radical*. London: Grafton, 1960.

Nead, Lynda. *The Female Nude: Art, Obscenity, and Sexuality*. New York: Routledge, 1992.

———. *Victorian Babylon: People, Streets, and Images in Nineteenth-Century London*. New Haven: Yale University Press, 2000.

Nord, Deborah Epstein. *Walking the Victorian Streets: Women, Representation, and the City*. Ithaca: Cornell University Press, 1995.

Nowell-Smith, Simon. *The House of Cassell, 1848–1958*. London: Cassell, 1958.

O'Connor, Maura. *The Romance of Italy and the English Political Imagination*. New York: St. Martin's, 1998.

Ogborn, Miles. *Spaces of Modernity: London's Geographies, 1680–1780*. New York: Guilford, 1998.

Olsen, Donald J. *The Growth of Victorian London*. New York: Holmes and Meier, 1976.

Otter, Christopher. "Cleansing and Clarifying: Technology and Perception in Nineteenth-Century London." *Journal of British Studies* 43 (1) (January 2004): 40–64.

Pagani, Catherine. "Chinese Material Culture and British Perceptions of China in the Mid–Nineteenth Century." In *Colonialism and the Object: Empire, Material Culture, and the Museum*, ed. Tim Barringer and Tom Flynn, 28–40. London: Routledge, 1998.

———. "Objects and the Press: Images of China in Nineteenth-Century Britain." In *Imperial Co-Histories: National Identities and the British and Colonial Press*, ed. Julie F. Codell, 147–66. Madison, Pa.: Fairleigh Dickinson University Press, 2003.

Parry, Linda, ed. *William Morris*. New York: Abrams, 1996.

Pearson, Nicholas. *The State and the Visual Arts*. Milton Keynes: Open University Press, 1982.

Pearson, Richard. "Thackeray and Punch at the Great Exhibition: Authority and Ambivalence in Verbal and Visual Caricatures." In *The Great Exhi-*

bition of 1851: New Interdisciplinary Essays, ed. Louise Purbrick, 170–205. Manchester: Manchester University Press, 2001.

Penny, H. Glenn. *Objects of Culture: Ethnology and Ethnographic Museums in Imperial Germany*. Chapel Hill: University of North Carolina Press, 2002.

Perot, Philippe. *Fashioning the Bourgeoisie*. Trans. Richard Bienvenu. Princeton: Princeton University Press, 1994.

Pevsner, Nikolaus. *Academies of Art Past and Present*. Cambridge: Cambridge University Press, 1940.

———. *High Victorian Design: A Study of the Exhibits of 1851*. London: Architectural Press, 1951.

———. *Pioneers of Modern Design: From William Morris to Walter Gropius*. 1936. Rpt.; New Haven: Yale University Press, 2005.

Physick, John. "The Government School of Design: Foundation, Rebellion, Investigation, and the Triumph of Henry Cole." In *Design of the Times: One Hundred Years of the Royal College of Art*, ed. Christopher Frayling and Claire Catterall, 14–19. London: Royal College of Art, 1996.

———. *The Victoria and Albert Museum: The History of Its Building*. London: Victoria and Albert Museum, 1982.

Pointon, Marcia, ed. *Art Apart: Art Institutions and Ideology across England and North America*. Manchester: Manchester University Press, 1994.

———. *William Dyce: A Critical Biography*. Oxford: Clarendon, 1979.

Poovey, Mary. "'Figures of Arithmetic, Figures of Speech': The Discourse of Statistics in the 1830s." *Critical Inquiry* 19 (winter 1993): 256–76.

———. *Making a Social Body: British Cultural Formation, 1830–1864*. Chicago: University of Chicago Press, 1995.

———. "The Man-of-Letters Hero: *David Copperfield* and the Professional Writer." In *Uneven Developments: The Ideological Work of Gender in Mid-Victorian England*, 89–125. Chicago: University of Chicago Press, 1988.

Port, M. H. *Imperial London: Civil Government Building in London, 1850–1914*. New Haven: Yale University Press, 1995.

Prothero, Iorworth. *Radical Artisans in England and France, 1830–1870*. Cambridge: Cambridge University Press, 1997.

Purbrick, Louise. "Building the House of Henry Cole." in *Art Apart: Art Institutions and Ideology across England and North America*, ed. Marcia Pointon, 69–86. Manchester: Manchester University Press, 1994.

———. "The Dream Machine: Charles Babbage and His Imaginary Computers." *Journal of Design History* 6 (1) (1993): 9–23.

———. "Ideologically Technical: Illustration, Automation, and Spinning Cotton around the Middle of the Nineteenth Century." *Journal of Design History* 11 (1998): 275–93.

———. "Introduction." In *The Great Exhibition of 1851: New Interdisciplinary*

Essays, ed. Louise Purbrick. 1–25. Manchester: Manchester University Press, 2001.

———. "Knowledge Is Property: Looking at Exhibits and Patents in 1851." *Oxford Art Journal* 20 (2) (1997): 53–60.

———. "Machines and the Mechanism of Representation: The Display of Design in Mid-Nineteenth-Century Britain." D.Phil. diss., University of Sussex, 1994.

Purbrick, Louise, ed. *The Great Exhibition of 1851: New Interdisciplinary Essays.* Manchester: Manchester University Press, 2001.

Rappaport, Erika. "Art, Commerce, or Empire? The Rebuilding of Regent Street, 1880–1927." *History Workshop Journal* 53 (2002): 94–117.

———. "'The Bombay Debt': Letter Writing, Domestic Economies, and Family Conflict in Colonial India." *Gender and History* 16 (2) (2004): 233–60.

———. "'A Husband and His Wife's Dresses': Consumer Credit and the Debtor Family in England." In *The Sex of Things: Gender and Consumption in Historical Perspective*, ed. Victoria de Grazia with Ellen Furlough, 163–87. Berkeley: University of California Press, 1996.

———. *Shopping for Pleasure: Women in the Making of London's West End.* Princeton: Princeton University Press, 2000.

Ray, Larry, and Andrew Sayer. "Introduction." In *Culture and Economy after the Cultural Turn*, ed. Larry Ray and Andrew Sayer, 1–24. London: Sage, 1999.

Reddy, William. *The Rise of Market Culture: The Textile Trade and French Society, 1750–1900.* Cambridge: Cambridge University Press, 1984.

Rich, Rachel. "Designing the Dinner Party: Advice on Dining and Décor in London and Paris, 1860–1914." *Journal of Design History* 16 (1) (2003): 49–61.

Richards, Sarah. "'A True Siberia': Art in Service to Commerce in the Dresden Academy and the Meissen Drawing School, 1764–1836." *Journal of Design History* 11 (2) (1998): 109–26.

Richards, Thomas. *The Commodity Culture of Victorian England: Advertising and Spectacle.* Palo Alto: Stanford University Press, 1990.

———. *The Imperial Archive: Knowledge and the Fantasy of Empire.* London: Verso, 1993.

Rieger, Bernhard, and Martin Daunton. "Introduction." In *Meanings of Modernity: Britain from the Late-Victorian Era to World War II*, ed. Martin Daunton and Bernhard Rieger, 1–21.: New York: Berg, 2001.

Rifkin, Adrian. "Success Disavowed: The Schools of Design in Mid-Nineteenth-Century Britain (an Allegory)." *Journal of Design History* 1 (2) (1988): 89–102.

Ritchie, Robert C. *Captain Kidd and the War against the Pirates.* Cambridge: Cambridge University Press, 1986.

Robbins, Derek. *The Work of Pierre Bourdieu: Recognizing Society*. Boulder: Westview, 1991.

Rogers, Helen. "Victorian Studies in the United Kingdom." In *The Victorians since 1901: Histories, Representations, and Revisions*, ed. Miles Taylor and Michael Wolff, 244–59. Manchester: Manchester University Press, 2004.

Rose, Mark. *Authors and Owners: The Invention of Copyright*. Cambridge: Cambridge University Press, 1993.

Ross, Ellen. *Love and Toil: Motherhood in Outcast London, 1870–1918*. New York: Oxford University Press, 2003.

Ross, Trevor. "Copyright and the Invention of Tradition." *Eighteenth-Century Studies* 26 (fall 1992): 1–27.

Rule, John. "The Property of Skill in the Period of Manufacture." In *The Historical Meanings of Work*, ed. Patrick Joyce, 99–118. Cambridge: Cambridge University Press, 1987.

Rydell, Robert W. *All the World's a Fair: Visions of Empire at American International Expositions, 1876–1916*. Chicago: University of Chicago Press, 1984.

Said, Edward. *Orientalism*. New York: Vintage, 1978.

Samuel, Raphael. "The Workshop of the World: Steam Power and Hand Technology in Mid-Victorian Britain." *History Workshop Journal* 3 (spring 1977): 6–72.

Saumarez Smith, Charles, Giles Waterfield, Tim Barringer, and Malcolm Baker. "The Victoria and Albert Museum: A Grand Design?" *Journal of Victorian Culture* 3 (1998): 349–81.

Saunders, David, and Ian Hunter. "Lessons from the 'Literary': How to Historicize Authorship." *Critical Inquiry* 17 (spring 1991): 479–509.

Schmiechen, James A. "The Victorians, the Historians, and the Idea of Modernism." *American Historical Review* 93 (2) (April 1998): 287–316.

Schneer, Jonathan. *London 1900: The Imperial Metropolis*. New Haven: Yale University Press, 1999.

Schwartz, Hillel. *The Culture of the Copy: Striking Likenesses, Unreasonable Facsimiles*. New York: Zone, 1996.

Schwartz, Vanessa. *Spectacular Realities: Early Mass Culture in Fin-de-Siècle Paris*. Berkeley: University of California Press, 1998.

Scott, Joan. *Gender and the Politics of History*. New York: Columbia University Press, 1988.

Scott, Katie. "Art and Industry, a Contradictory Union: Authors, Rights, and Copyrights during the Consulat." *Journal of Design History* 13 (1) (2000): 1–21.

Seed, John. "'Commerce and the Liberal Arts': The Political Economy of Art in Manchester, 1775–1860." In *The Culture of Capital: Art, Power, and* the *Nineteenth-Century Middle Class*, ed. John Seed and Janet Wolff. New York: St. Martin's, 1988.

Sen, Sudipta. *Empire of Free Trade: The East India Company and the Making of the Colonial Marketplace*. Philadelphia: University of Pennsylvania Press, 1998.

Senior, C. M. *A Nation of Pirates: English Piracy in Its Heyday*. Newton Abbott: David and Charles, 1976.

Sewell, William H. *Work and Revolution in France: The Language of Labor from the Old Regime to the Present*. Cambridge: Cambridge University Press, 1980.

Shannon, Brent. "ReFashioning Men: Fashion, Masculinity, and the Cultivation of the Male Consumer in Britain, 1860-1914." *Victorian Studies* 46 (4) (summer 2004): 597-630.

Sheppard, Francis. *London, 1808-1870: The Infernal Wen*. Berkeley: University of California Press, 1979.

Sheppard, Francis, ed. *Survey of London: The Museums Area of South Kensington and Westminster* 38. London: Athlone Press, 1983.

———. *Survey of London: South Kensington: Brompton* 41. London: Athlone Press, 1983.

Sherman, Daniel. *Worthy Monuments: Art Museums and the Politics of Culture in Nineteenth-Century France*. Cambridge: Harvard University Press, 1989.

Sherman, Daniel, and Irit Rogoff, eds. *Museum Culture: History, Discourses, Spectacles*. Minneapolis: University of Minnesota Press, 1994.

Siegel, Jonah. *Haunted Museum: Longing, Travel, and the Art-Romance Tradition*. Princeton: Princeton University Press, 2005.

Silverman, Debora. *Art Nouveau in Fin-de-Siècle France: Politics, Psychology, and Style*. Berkeley: University of California Press, 1989.

Sinha, Mrinalini. *Colonial Masculinities: The "Manly Englishman" and the "Effeminate Bengali" in the Late Nineteenth Century*. Manchester: Manchester University Press, 1995.

Smith, Alison. *Exposed: The Victorian Nude*. London: Tate, 2001.

———. *The Victorian Nude: Sexuality, Morality, and Art*. New York: Manchester University Press, 1996.

Snodin, Michael. "Who Led Taste?: Georgian Britain." In *Design and the Decorative Arts, Britain, 1500-1900*, ed. Michael Snodin and John Styles, 217-46. London: V & A Publications, 2001.

———. "Who Led Taste?: Victorian Britain." In *Design and the Decorative Arts, Britain, 1500-1900*, ed. Michael Snodin and John Styles, 369-97. London: V & A Publications, 2001.

Snodin, Michael, and John Styles. *Design and the Decorative Arts, Britain, 1500-1900*. London: V & A Publications, 2001.

Sparke, Penny. "Historical Revivals, Commercial Enterprise, and Public

Confusion: Negotiating Taste, 1860–1890." *Journal of Design History* 16 (1) (2003): 35–48.

Stansky, Peter. *Redesigning the World: William Morris, the 1880s, and the Arts and Crafts.* Princeton: Princeton University Press, 1985.

———. *William Morris.* Oxford: Oxford University Press, 1983.

———. *From William Morris to Sergeant Pepper: Studies in the Radical Domestic.* Palo Alto: Society for the Promotion of Science and Scholarship, 1999.

Starn, Randolph. "A Historian's Brief Guide to New Museum Studies." *American Historical Review* 110 (1) (2005): 68–98.

Steedman, Carolyn. *Landscape for a Good Woman.* New Brunswick: Rutgers University Press, 1992.

Steegman, John. *Victorian Taste: A Study of the Arts and Architecture from 1830 to 1870.* Rpt.; Boston: MIT Press, 1970. Originally published as *Consort of Taste, 1830–1870,* by Sidgwick and Jackson, 1950.

Stewart, Susan. *On Longing: Narratives of the Miniature, the Gigantic, the Souvenir, the Collection.* Baltimore: Johns Hopkins University Press, 1984.

Steyn, Juliet. "Inside-Out: Assumptions of 'English' Modernism in the Whitechapel Art Gallery, London, 1914." In *Art Apart: Art Institutions and Ideology across England and North America,* ed. Marcia Pointon, 212–330. Manchester: Manchester University Press, 1994.

Stocking, George, Jr. "Introduction." In *Objects and Others: Essays on Museums and Material Culture,* ed. George Stocking Jr., 16–43. Madison: University of Wisconsin Press, 1985.

Styles, John. "Manufacturing, Consumption, and Design in Eighteenth-Century England." In *Consumption and the World of Goods,* ed. John Brewer and Roy Porter, 527–54. London: Routledge, 1993.

———. "What Was New? Georgian Britain, 1714–1837." In *Design and the Decorative Arts, Britain, 1500–1900,* ed. Michael Snodin and John Styles, 281–307. London: V & A Publications, 2001.

Summerson, John Newenham. *The Architecture of Victorian London.* Charlottesville: University of Virginia Press, 1976.

———. *The London Building World of the Eighteen-Sixties.* London: Thames and Hudson, 1973.

Suny, Ronald Grigor. "Back and Beyond: Reversing the Cultural Turn?" *American Historical Review* 107 (5) (2002): 1476–99.

Sutherland, W. G. *The Royal Manchester Institution, Its Origins, Its Character, and Its Aims.* Manchester: Royal Manchester Institution, 1945.

Sweetman, John. *The Oriental Obsession: Islamic Inspiration in British and American Art and Architecture.* New York: Cambridge University Press, 1988.

Taylor, Brandon. *Art for the Nation: Exhibitions and the London Public, 1747–2001.* New Brunswick: Rutgers University Press, 1999.

Taylor, Miles. "Introduction." In *The Victorians since 1901: Histories, Representations, and Revisions*, ed. Miles Taylor and Michael Wolff, 1–13. Manchester: Manchester University Press, 2004.

Taylor, Miles, and Michael Wolff, eds. *The Victorians since 1901: Histories, Representations, and Revisions*. Manchester: Manchester University Press, 2004.

Thompson, E. P. *The Making of the English Working Class*. Vintage: New York, 1963.

———. *William Morris: Romantic to Revolutionary*. 1955. Rpt.; New York: Pantheon, 1977.

Tosh, John. *A Man's Place: Masculinity and the Middle-Class Home in Victorian England*. New Haven: Yale University Press, 1999.

Trippi, Peter. "Industrial Arts and the Exhibition Ideal." In *A Grand Design: The Art of the Victoria and Albert Museum*, ed. Malcolm Baker and Brenda Richardson, 79–88. New York: Harry N. Abrams, 1997.

Trodd, Colin. "Culture, Class, City: The National Gallery, London, and the Spaces of Education, 1822–57." In *Art Apart: Art Institutions and Ideology across England and North America*, ed. Marcia Pointon, 33–49. Manchester: Manchester University Press, 1994.

———. "The Paths to the National Gallery." In *Governing Cultures: Art Institutions in Victorian London*, ed. Paul Barlow and Colin Trodd, 29–43. Aldershot: Ashgate, 2000.

Turley, Hans. *Rum, Sodomy, and the Lash: Piracy, Sexuality, and Masculine Identity*. New York: New York University Press, 1999.

Turnbull, Geoffrey. *A History of the Calico Printing Industry of Great Britain*, ed. John G. Turnbull. Altrincham: John Sherratt and Son, 1951.

Turner, Eric. "Gas Jet." In *A Grand Design: The Art of the Victoria and Albert Museum*, ed. Malcolm Baker and Brenda Richardson, New York: Harry N. Abrams, 1997.

Vanden Bossche, Chris R. "The Value of Literature: Representations of Print Culture in the Copyright Debate of 1837–1842." *Victorian Studies* 38 (autumn 1994): 41–68.

Vergo, Peter, ed. *The New Museology*. London: Reaktion, 1989.

Vernon, James. "Who's Afraid of the 'Linguistic Turn'?" *Social History* 19 (1994): 81–97.

Waggoner, Diane. *The Beauty of Life: William Morris and the Art of Design*. New York: Thames and Hudson, 2003.

Wainwright, Clive. "Principles True and False: Pugin and the Foundation of the Museum of Manufactures." *Burlington Magazine* 136 (June 1994): 357–64

———. "Shopping for South Kensington: Fortnum and Henry Cole in Florence, 1858–59." *Journal of the History of Collections* 11 (1999): 171–85.

Wainwright, Clive, with Charlotte Gere. "The Making of the South Kensington Museum I: The Government Schools of Design and the Founding Collection." *Journal of the History of Collections* 14 (1) (2002): 3–23.

———. "The Making of the South Kensington Museum II: Collecting Modern Manufactures: 1851 and the Great Exhibition." *Journal of the History of Collections* 14 (1) (2002): 25–44.

———. "The Making of the South Kensington Museum III: Collecting Abroad." *Journal of the History of Collections* 14 (1) (2002): 45–51.

Walkowitz, Daniel J. "The Cultural Turn and a New Social History: Folk Dance and the Renovation of Labor History." *Journal of Social History* (spring 2006): 781–802.

Walkowitz, Judith R. *City of Dreadful Delight: Narratives of Sexual Danger in Late-Victorian London*. Chicago: University of Chicago Press, 1992.

———. "Going Public: Shopping, Street Harassment, and Streetwalking in Late Victorian London." *Representations* (62) (1998): 1–30.

———. "The Indian Woman, the Flower Girl, and the Jew: Photojournalism in Edwardian London." *Victorian Studies* 42 (1) (1998–99): 3–46.

———. "The 'Vision of Salome': Cosmopolitanism and Erotic Dancing in Central London, 1908–1918." *American Historical Review* 108 (2) (2003): 337–76.

Walsh, Clare. "Shop Design and the Display of Goods in Eighteenth-Century London." *Journal of Design History* 8 (3) (1995): 157–76.

Walton, Whitney. *France at the Crystal Palace: Bourgeois Taste and Artisan Manufacture in the Nineteenth Century*. Berkeley: University of California Press, 1992.

Walvin, James. *Fruits of Empire: Exotic Produce and British Taste, 1660–1800*. London: Macmillan, 1997.

Waterfield, Giles, ed. *Art for the People: Culture in the Slums of Late Victorian Britain*. Dulwich Picture Gallery: London, 1994.

Whitehead, Christopher. *The Public Art Museum in Nineteenth Century Britain: The Development of the National Gallery*. Burlington, Vt.: Ashgate, 2005.

Wiener, Martin. *English Culture and the Decline of the Industrial Spirit, 1850–1980*. Cambridge: Cambridge University Press, 1981.

Wilk, Christopher. "Foreword." In *Design and the Decorative Arts, Britain, 1500–1900*, ed. Michael Snodin and John Styles, vi–xi. London: V & A Publications, 2001.

Williams, Raymond. *Culture and Society, 1780–1950*. New York: Harper and Row, 1958.

Wills, John E., Jr. "European Consumption and Asian Production in the Seventeenth and Eighteenth Centuries." In *Consumption and the World of Goods*, ed. John Brewer and Roy Porter, 133–47. London: Routledge, 1993.

Winter, Emma L. "German Fresco Painting and the New Houses of Parliament at Westminster, 1834–1851." *Historical Journal* 47 (2004): 291–329.

Wolfe, Patrick. "Land, Labor, and Difference: Elementary Structures of Race." *American Historical Review* 106 (3) (2001): 866–906.

Wood, L. S., and A. Wilmore. *The Romance of the Cotton Industry in England.* London: Oxford University Press, 1927.

Woodmansee, Martha. "The Genius and the Copyright: Economic and Legal Conditions of the Emergence of the 'Author.'" *Eighteenth-Century Studies* 17 (summer 1984): 425–48.

Yanni, Carla. *Nature's Museums: Victorian Science and the Architecture of Display.* London: Athlone, 1999.

Cassell, John, 89, 97, 113, 115, 117–19, 121–22

Catalogue of the Museum of Ornamental Art, 127–28, 137–40, 145, 148. *See also* Museum of Ornamental Art

Catalogues: of Great Exhibition, 9–10, 15, 89–90, 102; of Museums and Exhibitions, 13. *See also individual catalogues*

Catholicism, 63, 64, 143, 152

Cellini, Benvenuto, 43

Ceramics: Chinese porcelain, 3, 194–95; French porcelain, 1, 108–11, 139; images of, 136, 141, 145, 147, 195; Museum of Ornamental Art and, 128, 139–40, 148, 156; Sèvres porcelain, 105, 108, 109, 110, 139; at South Kensington Museum, 178, 193–95; Summerly and, 131–33; Wedgwood and, 178, 194

Chadwick, Edwin, 66

Chamber of Horrors, 16, 145–50, 154–57

Chartism, 69, 180

China: craftsmen in, 120–21, 194–95; Great Britain and, 229 n. 142, 229 n. 144; images of, 42, 195; porcelain manufacture in, 3, 194–95; superior design in, 130

Chinoiserie, 41–42

Chromolithographs, 89, 113, 121

Clarke, Mrs. Jane, 105, 106

Clarkson, Thomas, 61–62, 72

Coalbrookdale Dome, 96; image of, 98

Cole, Henry, 3, 4, 5, 8; as Benthamite, 127, 130, 147; branch museums and, 178–82; Department of Practical Art and, 132; Great Exhibition and, 15, 87, 132; images of, 130, 196; retirement of, 194, 198, 201; School of Design and, 50, 87,

132; South Kensington Museum and, 159–61, 164–65, 167–68, 170, 191; Summerly's Art Manufactures and, 87, 131, 133, 137; vision and legacy of, 201–2, 252 n. 47

Collecting, 5, 3, 144, 160, 161, 189, 193–94, 197, 239 n. 3

Colonial Gothic, 143

Commodity: capitalism and, 13; fetishism of, 10, 90, 123; at Great Exhibition, 10, 15, 90, 222 n. 19; history of, 56. *See also* Spectacle

Conservatism, 53, 68–69

Consumers, 60, 96; as audience for design reform, 1, 3, 8, 160; families as, 154–59; Great Exhibition and, 123–25, 193; marketplace and, 61, 127, 201; Museum of Ornamental Art and, 127–30, 132–37, 140, 145–48, 193, 202; women as, 55–58, 71–72, 77, 124–25, 154, 163

Consumption, 1, 3, 6–8, 10, 55–56, 127–28, 130, 155, 201–2

Conway, Moncure Daniel, 3, 4, 6, 20, 144, 191–92, 196–200

Copy, 55, 59, 70; original vs., 76–77; as pedagogical practice, 36, 41

Copyright: acts governing, 58–59, 82–84, 147; case for extension of, 8, 14–15, 52, 53, 180, 197; French laws governing, 64; literary, 67–68

Corn Laws, 69, 74. *See also* Free trade

Cotton manufacture, 97

Coventry Ribbon, 123–24

Coventry School of Design, 44

Craftsmen, 9, 15. *See also* Artisans

Crane, Walter, 200–201

Credit, 155, 237 n. 110

Crystal Palace, 86–88, 96, 105, 123, 126, 130, 132, 146–49, 202; dismantling of, 164–65; images of, 88, 149. *See also* Great Exhibition

Cultural capital, 9, 12–14, 17, 107; artisans and, 16, 21–22, 45–46, 49, 54, 108, 123, 163; Manchester and, 211 n. 104; *Penny Magazine* and, 44–49; working man and, 163, 198

Cultural geography, 163, 189. *See also* Geography of art

Cultural history: critiques of, 207 n. 59; historiography of, 11–13; labor and, 3–5, 10–12, 163, 189, 202; state and, 204 n. 18

Cultural property, 9, 17, 170, 180, 189

Cultural turn, 11–13

Culture wars, 169, 189

Curvilinear design, 22, 26, 27, 78

Da Vinci, Leonardo, 46

Demand-side reform, 3, 4, 16, 127–28, 135. *See also* Consumers; Marketplace

Department of Practical Art, 132, 231 n. 20, 232 n. 21

Department of Science and Art, 132, 138, 161, 165

Department stores, 4, 177; consuming modernity and, 216 n. 51

Design: bad, 2, 15, 59, 127, 135; designers and, 14, 20, 59; good, 7, 15, 58, 125–28, 137–38, 199–200; morality and, 139, 160, 167, 180, 190, 236 n. 83; society and, 89, 122, 203 n. 11

Design education and training, 14, 20, 39, 50, 134; on the Continent, 33; Dyce and, 21–22, 31–36; Haydon and, 21–31; figure drawing and, 9, 21–31, 200–201; genius and, 28; public imagination and, 43; redefinition of, 132, 135

Design reform, 127, 193; arts and crafts movement and, 202; changing priorities of, 15–17, 197–98; success of, 199

Designs registry, 59, 80, 83, 147, 150, 199; prints from, 81, 83, 149, 151, plate 1, plate 8

Despotism, 64, 144, 152

Diorama, 78

Dickens, Charles, 41, 68, 70, 150

Digby Wyatt, Matthew, 89, 95–97, 105–7, 111–16, 120–24

Display, 6, 8, 10, 13, 15, 31, 61–62, 167. *See also* Great Exhibition; Spectacle

Domesticity: lower middle class and, 126, 128, 129, 150, 202; middle class and, 200; working man and, 169, 170. *See also* Women

Domestic periodicals, 126. *See also* Print culture

Drawing, 19–25, 34; from the antique, 29; design vs., 39; from the figure, 9, 21, 24–27, 29, 31–32, 200–201; from models, 28, 31, 38–40

Drawing Book of the Government School of Design, 34, 36

Drawing books and manuals, 13, 21, 22, 26, 34, 35

Dulwich Picture Gallery, 173, 189

Dyce, William, 14, 21–22, 40, 48, 54, 188; Continental training and, 33, 63, 107; figure training and, 31, 38–39; Governing Council and, 34; theories of design and, 32, 36, 39; workshop ideal and, 32–33

East End of London, 1, 163, 171, 180–87; new journalism and, 184, 187

East India Company: calicoes and, 55, 74; Great Exhibition and, 112, 144, 227 n. 108; museum of, 191, 193. *See also* Great Exhibition; India

Electroplating, 97

Elgin Marbles, 21, 25, 29

Elkington and Mason, 97

Ellis, Robert, 123

Empire, 3, 4, 6, 155, 167, 227 nn. 107–

Famine in, 101, 103; material culture and, 226 n. 66; women in, 103
Iron trade, 96–97
Islam, 152, 192
Italy, 108, 153, 178, 246 n. 30

Jamaica, 179–80
Jameson, Anna, 155
Jennings Buildings, 175
John Bull, 151–53. *See also* Patriotism; Provincial values
Jones, Owen, 132, 142, 143, 151, 152
Journal of Design and Manufactures, 84, 87, 96, 132, 135, 138, 139, 142, 145; images from, 73, 146

Kay, James Philips, 66
Kensington, 164, 173–77, 243 nn. 69–70
Kershaw, James, 66–67, 74, 77, 78; calico prints by, 83
Knight, Charles, 34, 45–46

Labor: aesthetic of, 193; as colonial category, 227 n. 114; design reform and, 2–7, 10–11, 16, 197–98; iconography of, 227 n. 115, 228 n. 132; theory of value and, 96
Laborers: Great Exhibition and, 10, 16, 86, 89–91, 97, 99, 105–12, 194, 197; in London, 163; museums and, 172, 178, 189; South Kensington Museum and, 163–71. *See also* Artisans; Working men
Lace, 103, 105; image of, 106
Ladies' Crafts, 103, 105, 106. *See also* Women
Lancashire: calico manufacture in, 56, 58, 59, 66; copyright extension opposed in, 53, 74; free trade and, 53, 69; manufacturers in, 38
Lane's Net, 78–81
Lee, Daniel, 74, 76, 77, 78
Letter to Lord Meadowbank, 32–33
Liberalism: design reform and, 12,

177; in government, 161; Great Exhibition and, 86, 89, 120; political economy and, 155; political reform and, 5, 17, 34, 161, 172; provincial, 53, 69, 151–53; museums and, 161, 172; the state and, 12. *See also* Exhibitionary complex; Free trade; Radicalism
Liberty, 53, 69, 151–53, 179
Linguistic turn, 11–12
Lithographs, 89, 140
Livingstone, Dr., 184
London: as artisanal manufacturing center, 56–59, 99; consumer culture and, 61–62; filth of, 173; geography of, 177; Great Exhibition and, 86; as heart of empire and metropole, 6, 56, 242 n. 56; homes of, 200; map of, 162; mobility in, 171–75, 180–81; museums in, 165, 181, 191, 202; neighborhood museums in, 178–88; railways in, 175, 181; suburbs of, 171, 174–76. *See also* Geography of art
London neighborhoods and streets: Bethnal Green, 163, 181–88; Bloomsbury, 176; Brixton, 127; Brompton, 162, 164; Charing Cross, 173; City, 62, 177; East End, 171, 181, 183, 184; Hackney, 173; Hoxton, 180; Islington, 179; Lambeth, 179; Leicester Square, 30–31; Lower Shadwell, 182; Pimlico, 171; Regent Street, 61; Soho, 43; South London, 126, 132; Spitalfields, 177; Sydenham, 132; Temple Bar, 177, Trafalgar Square, 162, 171–74; West End, 61, 62, 123, 126, 127, 132, 177–78; West London, 1, 161, 164, 175; Whitechapel, 177. *See also* Kensington; South Kensington
Lower middle class, 126, 128, 129, 150, 202; historiography of, 230

69; identity, performativity, and,
12; by printers, 15, 54, 64–70; by
working men, 1, 163, 180, 192, 202
Sèvres porcelain, 105, 108, 109, 139;
image of, 110
Shawls, 24, 58, 113, 116, 124
Sheepshanks, John, 167
Sheffield, 99–102, 193
Shilling Days, 87–88
Silk trade, 56, 107
Skill: artisans and, 1, 9, 13, 17, 163,
180, 197; Great Exhibition and, 9,
90, 92, 94–99; property of, 9, 13,
67, 68, 180
Slade School of Art, 200
Slaves, 6, 70, 92
Soane Museum, 137
Social history, 5, 9, 11–13, 202
Socialism, 69, 201
Society for Promoting Practical
Design, 30–31
Society for the Encouragement of
Arts and Manufactures, 87, 131
Somerset House, 19, 20, 29, 31, 37,
59, 199; image of, 30
South America, 60, 134
South Kensington: access to, 171–77,
180, 244 nn. 72–73; as aristocratic
stronghold, 144, 159, 175, 177; as
art district, 20, 144, 164, 177, 245
n. 93; Brompton and, 161, 164;
changing ideas of, 198, 245 n. 81;
estate, 17, 164, 173; as heart of
empire, 204 n. 19; International
Exhibition of 1862 and, 181; working man and, 17, 163, 171
South Kensington Art School, 194,
199
South Kensington Museum, 4–6,
17, 23, 46, 50, 122–23, 199, 202;
admission costs for, 161, 168;
architectural models at, 160; as
aristocratic stronghold, 144, 189;

Bethnal Green outpost of, 13, 178–
88; British Picture Galleries at,
1, 160, 167–68; Ceramic Court at,
193–95; collecting at, 3, 144, 160,
161, 178, 189, 193–94, 197, 239 n. 3;
commerce and, 239 n. 3; as exhibitionary complex, 161; gas light
and, 169–70; hours of, 161; Indian
Section at, 191–93, 197; influence
and success of, 199; introductory
lectures at, 160, 165, 167; lecture
hall at, 160, 168, 178; opening of,
160–61, 165; refreshment and dining rooms at, 168, 201; satellites
of, 178–80; South Court of, 178,
193; visitors to, 241 n. 37; working
man and, 163, 165, 167–70, 178, 180
Spectacle, 3, 5–6, 10, 15–16, 62, 85–
90, 93, 123, 144, 161, 185, 197. *See
also* Commodity; Great Exhibition
Steam engine, 96
Steel manufacture, 99
Style, 78, 80, 81, 135–36
Summerly, Felix [Henry Cole], 87,
131, 137; caricature of works by, 133
Sumptuary Laws, 56
Sunday openings, 160, 169, 179, 180,
199, 242 n. 41, 247 n. 109
Supply-side reform, 2, 4, 15, 127
Sykes, Godfrey, 178, 179, 193

*Tallis's History and Description of the
Crystal Palace*, 89, 103, 117, 120–21
Taste in design: bad, 2, 154; British
inferiority in, 151, 164; color and,
234 n. 43; critics of, 128; direct
imitation of nature principle of,
127, 138–39, 145–47, 150–51; foreign preoccupation with, 151–52;
French as masters of, 108, 217
n. 58; geometry principle of, 127,
138–38; good, 8, 21, 58, 63, 98, 122,
137–38; at Great Exhibition, 121;

education, 22, 50, 90–91, 142, 160; as audience for Great Exhibition and South Kensington Museum, 1, 17, 165–70, 175, 178, 12, 189, 193, 202; Bethnal Green Museum and, 181–88; domesticity and, 167, 169, 170; National Gallery and, 172, 174; as political subject, 178–80, 189. *See also* Artisans; Cultural capital; Laborers; Operatives

Working Men's Exhibitions, 179

Workshop, 21, 31–33, 49, 65, 66, 94, 96, 103

World's fairs, 6. *See also* Exhibitions; Great Exhibition

Wornum, Ralph Nicholson, 138

LARA KRIEGEL

is an associate professor

of history at Florida International

University.

Library of Congress Cataloging-in-Publication Data
Kriegel, Lara.
Grand Designs : labor, empire, and the museum
in victorian culture / Lara Kriegel.
p. cm. — (Radical perspectives)
Includes bibliographical references and index.
ISBN 978-0-8223-4051-5 (cloth : alk. paper)
ISBN 978-0-8223-4072-0 (pbk : alk. paper)
1. Design, Industrial—Great Britain.   I. Title.
TS57.K65 2007
745.20941—dc22   2007016092